Protecting Women

Protecting Women

Labor Legislation in Europe, the United States, and Australia, 1880–1920

Edited by Ulla Wikander,
Alice Kessler-Harris, and Jane Lewis

With the assistance of Jan Lambertz

University of Illinois Press ◆ Urbana and Chicago

© 1995 by the Board of Trustees of the University of Illinois
Manufactured in the United States of America
1 2 3 4 5 C P 5 4 3 2 1

This book is printed on acid-free paper.

Library of Congress Cataloging-in-Publication Data

Protecting women : labor legislation in Europe, the United States, and
Australia, 1880–1920 / edited by Ulla Wikander, Alice Kessler-Harris,
and Jane Lewis.

    p.   cm.
    Includes index.
    ISBN 0–252–02175–4 (cloth : acid-free paper). — ISBN 0–252–06464-X
(pbk. : acid-free paper)
    1. Women—Employment—Law and legislation—History.
I. Wikander, Ulla, 1940-   . II. Kessler-Harris, Alice. III. Lewis, Jane
(Jane E.)
K1824.P76   1995
344'.014—dc20
[342.414]   94-44875
                          CIP

Contents

Introduction   *Alice Kessler-Harris, Jane Lewis, and Ulla Wikander*   I

1. Some "Kept the Flag of Feminist Demands Waving": Debates at International Congresses on Protecting Women Workers   *Ulla Wikander*   29

2. Equality for Men? Factory Laws, Protective Legislation for Women in Switzerland, and the Swiss Effort for International Protection   *Regina Wecker*   63

3. "Let England Blush": Protective Labor Legislation, 1820–1914   *Jane Lewis and Sonya O. Rose*   91

4. "All These Forms of Women's Work Which Endanger Public Health and Public Welfare": Protective Labor Legislation for Women in Germany, 1878–1914   *Sabine Schmitt*   125

5. Special Labor Protection for Women in Austria, 1860–1918   *Margarete Grandner*   150

6. Women or Workers? The 1889 Labor Law and the Debate on Protective Legislation in the Netherlands   *Ulla Jansz*   188

7. "Lagging Far Behind All Civilized Nations": The Debate over Protective Labor Legislation for Women in Denmark, 1899–1913   *Anna-Birte Ravn*   210

8. The Beginning of a "Masculine Renaissance": The Debate on the 1909 Prohibition against Women's Night Work in Sweden   *Lynn Karlsson*   235

9. Protection or Equality? Debates on Protective Legislation in Norway   *Gro Hagemann*   267

10. "To the Most Weak and Needy": Women's Protective Labor
Legislation in Greece   *Efi Avdela*   290

11. A Paradise for Working Men but Not Working Women:
Women's Wagework and Protective Legislation in Australia,
1890–1914   *Renate Howe*   318

12. The Paradox of Motherhood: Night Work Restrictions in
the United States   *Alice Kessler-Harris*   337

Selected Readings   359

Contributors   365

Index   369

Acknowledgments

Our efforts to create a collective process have received generous help from several sources. At the Rockefeller Foundation's Bellagio Study and Research Center, in Lake Como, Italy, we benefited from our first opportunity to meet together in a beautiful and inspiring environment. We thank the foundation for hosting us at that 1989 meeting where we formed a group and started our comparative work. The Social Science Research Council (United States) provided grants to bring several participants in the project to the Eighth Berkshire Conference on the History of Women, in 1990, at Douglass College of Rutgers University in New Jersey. There, and at the Tenth International Economic History Conference, in 1990, at the University of Leuven, Belgium, we benefited from presenting our work to lively and encouraging audiences. The Swedish Council for Research in the Humanities and Social Sciences (HSFR), Stockholm, Sweden, provided the resources for our final gathering in Mariefred by Lake Mälaren, and it was there that we created the outlines of this book. Without these opportunities to meet across oceans, this book could never have emerged. We are enormously grateful for the support we received.

All of the authors received substantial help from our respective universities and institutions as well as from the many archivists, librarians, colleagues, seminar participants, and research councils on three continents that have supported our individual work. We cannot thank them all here, but we do want them to know how much we appreciate their efforts.

The final compilation of these essays was the product of many hands. Eileen Boris offered important criticism and a perspective on the whole at a crucial stage. At Rutgers University, Stephen Robertson and Liz Felter provided essential logistical support and final checks on material. Jan Lambertz managed to turn a group of essays that had originated in a variety of mother tongues into what we hope will be an entirely readable collection. Jan's astute readings and her intense scrutiny of the arguments led her to sharpen literally hundreds of sentences, to find more accurate formulations for many ideas, and in the process to clarify the larger meaning of the whole. Her contribution was essential to completing the book.

Finally, each of the editors wishes to thank the other editors as well as all the contributors. The process of putting this book together has taught us much about differences in national style and left us with enhanced respect for the difficulties of transcending intellectual borders. Working together has not only revealed the difficulties of creating a common ground from which to share ideas but has enhanced our sense of the critical importance of testing our ideas outside our own spheres.

Protecting Women

Introduction

Alice Kessler-Harris, Jane Lewis, and Ulla Wikander

In 1991, Russian women faced the quandary of special protective labor legislation for women. As their economy stumbled toward a market system, they discovered that the laws that had protected their capacity to fulfill family roles while they were employed could also have negative consequences. Male participants in newly developed cooperative enterprises (often the husbands and family members of women workers) began to resist special benefits for women. Eager to increase their profits, they no longer wanted to pay the extra costs involved in employing women. Some of the benefits available only to women and routinely utilized by them—such as absentee days for child care, pregnancy and maternity leaves, and early retirement—were proving expensive and inefficient. In an effort to increase productivity and diminish the cost of the labor force, newly market-conscious cooperatives began to lay off women and give preference to men. Women were too disunited to fight back. Many were tempted by the possibility of divesting themselves of their "double day" for the promise of a husband who could support them and their children. But others were unclear. What would be the financial and personal consequences of giving up their economic independence? Should they relinquish their special privileges in order to keep their jobs? Should they demand the same privileges for men?

These questions capture the central tension around women's efforts to juggle family and work responsibilities in the modern world. In different forms, they occupy a pivotal position in the debates of every industrial country, pitting the demand for equality in the workplace against the well-intentioned efforts of men and women to protect family life. Feminists have dubbed this issue the difference/equality question. But the euphonious phrase belies the hard choices that women must make when they choose between social policies that emphasize their differences from men and those that insist that men and women be treated as alike for workplace purposes. These choices are often blurred.

In the summer of 1991, the Court of Justice of the European Communities decreed that national provisions forbidding night work for women contradicted the Community's regulations. A Community Directive of 1976 had mandated equal opportunities in the labor market for men and women.[1] Both France and Italy had special night work laws for women—laws they had adopted in conformity with the conventions of the International Labour Organisation (ILO) and, they protested, were for women's own benefit. Lacking enforcement powers, the Court of Justice could do little but reiterate its position. Using equality of opportunity arguments to support its verdict, it claimed that prohibiting night work was no less than discrimination.[2] Women were not to be protected generally because of their biology but might have special protection when they were pregnant or had recently given birth. The court asserted that if the risks and dangers for women exceeded those for men, then employers should take measures against the hazards.

The French persisted: these laws, they argued, had never been rigidly applied; women could work at night if their trade unions agreed. They went on to note valid social reasons for the exclusions: women were more exposed to risks of violence or sexual assault, and their family responsibilities created extra work for them. But, the court averred, creating a deadlock that has not yet been resolved, the family responsibilities of women were not its concern; it was not the court's business to regulate the organization of the family or to get involved in deciding how responsibilities should be shared between partners.

The deadlock captures the conflict in which women themselves have been caught and which has produced particularly painful divisions in the United States. When the state of California passed a law in 1980 granting women (but not men) four months of unpaid leave with job security in the event of ill health during pregnancy and around childbirth, a California bank went to court, claiming that it was forced to discriminate against men by granting women a privilege it could not grant to men.[3] Influential women's groups split down the middle. To grant women this benefit, argued some, without allowing men comparable time off in the event of their own disability, would cause employers to discriminate against women. They advocated extending the law to men. But others objected that childbirth was unique to women, that it was in the interest of all women to recognize this difference, and that employers ought to be forced to accommodate the disparity. In this case, the U.S. Supreme Court finally ruled in favor of the state, agreeing that difference deserved to be accommodated and discounting the potential discriminatory effect.[4]

These examples illustrate some of the complexities of a sometimes bitter, century-long conflict over protective labor legislation for women only—a conflict that has historically pitted men against women, set government representatives and political parties against each other, and divided women among themselves. It is a conflict that begins with the question of what constitutes "protection" and moves to issues of equality between men and women at work and in the family. In between it raises profoundly disturbing issues of state intervention in family life and of the capacity of the state to redefine the nature of citizenship. No easy explanations can be found for the contentious nature of this debate. The measure of the distress it has caused is perhaps best captured by posing the kinds of questions its participants have often asked: What concepts of "women" and of "workers" are embodied in the legislation? How far has "protective" labor legislation been designed to enhance the well-being of women in the workplace rather than to encourage their activities in the home? To what extent does it further the interests of mothers in the health of their children as opposed to those of the state in child welfare? Does it enable women to maximize their work force contributions, or does it contribute to perpetuating and sharpening the sexual division of labor? Can protective labor legislation be said to serve the immediate interests of male workers in regulating the participation of women in the labor force? To what extent does it advance the interests of men as employees and employers to preserve male privilege at a time of technological change and shifting power relations in the workplace? Finally, how far did women support or oppose such legislation, and whose voices influenced politicians? These are among the crucial questions addressed in the essays that follow.

Because these questions have proved to be so intransigent, they have created controversy among historians as well as among policymakers. Virtually all Western countries began to adopt measures to moderate the effects of capitalism on labor at around the same time at the end of the nineteenth century. Generally, these took the form of health in-

surance, workmen's compensation, and old age pensions. Some have
viewed the initial passage of laws providing maternity benefits and
regulating women's hours at work in this context—as a part of an early
twentieth-century effort to alleviate the burdens of unfettered market
mechanisms by extending the benefits of state intervention to large
numbers of working people.[5] Seen in this light, protective labor legislation appears to be a part of the late nineteenth-century revaluation
of the efficacy of free market liberalism and a precursor of the modern
welfare state.

Others have argued that because in many countries protective laws
treated workers differently on the basis of gender, they are more appropriately viewed as extensions of employment law, as efforts to rationalize the labor market by affirming and extending the gendered division
of labor.[6] This suggests that the laws are often a response to technological change and to women's increasing economic opportunities: a way
to symbolically and literally put women back in their places.[7] To support the notion that protective laws for women were intended as an
extension of the state's regulatory powers to circumscribe the lives of
women in the interests of affirming male job rights and sustaining the
patriarchal state, historians cite several factors. Almost universally the
laws regulated only the industrial labor of women, generally in areas
that threatened the manhood of male workers if it did not challenge
their particular jobs. Household servants (by far the largest proportion
of women workers in this period), agricultural workers, and cannery
workers were everywhere excluded from the benefits of shorter hours
and night work restrictions. In many countries the law also exempted
nurses, waitresses, and employees in small workshops and nightclubs.
Generally, even the most benign laws, such as those that reduced hours
and provided maternity leaves, did so without providing compensatory
resources to enhance family life.[8]

Often, these distinctions blurred in a confusing array of assumptions
about what exactly constituted "protective" legislation and who, in fact,
was being protected. In general, maternity leaves and restrictions on
working hours, especially at night, constituted the core of such legislation in Europe; in the United States, hours and wages were typically
the focal point of female regulation; in Australia, wages and maternity
leaves provided the baseline. But labeling the categories does not begin
to suggest the meaning of the legislation. In Sweden and Norway, for
example, turn-of-the-century maternity leaves for women workers were

conceptualized by contemporaries as welfare policy in the sense that they were designed to preserve the health and well-being of mothers and children.[9] In Greece and the United States, they have historically been thought of as labor related, as part of an effort to enable or deter women's labor force participation. One result is that in the United States maternity leaves have been, until very recently, virtually non-existent. In Britain, where late nineteenth-century trades boards were empowered to regulate "sweated trades," they did so in the context of a general movement for liberal welfare reforms that included meals for needy schoolchildren, old age pensions, and national insurance against sickness and unemployment. A range of employment rules restricting women, passed in the same period in the name of "sweated mother-hood," could logically be seen as part of a much larger movement toward welfare legislation of all kinds. At the same time, in Australia, where national insurance failed to draw support and where the best pro-tection for workers was thought to be a good wage, regulating women's work seemed to fall more clearly into the category of labor legislation.

In an effort to sort out the confusion, the thirteen historians repre-sented in this book have attempted to clarify the motivations behind the movement for protective labor legislation when it first became a high priority in the final years of the last century and the early years of this one. We have looked closely at the origins of the legislation and the initial period of its operation in eleven countries and at the inter-national debates that surrounded them. Each essay addresses the par-ticular issues that motivated and inhibited action in one country and tries to sort out the major social and political concerns that informed the passage of complicated and sometimes controversial legislation. We have discovered an astonishing array of legislation, which differs dra-matically from country to country and defies easy generalization as to the meaning of protection or its intended consequences. We have also found exciting arenas of intersection. Together, the results provide some startling insights about why debates that originated more than a hundred years ago remain unresolved today.

◆ ◆

Our focus on the late nineteenth and early twentieth centuries re-flects the primacy the issue of protection assumed in these years. Efforts to regulate the labor conditions of adult workers began in Britain as early as 1819 and took center stage in Britain and Switzerland by the

1840s, with escalating concern for the impact of industrialization on the family lives of men and women. Friedrich Engels was among the earliest commentators to view with dismay the apparently topsy-turvy world of early British industrialization, where the labor of women and children was as much in demand as that of men and where the sanctity of the home appeared to be at risk. Threatened with profound disturbances in societal equilibrium, Europe buzzed with solutions to what became known as "The Social Question." Well-intentioned people asked what could be done about the poverty and squalor that seemed to go hand in hand with the spread of factory production. How much should the working masses be earning? What was a reasonable standard of living? Could the labor market be regulated without dramatically inhibiting the progress of the industrial machine?

Efforts to address these questions began slowly. The first steps taken to protect women involved restricting their freedom to work underground in mines. But early legislation also focused on the question of hours, particularly those worked by women at night, and on the conditions of work, especially women's safety around moving machinery. Later came measures more explicitly linked to the protection of women as actual or potential mothers, such as maternity leaves and prohibitions on work with toxic substances such as lead. In some, especially English-speaking countries, wages were made the subject of minimum wage legislation in trades deemed to be "sweated," which tended to employ a disproportionate number of women. While hours, wages, and reproduction were the major areas covered by labor laws, the three tended to overlap.

Britain, pioneer in the area, in 1842 prohibited women from working underground and in 1844 restricted their work at night. In 1847, the law restricted those working in the textile industry to ten hours a day. In 1848, at least one Swiss canton (Glarus) regulated the hours of both male and female workers in spinning factories—and, in 1864, in industry in general. At the same time, these and other countries, including Zurich in 1815, Britain in 1833, Prussia in 1839, France in 1841, Sweden in 1852, and Austria in 1859, restricted the numbers of daily hours that children of varying ages could work. By the 1870s, laws prohibiting children and young people from working at night and regulating their daytime hours were common all over Europe. These laws had varying impact. In Britain, where employers continued to work children in shifts, they were easily evaded. There and elsewhere, they sparked movements for factory inspection that not only continued into the twentieth century but also frequently became vehicles for women's involvement.

Muted debates concerning appropriate working hours and wages for adult workers erupted occasionally throughout the nineteenth century. These were generally sparked by organized protests of workers. But in industrializing countries class tensions and great disparities in living standards encouraged reformers and academics with a social conscience as well as some politicians to contemplate state intervention and expanded state responsibility. Still, legislation followed slowly. Not until the 1880s did most of Europe begin to seriously address the problem of hours, wages, and working conditions for industrial workers and, more specifically, to turn their attention to women workers. After 1890, in the wake of a series of international congresses and several national investigations of the situations of women and children in the labor force, women's roles as workers became the principal subject for debate. Female factory and sweatshop workers found themselves the center of a controversy about the social value of restricting their wagework.

In the end, three kinds of legislation emerged. One group of labor laws was explicitly gendered, connecting provisions for pregnancy, childbirth, and lactation to maternity leaves and benefits for childbirth. Such legislation generally applied to real women under specific conditions. Fundamentally rooted in biological differences, it provided little possibility for extending humane work conditions to men; yet, by relieving their wives' burdens, it could improve their family lives. A modified form of this kind of legislation accommodated and reinforced cultural practices by placing limits on the work of women with children and families to care for. Typical was the case of Switzerland, which in 1877 extended the length of the lunch break to women "who cared for a household." Germany, in 1891, gave shorter hours to all women on Saturdays and an extra half hour at lunchtime for those "who had to care for a household."

Other countries treated all women as if they had children and families to care for, or as if they were in preparation for these roles. Debates in the Netherlands, Norway, and Greece suggest that male legislators who initially wanted to reduce the hours only of married women found it easier to regulate those of all women. Greek legislators, eager to ensure married women's household services, imposed reduced hours on all women. Lawmakers in the Netherlands sought to provide married women with an extra half hour to prepare dinner but required employers to give the reduced hours to single women as well. Britain's 1874 act, motivated by the desire to reduce infant mortality, cut the working week for all women in regulated industries. Some laws utilized cultural practices to exclude women from desirable jobs. Typically, women were denied jobs around moving machinery on the grounds their hair might get caught in it.[10]

A second group of laws, which we might call gender neutral, addressed the problems of all workers. Sometimes these laws did so immediately and directly, as in the case of Swiss and Austrian limits on hours (1877 and 1885, respectively) and Australian insistence on minimum wages for all. But more frequently, proponents of gender-neutral laws began by advocating restrictions on women and children in the hope that curtailing the hours of most workers on the shop floor would necessarily yield shorter hours for adult men too; the goal, then, was to mandate the length of the working day for all workers. Because this kind of gender-neutral protective labor legislation was rooted in an economic theory that challenged images of "free labor," its effects on any one group of workers might be less pernicious than that of other kinds of legislation.

Finally, laws that might potentially have been gender neutral were, in practice, frequently limited to women. Restrictions on night work fall into this category. Illustrative is the case of Switzerland, where several cantons at first banned night work for both men and women. National legislation passed in 1877, however, allowed exemptions for men while refusing women permission to work at night under any circumstances. The practical effect of such actions was that legislation that could at first be characterized as potentially gender neutral ultimately imposed limits only on women. For this reason, proposals for night work legislation often created odd alliances across class lines and divisions between men and women as well as among women. In Denmark, social democratic as well as middle-class liberal women successfully opposed night work laws because they threatened the jobs of relatively well paid working women and raised the specter of unequal treatment. In Norway, liberal women also opposed night work regulation that applied only to women. They were joined by conservative men whose opposition stemmed from entirely different grounds: men opposed the laws partly because they violated free market principles and partly because they believed that women, having the right to vote, ought to be treated as equal citizens. In contrast, successful campaigns for night work legislation in Germany and Austria could and did derive support across the class divide and the political spectrum because they focused on women's capacity to care for children and families. The debates notwithstanding, most countries banned night work for women early on. Inevitably, the actual legislation treated all women as a homogeneous group without differences, thus creating or perpetuating a particular kind of family role for women and exacerbating the gender division of labor without promising men any relief from their harsh conditions.

In practice, the lines between these three kinds of legislation were difficult to draw. For example, laws that mandated extended maternity leaves could easily discourage employers from hiring women of childbearing age. This discriminatory effect has often been cited as the source of persistently high occupational sex segregation in the Scandinavian countries, where long maternity leaves are now customary. It also helps to explain why some women's groups opposed California's generous provision of disability benefits in the case of pregnancy-related illnesses but for no other disabilities. The reluctance of U.S. social reformers to advocate provisions for paid maternity leaves reflects the oft-spoken fear that men would take advantage of their wives' earning capacity to avoid their own responsibilities for family support.

The complex implications of protective labor legislation tell us something about why similarly situated people often took quite different positions with regard to its desirability. When applied to women only, potentially gender-neutral laws, such as those regulating hours and providing minimum wages, had the capacity to protect real and future motherhood; they also reaffirmed women's differences from men in ways that extended far beyond employment practices into issues of equal citizenship. Where women and men sharply distinguished between and valued one aspect or another of women's position, they could and did take firm positions either for or against protective legislation. The situations of Denmark and Sweden are instructive here. Swedish and Danish women (including women organized in trade unions, female members of the social democratic parties, and the middle class) objected to potentially gender-neutral legislation that was not applied neutrally. They opposed bans on night work that applied to women only; they welcomed proposals that would apply to all workers regardless of sex. Women's antagonism to these laws reflected their concern for equality. As a result, they saw no conflict between vigorously rejecting this kind of special legislation for women while simultaneously demanding maternity leaves for women workers. If early twentieth-century Scandinavian women could have used our vocabulary, they would have said that to use gender-neutral legislation in a gendered way was sexist. Such legislation ought to be neutrally applied to all. But in countries where the protection of motherhood seemed more important, such as the United States and England, night work laws proved more attractive to women across class lines.

Most male politicians approached the legislation quite differently. For them, government regulation of working conditions provided a way out of the proliferation of chaos, a way to lessen the suffering born of the free play of market forces. But not all men agreed on the reasons why governments should intervene. Some sought to smooth the functioning of the market, others to curb it. Some believed it possible to apply rules of fair competition over national boundaries; others thought of labor legislation as preparing the way for centrally planned and controlled economies. While in Norway liberal male politicians fought against women's protection as a matter of free market principles, in Denmark they divided on the question. Elsewhere, men with social democratic and conservative affiliations allied to pass legislation that would enable women to serve families, rationalizing the consequences for cherished economic principles and the potential impact on job opportunities for individual women. Here they were joined by many women, who also ranged from social democrats to middle-class reformers and who, like the Swedish reformer Ellen Key, believed that the issue of equality for poor women was merely an abstraction.

The essays in this collection demonstrate that debates over regulation and the outcomes of legislative discussion rested as much on particular political considerations as on theoretical niceties. Even a quick view of the escalating debates of the 1890s suggests that the issue became a vehicle through which several agendas were acted out. Among these were the issue of motherhood and maternalism; the question of difference and equality among women; the implications of new racialist thinking; and concerns for the public image of the nation in the international arena.

Chief among the factors that account for the prominence of the formulation of protective labor legislation as a woman's issue is the emergence of motherhood as a major source of concern. Maternalist discourses (broadly speaking, discourses that centered on the importance of motherhood) flowered in most Western countries at the end of the nineteenth century and the beginning of the twentieth. They came into prominence around the social problems of high infant mortality rates and low birth rates. Some proponents of maternalism (men as well as women) adopted a positive approach, emphasizing the importance of measures to improve the welfare of women and children, such as infant welfare clinics. Others were more inclined toward a restrictive approach stressing the things that mothers should not do, among which paid employment tended to figure strongly. Since the two were tied together by assumptions about the existence of a male breadwinner who earned a family wage, social reformers often conflated the protection of motherhood into a discourse that restricted female employment.[11]

Historians have debated the relative power of these discourses within maternalism. It was possible for maternalism to deliver real welfare benefits for women and their children or to offer protection on terms that, in the short run, simultaneously benefited them and controlled their behavior.[12] But it was also possible for maternalism to construct women's interests in opposition to those of their children and thus to insist that women subordinate their own interests to some greater good. Maternalist discourses seem to have been used in all these ways. In Britain, public health officials, eugenicists, and imperialists eager to improve the quality and increase the quantity of population joined with women philanthropists concerned with reducing infant mortality to launch a major educational campaign that culminated in a network of voluntary "schools for mothers" in the 1900s.[13] French pronatalism, primarily directed toward increasing the population, gave rise to some of the earliest infant welfare clinics—the Gouttes de Lait—which promoted breastfeeding, provided pure, modified cows' milk, and weighed babies.[14] In Austria, the Catholic church directed maternalist energies toward promoting explicit demands for married women to stay out of the work force in order to pay attention to their families.[15] Everywhere, concern over the birth rate had to do with race. In the United States, for example, efforts at enhancing child care were often directed at white urban immigrant populations in the early 1900s and later toward rural white women to the neglect of African-American women.

While the emphasis on motherhood brought some public health measures from which women benefited, the narrow focus of maternalism on what constituted good motherhood meant that many of the real needs of mothers went unmet. Its tendency to condemn mothers' paid work in particular exacerbated the difficulties of many poor women. By the 1880s, many doctors contended that going out to work obstructed women's breastfeeding and that carrying infants to nurse in the early morning exposed them to the dangers of respiratory infections. Some countries rapidly responded to these claims. Switzerland led the way in 1877, restricting women's right to work for two weeks before and six weeks after childbirth. Germany followed in 1878 with a three-week restriction. Austria imposed a four-week constraint in 1885, as did the Netherlands in 1889. When the Berlin Conference met in 1890 to consider an international program of protective legislation for all workers, it recommended a four-week maternity restriction. Many other countries fell into line. Britain adopted a four-week limit in 1891, the same year that Germany expanded its three-week minimum to six weeks and just before Norway's six-week restriction took effect in 1892. In 1900 Sweden provided for an obligatory four-week leave; Denmark joined the group in 1901; Greece, though relatively rural, complied by 1912.

As useful as these leaves might have been, their value was tempered by the all but total absence of provisions for wage replacement. The harsh working conditions of most poor women surely led them to welcome a respite from their double day. Yet a leave without pay might well have been impossible for many.[16] Apparently few legislators considered that mothers' employment might well be a lesser evil than grinding poverty. Some countries provided benefits to help pay the medical and nursing costs of confinement. These benefits began to spread after 1883 when Germany offered insured workers three weeks of pay at about half the average woman's wage. Austria did the same in 1887. Denmark set aside a limited fund to provide needy women with help on an ad hoc basis.[17] European countries responded equally slowly to calls for material help in the form of allowances to mothers who stayed home with their babies. Most countries did not provide for an "endowment" for mothers until after World War I.[18]

The United States constitutes something of an exception here. Little effort was made to provide new mothers with time off from work, and no state provided a maternity leave with the guarantee of job return. Convinced that women should simply quit work when they married or became pregnant, reformers who led the campaign to restrict women's work paid no attention at all to maternity leaves. The resulting hardships for wage-earning women strengthened arguments for a family wage for male breadwinners. Beginning about 1912, nearly half the states passed legislation calling for "pensions" for virtuous mothers who lacked male support. Ironically, most of these pensions proved to be so inadequate that they were generally given only to mothers physically able to undertake wagework as well.[19]

The power of maternalism can be understood only within the broader context of ideas about female citizenship, rights, and obligations. A dominant line of thinking defined women's citizenship in terms of a primary duty to bear children and to serve families. In return, women could expect the right to the protection of their husbands, the breadwinners within marriage, and, more controversially, of the state in the workplace. In this formulation, female citizens could expect little in the way of rights to suffrage or employment, but they could anticipate that the state would shield their family lives from excessive poverty or harsh work. Thus, protective legislation everywhere (with the possible exception of Australia) preceded the vote for women and perhaps served to diffuse women's efforts to secure the right to vote.

Maternalists could argue that far from being an impediment to free agency, protective legislation provided a richer family life. But the other side of the coin was that by constructing women as dependent on the state, the legislative shield supplanted the rights to citizenship to which many men were by now accustomed. Under these circumstances, women who accepted the fundamental premise of maternalist thinking (that the male family wage and restrictions against excessive work would provide women with protection at home) could hardly insist on freedom in the workplace as well. As the nineteenth century drew to a close, the efforts of increasing numbers of middle-class women to achieve equality of rights (which assumed that women could acquire economic independence by functioning much like men in the labor force) directly challenged the maternalist discourse (which assumed women's differences). In the early twentieth century, disagreements sharpened when some educated women who advocated independence from men developed a rationale based on the power of motherhood.

The issue was complicated by the class divisions embedded in it. Most of the women subject to regulation were poor. Though at any one time most working women were single, few expected to remain so. For married women, frequent pregnancy and little by way of domestic technology, or even running water, made household labor a difficult job in itself. Not until this changed would a majority of the wives of working men actively demand equal rights in the workplace. In the meantime, equality in the workplace seemed an abstract issue for many women workers.[20] To imagine themselves competing with men would challenge prevailing images of male breadwinning. And their ability to compete was, in any event, hindered by male control over definitions of what constituted "skill," and especially by defining women's competence as part of their "character" or "nature" rather than as knowledge acquired as part of the learning process.[21] Cultural emphases on different roles for women, along with gendered occupational segregation, meant that many white women stood to gain far more from protective legislation than they could hope to acquire from a fruitless battle for male prerogatives. There were exceptions, however. Skilled female typographers everywhere protested when legislation restricted their ability to take lucrative night jobs. In New York, a bitter struggle led the state to exempt them from night work laws that prohibited other women from working. But in France and Sweden, their protests did not change the law.

Questions of labor market access were often addressed by women who were themselves not poor and for whom the abstract meaning of equality loomed large. As the labor market constricted the lives of the poorest women workers, the spreading organization of middle-class women into societies with political and social purposes opened the possibility that other women could become citizens on a par with men. Egalitarian and individualistic values combined with democratic notions led many (usually bourgeois) women to hope that women and men could be treated equally in the eyes of the state. Feminists—organized sometimes in women's movements and clubs—advocated gender justice even when it might deprive poor workers of immediate comforts. At other times, as members of social democratic parties and as social reformers, educated women and men sought solutions to the social question through justice for all workers. For them, gender justice, which took the form of special treatment for women only, constituted a first step toward legislation that would include men as well.

The issue emerged most poignantly among social democratic women for whom class justice demanded that women be offered protection even if men were not, while their own sense of equality frequently pushed them toward insisting on equal treatment for men and women in the workforce. Germany's Clara Zetkin, for example, sharply opposed regulating women's hours and their night work until 1891, at which time she changed her mind and led other social democratic women into enthusiastic support for protection. Historians who have looked at the period between 1893 and 1913 have often dismissed those who complained about the negative effects of regulation on female equality as the special pleading of middle-class women. But national studies, such as those included here, indicate that no such easy division can be made. In the United States, well-off, reform-minded women led the charge for women's protective labor legislation, stifling the voices of opposition until the 1920s. In Sweden, Finland, and Denmark, however, even women in the social democratic parties spoke out for equality, joining with better-off and working-class women to oppose all protection except for maternity leaves. Such social democratic women refused to follow international mandates of social democracy and, as in Sweden, insisted on legislating in gender-neutral ways or not at all. The idea that protective labor legislation might inhibit female equality had been present at all the international congresses. It emerged dramatically at the Bern conference of 1913, when the Norwegian delegate rose to demand "equal legislation for men and women workers." Since that time, an ILO report of 1921 comments, "there has always been one section of opinion which lays particular stress on the equal competition of men and women, and which does not wish to destroy this equality by placing women in an inferior economic position merely in order to secure certain material advantages for them in the organization of labor."[22]

Contests over difference and equality were fought in an environment where many were worried about the vast social changes taking place and how to interpret them. Evolutionary ideas mingled science and social concerns, playing havoc with old ideas of stability and continuity. Everywhere, women's emancipation—their push toward equality—was said to weaken the capacity of men to respond and therefore threatened the virility of both men and society. Many feared a blurring of the sex barriers and saw in a dissolution of older gender norms a symptom of the decadence of society and the degeneration of humankind. The French philosopher Jacques Le Rider has called this moment a crisis of masculinity—one in which the male properties of creativity, strength, progress, and logic were threatened by the passive, sacrificing, weak, and irrational properties of the female. One result of this crisis was an increase in overt misogyny, which thrived among such influential philosophers as Friedrich Nietzsche, Otto Weininger, and August Comte. Literary artists like Schopenhauer and Baudelaire joined the woman-hating chorus. Weininger's *Geschlecht und Character* (Sex and Character) influenced many authors, including the Swedish August Strindberg.

The political expression of these trends emerged in the philosophy of Social Darwinism. As explicated by the British philosopher Herbert Spencer, Social Darwinism argued that the concept of evolutionary selection could be applied to societies: the least fit among humankind should be allowed to sink to the bottom of the heap. Such a view, which accommodated natural differences among all people, could readily be adapted to differences specifically between men and women. While arguments regarding biologically based sexual differences applied to all women, Victorian scientists built up their theories on the basis of assumptions regarding the behavior of women in their own social class. They used their own society as the model from which they formulated their ideas, which in turn justified the position of women as they found it. Having stopped women from acquiring certain capacities, especially with respect to education, science provided the justification for refusing rights on the grounds that those capacities were "naturally" absent. The idea of a "natural" basis for sexual difference, as opposed to patently artificial class differences, was powerful and long lived.[23] As among animals in the natural order, men and women were seen to have complementary functions that defined their separate roles and, by extension, their labor market positions. This rationale was most clearly articulated in the United States, where the notion that women were "mothers of the race" provided the basis for legislation that would otherwise have been constitutionally impermissible.

Ideas of biological and social evolutionary development had special consequences for looking at differences between the classes and the sexes. If the hierarchical structuring of society was natural, the working class could logically be considered as less developed than the middle and upper classes. By extension, working-class women occupied a lower position on the evolutionary scale than that occupied by the supposedly more highly developed women of the wealthier classes. This was confirmed by their apparently greater strength and capacity for hard work compared to women of the upper classes. They sometimes even worked in occupations similar to those of men. Advancing the civilizing process required bringing all women into more refined positions. That process would demand clearer barriers between men's and women's work, or, even better, it would discourage women from undertaking any type of wagework. Anchored in the educated classes, ideas about the survival of the fittest seemed to spread rapidly among workers as well. Everywhere, people quickly accepted that women were central to the civilizing process. Despite the class differences among women, and the material variations in how different women lived, the concept of the civilizing mother unified the discourse on women's roles. Assigning women responsibility for eugenic fitness and for the degeneration of the race provided the basis for state intervention in their lives at home and at work.

The combination of civilizing impulses and the needs of states to demonstrate their humane intentions provided a powerful rationale for the stream of protective labor legislation passed around the turn of the century. Among the series of international conferences documented in this volume are those called by the leading European nations to demonstrate their concern for the welfare of the working classes and to ensure that wage competition was kept within bounds. Beginning with Germany in 1890, followed by Switzerland, and attended by delegates from all of industrial Europe, these conferences demonstrated the importance of public expressions of commitment. The essays that follow reveal the extent to which leading male politicians felt pressured to adopt protective labor legislation for women only, not because they needed it, but lest they appear to be uncivilized in the face of national pressure to improve the "race" and international concern for humane conditions. Danish advocates made these impulses explicit when they suggested that passing legislation would admit the country to the "ranks of the civilized nations that did not tolerate the boundless exploitation of women." [24] In Denmark and in Norway, that argument failed to persuade legislators to restrict women's hours. But it did succeed in Sweden, which approved the Bern Convention of 1906 prohibiting night work more as a gesture of international goodwill than as a response to a real need for regulation. In Greece, too, protective laws were part of a state policy for institutional reform rather than a response to actual need or the demands of women. These examples suggest how strongly perceptions of national self-image influenced the development of protective labor legislation for women, making it the first line of defense against challenges to the state's presentation of itself as a protector of the weak.

Because protective legislation grew out of a variety of agendas, its passage appears to have been overdetermined. It was supported by male representatives of the most conservative political parties in countries like Austria, by liberals in Greece and Britain, and by a conservative Swedish government that was eventually joined by liberals and social democrats. Everywhere it drew support from such disparate groups as trade unionists, employers, citizen husbands, and social activists.

Women as feminists, as trade unionists, and as nonvoting fellow travelers with political parties also made their voices heard. The motives of protagonists varied. Employers looked for a cheap and abundant supply of workers and understood as well that if they exploited women too mercilessly, future generations of workers would suffer. Traditional voices, representing the church, were eager to preserve the mother for the family yet recognized that some married women, and unmarried daughters and widows, might need jobs to preserve family life. Women's organizations and those representing labor were also divided: in different ways each recognized that women's legitimate demands for economic independence rested on access to expanded roles in production, yet each wished to preserve some semblance of traditional family life with a mother's influence.

Given the variety of impulses supporting the movement, it is impossible to make generalizations about which groups hold primary responsibility for protective labor legislation. Historians of the United States have commented on the influence of middle-class women in getting legislation passed and in enforcing it afterward. Theda Skocpol, Robyn Muncy, and others credit the role of organized women's movements in conceiving and enacting mothers' pensions and protective labor legislation for women and in setting up the Children's Bureau to promote maternal and child welfare.[25] These historians concede that this legislation provided among the weakest set of protections of any industrial state. The essays in this volume do not support generalizations about the role of women in achieving labor legislation. In Australia and Switzerland, each of which created an impressive program of maternity leaves and night work regulation by 1900, women had little voice in the passage of legislation. Rather, the male leaders of political parties successfully fought for legislation to protect the wives of workers. In the Scandinavian countries, where women tended to oppose legislation, their success was mixed. In late nineteenth-century Britain, middle-class women constituted a significant, and partly successful, early opposition to extending protective legislation to workshops and homes. Large numbers of women were involved in local government and hence in the administration of poor relief and education, and in voluntary action of all kinds. But after 1900, women from all points of the political spectrum came out in favor of protective legislation. They did so in the name of protecting motherhood, although women were only one group among many campaigning for the Trades Board Act in 1909 that sought to put an end to "sweated labor" by providing a minimum wage for some occupations.

Continental European women's movements seem to have differed from those in Britain, Australia, and the United States in terms of form, strength, and goals.[26] The evidence in this book suggests that they were considerably more demanding with respect to protecting women's motherly roles and considerably more skeptical of the need for separate legislation with respect to women's employment. In many European countries, female social activists who expressed a belief in maternalism (in the sense of the importance of good mothering) formed alliances that were not necessarily entirely in poor women's interests. Susan Pedersen has described how, in France, the Catholic Union Feminine Civique et Sociale allied itself with pronatalists in its campaign for family allowances, but in so doing it found its commitment to the honor of motherhood and women's personhood hijacked by an illiberal maternalism.[27] In Britain, Beatrice Webb mounted a powerful campaign in favor of a minimum wage for certain categories of low-paid workers, male and female (although it was widely acknowledged that the vast majority were female), employing a range of efficiency arguments to do so—including the argument that minimum wages would promote the physical efficiency of sweated women workers who were also mothers of the race. Webb emphasized as well the idea that women would promote industrial efficiency. Thus, workers who were not capable of earning the minimum, such as elderly, infirm widows, would cease to be employed and have to resort to the poor law. As for the working women she wanted to help, their voices are often silent.

◆ ◆

Sorting through these issues has been a cooperative effort for a group of twelve women who live and work hundreds and thousands of miles apart and for most of whom English is a second or even a third language. What, we asked, were the different kinds of legislation passed? How did the forces that provoked such legislation differ across national lines? At what stage of the industrialization process did it begin? Who supported it? Was it pro woman? Or did it reflect an effort to regulate the labor force?

Our efforts to sort out the differences among countries and to see what generalizations might be made about the questions raised by protective labor legislation for women began in the early 1980s when Gro

Hagemann of Norway and Ulla Wikander of Sweden worked with other Nordic researchers to develop a Nordic comparison. That first attempt at comparison stumbled, but the idea blossomed again when the two arranged a session on "The Sexual Division of Labor" at an international congress on economic history held in Bern in 1986.[28] There, the three editors met for the first time.

The issues raised by the debates on labor market segregation at that meeting encouraged us to draw together a larger group that met three years later in Bellagio, Italy. Using contacts born of earlier involvements, personal recommendations, conferences, travels, and seminars, we tried to locate historians eager to expose their own research to international comparison. Our expanded group disagreed and discussed so adamantly that it was not until a third meeting in Leuven, Belgium, in 1990, that we began to see the shape of our project. Finally, the group met again in Mariefred, Sweden, in spring 1991 to sort out the project's final content. In between, encounters of two or three or four members of the whole took place; papers moved across national borders and oceans and language barriers; new angles were tackled, older ones dropped. Inevitably, and despite our best efforts, we did not manage to contact the relevant researchers in many countries. In particular, except for Greece, we missed any representation of southern Europe. Representation from other countries dropped out along the way. When a colleague from France withdrew, we mourned because the question of night work prohibition was so prominent among French feminists. We consoled ourselves by arguing that our effort at comparison was already so complicated that our work would merely provide a foundation on which others could build and which might be strengthened and shaped as more information emerged.

Early on we made several crucial decisions. To develop depth and provide some basis for comparison, we agreed to restrict our inquiry to the period before World War I. The decision provided us with a network of countries whose activists were more or less in touch with each other and whose success or failure to adopt legislation could not have gone unnoticed by other countries in the group. But restricting ourselves to the prewar period tended to exclude countries that had industrialized later. We added Greece in an effort to enrich the comparative frame.

When we agreed that our participants would, so far as possible, be working as historians in the country they wrote about, we thought the restriction offered a shared method and ground of analysis as well as common styles of presentation and research; but when we decided to publish the book first in the United States and in the English language, the differences came to the fore. For example, we differed dramatically on the question of when and how to present the hypothesis of an article and its result. Whereas academics from continental Europe tend to construct their essays like detective stories, taking readers by the hand and leading them through the arguments until they arrive at the surprise conclusion, Americans, English, and Australians present everything in an appetizing summary at first and from there go on to prove its validity by virtuoso manipulation of all the available evidence. This technique seemed a bit odd to the continental Europeans among us who made gracious efforts to accommodate to it in the present volume. The argument for the technique of the English-speaking participants seems to be that people will not read unless they are assured in advance that their efforts will be worthwhile. But continental Europeans argue that withholding the result tempts people to read who might refuse to do so if they know the result beforehand, and thus provides the possibility for changing closed minds.

In the end, we did not try to impose one method. Rather, we encouraged authors to follow their own judgments as to choice and presentation of data, style, and interpretation. Readers will find that continental European historians rely more on proofs in the text: long quotations are entered as evidence, while theoretical assumptions emerge only in brief and shadowy glimpses. The English-speaking style allows the voice of the researcher far more play: reflections and short summaries are interspersed in ways that appear decidedly unscientific to the continental researcher. Their emphasis on empirical facts may also reflect the relative paucity of writing in their own countries either on this topic specifically or on women's history generally. A far smaller common body of knowledge exists from which to start a discussion. Though we asked all the authors to keep the expectations of American academics in mind, we hope that in so doing we have not imposed restrictions that destroy the flavor of different academic traditions.

Since we have imposed few guidelines on either method or particular topic, each of the essays in this volume emphasizes what seems to be most important in the context of the national and international debate that influenced the thinking of the protagonists. Because protective labor legislation encompasses a broad rubric, the essays sometimes cover quite different ground. Each author has chosen to address the kind of legislation and the debates around it that are of most interest to her. This is not, in all cases, the most controversial issue, or the least. Rather, the author has chosen the issue or issues that seem in her judgment to have moved the debate. For countries such as Switzerland and Sweden, these efforts constitute reconstructions of the historical past not previously done. Other authors have had more leeway. In the case of Austria, Margarete Grandner has focused on the content of legislation, and the parliamentary maneuvers that produced it predominate. Efi Avdela and Anna Birte Ravn have identified the logic and motives of supporters and opponents of protective labor legislation. In the essays on Germany and the Netherlands, coalitions and disputes among supporters and opponents are placed in the context of differing theoretical assumptions. Sometimes, as for the United States, Australia, and Norway, the meaning of the legislation itself is unpacked. All the essays draw on the background of the international congresses laid out for us by Ulla Wikander.

Our effort has revealed not only the difficulty of making comparisons across national lines but also the complexities of the issues involved. For example, implicit in all these essays are efforts to interrogate the relationship of particular pieces of legislation to broader questions of family policy having to do with children and the male family wage. We begin to understand that such a relationship exists, but we are only just beginning to articulate the boundaries of the questions we must ask to reveal its intricacy. None of us has chosen to pursue the issue of state-sponsored enforcement, though its paucity runs like a thread through these essays, and several of us suggest that informal (gendered) mechanisms of enforcement might have been more powerful than factory inspectors could ever be. We have not attempted to obscure these complexities by seeking a common pattern. Instead, we hope that by encouraging each author to speak in her own voice, some generalizations might be possible. While it has sometimes seemed as if our comparative enterprise was rooted in the shifting sands of widely varying national circumstances and histories, we have taken comfort in discovering that the differences that make comparison so difficult also make it fruitful.

The rich details that emerge from the essays provide fertile ground for thinking out loud about the powerful symbolic meaning of the effort to regulate women's working lives that spread throughout the industrialized world in the early years of the twentieth century. At a moment when the emancipatory potential of workers' political aspirations reached their height, numerous nations, encouraged by a diverse array of international conferences, intervened to regulate the lives of women in ways that extended far beyond their concern for the welfare of workers. If the particular circumstances of different countries determined what positions were taken, and by whom and when, the general tenor everywhere was to see restrictions and benefits for women as a compromise between the perceived needs of family life and the demands of wagework. When applied to women only, protective legislation was directed less at their welfare than at reconciling the competing needs of women and families to meet a broader set of social purposes including sustaining the family wage male breadwinner ideology; supporting a sexually segregated labor market; and enhancing the possibilities of survival for future generations of workers. Because its reach was so broad, the terms of legislation were frequently contested. Applied to all workers, it seemed an unwarranted intervention in the free market. Applied to women only, it created special categories of workers. And since, in practice, legislation often affected certain categories of women more than others, it also produced divisions among women.

The authors of these essays take surprisingly similar positions in their overall evaluations of protective labor legislation. They share the interpretation that legislation shackled women to a male standard that substituted sameness for equality and turned difference into subordination. Their results thus challenge recent notions that maternalism provides an explanation for the passage of this legislation and its meaning as well as for the origins of the welfare state. Insofar as they suggest the stake of men in furthering the family-oriented and motherhood-preserving goals of nationalism, they call into question the value of the concept of maternalism itself. In elucidating the varied political interests in which protective legislation is located, these essays help us to understand something of the powerful and complicated meanings of regulating women. Many of the protagonists in the battle over regulation genuflected to the free labor market for men, even as they unapologetically intervened in it by reinforcing existing gender divisions and legitimizing new ones. The resulting legislation enabled many states to represent themselves as active agents in the search for humane values; and it simultaneously confirmed commonly held norms about women's special duties and natures while resisting challenges to the changing roles demanded of women by the new industrialism. The authors represented here find encoded within the politics and actions of legislators and reformers in different settings a series of messages about the roles of men and women, the meaning of the family, the importance of motherhood, the search for economic, political, and social equality or stability, and the nature of the state and the state's relation to its citizens. Perhaps, too simply, we might conclude that the legislation utilized women to rationalize the relationship of work to family life.

Notes

1. Directive 76/207/CEE article 5, 9 Feb. 1976, as reprinted in "Arrêt de la Cour du 25 Juillet, 1991. 'Égalité de traitement entre hommes et femmes—Interdiction legislative du travail de nuit des femmes,'" Arrêt C-345/89, Court of Justice of the European Communities, p. 3, no. 1.

2. Ibid., p. 10, no. 19. The following material is drawn from this document and from an appendix to it entitled "Rapport d'audience presenté dans l'affaire C-345/89"; see esp. pp. 3–4, 9.

3. California Fair Employment and Housing Act, Government Code 12845 (b). The California Federal Savings and Loan Association (CalFed) was initially taken to court in 1982 by Lillian Garland, a telephone operator who took a three-month pregnancy leave, after which the bank refused to return her to her original job. For a discussion of these issues before the adjudication of the CalFed case, see Nadine Taub, "From Parental Leaves to Nurturing Leaves," *New York University Review of Law and Social Change* 13:2 (1984–85): 381–405; and Lise Vogel, *Mothers on the Job: Maternity Policy in the U.S. Workplace* (New Brunswick, N.J.: Rutgers University Press, 1993).

4. See especially Brief of National Organization for Women et al., California Federal Savings and Loan Association et al. v. Mark Guerra et al., U.S. Court of Appeals for the Ninth Circuit, 1984 (nos. 84-5843 and 84-5844); and Brief of Equal Rights Advocates et al., California Federal Savings and Loan Association et al. v. Mark Guerra et al. to the Supreme Court of the United States, October term, 1985 (no. 85-494).

5. See, for example, Walter Korpi, *The Democratic Class Struggle* (London: Routledge, 1983); Mimi Abramovitz, *Regulating the Lives of Women: Social Welfare Policy from Colonial Times to the Present* (Boston: South End Press, 1988); Kathryn Kish Sklar, "'The Greater Part of the Petitioners Are Female': The Reduction of Women's Working Hours in the Paid Labor Force, 1840–1917," in *Worktime and Industrialization: An International History,* ed. Gary Cross (Philadelphia: Temple University Press, 1988). It is worth pointing out here that some of this legislation was adopted to protect workers' against employers who responded to accelerating competition by lowering wages and

firing inefficient workers, especially old people. Even in not-yet industrialized countries such as Australia, New Zealand, and Greece, legislators successfully argued that they needed to respond to the pressures of increased competition on employers by developing mechanisms for protecting workers.

6. For example, Eileen Boris and Peter Bardaglio, "The Transformation of Patriarchy: The Historic Role of the State," in *Families, Politics, and Public Policy: A Feminist Dialogue on Women and the State,* ed. Irene Diamond (New York: Longman, 1983); Alice Kessler-Harris, *Out to Work: A History of Wage-Earning Women in the United States* (New York: Oxford University Press, 1982); see also Efi Avdela, "To the Most Weak and Needy," in this volume.

7. On these points, see especially Judith Lown, *Women and Industrialization: Gender at Work in Nineteenth-Century England* (Cambridge: Polity Press, 1990), and Robert Gray, "Factory Legislation and the Gendering of Jobs in the North of England, 1830–60," *Gender and History* 5 (Spring 1993): 56–80.

8. Karen Offen, "Women, Work and the Politics of Motherhood in France," in *Maternity and Gender Policies: Women and the Rise of European Welfare States, 1880s–1950s,* ed. Gisela Block and Pat Thane (London: Routledge, 1991), points out the strength with which Catholic trade unions argued in favor of protective legislation in France, on the grounds that such laws would preserve gender divisions by keeping women in families. In Greece, this argument is put forward by legislators as a reason for creating protective labor laws.

9. See the essays in this volume by Lynn Karlsson, "The Beginning of a 'Masculine Renaissance,'" and Gro Hagemann, "Protection or Equality?" Denmark seems to have shifted positions: maternity leaves were part of the Poor Law of 1891 and the Sick Benefit Act of 1892, and also of the factory acts of 1901 and 1913. For this development, see the essay by Anna-Birte Ravn, "'Lagging Far Behind All Civilized Nations,'" in this volume.

10. Labor inspectors in Greece often used this argument to stress the need to enforce protective labor laws. Sweden, which debated such legislation in 1902–3, eventually found it unnecessary.

11. A discussion of these issues is provided by the essays in Seth Koven and Sonya Michel, *Mothers of a New World: Maternalist Politics and the Origins of Welfare States* (New York: Routledge, 1993), and by Alice Kessler-Harris, "Law and a Living: The Gendered Content of Free Labor in the Progressive Period," *A Woman's Wage: Historical Meanings and Social Consequences* (Lexington: University Press of Kentucky, 1990). A somewhat critical stance on the notion of maternalism is provided by Eileen Boris in her introduction to *Home to Work: Motherhood and the Politics of Industrial Homework in the United States* (New York: Cambridge University Press, 1994).

12. Robyn Muncy, *Creating a Female Dominion in American Reform, 1890–1935* (New York: Oxford University Press, 1991); Sonya Michel and Seth Koven, "Womanly Duties: Maternalist Politics and the Origins of Welfare States, in

France, Germany, Great Britain and the United States, 1880–1920," *American Historical Review* 95:4 (Oct. 1990): 1076–108.

13. Anna Davin, "Imperialism and Motherhood," *History Workshop* 5 (Spring 1978): 9–65; Jane Lewis, *The Politics of Motherhood: Child and Maternal Welfare in England, 1900–1939* (London: Croom Helm, 1980). During and after World War I, these "schools for mothers" increasingly became infant welfare clinics run by local government authorities.

14. Pierre Budin, *The Nursling* (London: Caxton Publishing, 1907); Gaston Variot, "Gouttes de Lait," *British Medical Journal* (May 14, 1904): 1125–26.

15. At the International Congress that met in Zurich in 1897, Catholic politicians discussed excluding married women from factory work altogether. See the following essays in this volume: Margarete Grandner, "Special Labor Protection for Women in Austria, 1860–1918"; Regina Wecker, "Equality for Men?" and Ulla Wikander, "Some 'Kept the Flag of Feminist Demands Waving.'"

16. Jane Lewis, "The Working Class Wife and Mother and State Intervention, 1870–1918," *Labour and Love: Women's Experience of Home and Family, 1850–1940* (London: Basil Blackwell, 1986); Elizabeth Roberts, *A Woman's Place: An Oral History of Working-Class Women, 1890–1940* (London: Basil Blackwell, 1984). In 1910, Greece also restricted work and provided no pay. Italy provided compulsory maternity insurance for women in childbirth but did not offer health insurance to male workers.

17. The International Congress of Working Women, which met in Washington in 1919, passed a resolution recommending that women restricted from working around childbirth be paid an income out of either public or insurance funds. But this does not seem to have been ratified by most European countries. For a rather optimistic summary of legislation as it existed in 1919, see Henry J. Harris, *Maternity Benefit Systems in Certain Foreign Countries,* U.S. Department of Labor, Children's Bureau, Publication No. 57 (Washington, D.C.: Government Printing Office, 1919).

18. John Macnicol, "Welfare, Wages and the Family: Child Endowment in Comparative Perspective, 1900–1950," in *In the Name of the Child: Health and Welfare, 1880–1940,* ed. Roger Cooter (London: Routledge, 1992).

19. Joanne Goodwin, "An American Experiment in Paid Motherhood: The Implementation of Mothers' Pensions in Early Twentieth Century Chicago," *Gender and History* 4 (Autumn 1992): 323–42; Molly Ladd-Taylor, *Mother-Work: Women, Child Welfare, and the State, 1890–1930* (Urbana: University of Illinois Press, 1994).

20. This conversation circled around, and in the United States largely ignored, issues of race. Married African-American women worked in proportions about three times as high as those of white women, and economic opportunity for their husbands was severely restricted. Most regulatory legislation

did not cover the occupations in which African-American women worked. Nor did national and international conversations about motherhood consider their needs.

21. Cynthia Cockburn, *Brothers: Male Dominance and Technological Change* (London: Pluto Press, 1983); Ava Baron, "Questions of Gender: Deskilling and Demasculinization in the U.S. Printing Trade, 1830–1915," *Gender and History* I (Summer 1989): 178–99; and Ava Baron, ed., *Work Engendered: A New History of American Labor* (Ithaca: Cornell University Press, 1991).

22. International Labour Office, "The International Protection of Women Workers: Early Measures of Protection," *Studies and Reports,* ser. 1, Oct. 15, 1921, 4. This position was in sharp contrast to that of Norway's social democratic women who had fought for a special night work ban for women. See Hagemann, "Protection or Equality?"

23. As the eminent physician Henry Maudlley put it in 1874, "sex is fundamental, lies deeper than culture, [and] cannot be ignored or defied with impunity" ("Sex in Mind and Education," *Fortnightly Review* 15 [1874]: 477).

24. See Ravn, " 'Lagging Far Behind All Civilized Nations.' "

25. Theda Skocpol, *Protecting Soldiers and Mothers: The Political Origins of Social Policy in the United States* (Cambridge: Harvard University Press, 1993); Muncy, *Creating a Female Dominion.*

26. For essays in a comparative frame, see Bock and Thane, *Maternity and Gender Policies;* and Koven and Michel, *Mothers of a New World.* On a more neglected area, see Efi Avdela and Angelica Psarro, *O feminismos stin Ellada ton Mesopolemon: Mia Anthologia* (Athens: Gnosi Publications, 1985).

27. Susan Pedersen, *Family Dependence and the Origins of the Welfare State, 1914–1945* (Cambridge: Cambridge University Press, 1993).

28. *The Sexual Division of Labor, 19th and 20th Centuries: Six Essays Presented at the Ninth International Economic History Congress, Bern, 1986.* Uppsala Papers in Economic History, Working Paper No. 7, Uppsala University, 1989.

· 1 ·

Some "Kept the Flag of Feminist Demands Waving"

Debates at International Congresses on Protecting Women Workers

Ulla Wikander

Protective labor legislation became a high priority in many circles during the final decades of the last century and the beginning of this one. In industrializing countries where class tensions and great disparities in living standards emerged, reformers and academics, women and men with a social conscience, as well as some politicians, employers, and workers' organizations began contemplating state intervention and expanded state responsibility. Their efforts were meant to come to terms with "The Social Question." For them, government regulation of working conditions provided a way out of a looming crisis brought on by the unimpeded play of market forces. Though individuals and groups differed in their reasons for supporting labor legislation, and especially in their opinions about what labor laws should encompass, they generally agreed that women needed a special kind of protection. Among men of different classes and nations, the consensus on this issue was especially strong. Sometimes, for very different reasons, they came to similar conclusions about the benefits of protective legislation for women only.

Women, by contrast, were divided over the question. Except for a few extreme free market liberals, the only significant dissent in the rising chorus of voices demanding special protection for women in the early twentieth century came from women themselves and a handful of male allies. Among working women as well as among so-called bourgeois women, vast disagreement existed over whether protective laws worked to women's advantage or disadvantage. While male society saw and treated women as an easily identified group for whom working conditions could be legislated unproblematically, women disagreed, recognizing that they belonged to many different groups with disparate interests. Their interpretations of the consequences of labor legislation differed widely.

This chapter compares the women's voices with those of concerned men—socialists and others—as they were heard at selected international congresses. All kinds of international gatherings became more and more frequent as the world grew smaller, as trains and steamers cut travel time dramatically. The 1880s and 1890s were the expansive decades for internationalization through congresses covering many areas and a multitude of topics, from statistics to anthropological criminology.[1] In this chapter, I introduce one of the vivid debates that developed in these new arenas of intellectual exchange.

Lacking easy access to public life, women sought to express themselves through several avenues. Some women joined male-dominated organizations and their congresses. Making themselves heard above the din, often as the bearers of unpopular minority opinions, proved hard going indeed. Weary of such battles, activist women attempted to circumvent their marginalization by forging public policy goals in largely women's circles. They created their own journals, societies, and regular meeting places. Other newly created spaces were major international women's congresses. These provided forums for skepticism about the course of labor policy and prevailing notions of the division of labor, suggesting differences and similarities in women's concern about the role of the state in regulating labor across the industrializing world.

Central in the debates of women's labor in all these congresses was the question—never resolved—about benefits or negative effects of special protective labor legislation to prohibit women from working at night. Around this question floated two distinct but interwoven discourses: first, that of male-female relationships in the labor market and workplace; and, second, the relationship of women's family duties to the needs of the state and the future of the "race." Arguments concerning such protective measures became a debate in part about the ideologies and principles underpinning the relations between men and women. They were also about the lack of choices confronting men and women in their struggle to come to terms with a rapidly changing and expanding labor market, in which "male" and "female" interests seemed on a collision course. Concepts of gender were at stake.

Beginning in the 1880s, women organized a series of international congresses to examine these and other questions across national boundaries. These congresses offer an especially important record for historians because they were among the few places where women could publicly speak their own minds in a supportive environment and determine the agenda themselves. The conferences were well prepared, and most women attending numbered among the activists for women's causes in their own home countries. As the essays in this volume indicate, female political activists across Europe had a lively interest in developments elsewhere and found these venues ideal for gauging the pulse of new developments and ideas, strategies and arguments.

I will examine four types of congresses here, each illuminating the way in which particular interest groups debated protective labor legislation for women. Two types were all-male or male-dominated arenas. The other congresses were all-female — the socialist women's congresses — or female-dominated.

The first type consists of congresses that focused on general protective labor legislation. These were semiofficial, sometimes government-sponsored gatherings and often brought together representatives from different nations. They remained few in number, beginning in Berlin in 1890, then meeting in 1897, 1900, 1905–6, and 1913. Eventually they grew into the International Association for Protective Labour Legislation with a bureau in Basel (1900), predecessor to the International Labour Organisation, which was founded after World War I (see appendix 1). They evinced more interest in fostering international cooperation between states, securing common legislation for equalizing the terms of trade between countries, and creating a friction-free labor market than in grappling consciously with relations between male and female labor. These congresses reflected widely held male views and produced legislative suggestions that were meant to be implemented on a national level.

The nine congresses of the Second International, held between 1889 and 1914, constitute the second discrete set of gatherings to be included in this chapter (see appendix 2). They became the regular international meeting points for socialists of various kinds. (At that time socialism and social democracy had not yet split into different movements.) The Second International was meant to stabilize the movement internally and internationally at the same time as it presented its demands and aims to the world. The Germans took the leading role in these congresses, competing with the French for this position, while other nations remained secondary actors.² Participants in the Second International showed keen interest in general international agreements on legislation about labor conditions, which regularly appeared on their agendas. These resolutions were far from gender-neutral. If at odds with bourgeois politicians on a multitude of issues, social democrats eventually came to act and argue very much like them on the question of special legislation for women.

Women who had joined the social democratic movement gathered at a third set of congresses. When it came to the question of protection of women at work, especially the prohibition of night work, the views of politically active socialist women in Europe varied widely.³ At first, they articulated their positions during the main congresses of the Second International. Beginning in 1907, however, socialist women were allowed to hold female "precongresses" to the Second International. These will form but a small part of the discussion here.

Finally, different opinions on the question of protective labor legislation were aired at a distinct set of international women's congresses organized by societies promoting women's causes with a wide range of political content. Such congresses—both small-scale or larger—met frequently after a first conference in Paris in 1878. From 1889 on, the topic of special legislation for women cropped up repeatedly in debates. By 1914 seventeen women's congresses encompassing general concerns had been held in various European capitals and in some of the larger cities in the United States and Canada (see appendix 3).⁴ Some, like the congresses sponsored by the International Council of Women, set very broad goals for themselves, taking up anything connected with women and inviting all women's organizations across the spectrum. Others dedicated themselves strictly to promoting equal rights for women; among these, several called themselves "feminist." Such was the Congrès Général des Sociétés Féministes,⁵ held in Paris in 1892. Over the years the number of women attending these different women's congresses grew from less than two hundred to several thousand, and they also became increasingly open to the general public, which could attend selected sessions. The heated debates generated by these assemblies reflected a vibrant and complex political culture that contemporary women had set in motion.

In this chapter, I lay bare some threads in the complex web of this world of congresses, seeking to show how differing positions on women and work arose and evolved in relation to protective labor legislation. In so doing, I will also trace the waning and waxing fortunes of the political value of "equality" for the women's movement—and the international roots of today's sometimes heated discussions about its content. During most of the period under discussion, "equality" and its counterpoint, generally called "peculiarity" by women at the time, were consistent subjects of discussion. Commitment to one or the other provided the basis for convictions as to what policies would best implement a better world for women. From "peculiarity" to a focus on "motherhood" was a short leap. The latter suggested a focus on women's lives as connected to duties toward children and family.

I go on to illustrate how the sharpest debates among activist women over the issue of protection and labor market conditions diminished after 1900, in a period when women's difference from men, as well as the primacy of promoting "motherhood," gained wide acceptance in the still-growing women's movement. Equalitarian arguments and positions were concurrently pushed to the margins of the movement or channeled into intense efforts to achieve suffrage for women. Nonetheless, a number of women, generally called "feminists," refused to relinquish their stance in opposition to special, gendered legislation.

◆ ◆

When the Second International held its inaugural meeting in Paris in 1889 (with the magnificent official title of Congrès International Ouvrier Socialiste de Paris 1889, issu des Congrès de Bordeaux, de Troyes et de la Conférence Internationale de La Haye),[6] protective labor legislation claimed a place high on the agenda, and delegates advocated organizing special international meetings and cooperative efforts on this question.[7] One resolution voted by the Parisian gathering dealt with general labor protection. It called for an eight-hour day for all workers and factory inspection to enforce state legislation. It also called for a night work ban for any worker, male or female, unless the nature of the work made night shifts indispensable.[8] Only two of the resolution's twelve paragraphs mentioned women separately: one stipulated that women workers should not be allowed into industrial jobs that endangered their "female organs"; and another, that women and young workers under age eighteen should not work at night.[9] The last formulation is difficult to evaluate from a gendered perspective. It was listed after the more encompassing demand that night work be generally prohibited unless absolutely indispensable and might be taken as a scaled-back compromise, all else failing. On the whole, this gathering of the International did not treat the case of women separately; rather, it included them in other demands for labor protection that also applied to men.

At this congress Clara Zetkin delivered her frequently cited speech on women's work "from a principled point of view." She argued that women's wagework was necessary in an industrial society not only for economic reasons but also as a matter of principle. Women's social and political equality with men (their *Gleichstellung*) depended on their economic independence, which could only be achieved through participation in wagework. At this point Zetkin opposed attempts to prohibit women from working outside the home, as well as any restrictions of that right. This, she argued, constituted an act of solidarity with the cause of workers.[10]

The equality stance seemed further confirmed at the next congress, held in Brussels two years later. Participants there were more or less provoked by the Belgian socialist leader Emile Vandervelde into conceding that women should be treated as equals to men. Women, he argued, were to live for their duties at home, not to have the same occupations as men. His formulation drew immediate fire and delegates confirmed their commitment to equality with only three dissenting votes.[11] Lest some women derived comfort from these beginnings, Vandervelde's rather orthodox drift was soon to resurface in the mainstream of socialist verities. The Second International again took up the subject at its third congress, in Zurich in 1893. There, protective labor legislation for women became the focus of special interests, which will be dealt with below.

Special treatment of women captured public attention when a very different kind of international conference focusing on labor legislation was assembled in the German capital, Berlin, in 1890. The first of the group of official and semiofficial congresses, this one was summoned by the new kaiser, Wilhelm II, who wanted to play a role in solving the ubiquitous social question. The Kaiser's positive stance toward protective legislation for workers seems to have emerged from his concerns about a strike wave plaguing German industries, especially in the expansive Ruhr area. At odds with his chancellor, Otto von Bismarck,[12]

Kaiser Wilhelm tried to strengthen his own national position as a leader capable of generating an international initiative. Bismarck's commitment to social insurance had been, Wilhelm thought, inadequate to contain worker discontent. Wilhelm proposed international cooperation around state regulation of working conditions. The kaiser sought an internationally agreed upon prohibition of labor on Sundays for all workers, as well as a reduction of the hours worked per week by women and children. He expressed his concern that the pace of industrialization had been so rapid that workers were physically taxed beyond their capacities ("squeezed like lemons").[13] His goal was to restore calm to labor relations, which was bound to benefit both the state and industry in the long run. Dealing with labor market regulations on an international level, he assumed, would mean that industry in all countries would face the same competitive possibilities and constraints. Armed with this rationale, state intervention into labor relations could be sold more easily to employers.[14]

At the international Arbeiterschutzkonferenz in Berlin, the representatives of several nations expressed doubts about the advisability of restricting work for adults, even if these were women. Despite this, the conference concluded that it was desirable that "girls and women . . . should not work at night." Seven countries out of fifteen, including Germany, voted in favor of a night work ban, while others such as Belgium, Italy, Portugal, and Spain voted against this formulation. France, Denmark, Sweden, and Norway abstained.[15]

Late in the day a French delegate at the gathering, Jules Simon, attributed his country's refusal to accept any restrictions on women's work to the tradition of individual freedom in France. Having explained that this was the official line, he declared his personal conviction that women were not individuals and thus could be protected without abrogating the principle of individual freedom for adults. Simon believed that women should be seen as mothers, as part of the family and home. Protecting them would halt a development that menaced the family and thus "the ethic of the human soul." Simon also alluded to women's "higher moral virtue." Others at the conference echoed his emphasis on "giving the mother back to the family" as the main goal for protective labor legislation for women.[16] His effort to associate all women with the concept of motherhood was by no means unusual at the time, though it contradicted the minority view of women's equality enunciated in the official French position.

Participants in the Berlin conference did not produce any binding agreements, but they did recommend that women not work at night or on Sundays, that their total workday not exceed eleven hours, and that they receive a break of at least one and a half hours each workday. They also recommended that women not be allowed back to work until four weeks after giving birth.[17] These resolutions became guidelines for future national initiatives for extending protective labor laws. They brought some uniformity to preexisting codes in Western countries and, by internationalizing them, gave them sanction.

Despite some recognition of their status as individuals in the official French stance, women emerged from the Berlin Congress lacking the self-evident right to be considered independent adults and ordinary citizens in this discourse of work and workers. Instead, every woman was assumed to be at the center of a family, an institution defined as the foundation of a stable society and important to the state. Barely hidden in the recommendations lay a set of assumptions about a woman's mission and her special role as a citizen. We have seen how support for the individual status of every adult, even females, quickly became blurred at this conference, with many state representatives responding positively to the proposal to exempt women from such status. Woman's special family duties received significant legitimation at a time when those duties conflicted with the demands of a labor market that used and needed women, and when other circles and assemblies had begun to object to women's special treatment as nonpolitical subjects and to take women's working conditions—and hence, women workers—very seriously.

The third congress of the Second International, in Zurich in 1893, reflected a dramatic transition to the opinion that had been explicit in Berlin. Women's equality, which had been taken as a matter of course in the two earlier socialist congresses, was thrown open to debate. The issue of special protective legislation for women received a prominent and visible place on the agenda. The Austrian Louise Kautsky presented a resolution calling for the protection of women workers.[18] It included an attack on the bourgeois women's movement, which she accused of rejecting out of hand protective legislation for women.[19] Capitalist society exploited both men and women, she argued, yet it was also necessary to "acknowledge the special role of women, based upon the differentiation of the sexes."[20] She proposed the following for women: an eight-hour day, prohibition of night work, prohibition of work two weeks before and four weeks after childbirth, and employment of a reasonable number of female factory inspectors.[21] Earlier demands for all workers, such as the prohibition of night work, were now confined to women.

Kautsky's proposals generated sharp disagreements, especially among the female delegates. One of them, the Belgian Emilie Claeys, argued that "this treatment will have the opposite effect of what [is] intended." She asked for equality in a strict sense, saying that "we cannot concur with a request for shorter working hours for women than for men. We do not demand any special rights for the woman."[22] Others joined her. Adelheid Dworschack[23] from Austria advocated "no special protection for us women" other than special protection concerning the period around childbirth. Further criticism of Kautsky's resolution revolved around the economic consequences of restricting women's wagework. Mrs. Nellie van Kol of Holland melodramatically warned that millions of unmarried women workers would have to choose between death by starvation or prostitution if protective laws were introduced.[24] An English delegate, Mrs. Irvin,[25] wanted to exclude the explicit attack on the bourgeois women's movement, hoping that channels for cooperation could be left open.[26]

Delegates from Belgium, Spain, Romania, Holland, Italy, France, and England raised the question of economic inequality by adding a demand for equal pay for equal work to the resolution. The Women Workers' Association of England and Ireland proposed an amendment that included the fight for equal pay and protective labor legislation for both men and women.[27] This double demand, stressing legal and economic equality, would also arise repeatedly at international feminist congresses from 1892 onward.[28] The prominent Social Democrat Clara Zetkin had by this time completely altered her earlier (1889) position and did not join the voices of dissent.[29] Together with Louise Kautsky she even spoke against the equal pay amendment.[30]

In the end the congress accepted the original resolution for the protection of female workers but softened the blow for its opponents by adding an equal pay amendment.[31] (Needless to say, men made up the majority of participants at the congress.) This combination of special protection for women plus the demand for equal pay was to become the standard position of the Second International on these issues during the decades that followed. The acceptance of the demand for equal pay without any discussion signals the double meaning adhering to

the slogan pointed out by Alice Kessler-Harris: for some it stood for
the protection of men's work from female competition and the pro-
motion of a gendered division of labor; for others it stood for justice
and equality.[32] Both advocates and opponents of special protection of
women could thus agree on equal pay for equal work.

The debate in Zurich shows that not all socialist women were at
ease with the German Social Democrats' position and the resolution
adopted by the Second International, and some of the German women
also remained reluctant to accept their party's official position. They
appear to have been brought in line.[33] Moving away from her position
of just a few years earlier, from 1893 on Clara Zetkin explicitly supported the demand for protective labor legislation for women.[34] Highly
influential, she set the norm for German socialist women and—as we
will see—carried her advocacy of this policy into later international
meetings of socialist women, where protection of women would stir up
controversy more than a decade later.[35]

◆ ◆

At the close of the 1890s, attitudes toward wage-earning women
within the working class and different working-class organizations were
at times negative, even resoundingly hostile. This rancor was much in
evidence at the International Congress on Protective Labor Legislation
in Zurich, in August 1897.[36] This congress falls outside the four categories of congresses outlined at the beginning of this chapter and must
be seen as a hybrid between the socialist Second International and a
kind of general congress to promote international labor legislation. It
represented a unique attempt to bring together representatives of organized workers, as well as other sympathizers of protective labor legislation, to discuss common strategies for implementing regulations. The
mass of congress-goers were trade union people but of different political and religious colors. Social Democrats constituted the majority.[37]

The Swiss Catholic Workers' Organization and its leader, the conservative Dr. Decurtins, organized this gathering.[38] Its debates illuminate
the depth and influence of religion on workplace policies and the conflicting ways in which the two trade union movements regarded working women, especially those who were married. Looking more closely
at this congress can reveal the prevailing uncertainty and defensiveness
of the socialist view in contrast to the Catholic view and provide as well
a more general perspective on the opinions of women, men, and fami-

lies as they appeared among active trade unionists. This is one of the few congresses with a majority of male participants where it is possible to discern some disagreement among men on the question of women workers. But these disagreements were at heart more political than practical, less directly concerned with perceptions of women and their social duties than with methods of promoting different ideologies.

Among the trade union delegates and other invited guests were some of the most important German *Kathedersocialisten*[39] (a term for academics who wanted to solve "The Social Question" by state intervention and legislation) and an impressive roster of German women, including Lily Braun, Clara Zetkin, Alice Salomon, and Jeanette Schwerin,[40] who represented both social democrats and activists from the bourgeois women's movement. Only six persons attended from France, among them Marie Bonnevial, representing a teacher's union and the Ligue pour le Droit des Femmes (Society for Women's Rights). In all, some thirty women took part as delegates or guests, together with more than five hundred men.[41]

While women were vastly outnumbered, women's wagework became one of the central flash points for disagreements. The journalist Gustav Maier, who was present at the congress, resorted to such melodramatic phrases as "a parliamentary battle field" dividing the congress into "two military camps" to describe how Catholics debated against Socialists. For Maier these high tensions indicated that a question of principle was at stake.[42] Yet the ferocity of the debate must have come as a surprise to many. Representing the preparatory Commission for Women's Work, two Swiss delegates, Jean Sigg and Margarete Greulich,[43] presented proposals for protection for women similar to those accepted in 1893 by the Second International's third congress. Carton de Wiart, delegate of the Belgian Social Christian Democratic Workers' party,[44] in turn offered up a provocative and unexpected counterproposal: "Women's work and especially married women's work in mines, quarries, and in large industries should gradually be eliminated."[45]

This proposal triggered a long debate. Best understood as a discussion of principle, it clearly differentiated the Catholics from the socialists.[46] The debate on women's work at this trade union and workers' congress did not focus on the workplace but, more pointedly, on the family and its meaning for a stable state. While wages were mentioned, the future of the family provided the subject at the core of Social Catholics' concern. The socialists responded defensively, surely a sign of their doubts about the views held by their own members on this question. Both sides laid claim to "facts," "science," and "rationality" as their own. In this constellation, socialist women had their work cut out for them: they wanted to defend not only woman's economic independence but also her special role in the family. The debate more or less ignored the issue of regulating work *in* the work force and focused instead on the unrealistic, but ideologically burning, question of *eliminating* at least married women *from* the work force. This standpoint heavily influenced the outcome of practical labor market policies.

Carton de Wiart defended the Catholic position by underscoring woman's weak physique and declaring that her role as mother demanded a healthy body, not one worn out by strenuous industrial labor. The results of women working outside their homes, he suggested, would be the dissolution of the family and the consequent undermining of society. Refusing to heed his message, he threatened, would lead to nothing less than "decadence." The Austrian baroness Marie von Vogelsang asserted that no working mother could possibly care for her children adequately.[47] Yet another speaker from this camp stressed that the family was a microcosm of the state, a "reflection of the state, and [here, too,] its Minister of the Interior must be responsible for something different than the Minister of Foreign Affairs."[48] If the image made clear that family responsibilities should be divided into public and private spheres, it simultaneously pointed to the interdependence of the two and evoked a popular contemporary metaphor: the family could be seen as a small state and the state as a large family.

Social Democrats such as Lily Braun, Clara Zetkin, and August Bebel defended women's right to work, even in industry. They accentuated a socialist belief in progress and articulated a conviction that women's wagework was necessary. But their arguments were often defensive. Braun first agreed that women's work in factories was too strenuous but tried to counterattack by saying that "a woman is not first a woman, just as a man is not first a man, but a human being. . . . She could only lay claim to the status of human being if she is economically independent."[49] Braun also claimed that to forbid wagework to women would foster prostitution and increase the number of children born out of wedlock because poor people could not afford to marry unless both worked. In the name of the family, then, wives had to be allowed to work in industry, but they ought to be legally protected.

On a different but equally family-oriented tack, Zetkin argued that working-class women should experience direct capitalist exploitation in the same way as men. This would make the working woman more conscious of her class position than a woman who was "nothing but a housewife" (*Nichts-als-Hausfrau*). Like Braun, she pointed out that a happy family life demanded an economically independent woman. She stressed that the socialists were not fighting for a mechanistic equality between men and women but sought harmonious individual development for women as wives and mothers. The wife was a husband's other half and, Zetkin often thought, the better half.[50] Her stress on complementarity inside the family, combined with personal economic independence for women, seems now like a compromise designed not to alienate her male trade union comrades.

The discussion culminated in a final verbal duel between the leaders of the two fractions.[51] When Decurtins argued that women ought to work primarily as mothers in the home, he drew on a range of arguments, from science to sociology, resorting even to Friedrich Engels's book on the condition of the working class in England and Marx's *Das Kapital* to underscore his argument that industrial work posed a menace to the family. Monogamous marriage, according to him, was God-given and thus natural, and the Christian family must remain the foundation of every sane society. Equality between man and woman was the sign of a dying culture.[52]

While both Zetkin and Braun had pointed to the importance of woman's economic independence, Bebel did not touch upon this. The leader of the German Social Democrats took up the theme of the family, denying that socialists wanted to destroy it. He deplored the need for millions of married women to work outside the home, thus abandoning their family duties. But, he argued, prohibiting them from working would not improve their condition. Bebel labeled his adversaries as atavistic, for they clung to an ideal of a bygone society, the petit bourgeois social order. By contrast, the socialists were moving forward and were going to move capitalist society to a higher stage, the socialist society. This idea constituted the fundamental difference between their worldviews.[53]

In the end, the social democratic majority at the congress rejected the controversial proposal to prohibit married women in particular from waged work.[54] The Zurich congress instead settled on a resolution that had been proposed early in its deliberations demanding far-reaching labor protection for women workers in large and small industries, work-

shops, commercial enterprises, transport, and communication jobs, as
well as in home industry. Delegates called for a maximum eight-hour
day for women and a forty-four-hour week, free Saturday afternoons,
and weekends comprised of forty-two hours uninterrupted by wagework. They also demanded an eight-week rest for mothers around the
time of childbirth, with a state maternity allowance, and equal pay
for equal work. These demands were approved without objection and
without discussion of such issues as women's individual rights. The congress also tackled the prohibition of night work in a later and separate
resolution, in principle demanding the ban for both male and female
workers.[55]

After the unrealistic suggestion to bar married women from doing
any wagework, the proposal that women be protected must have
seemed very moderate and sensible to everyone present. The debate
on women's paid work had included the voices of several women, in
itself an unusual occurrence at this congress, where at other sessions
most women kept quiet. The only exception to the general consensus
was Marie Bonnevial, who early during the congress dared to demand
women's right to work on equal terms with men. This conferred on
her the dubious honor of being referred to as the only one who "kept
the flag of feminist demands waving" (*tient le drapeau des revendica-
tions féministes*) at this congress.[56] Bonnevial argued that no distinction
be made between adult men and women when it came to labor legislation, for both needed protection. The first time she spoke the other
speakers ignored her, treating the matter as irrelevant.[57]

After the big debate on women's right to work, Bonnevial again
came forward with her call for equal legislation for men and women
and spoke against all curbing of women's right to work.[58] Her speeches
are hard to reconstruct, surviving in summary form or in secondhand
accounts only. Her comments were evidently considered less significant than those of Braun, for example, or Zetkin, whose words were
recorded in detail. A French report said that Bonnevial spoke "general
words on women's work and woman's emancipation." The official German protocol did not say much more.[59] After Bonnevial's contribution
to the forum, Decurtins commented—his sarcasm ringing loud and
clear—that only his chivalry had prevented him from interrupting her
earlier; even women must learn to keep the time when they become
emancipated, he jabbed.[60]

Bonnevial's compatriots at the congress categorized her as a feminist,[61] and she probably defined herself as such. She had been active at two earlier international feminist congresses held in Paris in 1892 and 1896. Both congresses had passed resolutions against protective labor legislation for women only and for both women and men.[62] Such was also the outcome of an international feminist congress that had taken place in Brussels only a couple of weeks earlier.[63]

Bebel, by contrast, lingered on the inconveniences that women's wagework had for women, men, and their families. His speech was a delicate balancing act between the conflicting opinions he must have known existed inside his own party. Bonnevial articulated the only feminist demand, which was not merely ignored by women as well as men but also subjected her to ridicule. Her insistence on raising the question of legal equality between the sexes among male trade unionists seems to have been an almost heroic, if hopeless, deed.

◆ ◆

While the reception of Bonnevial's interventions in Zurich suggests that most socialist leaders of both sexes had shelved questions of equality in favor of protecting women as mothers, the issue had not yet died for all socialists. Bonnevial belonged to a group of French feminists who simultaneously thought of themselves as socialists, trying to unite both these convictions.

They confronted a world where by 1900 many countries had already introduced labor laws for women only and other countries were contemplating such legislation. On an international level, several male initiatives on labor protection took the logic of women's special protection as self-evident, either as a first step toward general sex-blind legislation or with reference to women's difference. Among women, however, the question was far from settled.

Suffrage, a divisive subject even among female emancipationists during the 1890s, became a question that united more and more of them with the new century. It did not demand a revision of the gendered division of labor and so drew into a growing women's movement increasing numbers of women who accepted motherhood as woman's main duty. At the same time leading feminist activists began to support protective labor legislation. Equality in the labor market lost its self-evident position at many international women's congresses and turned instead into a highly volatile question when its revolutionary potential became apparent. But abandoning the idea of an egalitarian labor market in favor of political equality for women was not an easy process, and the expanding discourse on motherhood helped immeasurably to smooth the path. In one sense, the debates on protective labor legislation measure the transformation from interest in labor market conditions to the centrality of the family, a change that parallels the growth of the women's movement.

During the 1890s some of the international women's congresses had called themselves feminist and promoted egalitarian resolutions, beginning with the Congrès Général des Sociétés Féministes (General Congress of Feminist Societies) in 1892.[64] At such feminist congresses, resistance to special labor protection for women was especially strong. Precedent had been set in France with the Congrès Français et International du Droit des Femmes (French and International Congress on the Rights of Women), held in Paris in June 1889. This congress emerged when French feminists resisted official conditions for setting up a women's congress in connection with the Universal Exposition held that year to commemorate the French Revolution. Among other things, they objected to the official organizers' proposal that Jules Simon, a well-known protectionist, serve as president of the congress. Maria Deraismes became the main organizer of an independent congress for women's rights that protested the official view on labor laws for women. Thus, that jubilee summer saw two women's congresses instead of one.[65]

In the inaugural address of her free congress, Deraismes argued against the protection of women from the standpoint of liberal and equal rights. She derided special legislation, calling it restrictive and oppressive.[66] Later speakers denounced this kind of legislation because it would keep women out of certain respectable professions. A law prohibiting night work would limit women's liberty and was nothing less than a "law of slavery."[67] Such formulations set a precedent for several congresses in Paris for decades to come.

In 1892 the French parliament introduced a night work prohibition for women. The Congrès Général des Sociétés Féministes took a dim view of the decision and responded by demanding suffrage for women as well as a night work prohibition for *all* workers.[68] The same demands arose at the next Congrès Féministe International held in Paris in 1896. Resolutions called for no restrictions for women unless they also applied to men; apart from this, demands were for an eight-hour day for all workers and equal pay for equal work.[69] This congress was probably the inspiration for what Bonnevial was to offer the following year in

Zurich. Present at both congresses in 1892 and 1896,[70] she must have known that her daring demands had clear support in radical circles. This equality-based demand was to remain the basic feminist formula through the years up until World War I.

"Feminism"—defined as the organized demand for equality with men—was spreading as a concept and an agenda in neighboring Belgium as well. In early August 1897, for instance, the Congrès Féministe International met in Brussels. It was organized by the Ligue Belge du Droit des Femmes and presided over by Dr. Marie Popelin. A fairly small congress, it produced a rigid policy concerning special legislation. Popelin considered two questions as the most burning for feminist mobilization: unfair limitations on job opportunities and the regulation of prostitution.[71]

Women's right of access to all professions and all kinds of employment, as well as equal pay for equal work, was the theme of a half-day session on economic rights. Here contributors agreed that men had introduced legal protection to save the best jobs for themselves and escape female competition. The fact that women had finally begun to have access to more than a rudimentary education had led to "feminism, that is, the necessity for the woman to attain an independent position and be prepared to fend for herself in the same way as a man," wrote Maria Martin, editor of the Paris-based *Journal des Femmes*. Congressgoers called protective laws for women oppressive and insisted that economic independence was vital if women wanted to get away from the exploitation that many of them had to suffer in their own homes.[72]

"The liberty to work" was proclaimed again and again at this congress. Women were not demanding "more than men had already gotten," merely equality in the face of the law and the right to work. Wilhelmina Drucker of Amsterdam declared that she did not worry too much about suffrage; women would get that easily. Striking a gloomier note, she warned that the right to work on the same terms as men was going to be far harder to achieve. The liberty for women to work was not accepted by any man, be he a minister or a worker.[73]

Often underlying such claims was a presumed normal state of affairs. Male-female relations were expected to go on "as usual"; economic independence should be a possible choice, but not a duty for every woman. A few solitary voices could be heard demanding instead a clear-cut gendered division of labor,[74] or else insisting that married women should have a legal right to part of their husbands' income.[75]

The congress offered a militant plea for women's equality with men.[76]

Most speakers intended to expose the male-female competition for jobs and what they saw as more or less open warfare exploding around work and economic independence; they accused men of taking advantage of masculine political privileges and using their power to hinder women's opportunities. This congress—in contrast to the two that preceded it in Paris—had a more bourgeois character and was partly ignored by the French socialist feminists, despite its very similar analysis of protective labor legislation. In Brussels there was feminism without socialism, so to speak. Not all international women's congresses, however, had an equally clear feminist position.

The International Council of Women (ICW) had, since its inception in Washington, D.C., in 1888, ducked firm resolutions on controversial questions in an attempt to build a truly broad coalition of women's societies. Still, debates were allowed and flourished at its congresses.[77] The ICW had in fact dealt so reluctantly with the question of suffrage that the International Woman Suffrage Alliance (IWSA) was founded in Berlin in 1904 as a protest and way of mobilizing an offensive across national borders. This umbrella strategy of the ICW—to encompass extremely disparate elements while trying to avoid internal controversy—signaled its approach to the question of protective labor legislation and its special concern with women's night work.

On the positive side, this strategy allowed latter-day historians to follow heated discussions at some of the ICW's major gatherings. From a negative perspective, the organization—having no policy of its own and allowing no resolutions to be voted—appears to have given its tacit consent to the inclinations of a majority of its members when the organization grew. The ICW essentially, if not openly, took the side of advocates of special protective legislation for women, as we will see below. But its policy of indecision frustrated women on both sides of the question.

In 1899, at its International Congress of Women in London, the ICW brought up for discussion the issue of labor protection for women. The debate revealed the range of conflicts plaguing so-called bourgeois women. Alice Salomon began, painting a bright picture of the consensus recently reached on women's protection in her country, Germany.[78] She characterized such legislation as a positive development, for in her eyes it confirmed a natural sexual division of labor: "Such legislation will produce for the laboring classes what we must struggle to attain for all classes of humanity—a division of work according to sex on the basis of special qualities; it will put, in place of a mechanical or organic division of work, a division according to characters and constitutions!"[79] Salomon was thus aware of the potential consequences of the legislation in structuring the labor market and eager to have sexual divisions recognized, assessing them as favorable to women. This influential German social reformer hoped that the popular German concept *Eigenart* (translated as "peculiarity" in her speech and in congress protocols) would have positive consequences for women. The term "peculiarity" pointed up women's difference and transformed it into a valuable complement to men's particular gender characteristics.

Beatrice Webb of England followed up this defense of protection for women, blaming women themselves for their bad position in the labor market. She believed in different wage levels for men and women because of differences in "their particular circumstances." Male compositors had a right to high wages and to "a man's standard of life." She took the side of male compositors in a controversial debate over typographical work, a sector women often referred to when arguing against protective legislation; opponents of such laws often pointed to the fact that protective laws had had especially negative consequences in the printing industry.

That some kind of special protection was always necessary was another of Webb's arguments: it would always be required for certain work, or for the operation of certain machinery, or it would be "at times connected to sex." To make her point, she mentioned childbearing and the special needs of mothers after giving birth. Thus, when she required a safe argument for the protection of women, she emphasized the actual experience of childbirth, not the potential needs of motherhood, that underlay general claims for protection. Webb thereby fused the distinction between two kinds of protection, one general—for all women as possible mothers—and one specifically aimed at the individual woman giving birth. Other women at the time made such a distinction, demanding paid maternity leave for mothers.[80] Webb also raised the question of citizenship and the state, insisting that to "retain a high standard of citizenship, it is not in the interest of women to insist that they should be free to do whatever the men do."[81] Without different protection for women and men "the nation will not reach its maximum strength, and women, therefore, will fail to attain their maximum development."[82]

Webb's different definitions of citizenship for women and men was, as Jane Lewis has pointed out, a typical way of understanding citizenship at the time.[83] For Webb, citizenship was a duty toward the state; the question was what the state needed from its citizens of *different* sexes and not questions or demands for legal equality. She wanted favorable conditions in the labor market, including protection when needed, for the sake of the nation and its strength.

In response, Camille Bélilon, a Frenchwoman and contributor to the *Journal des Femmes,* fired off a polemical speech directed against Webb. She began by informing her audience that when paid work opportunities expanded, men of all classes tried to forbid certain work for women. She accused trade unions of acting in an *esprit misogynique,* for which she provided several examples. In the case of typographers, she decried union feelings toward women as nothing less than hatred (*haine*). Workers had plotted to get women out of their way by using the new protective laws. To that end they had even managed to fool members of Parliament by talking about child mortality and about the sorry state of the nation. With bitter irony she contrasted their eagerness in this case with their utter lack of concern about the damage to the race caused by alcohol. Women's economic independence could be halted through special legislation. There were people, Bélilon remarked in a pointed jab at Webb, who scolded women workers for taking low wages while at the same time supporting legislation that put women out of work. She proclaimed that to regulate *only* women's work was to abandon a feminist stance, a stance that called for the same freedom for women as for men.[84]

Alexandra Gripenberg of Finland argued that the "idea of special labor legislation for women is an outcome of the principle that women must have privileges, not rights, that they must be protected instead of having the power to protect themselves, that they are—as the national economists say—'A people's most precious property,' instead of forming a part of the people itself." She wanted women to be citizens on the same terms as men, not property to be protected.[85]

The last scheduled speaker, Harriot Stanton Blatch—an American and the daughter of Elizabeth Cady Stanton—had lived near London since 1882.[86] She argued that the "legal restriction" of women had "handicapped the evolution of women's economic position" and had increased the employment of children by placing women and children in the same category. She further suggested that such restriction had led to "indifference to the interests of men, and helped to destroy the balance in the number between the sexes." She also saw regulations as a barrier against women's entry into more skilled trades and professions. Blatch demanded equality because "the principle reason for making legislation equal is that men need legal protection as much as women."[87] Two English trade union representatives, one male and one female, enthusiastically spoke in favor of protection for women during the open debate that followed, calling it beneficial to the whole of society.[88]

The eloquent feminists present at this congress turned protective legislatinon into a gender conflict, objecting particularly to the disadvantages it carried for women workers. Blatch argued strategically that it was unfair to men not to protect them as well. The advocates of special protection by contrast pointed to women's difference and the interests of creating a harmonious society. A gendered division of labor was nothing to fear, they insisted. The line between the groups was already clear by this period, but the verbal sparring about practical and political outcomes would go on at international women's meetings for years to come.

No clear-cut political boundaries can be drawn to delineate the development of the controversies. German socialist and bourgeois women had joined in a pro-protection stance but did not otherwise cooperate. In other countries the alliances looked different. At the international level a geographical, national consensus between women can be seen developing in some arenas, for example, in France. In 1900, two international congresses for women were again held in Paris. This time, both of them passed resolutions against special protective labor legislation for women. The antiprotection stance had now spread to both the groups involved in setting up congresses. One congress, the Congrès International des Oeuvres et Institutions Féminines, took greater pains to emphasize women's capacities. Its participants, possessed by a strong liberal inclination, not only took a stance against labor protection for women but against *all* labor protection.[89] The autumn congress, the Congrès International de la Condition et des Droits des Femmes, stuck to the earlier established feminist line of asking for labor protection laws for all but no special laws for women. Bonnevial was one of the four discussants for the session dealing with women's work and protection.[90]

The international women's congress in Berlin, Der Internationale Frauen-Kongress in Berlin, held in the summer of 1904,[91] was organized by the German National Council of Women. The congress was a large one, with two thousand participants and six thousand visitors,[92] and represented the high point of emotional debate over protective labor legislation. Yet, as in London five years earlier, the heated discussion reflected little of the legislative process that was underway.

In her inaugural speech, Marie Stritt called the question of women in industry "the most burning women's question, the bread question."[93] Several sessions took up the issue of women's work.[94] Chairing the meeting on labor protection, Alice Salomon pointed out that such legislation was still a controversial question internationally. She suggested that the issue, which in her view was vitally important, distilled the character of the whole of the women's movement.[95]

The congress seemed generally favorable toward labor protection for women, despite the fact that no formal resolutions were made to demonstrate this position decisively. Three women spoke against such laws: Dora Montefiore of England, Alexandra Gripenberg of Finland, and Marie Rutgers-Hoitsema of Holland.[96] The congress organizers' positive inclination toward protection was, for example, registered by the treatment accorded the Rutgers-Hoitsema speech; it was duly summarized on one page, while the speech of an advocate of protection, such as Helene Simon of Berlin, sprawled over five pages.[97] Rutgers-Hoitsema's contribution was evidently appreciated by the Swedish participants, for *Dagny,* the journal of the women's movement in Sweden, published it in a translation covering seven pages.[98]

Women discussed but men ultimately made the decisions, for very few countries had given women the right to vote by this juncture. Protective labor laws for women were promoted by more influential male congresses with direct connections to the legislative bodies of states, and here a single dissenting voice was rare indeed.

◆ ◆

The final victory of advocates of protective labor legislation for women came in the series of international conferences started by the German emperor and then followed up by initiatives of a semiofficial kind from circles of concerned academics and state representatives. The latter were eager to equalize the conditions for competition throughout the industrialized world even as they tried to accommodate the expanding socialist movement. This cooperation materialized with the founding in Paris, in 1900, of the International Association for Protective Labour Legislation. Headquartered in Basel, Switzerland, it linked national associations for labor protection and aimed to coordinate, support, provide information about, investigate, and promote the spread of international labor agreements. In 1906 the association arranged a meeting in Bern that was attended by governmental representatives from fifteen countries. These representatives agreed to two international conventions, one prohibiting the use of white phosphorus in the match production industry and the other prohibiting women's night work in industry.[99] They constituted the first two international conventions on labor protection and laid the foundation for further cooperation between states on the structure of industry and work.

The convention on the prohibition of night work appears to have come about on the recommendation of the French National Association for Labor Legislation.[100] The contemporary French writer Marcel Caté reported that night work was at the top of the agenda because it was considered "the most important, the most urgent, and the easiest to take care of."[101] Considerations about "the economic value of the race" had been particularly relevant as an explanation of the importance of the recommendation.[102] To become valid, the convention had to be ratified by each national parliament and converted into national law. In contrast to most western European countries, legislators in Denmark and Norway never approved it, and Finland and Greece only passed it decades later, after World War II.

Conference participants in Bern steered completely clear of the question of the individual rights of women. As at earlier, male-dominated congresses on labor protection, almost no discussion took place about the contradiction between the political ideology of equality of humankind and special legislation for women. In this context, the short discussion in Berlin in 1890, initiated by the French delegate Jules Simon, must be seen as an anomaly. In Bern, some of the potential negative consequences of the legislation, such as that it might force a woman into home industrial work, prompted only brief remarks. The proposed solution to this kind of exploitation was for the conference to articulate its commitment to an extension of the night work prohibition for women to paid work at home.[103]

In the congresses on labor protection as well as at the congresses of the Second International, men had easily agreed on banning women's night work.[104] Inside the Second International, reactions to one dissenting male voice are telling. In 1910, at the Eighth International Socialist Congress in Copenhagen, the lord mayor of Stockholm, former Liberal turned Social Democrat Carl Lindhagen, put forward the suggestion that a night work prohibition had to be instituted for men also. He said

that the formulation in the congress's resolution on labor protection—
largely built on the older programs—was old-fashioned in the absence
of an amendment to include men. His suggestion provoked no comment.[105]

At the Second International Socialist Women's Conference, held
just before this 1910 general congress, Danish and Swedish women
disturbed the German-led united front among socialist women. They
argued against special legislation, demanding *equal* protection of all
workers; and until that could be attained, they wanted no special protection for women.[106] They brought up—in a purely socialist context—
the demands that feminists had raised again and again at women's
congresses, demands that had not been heard inside the Second International since 1893. Following the party lead on this question had been
significant for socialist women in Europe, but the Scandinavian arena
revealed quite a number of opponents to the simple party line of protecting women by denying them night work. It is of course doubtful
whether or not these dissenting socialist women would have labeled
themselves feminists, but—as this book demonstrates[107]—political decisions by men were not always accepted by women in the workers'
movement.

◆ ◆

On an international level it was mainly men who initiated the drive
for special labor legislation for women, culminating in an international
convention that banned women's night work in industry. When the
International Labour Organisation formed in 1919, it stood firmly behind the ban, even as it became one of the most controversial international labor conventions of the 1920s and 1930s. In fact, it remains
controversial to this day, contradicting edicts condemning discrimination against particular categories of workers.

For a short period, women activists claimed a share of the international spotlight by airing their positions on what was for them a burning question. But their opportunities for influencing national policies
remained limited. Women who organized together with men tended to
conform and accept special prohibitions for women. Female factory inspectors—in most countries where there were any—also were more or
less closely connected to official social policy institutions. Julie Arenholt of Denmark, Vera Hjelt of Finland, and to some extent Kerstin
Hesselgren of Sweden remained exceptions.

Strong opposition to the special night work ban was raised by women who called themselves feminists, especially those from France, Holland, and Belgium, but some from England and the United States as well, and their opposition died hard. Organized bourgeois women in Denmark, Sweden, Norway, and Finland also protested against the ban. In some of these countries, such as Denmark and Sweden, unity on this question developed across class boundaries, contradicting the anticooperative spirit that German Social Democrats had tried to foster to make the rift between women of different classes unbridgeable. In other countries most women accepted the principle of special protection, and by the first decade of the twentieth century few female voices—except those mentioned—were raised against special labor laws for women. There was no clear class division on the question, but it seems that socialist women were under greater pressure everywhere to accept these types of laws than were the more independently organized bourgeois women.

In contrast, the women's international congresses examined here highlight the competing discourses about women and work. Unlike male-dominated groups, women explicitly raised the issue of equality and discussed its complications for women. Since the 1890s, the International Council of Women had moved very cautiously, not really wanting to take a stand on the most controversial questions concerning women—neither on suffrage nor on protection. Inside the influential ICW the question of protection was never settled. But many other international women's congresses resolutely opposed special legislation for women even after 1900 and explicitly raised the feminist double demand of equal pay and equal protection. Even the 1913 Parisian congress, meeting under the auspices of the ICW, insisted on such a formulation.

Debates about protective labor legislation connected women's economic independence to new constructions of the sexual division of labor. This can be seen in the actions of women who regarded the labor market as the place where competition prevailed between men and women, with men having the upper hand. These women led an abortive attempt to organize a new international, truly feminist organization focusing on the labor market. Following the lead of the International Woman Suffrage Alliance, which had organized separately around suffrage, they created an organization called International Correspondance to oppose the movement to ban women's work at night. Founded in Stockholm in 1911, with headquarters in The Hague, and led by Marie Rutgers-Hoitsema, it vehemently opposed the Bern Convention of 1906 and promoted women's legal equality with men at work. For different reasons this organization folded after some years of activity.[108]

Deep-seated principles or prejudices about women—rarely discussed by men explicitly—lay behind the night work prohibition and were translated into the concrete division of a gendered labor market through legislation. The result was widespread acceptance of social conventions that assigned different jobs to men and women. Social practice was reinforced by repeated arguments about women's special nature and about motherhood and its consequences, arguments that reverberated in the labor market as well as in the family. Many women also accepted the general analysis that saw women and men as essentially different quantities; their numbers increased from the mid-1890s onward. In Germany this tendency was launched under the expression *Eigenart,* meaning "special or peculiar species," hinting at great and natural differences of a directly complementary kind.

A sexual division of labor was thus accepted by various women who, through their analyses of women's "peculiarities," became influential. A prime example was the Swedish author, Ellen Key, whose book *The Century of the Child* appeared in 1901 and was translated into many languages. It contains a long and elaborate defense of special protective labor laws for women, seeing them as beneficial to both mother and child. Even when such women demanded suffrage, they tolerated special "natural" occupations for women and thought women especially well suited to care for homes and children. Thus men and most women united in an analysis of women and men as different and complementary—and the labor market of this century was organized accordingly. Congresses helped to internationalize such attitudes and also to spread legislation confirming conventional ideas about women and work in a time of great possibilities and of real changes in the structure of workplaces and identities.

Appendix 1:

International Congresses on Protective Labor Legislation before World War I

1890   Der Internationalen Arbeiterschutzkonferenz in Berlin, 15–29 March
1897   Internationaler Kongress für Arbeiterschutz in Zurich, 23–28 August
1897   Congrès International de Législation du Travail, tenu à Bruxelles, 27–30 September

1900   Congrès International pour la Protection Légale des Travailleurs, Tenu à Paris, 25–28 July

1906   Conference Diplomatique pour la Protection Ouvrière, Réunie à Berne, 17–24 September, which had been prepared by a technical conference in 1905

1913   Technical Preparatory Conference in Basel, in September. Because of the war, a diplomatic conference scheduled for 1914 never took place.

Appendix 2:
Congresses of the Second Socialist International, 1889 to World War I

Congresses were held in the following cities:

1889   Paris
1891   Brussels
1893   Zurich
1896   London
1900   Paris
1904   Amsterdam
1907   Stuttgart (with a socialist women's precongress)
1910   Copenhagen (with a socialist women's precongress)
1912   Basel

A congress planned for 1914 in Vienna was never held.

Appendix 3:
Official Names of General International Women's Congresses from 1878 to 1914

1. 1878 in Paris: Congrès International du Droit des Femmes, 25 July–7 August
2. 1888 in Washington, D.C.: a preliminary International Council of Women congress, 25 March–1 April
3. 1889 in Paris: Congrès Français et International du Droit des Femmes, 25–29 June
4. 1889 in Paris: Congrès International des Oeuvres et Institutions Féminines, 12–18 July
5. 1892 in Paris: Congrès Général des Sociétés Féministes, 13–18 May
6. 1893 in Chicago: World's Congress of Representative Women (official beginning of the International Council of Women), 15–22 May
7. 1896 in Paris: Congrès Féministe International, 8–12 April

8. 1896 in Berlin: Der Internationale Kongress für Frauenwerke und Frauenbestrebungen, 19–26 September
9. 1897 in Brussels: Congrès Féministe International de Bruxelles, 4–7 August
10. 1899 in London: International Congress of Women (jointly with the quin-
    quennial meetings of the ICW), 26 June–5 July
11. 1900 in Paris: Congrès International des Oeuvres et Institutions Fémi-
    nines, 18–23 June
12. 1900 in Paris: Congrès International de la Condition et des Droits des
    Femmes, 5–8 September
13. 1904 in Berlin: Der Internationale Frauen-Kongress in Berlin (jointly with
    the quinquennial meetings of the ICW), 12–18 June
14. 1909 in Toronto: International Congress of Women (jointly with the quin-
    quennial meetings of the ICW), 24–30 June
15. 1912 in Brussels: Congrès Féministe International de Bruxelles 1912, 28–
    30 April
16. 1913 in Paris: Dixième Congrès International des Femmes—Oeuvres et
    Institutions Féminine—Droits des Femmes (jointly with the ICW), 2–
    10 June
17. 1914 in Rome: International Congress of Women (jointly with the quin-
    quennial meetings of the ICW), 16–23 May

Notes

1. *Mil neuf cent: Revue d'histoire intellectuelle.* Special issue: "Les congrès
lieux de l'échange intellectuel 1850–1914," no. 7 (1989): 13.

2. James Joll, *The Second International, 1889–1914* (1955; rpt., London: Routledge, 1974).

3. Researchers have tended to neglect the differences among socialist
women, to ignore the Scandinavian arena, and instead to take the later German or Austrian positions as the representative European case. See, for example, Eleanor S. Riemer and John C. Fout, eds., *European Women: A Docu-
mentary History, 1789–1945* (New York: Schocken, 1980), 88, 91. In contrast to
my findings, Riemer and Fout blame "male-led socialist parties" for having
objected to and delayed special legislation for women and assume women
were unified in their desire for these laws.

4. More specialized international women's congresses—for example, on
peace, suffrage, or the white slave trade—are not examined here.

5. I use "feminist" in this essay strictly as it was used at the international
women's congresses. There it was connected to women demanding equal rights
with men in the labor market, in education, and before the law. Thus far I
have not found the term used in any other broader sense at these congresses.

Several of these feminists also called themselves socialists, especially during the 1890s in France. See Ulla Wikander, "International Women's Congresses, 1878–1914: The Controversy over Equality and Special Labour Legislation," in *Rethinking Change: Current Swedish Feminist Research*, ed. Maud L. Eduards et al. (Stockholm: HSFR, 1992).

6. George Haupt, *La Deuxième Internationale, 1889–1914: Étude critique des sources, essai bibliographique* (Paris: Mouton, 1964), 105n.3.

7. *Histoire de la IIe Internationale*, vols. 6–7: *Protokoll des Internationalen Arbeiter-Congresses zu Paris, Abgehalten vom 14. bis 20.Juli 1889: Deutsche Uebersetzung* (Nürnberg, 1890) (Geneva: Minkoff Reprint, 1976), 168.

8. Ibid., 170.

9. Ibid.

10. Ibid., 128–32.

11. Ibid., vol. 8: *Congrès International Ouvrier Socialiste, . . . Bruxelles du 16 au 23 août 1891*, 118–19; *Verhandlungen und Beschlüsse des Internationalen Arbeiter-Kongresses zu Brüssel (16.–22. August 1891)* (Berlin, 1893), 314.

12. Ernst Gagliardi, *Bismarcks Entlassung: Erster Teil: Die Innenpolitik* (Tübingen: Mohr, 1927), 31. For an evaluation of this social policy and the crisis with Bismarck, see Sabine Schmitt, " 'All These Forms of Women's Work Which Endanger Public Health and Public Welfare,' " in this volume.

13. Gagliardi, *Bismarcks Entlassung*, 35–36; Werner Trappe, *Dr. Hans Freiherr von Berlepsch als Sozialpolitiker* (Essen a.d. Ruhr: Diss. Univ. Köln, 1934), 15ff.

14. For international cooperation in this field, see Regina Wecker, "Equality for Men?" in this volume.

15. *Die Protokolle der internationalen Arbeiterschutzkonferenz* (Im amtlichen Auftrag) (Leipzig: Duncker und Humblot, 1890), 89–91, 132.

16. Ibid., 154–55.

17. *Conférence internationale concernant le règlement du travail aux établissement industriels et dans les mines* (Par autorisation officielle) (Leipzig: Duncker et Humblot, 1890), 82.

18. Schmitt, " 'All These Forms of Women's Work Which Endanger Public Health and Public Welfare,' " discusses the congress, further connecting it to developments inside the influential German Social Democratic movement. Louise Kautsky was the former wife of the prominent German socialist leader Karl Kautsky. After her divorce she lived in London as Friedrich Engels's secretary. From there she wrote for the Austrian *Arbeiterinnenzeitung*, which focused on women workers.

19. *Protokoll des Internationalen Sozialistischen Kongresses in der Tonhalle Zürich vom 6. bis 12.August 1893*, ed. the Organisationskomite (Zürich: Grütlivereins, 1894), 36ff.

20. Ibid., 37.

21. Ibid., 36–37.

22. Ibid., 38, 55.

23. Later, she became well known as Adelheid Popp and eventually changed her opinion.

24. Ibid., 39. Nellie van Kol was married to the Social Democrat H. van Kol, who was at the congress as a representative of Holland. She and her husband lived in Belgium, near Liège. She is not mentioned in the list of the participants of the congress (ibid., 55ff.) but apparently still took part in the discussions. "That same summer of 1893, Nellie van Kol together with Emilie Claeys founded a Dutch-Flemish Women's Association (Hollanda-Vlaamse Vrouwenbond), which did not last very long" (Ulla Jansz, personal communication).

25. List of participants: "Marguerite Irwin, Glasgow, Women's Provident Protective League." Ibid., 58.

26. Ibid., 37–39.

27. Ibid., 38.

28. Wikander, "International Women's Congresses."

29. Her change during these years can be followed in several articles appearing under her name in her journal *Die Gleichheit*. See Schmitt, "'All These Forms of Women's Work Which Endanger Public Health and Public Welfare.'"

30. *Protokoll des Internationalen . . . Zürich . . . 1893,* 39–40.

31. Ibid., 40.

32. Alice Kessler-Harris, *A Woman's Wage: Historical Meanings and Social Consequences* (Lexington: University Press of Kentucky, 1990), 81ff.

33. *Report to the First International Conference of Socialist Women* (1907), 10–11. Here, women admit in an account of their own history that German Socialist women had opposed protective labor legislation up until 1893. Schmitt, "'All These Forms of Women's Work Which Endanger Public Health and Public Welfare,'" discusses this in more detail.

34. See *Die Gleichheit* 3, nos. 16, 18, 19, 20 (1893).

35. See Anna-Birte Ravn, "'Lagging Far Behind All Civilized Nations,'" in this volume.

36. In German, "Der internationale Kongress für Arbeiterschutz in Zürich." See Wecker, "Equality for Men?"

37. *Internationaler Kongress für Arbeiterschutz in Zürich vom 23. bis 28. August 1897: Die Cirkuläre des Organisationskomites; Referate und Anträge und Vorläufiges Verzeichniss der Kongresstheilnehmer* (Zürich: Grütlivereins, 1897), 3. Social Democrats had earlier rejected invitations from the separate Christian trade union movement for a meeting but agreed to accept if they were allowed to be the majority. See *Musée Social, Série B, Circulaire No. 14,* special number: "Le congrès de la protection ouvrière à Zürich" (protocols and comments to the congress in Zurich) (Paris, Oct. 15, 1897), 402.

38. For a discussion of Decurtins, see Wecker, "Equality for Men?"

39. Report of Gustav Maier in *Die Verhandlungen und Beschlüsse des internationalen Kongresses für Arbeiterschutz in Zürich (23.–28. August 1897)* (Bern: Verlag von Steiger & Cie, 1897), 4; *Internationaler Kongress*, 273, 278. For example, the professors Adolf Wagner, Heinrich Herkner, Werner Sombart and Ferdinand Tönnies. It seems as if only Herkner really participated, whereas the others gave their support in absentia.

40. Maier, in *Die Verhandlungen*, 4; *Internationaler Kongress*, 278. Minna Cauer and Elisabeth Gnauck-Kühne gave their support in absentia.

41. *Internationaler Kongress*, 261ff.

42. Maier, in *Die Verhandlungen*, 21–22.

43. *Internationaler Kongress*, 198–206.

44. "Herr Carton de Wiart, der bekannte belgische Deputierte und Wortführer der dortigen demokratisch-christlich-socialen Arbeiterpartei" (Maier, in *Die Verhandlungen*, 22).

45. *Internationaler Kongress*, 206.

46. According to judgments by French delegates from the Musée Social, Paris, Wiart's proposition was never considered a realistic one. It was more intended to emphasize the differences between the Catholics and the socialists than to be accepted (*Musée Social*, 419n.1).

47. Ibid., 421.

48. Maier, in *Die Verhandlungen*, 24–25.

49. *Internationaler Kongress*, 207.

50. Ibid., 210–13.

51. Ibid., 215. Fifteen persons were waiting to speak when the discussion was limited to only two final speakers, with one chosen by each side.

52. Ibid., 217.

53. Ibid., 217–20.

54. Ibid., 220. There were 165 votes against 98.

55. Ibid., 198, 227ff.

56. *Musée Social*, 404. This was how her compatriots described her contribution to the congress in their report.

57. Ibid., 414.

58. *Internationaler Kongress*, 220.

59. *Musée Social*, 404, 424; *Internationaler Kongress*, 220. The German protocol added that she spoke in favor of an international coalition on working women.

60. *Musée Social*, 220–21. Bonnevial had been given ten minutes to make her unpopular case. Her contribution received all of four lines in the protocol, as many as Decurtins's sneering remark.

61. To be called a feminist in this context was demeaning. It was what French equality feminists with leanings toward a socialist worldview called

themselves at the international congress in Paris in 1892. From that congress on, "feminism" implied the demand for equal treatment. See Wikander, "International Women's Congresses."

62. Ibid.

63. *Actes du Congrès Féministe International de Bruxelles, (4–7 août) 1897* (publié par les soins de Mlle. Marie Popelin, docteur en droit, secrétaire générale du congrès) (Bruxelles: Impr. Scientifique, 1898); and Léopold Lacour, "Le congrès féministe de Bruxelles," *Le Journal,* Aug. 3, 4, 9, and 10, 1897.

64. *Le Journal des femmes* (a woman's journal presenting the agenda, discussions, and resolutions of this congress), no. 7 (June 1892) and no. 8 (July 1892); *Le Matin,* May 14, 1892; *La Lanterne,* May 17, 1892.

65. *Congrès Français et International du Droit des Femmes, 1889* (tenu à Paris, salle de Géographie du 25 au 29 juin) (Paris: E. Dentu, 1889). See appendix 2 for the name of the other officially acknowledged congress, which did not discuss protective labor legislation. Wikander, "International Women's Congresses"; Patrick Kay Bidelman, *Pariahs Stand Up! The Founding of the Liberal Feminist Movement in France, 1858–1889* (Westport, Conn.: Greenwood Press, 1982), 173ff.; Laurence Klejman and Florence Rochefort, "L'égalité en marche: Histoire du mouvement féministe en France" (Diss., Université Paris Sept), 425ff., and a later, shorter version printed as *L'égalité en marche: Le Féminisme sous la Troisième République* (Paris: des femmes, 1989).

66. *Congrès Français,* 3ff.

67. Ibid., 122.

68. *Le Journal des femmes,* no. 7 (June 1892) and no. 8 (July 1892).

69. "Voeux adoptés par le Congrès Féministe International, 1896," Dossier 37, Bibliothèque Marguerite Durand (BMD), Paris.

70. Ibid.; *Le Temps,* May 14, 1892; Patrick Kay Bidelman, "The Feminist Movement in France: The Formative Years, 1858–1889" (Ph.D. diss., University of Michigan, 1975), 382, appendix J; "Congrès 1896—Paris," Dossier 37, BMD, Paris.

71. *Congrès Féministe.*

72. Ibid., 53, 56–58, 60, 66.

73. Ibid., 69–71.

74. Among them were Hanna Bieber-Böhm of Germany and Mme. Kergomard of France. See ibid., 77–79, and the brochure by Mme. Vincent, "Congrès féministe international de Bruxelles, en 1897" (Paris: 1898), 4.

75. *Congrès Féministe,* 75–76.

76. Ibid.; Lacour, "Le congrès féministe de Bruxelles."

77. Wikander, "International Women's Congresses."

78. *The International Congress of Women, London, July 1899,* vol. 2, ed. Isabel Maria Gordon, Countess of Aberdeen (London: T. Fisher Unwin, 1900), ix, 36–40.

79. Ibid., 39.

80. See the following chapters in this volume: Ravn, "'Lagging Far Behind All Civilized Nations'"; Lynn Karlsson, "The Beginning of a 'Masculine Renaissance'"; and Margarete Grandner, "Special Labor Protection for Women in Austria, 1860–1918." Such a distinction was made in Scandinavia as well as in Austria.

81. *The International Congress of Women*, 39.

82. Ibid., 43.

83. Jane Lewis, *Women and Social Action in Victorian and Edwardian England* (Hants: Edward Elgar, 1991), 7ff.

84. *The International Congress of Women*, 43–48.

85. Ibid., 48–50; the quotation appears on p. 43.

86. Ibid. Stanton Blatch (mistakenly named "Black" in part of the protocol) was one of the nine convenors of the session on industry and legislation. (Her name is spelled correctly on the unpaginated list of convenors.) See Elisabeth Griffith, *In Her Own Right: The Life of Elizabeth Cady Stanton* (New York: Oxford University Press, 1984), 181, 214, 229. Blatch's full name was Harriot Eaton Stanton Blatch. Born in 1856, she had a home in Basingstoke, west of London, since her marriage in 1882. Susan B. Anthony, leader of the U.S. delegation to the meeting in 1899, stayed with her during the congress. See Ellen Carol DuBois, "Working Women, Class Relations, and Suffrage Militance: Harriot Stanton Blatch and the New York Woman Suffrage Movement, 1894–1909," in *Unequal Sisters: A Multicultural Reader in U.S. Women's History*, ed. Ellen C. DuBois and Vicky L. Ruiz (New York: Routledge, 1990).

87. *The International Congress of Women*, 50–54.

88. Ibid., 57–58. Mrs. Amie Hicks, president of the Ropemakers' Union, and Mr. Herbert Burrows, secretary of the Matchmakers' Union.

89. *2e Congrès International des Oeuvres et Institutions Féminines, tenu au Palais des Congrès de l'Exposition Universelle de 1900* (sous la présidence d'honneurs de M Léon Bourgeois et sous la présidence de Mlle Sarah Monod, compte rendu des travaux par Mme Pégard, Chevalier de la Légion d'honneur, secrétaire générales du congrès), 4 vols. (Paris: Impr. de Charles Blot, 1902), 1:91.

90. *Congrès International de la Condition et des Droits des Femmes* (tenu les 5, 6, 7 et 8 Septembre 1900 a l'exposition universelle au Palais de l'Economie Sociale et des Congrès. Questions économique, morales et sociales. Éducation. Législation: droit privé, droit public.) (Paris: Impr. des Arts et Manufactures, 1901), 54–55.

91. *Der internationale Frauen-Kongress in Berlin 1904: Bericht mit ausgewählten Referaten* (Herausgegeben im Auftrage des Vorstandes des Bundes Deutscher Frauenvereine von Marie Stritt) (Berlin: Habel, 1905), xxi–xxv.

92. Ibid., 1ff.

93. Ibid., 4.

94. Ibid., 177.

95. Ibid., 444–45.

96. Ibid., 444ff.

97. Ibid., 445–51.

98. *Dagny* (1904): 377–83. See Karlsson, "The Beginning of a 'Masculine Renaissance.'"

99. *Bulletin de l'Office International* (1905–6).

100. Alexandre Millerand, "La Conference Officielle de Berne," in *La Protection Légale des Travailleurs: Discussions de la Section Nationale Française, de l'Association Internationale pour la Protection Légale des Travailleurs,* ser. 3 (Paris: Musée Social, 1907).

101. Marcel Caté, *La Convention de Berne de 1906, sur l'interdiction du travail de nuit des femmes employées dans l'industrie* (Thèse pour le doctorat. Université de Paris. Faculté de droit) (Paris: Emile Larose, libraire-éditeur, 1911), 18–19.

102. Ibid., 26.

103. The "Résumé des arguments évoqués pour et contre le travail de nuit des femmes"; it also exists in a German version: Pre-ILO 10 403, ILO archives, Geneva.

104. In fact, very few dissenting voices were heard at some of the congresses that I have not dealt with here, for instance, one in Brussels in 1897. See *Congrès International de Législation du Travail, tenu à Bruxelles du 27 au 30 septembre 1897* (Rapports et compte rendu analytique des séances publié par le bureau de la commission d'organisation) (Bruxelles: Weissenbruch, 1898). Those voices belonged to extreme liberals, however, who were also against labor protection across the board and advocated a totally free labor market.

105. *Congrès Socialist International* (Copenhagen, August 28–September 3, 1910), reprinted in *Histoire de la IIe Internationale,* vols. 19–21 (Geneva: Minkoff Reprint, 1981), 471–72.

106. See also Ravn, "'Lagging Far Behind All Civilized Nations.'"

107. See the following essays in this volume: Ravn, "'Lagging Far Behind All Civilized Nations'"; Gro Hagemann, "Protection or Equality?"; and Karlsson, "The Beginning of a 'Masculine Renaissance.'"

108. In its planning stages, this organization was called the International Women's Labor Association. See the Rutgers-Hoitsema papers at the International Archives for the women's movement in Amsterdam. I will explore this aborted attempt further in a forthcoming book.

· 2 ·

Equality for Men?
Factory Laws, Protective Legislation for Women in Switzerland, and the Swiss Effort for International Protection

Regina Wecker

In a report by the British Royal Commission of Labour on Switzerland presented to Parliament in London in 1893, the commentator remarked,

> It is a remarkable fact that Swiss law contains so few provisions for the protection of women and children. The same working hours, with the same intervals are legal for all persons employed in factories whatever may be their age or sex. . . . Women are altogether forbidden to work at night. . . . A large number of women and children are, however, employed in factory work, and some cases occur in which children are allowed to begin work too early, or women are employed in dangerous work or kept at work all night.[1]

From a foreign perspective, provisions in the Swiss factory law of 1877 (Bundesgesetz betreffend die Arbeit in den Fabriken) exclusively regulating women's work were few. Swiss politicians, however, believed that men and women in their country benefited from a very high degree of protection compared to other countries.[2] Switzerland had already implemented gender-neutral measures with regard to maximum hours, safety regulations, and the prohibition of night work. Moreover, the Swiss vigorously advocated protective legislation on an international level, writing to foreign embassies and governments on the subject, organizing conferences, and spreading the idea of international treaties covering labor regulations. Because the earliest Swiss factory laws af-

fected men as well as women, a kind of relative equality existed in
the control of working conditions in the first decades of Switzerland's
industrial revolution.[3]

In the latter half of the nineteenth century and the first years of the
twentieth century, equal treatment underwent a progressive erosion,
aided and abetted by a series of laws regulating factory work—some
regional, some national, and some mirrored in initiatives to establish
an international agenda for labor and industrial production. This chapter will delineate that history and explore the gradual creation of labor
protection into the antithesis of gender equality and its attempted export beyond national borders. Swiss protective labor legislation would
introduce a new, defining element into workplace gender divisions, pro-
gressively molding female labor into a separate category. In turn, Swiss
male industrial labor not only lost its ambivalent "protected" status—
which a legally encoded "equal weakness" in the work force had afforded—but won the hypothetical protection of constraints placed on
female labor, constraints encoded in labor law. If "protection" was re-
written, "equality" also took on a different, highly ambiguous tenor,
one that troubles feminists in Switzerland to this day.

Gender difference and inequality of course rested on much more
than whether those holding late-night jobs were men or women. Yet
the history of the gendering of protection for workers is central to
understanding the trade-offs made—by industrialists, male and female
workers alike, women's welfare advocates, and politicians wary of the
"anarchy of production"—for making the new industrial order more
palatable, if not profitable. Unique in this Swiss story is not only the
seemingly genderless genesis of protective laws but also the later vigorous attempts by the Swiss to export the gender-bound version of
protection they had wrought. This chapter will explore that journey.

◆ ◆

In Switzerland, the attempt to regulate factory work via labor legislation began in the early nineteenth century, roughly coinciding with
the country's industrial take-off in the years between 1800 and 1830.
The form such legislation initially took was bound up with the character of the country's industrialization, the work force populating its
major industries, and its political institutions and their development.
In this early period Switzerland had about 1.7 million inhabitants,[4] and
textiles was the main industry. Once an important market for British

cotton cloth, this small country became Britain's competitor in markets the world over.[5] Indigenous chemical and machine industries had grown up around textiles, the former producing dye for cloth and the latter revolving around the production and repair of textile machinery. Neither of these industries would attain independent importance until the twentieth century.

Swiss industrialization claimed a place in the countryside as well as a place in town; it basically remained decentralized. Although Swiss towns were growing, industrialization was not accompanied by a rapid expansion of urban agglomerations. Perhaps because industrialization remained rather small-scale, class antagonism was less pronounced than in most industrializing countries. Decentralized industry and concentration of workers made it more difficult for the new labor force to organize, and a large portion of factory workers kept "proletarian" identity at arm's length. Many industrial workers in fact still owned some farming land and garden plots, and sometimes even owned the houses they lived in. By involving the entire family in some additional agricultural work, the cost of living could often be kept to a minimum. Yet the scene is much less idyllic than some historians would have us believe.[6]

With no access to the sea, Switzerland was locked into a highly unfavorable geographical position and forced to import all its raw materials. In pursuit of high returns, industrialists relied on the skilled work produced in the cloth finishing industries and the staple of low wages. Much skilled work also came relatively cheaply, for a large proportion of industrial workers were female. While the proportion of women in the work force decreased during the nineteenth century, as late as 1882 nearly half the workers in factories were women, and in the textile industry women made up 65–70 percent of all workers.[7]

The Swiss state has a federal structure and consists of twenty-six[8] member states (cantons) that enjoy considerable autonomy and differ in their political structure and institutions. Historically, the cantons came first and were slow (and reluctant) to transfer powers to the national government and the national parliament, a process that was at its height in the nineteenth century. The history of protective legislation in Switzerland was both a mirror and an incentive for the transfer of power from the cantonal to the national level. After the Napoleonic Empire collapsed in 1814, Switzerland could still be considered a *Staatenbund,* a confederation of states.[9] Only in 1848 did it take the decisive step of becoming a federal state and forming a parliamentary system that strove to find a synthesis between federalism and centralism.[10] But civil, penal, mercantile, and labor matters were still decided on the cantonal level or by rather complicated agreements among the cantons, a disadvantage in the rapid industrialization process. The situation did not change until 1874, when the revised constitution conferred more power on the federal institutions.

Legal and constitutional developments ensured that the cantons would be first to take the initiative in matters of protective legislation. At the beginning of the nineteenth century, the cheap labor force still included a large number of children. Opponents of child labor argued that children's physical development suffered and that they failed to get the schooling the republic expected of its future citizens. Therefore, some cantons passed legislation addressing children's hours and conditions of work. In Zurich, in 1815, a decree excluded children under nine from factory work and limited working hours of those under sixteen to a maximum of twelve to fourteen hours a day. The canton of Thurgau attempted to institute similar restrictions.[11] Major industrialists vigorously opposed the regulations, as did parents who relied on their offspring's income. Cantonal authorities in fact had no means of enforcing this legislation, yet the state had set in motion a precedent for interfering in private contracts and "violating" the idea of free enterprise and free contracts.

Glarus, a major center of textile production early in the century, began the process of passing comprehensive factory legislation in 1824. It forbade night work after 9 P.M. for all workers in spinning factories. If this canton made a move long before others, its commitment came in fits and starts, and the well-being of Glarus mill laborers was probably not at the forefront of legislative deliberations. The aim of the 1824 provision seems to have been to protect the neighborhoods surrounding the factories from fire hazards. Glarus continued its efforts to regulate the working lives of all workers by introducing the thirteen-hour day in the cotton-spinning industry in 1848.[12] Though many women were its de facto beneficiaries, this piece of legislation contained no special rules pertaining to women. In 1864 the same canton unveiled the first factory law applying to *all* factories in its territory, instituting a twelve-hour day and prohibiting night work for men and women alike.[13]

The parliament of Glarus had originally intended the 1864 law only to regulate working hours for women and children, "adult men being able to negotiate for themselves."[14] Coupling this argument with laborers' economic need and the financial straits of the canton's entrepreneurs, the parliament of Glarus turned down the general prohibition of night work as well, limiting it to women and children. In a famous debate in the Landsgemeinde (the cantonal assembly of all enfranchised citizens), working men, supported by physicians and ministers, altered the law. Calling the assertion that adult men were able to protect themselves from exploitation a "bad joke," they insisted that working hours and the prohibition of night work should be the same for men and women. Viewed from a gender perspective, the debate reveals men—still a minority among factory workers in Glarus, but in possession of the "manly" power to legislate—as the successful defenders of de facto male "equality with women." [15] In the final law, only one provision explicitly dealing with women remained: it forbade women from working for six weeks after childbirth.

Men in the Landsgemeinde revealed their clear antipathy toward special legislation and special protections for women, be it for night work or gender-specific maximum hours. Those who argued against comprehensive provisions in the assembly asserted that women were especially vulnerable. In the end, a majority rejected the notion that only women and children required protection and had separable interests from men. In the middle of the nineteenth century, Swiss families depended on more than one income to survive; and in the laboring classes in particular, wives, daughters, and sons were all expected to contribute to the family income. Reducing the maximum hours of women and children alone may arguably have led to a reduction of family income without offering any advantages to men. There were no immediate, obvious gains for "male privilege" to claim by strengthening gender differentiation at this juncture and in this way; the currency of the "male family wage" arguably remained too weak to support such a move. Male workers in the Landsgemeinde had spoken out, insisting that they did not feel strong enough to negotiate with private employers or to strike for better conditions.[16] Perversely put, their egalitarian position was probably elicited by a feeling of equal weakness. Regardless, factory legislation affected more women than men simply because they constituted a majority of the canton's factory workers.[17] Echoing the Swiss labor historian Erich Gruner, Swiss historians concur that the 1864 law served as a model for the subsequent cantonal as well as federal legislation and that it determined the form of future protective legislation.[18] This view can only be partly true if we take the peculiar position of women seriously.

Four other cantons (out of twenty-five) followed Glarus and imposed factory laws: Basel-Land (in 1868), Basel-Stadt (in 1869), Schaffhausen (in 1873), and the Ticino (in 1873). The electorate of two cantons (Zurich and St. Gallen) rejected such legislation.[19] While the law of Basel-Land and that of Shaffhouse mainly aimed at protecting young people, the factory law of Basel-Stadt closely followed that of Glarus: it instituted a twelve-hour day and banned night work for both men and women. The issue of shorter working hours for women was raised, but it was quickly dropped because MPs feared that this would endanger the legislation as a whole. Identical maximum hours were thus set up for men and women. As a compromise, the law entitled the government to reduce working hours for women and children "if necessary."[20] A further provision is of interest: married women could take a longer midday meal break on request, presumably tied up more with familial provisioning than with chivalrous generosity. Although Basel-Stadt clearly modeled its law on that of Glarus, it contained special provisions for women, at least in theory: the longer midday meal break was optional and women often could not take advantage of it even if they wanted to, for it reduced their income. The government never made use of its right to impose shorter working hours for women. Intervention on behalf of children, then, set a general precedent for government involvement in industrial relations during the early and mid-nineteenth century in Switzerland. Beyond intervention for children, the question of whether or not the state should participate in the creation of gender divisions through regulation of working conditions would remain a far more ambiguous proposition in these years, antipathy toward special legislation and special protection for women being predominant.

◆ ◆

The era of cantonal regulations ended in 1877 as a result of changes in the Constitution of 1874, which gave the federal Parliament the right to legislate conditions of work "for children and adults."[21] Parliament soon made use of this new capacity. This shift made more systematic responses to industrialization possible, and, crucially, it opened the way for transforming the Swiss dialogue between work and gender divisions.

The new 1877 Federal Law on Work in Factories[22] expanded on and differed from its cantonal predecessors in various ways. It instituted an eleven-hour day. It also forbade night work for men and women but decreed that night work might be permitted in emergencies and that in special cases permits for exceptions might be issued to men but not to women (Article 15).[23] The law decreed that women with "household duties" could request a break of ninety minutes at lunchtime, which they would take at their own expense. Married women were not allowed to perform auxiliary work outside normal working hours, and women were generally not allowed to clean running machinery. The law mandated a maternity leave of eight weeks (two before and six weeks after childbirth). It instructed the Federal Council to publish a list of industries and jobs (*Fabrikationszweige*) in which pregnant women would not be allowed to work. Finally, children under age fourteen were barred from factory work altogether.

In Switzerland, before a draft becomes federal law it must pass several stages, the first of which involves submitting the draft to a public consultation procedure (*Vernehmlassung*), where the governments of the cantons, political parties, unions, interest and pressure groups, and concerned individuals submit their opinions.[24] The federal government then presents it to Parliament with a written report that contains the major arguments of all groups and institutions who participated in the consultation process. The two chambers of Parliament deliberate and vote on the proposed law.[25] Finally, the bill is submitted to a plebiscite if a certain number of voters ask for this.[26] It is then accepted or rejected by a majority of the voters.

In the *Vernehmlassung* the government received sixty written statements. Responding to the proposed prohibition of women's night work, a group of 272 textile industrialists wrote that they could not accept the law; it would be the deathblow for night work in general, for most textile workers were women.[27] Apart from this, little opposition to the ban was registered. The Association of Industrialists (Handels-und Gewerbeverein), the most important pressure group of entrepreneurs, accepted it. The national Working Man's Association (Arbeiterbund) argued for shorter working hours for women and for a maternity leave of twelve weeks, a shift from its earlier position. When the association was founded in 1873, it proposed equal working hours and equal pay for men and women as part of its program. Now it claimed that most of its members wanted to abolish factory work for women. Even the best legislation, it argued, could not make up for the harm done to households and families by the absence of a housewife and mother.[28]

Apart from the question of whether or not the federal authorities might legitimately have a hand in legislating working conditions (an issue that revealed how large the obstacles to national legislation were), the main discussion in Parliament revolved around limiting the work-day to eleven hours for all workers. Opponents of the law had both tacitly and openly agreed that if protective legislation was inevitable, it was better to increase protection of women and children than to impose stricter rules on the whole work force. They concentrated their efforts on blocking the eleven-hour day in the parliamentary debate. This strategy failed, for Parliament accepted the eleven-hour stipulation. Judging from the "letter of the law," the difference between protection of men and protection of women with respect to night work was small; night work could in general only be performed in exceptional cases. The difference became more obvious, however, when exceptions for male workers were obtained rather easily.

The Swiss Parliament passed the law by a large majority.[29] Opponents of the law then submitted it to a plebiscite. It was the Association of Industrialists of the canton of Aargau that started the referendum. The association was backed by other industrialists and entrepreneurs. In the campaign that followed, the eleven-hour day once again became the most important issue, but there is not much leeway in a plebiscite for subtle arguments. Prohibition of night work, a ninety-minute mid-day meal break for women with household duties, exclusion of children under age fourteen, and an eleven-hour day for all workers were part and parcel of one law that could either be accepted or rejected but no longer amended. Supporters and opponents concentrated their efforts on discussing the consequences of an eleven-hour day for all factory workers rather than, for instance, the strict ban on women's night work. Protection of women and children had become more accepted. The absence of any discussion of an absolute ban on night work constituting a positive feature of the law may well have derived from the fact that women did not have the vote; their support for the law was thus dispensable.

Indeed, women's organizations at the time were not active in discussions about factory legislation. The new type of bourgeois women's organization,[30] which would deal with political questions, did not appear in Switzerland until the early 1890s.[31] Furthermore, public discussions of female labor had started rather late in the 1860s and 1870s, when the Swiss Welfare Societies[32] and their female adherents dealt with the problems of women's work by developing models of female education that were primarily aimed at promoting better housekeeping. These societies were convinced that a solution of "The Social Question"— as they called the growing misery caused by rapid industrial development—lay in good cooking and thrifty housekeeping. Their model for education was ambivalent. In the 1880s, they developed vocational courses in sewing, ironing, or knitting. They aimed to improve women's knowledge in an area that would be useful both at home and in industry.[33] Working Women's Associations, which represented working-class women and later defended protective legislation, were only founded toward the end of the 1880s and therefore did not take part in this discussion. If we tap into the opinions of individual working women on the matter, we find that they were in favor of measures such as longer midday meal breaks.[34]

Male Swiss voters accepted the law by a small majority. Thus, the total exclusion of women from night work went into effect, as did other special provisions. Women were thus doubly protected, as workers and as women, though not entirely for their own benefit: they were supposed to rush home to cook meals, and they had to stay home from jobs for eight weeks around the period of childbirth, with no provisions made to replace wages lost during this time. Furthermore, they could be dismissed when they became pregnant if they worked in a so-called dangerous occupation.

The ambiguities radiating from the provisions regulating women's work were not publicly discussed in Switzerland at the time. Perhaps the implications were barely clear, too tangled in mixed objectives and political strategizing by both defenders and opponents of the measures. Neither the possibility that special protection might weaken women's position in the labor market nor the issue of whether or not protection of women was a viable strategy for reducing the harsh toll of factory work entered the public record. Rather, a consensus seems to have developed, a feeling that female factory workers suffered from a double burden of housework and factory work and that any possible provision to alleviate it ought to be welcome. Women's position in the family and the workplace seemed different from that of men, and their capacity to bear children seemed to make special regulations necessary.

The plebiscite results may be taken as a sign that the concept of the male breadwinner was gaining ground in the working classes. It was arguably accompanied by a shift from the assumption that women belonged in the family wage economy to a more middle-class norm: a woman was primarily mother and housewife and required protection. Work outside the family economy—common in an industrialized society—may have in theory created conditions for an economically

independent existence for women, and Swiss legal developments also
pointed in this direction.[35] But opportunities for such independence
were destroyed even before they were put into practice. On the legal
level, the new Civil Code (*Zivilgesetzbuch*) drove this message home in
its definition of both women's property rights and the rights and duties
of husband and wife;[36] on an economic level, the ideas of man as the
breadwinner and woman's wage as supplementary gained credence. The
1877 factory act, with its special regulations for women, essentially mirrored these trends. It helped to reassert differences between male and
female in the workplace. Offering a distinct new set of rights for men,
it shored up male dominance, which was losing confidence in the face
of a new machine age in which the value of traditional male labor and
skills was itself being undermined and eroded. Still, its consequences
for the shape of male labor probably remained veiled for many contemporaries. Would it help to firm up the sexual division of labor before
de-skilling put in an appearance, or would it help restructure mixed-
sex industries to benefit all workers?

◆ ◆

While notions of protection for women and children had circulated
from the earliest days of Swiss industrialization, the 1877 federal law
and the international initiatives that followed were to prove powerful
steps toward the creation of women as a special class of workers and
the construction of gender differences. In 1864, night work prohibition
was still a question of social justice: night work was forbidden with no
exceptions because it was harmful to women and men. In 1877, a concern with gender difference—the protection of women—encouraged
parliamentarians and male voters at large to make exceptions to the
night work ban for men.[37] Longer midday meal breaks and a maternity
leave acknowledged women's family role but arguably also made that
role a self-fulfilling prophecy. And they offered a new version of "protection of men." It was as though legislators wanted to demonstrate
that while working men lived and worked under bad conditions and
had few rights, they had a right to wives who looked after them and
their offspring.[38]

The 1877 law, then, functioned as an opening wedge not only for the
terms of international protective legislation but also for a retooled conception of protection: special protection for women only. In the canton
of Basel-Stadt, for instance, it underwrote the argument that if women

were not allowed to work in factories for more than eleven hours, then making dresses in sweatshops, selling goods in unhealthy shops, or working in offices (including on Sundays) was no more acceptable. This kind of argument could well have been extended to men's work, but it was used to address women's labor alone for the first time. Basel was the first canton to go beyond the federal law and apply both the eleven-hour day and night work prohibition to all women working in millinery production and other trades that were not defined as factories and employed more than three women (1884).[39] In 1888, the canton extended protection to all enterprises (except retail shops) employing three or more women or any woman under the age of eighteen.[40] The 1888 law mandated a maternity leave of eight weeks. In 1904, Basel altered its law again to include protection for women working in retail shops as well. Only servants remained excluded, an omission hardly out of step with other European countries but an interesting comment on conceptions of domestic labor.

Up to 1904, seven cantons[41] had introduced laws specifically regulating women's work outside factories along the lines of factory regulations; these introduced an eleven-hour day,[42] maternity leave,[43] and a ban on night work and Sunday employment.[44] Apparently, women's organizations did not challenge them. The Working Women's Association as well as individual women supported the 1888 law when an amendment was again discussed in Basel in 1904.[45]

◆ ◆

Swiss politicians thought protection for men and women in Switzerland compared very favorably with the provisions made by other countries.[46] Special measures for women workers had grown out of a broader tradition of factory legislation for all workers. These general provisions were supported by politicians and trade unions of different political persuasions. For some, the idea needed to be extended even further, be it in gendered terms or carried into the international realm. Here, Swiss protection initiatives were a point of pride and of calculation. As these initiatives developed from the latter half of the nineteenth century, they would mirror the same divisions and ambiguities surrounding gender questions that beset protection debates within Switzerland.

The idea of promoting labor protection internationally had a long history in Switzerland. It originated with industrialists from the Swiss canton of Glarus, the canton that was furthest along in creating protective measures. Already in 1855, these men tried to convince other Swiss cantons of the necessity of a "concordat"[47] on factory legislation. More calculating than worker-friendly, they sought "equal conditions" for employers in the cotton-spinning industry. At the same time and in a similar vein they were already toying with the idea of international agreements as a weapon for improving their competitive position in both Swiss and international markets. Last but not least, they sought to reduce productivity, seeing "overproduction" as a threat to economic stability.

Emil Frey, later a member of the Swiss government, made an early important contribution to the internationalization of factory legislation. In his parting address after a year as president of the Swiss National Council in 1876, he proposed that Switzerland should initiate international conferences and treaties and create equal conditions for production of all industrialized European countries. This intention was based on economic and political calculations: the Swiss Parliament was at that time discussing the factory law, and employers complained that the legislation would put them at a disadvantage in other European markets. Frey, a member of the Liberal party (Freisinnig-demokratische Partei), was an ardent defender of the factory law. Such a law, he argued, was in keeping with a humane worldview and the notion of social stability.

Frey promoted the idea that Switzerland should take the first steps toward an all-inclusive labor legislation stretching beyond its borders. According to him, no other country had quite the same obligation to creating better working conditions. Although conditions were not especially bad in Switzerland, he argued, it was nevertheless the responsibility of a republican and democratic Swiss state to care for those who could not care for themselves. In a state like Switzerland, poor living conditions for a large group of citizens should not be countenanced and had to be abolished by legislation. Unchecked social inequality would only increase and eventually endanger political equality, the basis of a democracy. Furthermore, because the Swiss state gave its citizens the right to exert direct influence on political issues, it was, according to Frey, obliged to care for the welfare of those who influenced its politics. If by this intervention the basis of production and competitive viability were to suffer, it was Switzerland's duty to underwrite more expansive equal opportunity through international treaties.[48]

Although Frey's concept of protective legislation contained special passages for women (a strict prohibition on night work, provision of maternity leaves, exclusion from dangerous jobs), his notion of the citizen who required protection appears above all to have been the citizen who had the power to legislate and influence politics—that is, the male citizen who might be influenced by Marxist ideology, who might cause upheavals or revolutions, and for whom the state had to procure acceptable working conditions.

In response to Frey's address, Swiss newspapers dealt at length with international protection for the first time; from then on, the subject became a matter of parliamentary and public discussion. In addition to humane considerations, internationalizing protective measures was arguably a means of ameliorating working conditions at home without creating economic disadvantages abroad.

Frey's address did not go unchallenged. In the French-speaking part of Switzerland in particular he was tagged a *socialiste* and *utopiste*.[49] Nevertheless, the idea of international protection gained ground after the proposed factory legislation rode out the plebiscite and the attempts to rescind it shortly afterward derailed.[50] The results of different cantonal plebiscites showed that some workers remained opposed to protective legislation, but the leaders of the workers' association had always advocated protection on a national level and now pushed the idea of international legislation. In 1880, the Arbeiterbund[51] took up the idea and demanded action from the federal government. Political forces such as the Grütliverein, a moderate political party, and the parliament of the canton of Grisons supported the association's call. Later in the same year, Emil Frey, still a member of the Swiss Parliament, submitted a motion that obliged the government to take concrete steps toward international protective legislation. This first attempt failed.

Almost a decade lapsed (1888) before two members of Parliament, Caspar Decurtins of the canton of Grisons and Georges Favon from Geneva, submitted a second motion. Decurtins,[52] a member of the Catholic Conservative faction in the National Council, argued that because modern industrialization had produced the same conditions of work and the same grievances everywhere, a common effort should be mobilized to address them. According to Decurtins, overproduction was the main danger of the modern system, and international workers' protection provided a means of stopping the "anarchy of production." From elsewhere on the political spectrum, Favon, a member of the Council of States for Geneva and a Radical (*Radikal-Demokrat*), saw the

move as a necessary step toward "uniting all friends of social reform."[53]
It seems obvious that at least Decurtins also had a specific agenda for
the future of female labor: he considered factories thoroughly unfit for
women and saw protective legislation as a way to abolish factory work
for women in the long term.[54]

The Swiss government accepted the motion and planned a congress
in Bern for 1890. Representatives were invited from Belgium, Denmark,
Germany, France, Great Britain, Italy, Luxembourg, the Netherlands,
Austria, Portugal, Russia, Sweden, Norway, and Spain. The agenda included the abolition of work on Sundays, minimum age laws for child
labor, maximum hours for young people, the abolition of work for
young people and women in dangerous industries, a ban on women's
night work, and enforcement and control of these regulations through
an international treaty.

Before the Bern Congress could be held, Germany stole the show.
The kaiser seized the initiative and invited representatives of the various
nations to Berlin for the same purpose. Like most countries, Switzerland accepted the invitation. The program at the Berlin Congress was
very similar to what had been planned for Bern, but the results were a
far cry from the original plans laid by the Swiss: measures encoded in
treaties were not on the agenda, and congress participants could merely
agree to proposals.

Switzerland took the initiative for a second time in the wake of the
Berlin meeting. This time, the workers' association seized the reins.
On the one hand, the idea of protective legislation had become more
prevalent among socialists following the Second International of 1889
and its demand for an eight-hour day. On the other hand, the issue now
attracted Catholic politicians because of Pope Leo XIII's 1891 Rerum
Novarum encyclical, which advocated workers' protection.[55] The First
Congress on Workers' Protection was ultimately delayed, however, because German and Austrian socialists refused to participate if members
of nonsocialist parties or unions were allowed to attend.

The congress finally took place in Zurich in 1897 and was attended
by 391 delegates. Most were members of unions and workers' organizations, but attendance was not limited to those of a socialist persua-
sion. The most prominent participant of the Social Democratic party
(SPS) of Switzerland was *Arbeiter-Sekretär* Hermann Greulich, his position created to mediate between the federal government and workers'
unions. Apart from delegates of the workers' organizations and unions,

several Swiss cantonal governments sent delegates as well. The official delegate of the federal government was Fridolin Schuler, a physician from Glarus and the first Swiss factory inspector. To demonstrate that protective legislation was a matter of broad public (not merely socialist) concern, the Swiss government granted organizers 4000 SFr toward the expenses of the congress. The program featured all the "usual" points. The speakers were all Swiss, among them Margarete Greulich,[56] who was one of the main lecturers in the congress segment devoted to women's work.

As in Berlin, Zurich delegates also lacked the authority to formalize international treaties, though the congress reached unanimous agreement on most questions.[57] Special protection for women remained the exception, and three different positions emerged: total exclusion of married women from "mines, quarries, and from heavy industry"[58] (meaning all factories); a halfway house of special protection for women; and equal protection for men and women.[59] Some of the Swiss delegates—among them Decurtins—belonged to a minority at the congress who advocated total exclusion. Most of the delegates were in favor of special protection for women short of such an across-the-board exclusion, among them probably all the Swiss women present. Equal protection for men and women, the third position and once the theme of such legislation in Glarus, went unsupported by the delegates.[60]

With factory legislation on the books—defended by the government and different workers' organizations—protection for men and special regulations for women had clearly become an unchallenged tenet in Switzerland. Quite apart from its practical effects, however, its meanings remained wide open: some viewed protective legislation as the first step in a march toward abolishing factory work for women altogether (Decurtins), while others remained convinced that it opened up a route for ensuring further protection for men as well (Margarethe and Hermann Greulich). Its potential meanings had also moved beyond the country's borders.

Kaiser Wilhelm notwithstanding, the importance of the Swiss role in matters of international protective agreements seems to have been confirmed by the founding of the International Labour Office (ILO), which was established in Basel in 1901. The shift in Swiss activities around protection was not just a matter of scale, however. It was symptomatic for a major recasting of the gendering of labor issues in Switzerland at the close of the century.

Of the twenty-one articles of the Swiss factory law of 1877, only two dealt with women. Moreover, such legislation was historically designed to protect all workers, and special protection for women was once considered a threat to factory legislation.[61] Given this history, it is retrospectively stunning how easily Swiss delegations attending turn-of-the-century conferences opted to attach protective regulations to women's work exclusively. Here was proof again that attitudes toward women's work had changed significantly since the early days of factory legislation.

◆ ◆

While Switzerland was consolidating its international position with regard to protective laws for women, there were strong demands for the revision of the 1877 national factory law. The eleven-hour day in particular was no longer acceptable to the unions; in its place they demanded a forty-eight-hour week. The attempt at revision was started in 1910. Regarding night work, the governmental report did not question the absolute ban for women: "There is nothing to say against it," the report stated.[62] In the parliamentary debate in 1913, however, a demand arose to grant exemptions for factories producing canned goods, especially those processing canned fruit. The National Council turned down the motion, although the person proposing it—an industrialist— had argued that only women could do this particular kind of work for it was "woman's work."[63] But a very important change had occurred between the 1888 law and the revision process that illustrates what Alice Kessler-Harris, at a conference on protective labor legislation, called "the creation and precise definition of the concept of 'universal woman.'"[64] In 1877, the government listed the jobs *pregnant* women should not hold. Some thirty years later, a movement to amend the law expanded the categories of work from which *all* women were prohibited to include such things as lifting heavy loads or handling poisonous materials. In addition, the ninety-minute midday meal break was now explicitly defined as a right for all women if they had household duties, whether they were married or not. Women who were responsible for housework were also entitled to stay at home on Saturday afternoons.

The government anticipated opposition to this new "British idea" by saying that only some women would really benefit, "the loss of earnings being a discouragement."[65] When Parliament discussed the Saturday afternoon housework issue, most of the National Council agreed with M.P. Albert Schwander, who asserted that a working woman should have the time "to clean the house for Sunday." [66] Schwander, a politician from the canton of Basel-Land and popular with the Social Democrats, said the number of female factory workers who were housewives—about twenty-eight thousand—was "disquieting." (At stake were benefits for about a fourth of all female factory workers or a third of all female factory workers over eighteen.) Those women could not possibly fulfill their "proper duty," looking after their children and households, lamented Schwander. Some textile industrialists opposed the provision. Given the large proportion of women in the textile industry, a free Saturday afternoon for women would cause difficulties in terms of the industry's work schedule. The compromise finally reached was to delay enforcement of this particular provision for five years after the amended factory law came into force. This move purportedly ensured that the textile industry had sufficient time to adapt its schedules.[67]

An increasing emphasis on women's "proper duty" gave gender-based protective legislation a more distinct character, temporarily imposing greater fixity on its meaning. But there were limits put on the recognition of workers as "women." Maternity leaves were shortened to the six weeks after confinement, justified by the argument that health insurance policies only covered these six weeks.[68] At the beginning of the debate on revisions, the National Council changed the proposal to eight weeks, but the Council of States later overturned this.

Arguments for protection entertained at the time by various strands of the Swiss women's movement remain fairly opaque, the choices strewn with complications. Two women's organizations—the newly founded umbrella organization of the Swiss feminist movement, Bund Schweizerischer Frauenvereine (BSF); and the Union Féministe de Neuchâtel—offered written opinions on the law in 1910. Neither objected to protective legislation in general, although the Swiss feminist movement had by this time accumulated some evidence of the negative impact of protection. When the Union für Frauenbestrebungen, a progressive bourgeois women's organization, advocated equal pay for men and women working in the state mail and telephone company, they were told that women earned less because they were not allowed to work at night.[69] The question of maternity leave also revealed complications. The BSF and the Organization for Women's Welfare (Gemeinnütziger Frauenverein) had in a late phase of the discussion argued that the law on health insurance and the revised factory law provisions for maternity leave should be brought in line with each other. The Council of States coolly considered this an argument for a six weeks' leave, which finally became law.

Not until the 1920s did a section of the bourgeois feminist movement in Switzerland challenge special protective measures for women.[70] At the Second Women's Congress (Kongress für Fraueninteressen) in 1921, for instance, Annie Leuch, a member of the organizing committee of the congress and later president of the Swiss Union for Women's Suffrage (Schweizerischer Verband für Frauenstimmrecht),[71] advocated equal protection for men *and* women. Leuch opposed shorter hours and other restrictions on the basis that protection tended to weaken women's economic position and their claim for political participation. She pointed to the example of book printing to show that protection carried a price, that of exclusion from a trade "profitable and suitable for a woman."[72]

In the 1920s, many Swiss unions were in fact stepping up efforts to exclude women from certain trades. The more powerful a union was, the more successful it proved to be in this pursuit. The Typographers' Union, a section of the Swiss Union of Workers (Schweizerischer Gewerkschaftsbund [SGB]) managed to exclude women by regulations encoded in the Labor and Collective Bargaining Agreement. The Typographers' Union had already tried to exclude women from printing jobs in 1899. Casting their work as a "dangerous trade," the Typographia Bern and fourteen other local sections asked the federal government to intervene to expel women from book printing. The provisions of the factory law of 1877 were not considered sufficient to exclude all women,[73] and the federal government did not comply with their request.[74] On the basis of the amended factory law of 1914—which was only put into effect after World War I—women could eventually be legally excluded from all skilled work and from apprenticeships in the book-printing trade because lead (a staple of the trade) was on the government's list of dangerous substances, something no woman was allowed to handle. Women were not, however, excluded from *unskilled* work in the printing industry.

No independent women's union existed to oppose the policy of the Typographers' and Lithographers' Union. The Working Women's Association was hardly a candidate. It had been part of the Social Democratic party from 1912 on, and the Social Democrats had always defended protective legislation. Women's position in the Swiss trade unions was generally very weak.[75] While not typical, the example of the typographers leaves little to the imagination: once made acceptable, special protective laws for women could be seamlessly conjoined with disputes over the sexual division of labor. Even if organized women had begged to differ on the matter, they were also tangled in alliances that made integration crucial, dissent difficult, and special protection a reasonable proposition in many contexts.

On the whole, the group of women opposing protective legislation seems to have been a minority even in the bourgeois feminist movement. At the Congress for Female Suffrage in Paris in 1927—where a majority of the delegates opposed protective legislation—the Swiss voted with a minority that passed a counterresolution in favor of such legislation.[76] Even opponents acknowledged the need for maternity leave and the protection of pregnant women. Thus, opponents supported benefits for actual mothers through maternity insurance and a paid maternity leave rather than measures that assumed that all women were or would be mothers. Here they found common ground with the social democratic position.

◆ ◆

"Protection" has a long legacy in Switzerland and "equality," a complex pedigree. According to the letter of the law, night work is still not permitted in Swiss industry.[77] The Ministry of Industry, Trade and Labor (BIGA) issues special permits exempting exceptional cases, and these only go to male employees. The 1964 law continues to protect women, in keeping with the tradition of the 1914 law. It construes all women to be mothers or potentially pregnant, whether they are married or not, whether they have children or not, whether they are aged sixteen, twenty-five, or sixty-two.

Women are not allowed to work on Sundays. Maximum working hours are the same for men and women, but women who have "household duties" need not work overtime. Some special regulations exist on the relation between leisure and work, with regard to women, and on their maximum weekly hours (article 34 of the 1964 law). These special provisions all feed the impression that women are a very special category in the Swiss labor market. Special regulations other than those connected with pregnancy—particularly night work regulations—run contrary to the Equal Rights Amendment of the Swiss Constitution passed in 1984. As a result, the Swiss government was forced to amend its Law on Work. In the current draft, women will be allowed to work night shifts in industry.

Will the abolition of such special regulations prove to be a successful way of improving women's position in the labor market? The development of protective legislation for men and women during Switzerland's 150-year history helped to create and still reflects the development of the notion that a woman combining family work with wagework is undesirable, harmful for her family. This notion and special protective legislation for women were the products of the end of the nineteenth century; developments in the twentieth century gradually reinforced their thrust. While this standard is now questioned, the social security system and the absence of a child-care system bear witness to the tenacity of Switzerland's basic assumptions and spirit. Abolishing only one feature of that standard (the night work ban for women) in only one part of the legal system (labor legislation) does not automatically represent a step toward equality. A modification of the labor laws alone will not advance women's position in Swiss society.

Women still earn less than men. A recent report revealed that the differential could not be a result of women's lesser qualifications or training but rather of the simple fact that women are paid less because of their sex. In middle- and upper-management jobs women typically earn one-third less than men with the same qualifications and types of jobs. Although protective legislation had been used as an argument against equal pay from early on,[78] it is clearly responsible neither for the financial disadvantages and poor position of women in the Swiss labor market nor for the peculiar Swiss social security system. However, special protective legislation for women and the standard on which it is based derive their strength from the same kind of ideological assumptions: the notion that all women are wives and mothers and that a woman's proper place is with her family. A sex-segregated labor market and protective legislation tend to back on each other in a pernicious way, reinforcing the impression that women are something exceptional and a special category in the labor market. Consequently, the better jobs, higher pay, and attendant influence these carry in Swiss society today remain the preserve of men.

With this in mind, some progressive women's organizations, the Catholic women's movement, the Social Democratic party, and the trade unions opposed the work of the commission. The umbrella organization of the Swiss women's movement (BSF) did not object, however. The oppositional alliance only formed recently, and the arguments they have mobilized are also new. They believe that under the pretext of equality employers attempted to introduce night work for women in industry without complying with other important elements of the amendment: equal pay and equal opportunity. The trade unions, which still view employers as interested in using women largely because they are paid less, believe that the new regulations would increase the overall number of people forced to work the night shift. "Night work is harmful for men and women," the SGB has argued, "but instead of diminishing the number of night workers, the federal government tends to increase it."

Organized women opponents of the new regulations now believe that equal opportunities for Swiss women can be attained only by raising salaries, changing social security regulations, and establishing a system of child care that would give women a choice about whether or not to work at night. Until those conditions are fulfilled, they will not agree to the amended law.[79] In 1991 women therefore faced a situation in which they opposed what was planned in the name of equality and laid claim to special regulations because of women's position in society. They opposed this kind of equality because it would again force women to adjust to male standards.

Writing about the Sears case in the United States, Joan Scott described the kind of difficulties that have also ensnared Swiss women: "When equality and difference are paired dichotomously, they structure an impossible choice. If one opts for equality, one is forced to accept the notion that difference is antithetical to it. If one opts for difference, one admits that equality is unattainable."[80] Women's organizations in Switzerland refused to structure their choices in the framework of this simple binary opposition. Their political strategy was not to claim categorical difference, but they also rejected the notion that sameness should be the basis for political equality. They escaped falling into what—in the process of adapting Swiss law to the principle of gender equality—has been called "the equality trap." Despite their protest, the Swiss federal government rejected the ILO's Convention 89 (the ban on night work for women) in February 1992. An alteration of the Swiss law would probably lead to a popular referendum.[81] A second *Vernehmlassung* (consultation) was started in the summer of 1993, but the opinions are not yet publicly known or published. The outcome is uncertain, as is the outcome of a (possible) plebiscite. The effects of the recent economic crisis arrived in Switzerland after some delay, but the unemployment rate has now grown considerably. The unemployment rate of women is even higher than that of men, which might weaken the position of those who resist abolition of the night work provision for women. Employers interested in the abolition of special protective legislation for women can create public pressure by threatening to transfer factory production abroad. Women may fear losing their jobs and accept the change.

The factory law of Glarus was a remarkable step in the history of Swiss factory legislation: men claimed to be equally protected and considered their health too valuable to be ruined on the night shift. Would this not be an opportune moment and context in which to return to an understanding of protection that once was?

Notes

1. Royal Commission of Labour, *Foreign Report*, vol. 7: *Switzerland* (London: HMSO, 1893), 25.

2. See "Arbeiterschutz (internationaler Arbeiterschutz)," in *Handwörterbuch der Schweizerischen Volkswirtschaft*, vol. 1, ed. Naum Reichesberg (Bern: Verlag Encyclopaedie, n.d.), 130.

3. Unfortunately, no new research has been done on the history of protective legislation in Switzerland in general, apart from Dominique Grobéty, *La Suisse aux origines du droit ouvrier* (Zurich: Juris, 1979). There are, however, some very useful juridical abstracts and studies that provide a short summary of the history of this question, e.g., Isabell Mahrer, *Die Sonderschutzvorschriften für weibliche Arbeitnehmer in der Schweiz* (Bern: Eidgenöss. Kommission für Frauenfragen, 1985), and Alexandre Berenstein, "L'influence des conventions internationales du travail sur législation suisse," *Revue internationale du travail* 77 (1958): 553–78. As a result of research done for this essay, I have published some short essays on the development in the Swiss cantons, e.g., Regina Wecker, "Sauber und blank für den Sonntag," in *Alles was Recht ist! Baselbieterinnen auf dem Weg zu Gleichberechtigung und Gleichstellung*, ed. Pascale Meyer and Sabine Kubli (Liestal: Archäologie und Museum, Heft 024, 1992). In October 1993 I started a new research project on the development of protective legislation in Switzerland between 1920 and 1964, financed by the Swiss Science Foundation.

4. In 1850 there were 2,400,000 inhabitants; in 1900, 3,320,000; and in 1980, 6,360,000.

5. B. M. Biucchi, "The Industrial Revolution in Switzerland," in *The*

Fontana Economic History of Europe, vol. 4, pt. 2, ed. Carlo M. Cipolla (London: Fontana/Collins, 1973).

6. See ibid.

7. In 1888 about 17 percent of the female work force was employed in factories.

8. The twenty-sixth canton was only accepted in 1978. In the nineteenth century there were twenty-five cantons.

9. There were few restrictions on the cantons' autonomy, mainly in matters of foreign policy. There was no central government but rather a sort of traveling secretariat that rotated every two years among Zurich, Bern, and Lucerne. Of course there was no federal law regulating labor conditions in this loose confederation.

10. A bicameral parliamentary system was created on the American model. The Nationalrat (National Council) represented the whole of the Swiss people and the Ständerat (Council of States) represented the cantons. In the National Council the fixed number of 200 seats is distributed according to population, while each canton sends two representatives to the Council of States. The four annual sessions of Parliament, taken together, last twelve weeks. Important and perhaps strange in comparison to other political systems is that parliamentarians are not professional politicians but have other professions. (This is true on the national as well as on the cantonal level.) In the nineteenth century a considerable number of parliamentarians were industrialists and owned enterprises. While both chambers usually meet separately, they have the same powers and duties. The consent of both is necessary for the adoption of new laws. Both houses sit together for elections and votes are not counted separately. This so-called Vereinigte Bundesversammlung (United Federal Assembly) elects the seven members of the government, called Bundesrat (Federal Council). They come from the major political parties, and at present four political parties have a member. It is a "collegial government": for instance, all members have the same rights, the chairmanship—or presidency—is rotated annually, but the position actually involves no additional power.

11. See Victor Schiwoff, *Die Beschränkung der Arbeitszeit durch kantonale Gesetzgebung und durch das erste eidgenössische Fabrikgesetz 1877* (Bern: Haupt, 1952), 17.

12. "Gesetz über das Arbeiten in den Spinnmaschinen 1848 erlassen von der Landsgemeinde," *Landsbuch des Kantons Glarus* (Glarus, 1854).

13. "Gesetz über die Fabrikpolizei, erlassen von der Landsgemeinde 1864," *Amtliche Sammlung der Gesetze und Verordnungen des Kantons Glarus* (Glarus, 1864), 44. Four factory workers initiated the law in 1863. Referring to the situation in England, they asked for state protection. They demanded the eleven-hour day for all workers in Glarus and improvement of workplace sanitary provisions. A commission formed to examine working conditions, and it finally drafted a law for Parliament.

14. See Heinz Dällenbach, *Kantone, Bund und Fabrikgesetzgebung* (Zurich: Juris, 1961), 72ff.

15. In 1865 ten thousand inhabitants, or a third of the canton's population, worked in factories. More than 50 percent of the adult workers (in these establishments) were women.

16. They had the power to use legislative means to bargain around working conditions, which they preferred to negotiating privately or collectively with employers. They were well placed to influence political decisions in each canton because of their ready access to the Landsgemeinde. Major political decisions were reached in these bodies rather than in a more distant parliament.

17. As late as 1895, 55.5 percent of factory workers in the canton of Glarus were women (4,551 of 8,204). In Switzerland as a whole, the first factory census in 1882 showed that 64,498 women were factory workers, i.e., 47.8 percent of all workers employed in factories. The percentage of women was decreasing, but as late as 1895 some 40.5 percent of these workers were women (80,995 of 200,199).

18. Erich Gruner, *Die Arbeiter in der Schweiz im 19. Jahrhundert* (Bern: Francke, 1968), 230. See also *Geschichte der Schweiz und der Schweizer,* vol. 2, ed. Beatrix Mesmer, Jean-Claude Favez, and Romano Broggini (Basel: Helbing und Lichtenhahn, 1983), 46.

19. See Dällenbach, *Kantone;* Eduard Weckerle, *Herman Greulich* (Zurich: Büchergilde Gutenberg, 1947), 91ff.

20. "Fabrikgesetz des Kantons Basel-Stadt," Nov. 15, 1869, par. 3.

21. Article 34 of the Federal Constitution of 1874.

22. The law was passed on March 23, 1877.

23. Article 15 reads (my emphasis): "Frauenspersonen sollen *unter keinen Umständen* zur Sonntags-oder Nachtarbeit verwendet werden." (Female persons shall not be used for Sunday or night work *for any reasons whatsoever.*)

24. The Vernehmlassung is considered a very important test for the chances of a draft bill in the political arena. Parliament often changes a law considerably if it becomes obvious that a political party or pressure group that lacks strong numbers in Parliament but is strong enough to launch a referendum opposes part of the draft or bill.

25. Both chambers must consent to adoption of a law.

26. In 1877 a bill had to be put to a referendum if 30,000 eligible citizens petitioned for it. All male Swiss citizens above age twenty were eligible to sign. Today, 50,000 signatures are required (women's enfranchisement was an argument for this increase).

27. "Botschaft des Bundesrates betr. den Gesetzesentwurf über die Arbeit in den Fabriken vom 6. Dezember 1875," *Bundesblatt* 4 (1875): 952–53.

28. Dällenbach, *Kantone,* 162. This must not be considered a shift as the demand for equal pay may contain an element of exclusion of female labor.

29. The National Council accepted it by a margin of eighty to twelve, and five other men abstained. The Council of States approved it by a margin of twenty-one to sixteen.

30. The first feminist organization, the International Women's League, founded by Marie Goegg in Geneva in 1867, lost its influence toward the end of the 1870s. See Susanna Woodtli, *Gleichberechtigung* (Frauenfeld: Huber, 1975), 24ff.

31. Working women's associations (*Arbeiterinnenvereine*) were founded toward the end of the 1880s. Middle-class women's organizations started up at the beginning of the 1890s. See Beatrix Mesmer, *Ausgeklammert Eingeklammert: Frauen und Frauenorganisationen in der Schweiz des 19. Jahrhunderts* (Basel: Helbing und Lichtenhahn, 1988), 196.

32. Schweizerische Gemeinnützige Gesellschaften (SGG).

33. See Mesmer, *Ausgeklammert*, 117–18.

34. In Basel a group of eleven factory workers in 1870 asked their employer for the longer break. See Staatsarchiv Basel-Stadt, Handel und Gewerbe MM 2,16.

35. These included, for instance, the abolition of male custody over women in 1881; the possibility for widows to inherit an equal share of property, which some Swiss cantons introduced in the nineteenth century; and a woman's right to an equal share of property after a divorce.

36. For instance, the Civil Code defined the husband as head of the family, and he had to give his consent if his wife wanted to take up employment. Property provisions were also less favorable for women than they had been in some of the cantonal laws.

37. Until 1877, five cantons had factory laws: Glarus, Basel-Stadt, Basel-Land, Schaffhausen, and the Ticino. Attempts to institute such laws in Zurich and St. Gallen were rejected.

38. Perhaps their "rights" were seen to include the right to a wife who was sexually available (although this was never declared openly).

39. "Gesetz betreffend die Arbeitszeit der weiblichen Arbeiter" (Basel-Stadt, 1884).

40. "Gesetz betreffend den Schutz der Arbeiterinnen" (Basel-Stadt, 1888).

41. There were twenty-five cantons. Most of those that instituted special legislation for women were industrialized but also had a large female population engaged in trades, in workplaces not defined as factories.

42. In some cantons, a ten-hour maximum was stipulated.

43. Maternity leave was usually set at four to six weeks after childbirth, and in some cantons (Basel and Glarus) it also included the two weeks before confinement.

44. Fanny Goldstein, *Der Arbeiterschutz zu gunsten der Kinder und Frauen in der Schweiz* (Bern: Francke, 1904), 54–55.

45. One argument ran that work in retail shops was just as unhealthy and exhausting as factory work. See Regina Wecker, *Frauen in der Schweiz-von den Problemen einer Mehrheit* (Zug: Klett und Ballmer, 1983), 48–49.

46. See "Arbeiterschutz," in *Handwörterbuch*, 130.

47. Ibid.

48. Fritz Grieder, *Der Baselbieter Bundesrat Emil Frey* (Liestal: Verlag des Kantons Basel-Landschaft, 1988), 157.

49. Ibid., 158–59.

50. Industrialists had tried to abolish factory legislation in the 1880s.

51. The Arbeiterbund was the umbrella organization of workers up to the foundation of the Social Democratic party in 1888. It bore features of a political party as well as of a trade union federation.

52. Caspar Decurtins (1855–1916) belonged to the social wing of the Catholic Conservatives. In matters of protective legislation, he was the leading force of this party and later became one of the organizers of the International Congress in Zurich in 1897, presiding at that congress. See Erich Gruner, *Die Schweizerische Bundesversammlung 1848–1920, Biographien* (Bern: Francke, 1966), 613–14.

53. *Internationaler Kongress für Arbeiterschutz, Zürich 1897: Amtlicher Bericht* (Zurich, 1898), 129–30. Favon and Decurtins wanted international legislation on the protection of children, limitation of female work, a ban on Sunday work, and maximum hours.

54. Decurtins expressed his vision of society in the future and the proper place of women—the home, of course—in his speeches at the congress in 1897.

55. Caspar Decurtins is said to have instigated the encyclical in which the Pope advocated protection of workers. See Gruner, *Schweizerische Bundesversammlung*, 614.

56. Margarete Greulich, eldest daughter of the *Arbeitersekretär* Hermann Greulich, was the delegate of the Labor Office of the city of Zurich.

57. Wilhelm Liebknecht, the German socialist, reportedly spoke of a notion of *Gottesfriede* (truce of God) at the congress. For details of the congress, see Ulla Wikander, "Some 'Kept the Flag of Feminist Demands Waving,' " in this volume.

58. This was demanded by the Belgian delegate, Carton de Wiart. See *Amtlicher Bericht*, 206, for the congress.

59. The French speaker Marie Bonnevial, delegate of the International Working Women's Coalition, demanded this. See ibid., 220–21.

60. Marie Villiger of Zurich advocated legislation for heavy and light industry, for she felt that exploitation seemed even more severe in the latter. No Swiss delegate opposed the legislation for women's work.

61. See the aforementioned discussion in the Basel Parliament in 1869.

62. "Botschaft des Bundesrates an die Bundesversammlung betreffend die Revision des Fabrikgesetzes vom 6.5.1910," *Schweizerisches Bundesblatt 3* (1910): 643ff.

63. "C'est un travail que ne peut pas être fait par une main masculine. Il n'y a que des femmes qui puissent faire ce travail, non pas que le travail féminin soit plus économique, ce n'est pas a cause de cela que les femmes sont employées, mais parce que ce n'est pas un travail d'hommes" (*Amtliches Stenographisches Bulletin der schweizerischen Bundesversammlung* [NR 1913], 761).

64. Bellagio Conference on comparative protective labor legislation for women only (1989).

65. "Botschaft des Bundesrates," 645.

66. *Amtliches Stenographisches Bulletin der schweizerischen Bundesversammlung* (NR, 1913), 764.

67. This discussion was held in 1913. The amended law was only enforced as of 1919 because of World War I, and the free Saturday afternoon rule was enforced as of 1925.

68. The Law on Health Insurance was instituted in 1912. Health insurance was not compulsory, so it only covered expenses for those who had already been members for a certain period.

69. The company also told them, for instance, that a man's income was a "family income" and that men had more obligations. See Mesmer, *Ausgeklammert,* 205.

70. See Margarete Gagg, *Die Frau in der schweizerischen Industrie* (Zurich: Orell Füssli, 1928), 296.

71. Ibid., vii; Annie Leuch, *Die Stellung der Frau in der schweizerischen Gesetzgebung: Bericht über den zweiten Kongress für Fraueninteressen 1921* (Bern: Staempfli, 1921), 468ff.

72. Leuch, *Die Stellung,* 471.

73. They referred to pregnant women only.

74. See Christine Ragaz, *Die Frau in der schweizerischen Gewerkschaftsbewegung* (Stuttgart: Kohlhammer, 1933), 67.

75. The unions were reluctant to organize women. In the 1920s between 8 and 10 percent of the members of the Swiss trade union SGB, the most important union, were women (ibid., 150). At the International Congress of Working Women in Paris in 1927, Swiss delegates were on the side of protection advocates.

76. See Gagg, *Die Frau,* 292–93.

77. "Arbeitsgesetz vom 13.3.1964," article 16.

78. Compare the aforementioned argument made against equal pay in postal and telephone offices.

79. Many women's organizations have expressed their desire to the government to have night work generally reduced to a minimum.

80. Joan W. Scott, "The Sears Case," in *Gender and the Politics of History,* ed. Joan W. Scott (New York: Columbia University Press, 1988), 172.

81. It would be the first time in Swiss history that women had a say in the revision of the Law on Work. Swiss women were only granted the vote in 1971.

· 3 ·

"Let England Blush"
Protective Labor Legislation, 1820–1914

Jane Lewis and Sonya O. Rose

Legal restrictions on women's work were first established in England in the 1840s. Public discussion about regulating women's employment reflected growing apprehension about the consequences of industrial transformation for women's roles coupled with emerging general concerns about the changing industrial order and the state of the nation.[1] Numerous contemporary commentators, including Engels, remarked on both the social and moral consequences of women working in factories.[2] In fact, for nineteenth-century reformers and observers, social analysis and moral assessment often were conjoined.[3]

The debates leading to the enactment of protective labor legislation helped to construct ideas about women and about the nature of work. They contributed to the notion that women were to be defined primarily by their domestic roles while wagework, especially employment in rationalized workplaces, was structured for men. They advanced and strengthened the idea that the "working woman" and, later, the "working mother" were contradictory terms. When it came to employment, women were and would continue to be the special case, not the norm. In this essay, we will focus on these debates, especially on the rhetoric of those who were the major participants in the public dialogue about women and work. The rhetorical ploys that were effective in securing protective labor legislation, as well as the acts themselves, had a long-lasting impact on working-class lives as many of the arguments about the social and moral condition of women workers came to dominate the ways that people thought about women and structured their opportunities for employment.

The primary focus of protective legislation for most of the nine-teenth century concerned the restriction of women's hours of work. Debates focused on the total number of hours of work in factories and workshops rather than on the issue of night work. When lawmakers limited the working day, they assumed, with very little if any discussion, that working hours would be during the day.[4] In the absence of *any* gov-ernmental control, factories were kept operating as long as employers wished, and workers—men, women, and children—toiled at an unre-lenting pace for twelve or fourteen hours a day. Initially, male operatives sought state regulation of factory hours for all workers, including adult men, but they were constrained by the developing hegemony of classical political economy that dominated the thinking of many industrialists and their representatives in Parliament. Central to these ideas was the principle that autonomous individuals should freely establish contracts without government interference. Working men could not seriously challenge these principles, and so they proposed legislation that would affect only women and children, knowing that men's hours also would be shortened because of the interdependence of everyone's work in the textile factories. By focusing on women and children, advocates of fac-tory reform could play on public concerns about sexual morality, the sanctity of childhood, and maternal duty to address the need for social reform.

This was a strategy that often proved acceptable to another powerful group of male actors in the debates, the employers, especially those who were anxious to appease male trade unionists. Industrialists' views also were informed by considerations of profit and loss, which became more acute in the face of increased international competition in the third quarter of the century. Some, especially those who did not command large enterprises, feared that legislation would place them at a disadvan-tage. Others turned to the practice of a "new paternalism" in the work-place that combined a theory of dependence with individualist prin-ciples of self-help. In practice this meant that industrialists combined their use of cheap female workers with strategies that included domes-tic economy lessons for young women employees, sexually segregated entrances and eating facilities, and support for protective legislation.[5]

Male legislators played up the more overt arguments about sexual difference that underpinned the whole debate. In the first half of the nineteenth century, legislation covered the work of women in heavy industry, especially in textile factories and underground in coal mines, and the main focus of attention for legislators was the issue of morality: could men and women mix "promiscuously" in the public sphere? What was at issue in this early period was not women's employment per se but their role as independent economic actors who earned wages outside family units.

Large numbers of women and children had been drawn into the textile factories in the early phase of industrialization. Over the whole period, the percentage of women listed in the census as employed varied between 34 and 36 percent from 1851 to 1891, declining to about 32 percent in 1901 and 1911.[6] Of these, the percentage working in textiles was at its height of 22.4 percent in 1851, declining to 16 percent in 1911. At the same time, the percentage of women working as domestic workers increased from 40 percent in 1851 to 45 percent in 1891, declining in censuses taken after the turn of the century.

By the end of the nineteenth century, in the context of increasing concern about national efficiency—which included the health and welfare of the population based on increased investigation of and knowledge about the conditions of working-class family life—the rationale for legislation centered on the protection of women as actual or potential "mothers of the race." Evidence about the numbers of working mothers is very sketchy, and the available data suggest that fewer married women were employed in late nineteenth- and early twentieth-century industry than during the early phase of industrialization. But the census did not distinguish the number of married women workers from unmarried ones until 1911, at which point it showed only 10 percent of the former to be gainfully employed, although this figure undoubtedly failed to include large numbers of married women who took casual employment—for example, hawking fruit or doing a day's washing (and whose income was vital to the fragile family economy). The declining number of married women in regular, full-time employment was probably a response to the development of an ideology of working-class domesticity for women connected with emerging ideas about working-class male respectability that attached considerable importance to the ability to "keep" a wife and children, as well as with the capacity of the most skilled male workers to earn a "family wage."[7]

The government's concern with promoting the primacy of women's role as mothers nevertheless ran counter to its desire to limit the extent of state regulation of the private sphere of the family. The two areas causing the greatest debate in relation to the expansion of the factory acts at the end of the century were, first, the extent to which home-work was to be regulated and, second, the application of legislation to laundry work, a predominantly female occupation believed to be, like any domestic work, manifestly suitable for women whether carried out in homes or in small and large workplaces.

The shift toward motherhood as the main rationale for protective legislation was reflected in the broadening of legislation in the 1890s to include the introduction of mandatory maternity leave and the prohibition of work with toxic substances. Finally, in the 1900s, minimum wage legislation was introduced for a limited number of trades in which the work force was predominantly female and which were deemed "sweated." Again, it was the deleterious effect that sweating women workers might have on the national health and welfare that captured the public and political imagination.

Throughout the period, legislators who advocated protective legislation maintained that such laws were in the national interest. Although the specific focus of their concerns shifted from sexuality and the importance of domesticity as a corrective to immorality to the "mothers of the race," legislators portrayed the control of women, as workers, as fundamental to social order and the health of the body politic. At least in the context of a polity that excluded women as citizens, ideas about their autonomy were deeply threatening.

Although discussions about the hours and conditions of women's employment began early in the nineteenth century, until the 1870s public deliberations about state regulation of women's employment were conducted primarily by men. Women's voices, particularly those of the working women themselves, were rarely heard on the subject, no less taken into account. From the 1870s the public consideration of the regulation of women's work drew in largely middle-class women, who united with female trade unionists to oppose protective legislation. But by the 1890s, in the context of changes in economic ideas, in political views about the role of the state and the increased emphasis placed on women's welfare as mothers, female opponents of protective legislation became a minority.

Both opponents and proponents of legislation argued within parameters set by the doctrine of free agency from political economy, on the one hand, and ideas from social and medical scientists who insisted on the essentialist properties of sexual differences between men and women, on the other. These constructions constrained the terms of the debates. In particular, those who opposed protective labor legislation for women argued that women, like men, were autonomous agents capable of negotiating the terms of employment for themselves. Those who argued for protective legislation stressed women's differences from men as the reasons that protection was especially warranted for them. The debate over protective legislation in the nineteenth and early twentieth centuries was thus a debate about women's nature and place.

◆ ◆

Between 1830 and 1850, male textile operatives in Lancashire and Yorkshire led a massive campaign to limit working hours in factories to a ten-hour day. The campaign was opposed by industrialists, academics, and their representatives in Parliament, who believed that any limitation in the hours of factory operation would lower profits and hinder competition, and those who held firmly to the principle that government should not intervene in the relations between capital and labor. As early as 1818, the Lancashire cotton spinners had petitioned Parliament for a universal ten-and-a-half-hour day, of which nine hours would be for work.[8] These early appeals fell on deaf ears.

In 1830, what became known as the Ten Hours Movement began to advocate a reduction in the hours that children could be employed in textile factories. Although the male operatives and their supporters expressed concern for the children who worked more than fifteen or sixteen hours a day, they hoped that by shortening the workday for those under eighteen years of age, their own hours would be shortened as well.[9] The spinners reasoned that because children were employed as their assistants and to do other processes that were ancillary to the production of yarn, a limitation on their hours would result in limiting hours for everyone. They had to convince members of Parliament and the general public, however, that legislation of children's hours was warranted.

To make their case, reformers used tactics and rhetorical ploys that were to be repeated in future campaigns to legislate restrictions on women's work. Commissions of inquiry were structured in ways that helped to achieve the ends of those who organized them. By portraying women and children as victims of ruthless employers and the factory system, one such investigatory committee that collected testimony throughout 1832 shocked public sensibilities with accounts of the cruel and inhumane conditions children suffered in the mills.[10] As

Robert Gray has suggested, patriarchal values pervaded the inquiry as husbands and fathers were called on to advocate on behalf of these victims of industry.[11]

Although gender difference was not a stated focus of the debates in the early 1830s, both proponents and opponents of factory legislation were preoccupied with a concern for the morals of young girls and their fitness to be wives and mothers.[12] Reformers expressed anxiety about how physical deformities might impair the ability of boys to do men's work in the future, but they focused on the moral welfare of girls and their fitness for domesticity.[13] Playing on bourgeois sexual fears, Michael Sadler, a committee organizer and author of a ten hours bill for children, told Parliament that the mills were "little better than brothels," and agitators for reform "painted the factories as dens of vice in which masters seduced female operatives freely."[14] To challenge sentiments of national pride, orators used images of females as morally debased and degraded. In a letter to a newspaper about drunken "factory girls," Richard Oastler, a major Ten Hours agitator, wrote "LET ENGLAND BLUSH!"[15] The connection between the moral degradation of females and national identity would be a powerful rhetorical strategy in obtaining state protection of women workers in the 1840s.

To delay action amid demonstrations and protests in favor of factory reform throughout the country in 1833, the government set up a new parliamentary commission to moderate the accusations of cruelty to children detailed by Sadler's committee. Continuing public pressure for a measure to help the children led these new commissioners to moderate their principle of noninterference by the state in private contracts. The commissioners argued that "at the age when children suffer these injuries from the labour they undergo, they are not free agents but are let out to hire" by their parents.[16] The commissioners shifted the blame for overworking the children from mill owners to working-class parents, and by doing so they created a rationale for why children should not be seen as autonomous agents.[17]

The resulting factory act of 1833 banned children under nine years of age from working in textile factories and reduced the working day for those between the ages of thirteen and eighteen to twelve hours a day; younger children were restricted to an eight-hour day. The act placed no limits, however, on when the eight hours had to be worked. It therefore fell far short of the ten-hour day for which the Short Time Committees of working men had been pressing. Because children could be worked in relays, the hours of adult workers were not affected by the act at all.

By 1840 it was evident to the operatives that the act of 1833 was not effective. In addition to working young children in relays of eight hours, some manufacturers replaced thirteen- to eighteen-year-olds with adult women in order to keep their factories operating for longer than twelve hours a day. Also, some male operatives began to fear women as a threat to their own employment, and if exclusion was impossible, then restriction would be the next best solution.[18] Using language that drew together the themes of women as victims, the morally degrading nature of factory employment, and the threat to domesticity posed by mill work, a deputation of Ten Hours advocates from West Riding to Parliament and government ministers urged the "gradual withdrawal of all females from factories."[19] Supporters evidently believed that their best chance of securing a reduction of hours for all textile factory workers was to focus on the evils of women's employment and to have their hours of work restricted along with those of children and young people.

The cause of the Ten Hours Movement was aided by the riveting of national public attention on women's employment in the coal mines by a new parliamentary commission, which began its work in 1841. As a consequence of the commission's revelations, the Mines and Collieries Act of 1842 was passed, and it had as its first clause the exclusion of all females from underground work.[20]

The commission findings featured evidence alleging immorality involving the women mine workers, replete with portrayals of women and men working scantily clad and bare-chested and with testimony about the illegitimate births that supposedly resulted from women working underground. Most of the witnesses were queried about whether or not the men took "liberties" with the women in the pits, about the women's clothing, and about their chastity.[21] In addition, the commission report decried the poor state of the homes of the collier women and their lack of skill in caring for their husbands and children. Commissioners and subcommissioners linked morality with domesticity: "let her attend to a mother's and a housewife's duties; and you will soon change the moral condition of the collier."[22]

In the debates in Parliament, lawmakers virtually ignored the testimony from clergymen, as well as from the workers themselves, that countered the accusations of immorality. In addition, although the report described in detail the backbreaking labor engaged in by the collier women, and how women continued to work through their pregnancies and often miscarried or their babies died at birth, surprisingly little was made of these revelations in Parliament.[23]

Lord Ashley's speech presenting the bill to ban women and children from working underground noted the harmful effects of the brutally hard work on pregnant women, but he exploited the sensationalism in the reports to excite the moral outrage of his fellow legislators: "In the West Riding girls seven to twenty-one work naked down to the waist and are dressed—as far as they are dressed at all—in a loose pair of trousers. These are seldom whole on either sex. In many collieries the adult colliers, whom these girls serve, work perfectly naked."[24] Ashley, who was the parliamentary standard-bearer of the Ten Hours Movement, also linked collier women's supposed "ignorance of domestic duties" with immorality: "But now mark the effect of the system on women: it causes a total ignorance of all domestic duties; they . . . become utterly demoralized. . . . If you corrupt the women, you poison the waters of life at the very fountain."[25]

The nation's image of itself, shaped by the humanitarian sentiments of enlightened industrialists and landowners, fostered by Evangelicalism, and fashioned by colonialist rhetoric, had been badly tarnished. As one of the mines and collieries subcommissioners put it:

> The estimation of the sex [women] has ever been held a test of the civilisation of a people. Shall it then be said that in the heart of our own country—from which missions are daily sent to teach God's law, and millions upon millions have been generously poured forth for the manumission of hosts in a distant land—that there shall exist a state of society in which hundreds of young girls are sacrificed to such shameless indecencies, filthy abominations and cruel slavery as is found to exist in our coal pits?[26]

Disorderly and degraded women who were incapable of domesticity were a threat to national honor, and it was deemed in the national interest that the state should intervene.[27]

The exclusion of females from working underground produced relatively little debate. What dissent there was primarily focused on the economic plight of the women and families that depended on their wages.[28] The sensationalism of the issue of immorality silenced those who were concerned with the principles of political economy and the state regulation of industry.[29] In the House of Lords, the Earl of Devon argued that it was "the duty of the Legislature to interfere to prevent the demoralization of the rising generation. He had no wish to contravene the principles of political economy, but there were higher duties than any that political economy could teach." [30]

The Mines and Collieries Act of 1842—and the debates that interlaced themes of moral degradation, lack of domesticity, and a blight on the national character caused by this particular form of women's employment—set the stage for a new round of legislative efforts to secure a ten hours bill. [31] The next year the government introduced a factory bill to include women under the twelve-hour work limit for young persons that had been defined by the act of 1833. [32] The bill, which passed in 1844, limited women to a twelve-hour day, barred them from working at night, and defined them to be, like children, "unfree agents" in the labor market.

Lord Ashley's speech to the House of Commons (introducing an amendment to limit factory hours to a ten-hour day) mentioned the consequences of women's long hours of labor for childbearing and their exploitation at the hands of unscrupulous employers who forced them to do exhausting work. However, as in his discussions about collier women, Ashley regaled the House with reports about the factory women's incompetence in household duties and their immorality.

New to parliamentary discussion about women workers was Ashley's accusation that women were replacing men as family breadwinners. He related an incident in which a man carrying a baby came into a club (where women met "to drink, talk and smoke") to get his wife to come home to attend to her household duties. She refused to go because she wanted to drink a second pint of ale. Ashley commented: "Whence is it that this singular and unnatural change is taking place? Because that on women are imposed the duty and burthen of supporting their husbands and families, a perversion as it were of nature, which has the inevitable effect of introducing into families disorder, insubordination, and conflict." [33] Calling on the lawmakers' national pride, Ashley said: "The toil of the females has hitherto been considered the characteristic of savage life; but we, in the height of our refinement, impose on the wives and daughters of England a burthen from which, at least during pregnancy, they would be exempted even in slave-holding states, and among the Indians of America." [34] Ashley had identified both female domesticity and male breadwinning as the test of a civilized society, as other influential commentators, notably Herbert Spencer, continued to do throughout the century. [35]

Ashley was bringing to the national stage fears about women workers that were being articulated by Ten Hours Movement leaders and male unionists. Chartists also were espousing the ideology of female domesticity in their tracts and public speeches. Unionists, Ten Hours men, and Chartists usually were speaking to members of their own communities in addition to attempting to enlist the sympathy of the elite classes. They were creating working-class versions of the ideology of domesticity for women and breadwinning for men. Ashley, however, was connecting images of role reversal and women's immorality to fears of social disorder that were preoccupying members of the ruling classes.

The years 1841 and 1842 were ones of dire economic distress; massive unemployment produced severe hardship in the factory districts. In 1842, Chartist agitation and the economic duress experienced by the working classes led to strikes and disturbances throughout the factory districts, culminating late that summer in pitched battles between strikers and troops called in to quell the insurrections.[36] Ashley alluded to these events in his speech to Parliament by calling the lawmakers' attention to the "ferocity of conduct exhibited . . . in the manufacturing towns" in the disturbances of 1842 and the "share born by girls and women."[37] He then quoted a Manchester police superintendent who said that factory women "lose the station ordained them by Providence . . . wearing the garb of women, but actuated by the worst passions of men. The women are the leaders and exciters of the young men to violence in every riot and outbreak in the manufacturing districts, and the language they indulge in is of a horrid description. While they are themselves demoralised, they contaminate all that comes within their reach."[38] Ashley was portraying social chaos as caused by disorderly women who had been degraded by becoming breadwinners. Social order, then, was predicated on patriarchal control. His vision made it clear that to think about women as independent adults was a recipe for anarchy.

In 1844, most members of Parliament seem to have agreed that women's hours should be restricted, and the only question to be considered was whether or not manufacturers' competitive position would be too severely disadvantaged to legislate the ten-hour day that Ashley had proposed. M.P. J. Roebuck was the arch defender of political economy, arguing in opposition to any restriction on women's labor. He made a formal motion to make it a matter of state policy that there should be no interference with "adult labour in factories to make contracts respecting their hours."[39] Sir James Graham, home minister who had introduced the government's bill, argued with Roebuck that women were forced to work beyond twelve hours by employers who were evading the act of 1833. He added: "Married women might clearly be influenced by their husbands, for the sake of gaining higher wages, and thus to overwork themselves, and generally as to females, considering that they were the weaker portion of the community, having a claim by nature on our compassion . . . were more peculiarly entitled to the protection of the Legislature."[40] Supporters of factory reform in Parliament argued that, for a variety of reasons, women were not free agents. A favored argument was to blame working-class husbands for forcing their wives to work.

With these debates in Parliament about the legitimacy of the state to regulate the work of adult women, and the subsequent passage of the 1844 factory act, the state formally included women with children as needing its protection. As far as Parliament was concerned, hours legislation would be secured from "behind the women's petticoats."[41] The Ten Hours Bill (for women and children) was passed in 1847, and until the early 1870s there were no further legislative attempts to reduce the length of the working day.

◆ ◆

Skilled working men in several trades began demanding a nine-hour day from their employers in the 1850s.[42] They were unsuccessful until 1871, when a five-month-long strike of engineers in Newcastle was victorious. Valiant efforts by the Oldham cotton textile operatives were unsuccessful in negotiating a reduction of their hours. They turned to A. J. Mundella, member of Parliament from Sheffield and hosiery manufacturer from Nottingham with known sympathies to the trade union movement, to introduce a nine hours bill in Parliament. The unionists were joined by several cloth manufacturers who were sympathetic to their cause and who were anxious for a uniform reduction in the hours of work in the textile factories in order to slow down the production of cotton cloth and raise the prices for manufactured goods on the market. It was evident to all the protagonists that a nine hours bill, which directly and formally included men, was out of the question.

Like their forebears in the 1840s, the Factory Acts Reform Association requested a bill for the protection of women and children knowing that their own hours also would be limited. Mundella's nine hours bill was debated in 1872 and 1873, and in 1874 the Tory government under

Benjamin Disraeli introduced the "Factories (Health of Women etc.) Bill." In becoming law, it restricted the working hours of women, children, and young persons employed in textile factories to 56½ hours per week.

Supporters of these measures, like those in the 1840s, had to make the argument for factory act reform specific to women. Unlike their counterparts in the 1840s, they did not focus on women generally but on married women and especially mothers. The Factory Acts Reform Association enlisted orators like the Reverend Stephens, a former Chartist activist, to argue their case for protecting motherhood. Legislators and other middle-class commentators who debated the measures also focused their arguments on the ill effects of married women's work on family life. Like their counterparts earlier in the century, they accused working-class husbands of forcing their wives to work. Once the debates were underway in the House of Commons, working men lost control over the discourse about mothers, wagework, and the hours of labor.

The controversy about married women's employment and its causes articulated in these debates was part of a larger public discussion about the working-class family that began in the 1870s. In 1870 the Married Women's Property Act, a measure designed to protect the earnings of working-class women, was passed. In the hearings that led to the framing of the legislation, proponents argued that the law would enhance the mother's role as educator of her children and would protect her earnings from feckless men.[43] Mundella viewed the Married Women's Property Act of 1870 as coming from the same public concern that justified the regulation of women's hours under the factory acts.[44]

The government appointed two physicians to investigate the effects of factory life on women and children. The physicians noted high rates of infant mortality in the factory districts and argued that these high rates were caused by the employment of mothers. Their findings about infant mortality were interpreted by legislators and industrialists as portents of a decline in the quality of the English working population. The public concern with motherhood was increasingly linked to concerns about the quality of the race.[45] In the last quarter of the nineteenth century, motherhood became an obligation women had not simply to their individual families but to the nation. Again women were linked to the national interest; now the focus was not on women and morality but on women's maternal obligations.

Both opponents and proponents accepted and used the findings about infant mortality and its causes, but to different ends. Employers and legislators who opposed the legislation argued that only "the gradual removal of women from the factories and the resumption of the motherly duties they owe to their offspring" would solve the problem.[46] One of the lawmakers who favored the bill said, "As far as he was concerned, he hoped and believed that the time was not far distant when working men would be ashamed to allow their wives to work in factories at all. The sooner that time arrived the better it would be for England; but until then he thought we ought to legislate in such a way as to render the evil of the present system as small as possible." [47]

Organized opposition to the measures came principally from some employers who feared that a reduction in the hours of labor would put them at a disadvantage in international competition. Joining the opposition were members of Parliament and academics who maintained that the state should not intervene in the labor contracts of adults. Although women's labor had been protected by the state for about thirty years, this argument was made at least as forcefully as it was earlier—if not more so.

A combination of factors contributed to a new round of discussion about whether or not women were autonomous agents who could enter into contracts on their own. The growing women's suffrage movement and the first Married Women's Property Act contributed to the idea that women could claim some of the same rights as men. In addition, many male workers in the factory districts had secured the franchise, making the distinction between these working-class men and all women very evident. In the 1870s bourgeois egalitarian feminists entered the debates about women and work.[48] They concerned themselves with opening up women's options for employment and viewed legal gender distinctions to be a barrier to gender equality. In effect, they argued the classic liberal feminist position that women are the same as men only female. They asserted that women, like men, were free agents and should not be seen as children who needed the protection of the government. In the early 1870s, their position of noninterference with adult women's labor was undermined and ultimately defeated by prevailing views— about women workers, married women's labor, and men's responsibilities toward families—held by the proponents and opponents of factory legislation alike.

Factory act reformers persisted in maintaining in the 1870s that women were not free agents. In making their case they argued that women and girls were forced to work by their husbands, by cruel employers, or even by their maternal instinct to care for their children.[49] Opposing them was a women's rights organization, the Vigilance Association for the Defence of Personal Rights and for the Amendment of the Law in Points wherein it is Injurious to Women. The group, made up primarily of bourgeois egalitarian feminists and libertarians, had been formed in 1871 to fight the Contagious Diseases Act. Although the writings of the Vigilance Association maintained that women were free agents, they often appealed to the same gender ideology as those whom they opposed. For example, the association suggested that a woman be given the power to request that her husband's wages be attached if he consistently neglected to maintain her; in this way women "would . . . voluntarily and without compulsion of law, withdraw from labour pursued elsewhere than in their own homes, and would devote themselves to maternal and domestic duties."[50] To these middle-class observers women were responsible for domesticity, but men were to blame if women could not do their motherly duties.[51]

The Vigilance Association made efforts to influence the proceedings both by appealing to the Trades Union Congress and to Home Secretary Asheton Cross, to no avail. The primary influence of these women's rights activists on the legislative considerations was through the Fawcetts. Millicent Fawcett, women's rights leader and suffragist, argued the noninterventionist position in a letter to the *Times* (London), and her husband, Henry, a member of Parliament for Cambridge, brought the argument to the House of Commons. A major weapon used against these particular opponents of the legislation was that they were women of privilege. Supporters of the acts countered their arguments by saying that they adopted their position because "they did not belong to the humble class who were so shamefully overworked."[52]

We know very little about working-women's opinions concerning factory legislation. When their jobs were threatened, women fought to protect their livelihoods. For example, when a newspaper in 1832 suggested that "females of any age" should gradually be excluded from manufacturing, the female operatives of Todmorden replied,

> for the thousands of females who are employed in manufactories, who have no legitimate claim on any male relatives for support, and who have, through a variety of circumstances, been early thrown on

their own resources for a livelihood, what is to become of them? . . .
Now, then as we are a class of society who will be materially affected by any alteration of the present laws, we put it seriously to
you, whether, as you have deprived us of our means of earning our
bread, you are not bound to point out a more eligible and suitable
employment for us?[53]

In addition, they had undoubtedly supported initiatives to shorten
their working hours.[54] But they lacked their own trade union organizations, which might have argued on their behalf.

In 1874, Emma Paterson founded the Women's Protective and Provident League to encourage the formation of unions of working women.
Paterson, a middle-class woman who had apprenticed as a bookbinder,
believed that women could improve their economic position by union-
izing.[55] She was outspoken about the "sweated conditions of female
labor" and argued that women "more than ever need the protection
afforded by combination; for at present the women affected by the
proposed restrictions have no means of making known their collective
opinions."[56] Her goal was to create a cross-class alliance of women that
would assist working women to gain higher wages and shorter hours
without relying on the state.[57]

Paterson and the league, as well as women workers who were members of unions affiliated with the league, actively protested against extending restrictions on female labor proposed in a new act, the Factory
and Workshops Consolidation Bill, which was made law in 1878. They
spoke out against further restrictions in commission hearings held before the introduction of legislation, despite considerable resistance expressed by the commissioners to their point of view. For example, "a
meeting of Ladies" who opposed restrictions on women appeared before the commissioners to argue that such restrictions forced women
out of well-paid employment and into other trades that then became
"over-crowded."[58] Mrs. Fray, who appeared on behalf of the Leicestershire Stitchers and Seamers Association, an association of homeworkers
that had been organized with the assistance of Paterson's league, argued
against state regulations of homeworking hosiery workers.[59]

Like the opposition from the bourgeois women's movement to the
legislation of 1874, the women's unions and the Women's Protective and
Provident League were denied the opportunity to send a deputation to
the home secretary and were constrained to register their opposition to

the proposed legislation in a memorial. Although they could exert little direct influence on the debates on the 1878 act, their cause was again joined by legislators opposed to any governmental intervention in labor contracts. Henry Fawcett, supported by several other lawmakers, attempted to have the word "woman" omitted from various clauses of the bill, but they were only successful in excluding home workshops from the measure.[60] The commissioners who investigated the issue in 1876 accepted that it was "desirable to interfere as little as possible with the habits and arrangements of families."[61] Education provided by middle-class "visitors" rather than direct legislative fiat was considered by legislators to be appropriate intervention in the working-class family.

During this period, male trade unionists were espousing the values of domesticity for women and breadwinning for men. Although the evidence is quite clear that they had pushed for a nine hours bill to gain advantages for all workers in factories, not just for women, they often espoused the idea that women were "naturally" different from and weaker than men. The Labor leader George Howell, who headed the influential Parliamentary Committee of the Trade Union Congress in the last quarter of the century, wrote: "Women are essentially weak. . . . Some of the causes of this weakness lie deep and hidden in human nature, others are not far to seek. The fact, however, is patent; woman needs protection."[62] Male trade unionists and the Women's Protective and Provident League became increasingly hostile to one another. Henry Broadhurst's disdain for the women unionists was palpable. At the Trades Union Congress of 1878, at which Paterson and others were present, Broadhurst argued against a proposal advocating that women be hired as factory inspectors: "he had doubted the wisdom even of inviting ladies to the Congress as delegates . . . because he feared that under their persuasive eloquence the Congress would . . . be led into the illogical position that men could be placed in and would vote for a proposition which they would not entertain in their clearer and more rational moments."[63] At a meeting of the Leicestershire Seamers and Stitchers in 1877, the women barred men from the meeting room.[64] Women trade unionists associated with the Women's Protective and Provident League and many of their advocates believed that male unionists were advocating protective legislation because they feared women's competition for employment.[65]

Male trade unionists and members of women's rights organizations took opposing positions on the next significant attempt to restrict women's work. In the mid-1880s, the Miners' Federation promoted the exclusion of women from working at the pit brows. Although there had been sporadic criticisms of women working at the surface of mines since midcentury, these attacks coalesced in the 1880s. As Angela John has proposed, the move to eliminate women from mine work was given new vigor by the debates and subsequent passage of the hours bills of the 1870s.[66]

The advocates of complete exclusion of females from mine work attempted to make their case in ways similar to the advocates of exclusion in 1842. Bourgeois reformers spoke of the moral degradation and the debasement of women due to their work at the mine face. The pit brow women were "seen as a moral threat, a challenge to the cult of motherhood and another forceful image of darkest England."[67] Proponents of exclusion focused on the unsuitability of their work and on their dress. This campaign was ultimately unsuccessful as coal owners from female employing areas, anxious to retain the system because it kept wages low, and members of suffrage organizations and the Vigilance Association, each for reasons of their own, supported the pit brow women who demanded their right to work.[68] The Mines and Collieries Act of 1887 permitted any female over the age of twelve to continue to be employed at the pit top.

◆ ◆

In spite of this consolidated front against exclusion of the pit brow women, the unified opposition to protective legislation by the various women's movement organizations was beginning to unravel. By the 1890s, the Women's Protective and Provident League reversed its position on state regulation of women's work.[69] Even earlier there was some dissension within its ranks, but the death of Emma Paterson and the accession to leadership of the women's trade union movement of women with differing views contributed to a dramatic change in the policies of the league, which also had exhibited a rather poor record of success in organizing women workers.

As Rosemary Feurer has argued, the change must also be set in the context of shifts in economic and political ideas and in relation to changes in male trade unionism.[70] The voice of neoclassical economists, most notably Alfred Marshall, was heard on government committees of inquiry setting the parameters within which a new enabling role for the state could be justified, and New Liberal theorists produced arguments to justify the greater use of collectivist means in order to secure the full development of the individual.[71] With the increased pressure exerted by employers on labor at the end of the century, historians have suggested that the "respectable" members of the unions of skilled working men, and new unionists among the unskilled, became increasingly militant.[72] In the 1890s men's trade unions began to push for a general eight-hour day. The *Cotton Factory Times* quoted a union leader as saying, "now the veil must be lifted and the agitation carried on under its true colours. Women and children must no longer be made the pretext for securing a reduction of working hours for men."[73]

However, those who spoke for the realigned women trade unionists rarely argued that men also needed state protection. Rather, they justified protective labor legislation for women on the grounds that women and children "do not, or cannot, combine for self-defense, and their competition in the absence of a legal limitation of hours would continually weaken the workingday for all."[74] They were joined by a broad political coalition of women philanthropists and social investigators. Many female leaders of the campaign to extend protective legislation were also antisuffragists. This position should not be surprising. Women's claim for the vote, as Carole Pateman has pointed out, was a claim for independence, and the whole basis of the antisuffrage case was grounded in sexual difference and in women's natural dependency and need for protection.[75] As a leader of the antisuffragist movement, Mary Ward argued that the extension of protective legislation met women's real needs and also demonstrated that the vote was unnecessary.[76] This was an extreme view; campaigners for protective legislation also included many suffragists. But in calling for protection for women workers, the vast majority of women reformers also accepted that women's work was of inferior value to that of men. Women proponents of protective legislation fundamentally shared the view that some jobs were more suitable for women than others and that married women's primary responsibility was to home and family. Within these limits, both opponents and proponents desired as wide a range of occupations as possible to be open to women, as well as better pay and working conditions. Differences in the 1890s arose primarily over the role of the state in obtaining these, although any simple division between individualists and collectivists would be misleading. By the 1890s there was a spectrum of views. There were proponents of protective legislation who campaigned for factory inspection but not for minimum wage legislation, and opponents who would nevertheless accept a measure of inspection under the public health acts. Only those egalitarian feminists attached to the *Englishwoman's Review,* such as Jessie Boucherette and Helen Blackburn, continued in diehard opposition to all protection, insisting that it would only increase female dependence and that legislators who treated women as helpless made them helpless.[77]

Proponents of protection found it increasingly easy to cut away egalitarian arguments during the 1890s. Beatrice Webb's contributions were both the most influential and the most sophisticated. She effectively dismissed the major practical concern of the egalitarians regarding the effect of protective legislation on women's competitive position in the labor market, pointing out that because of sexual segregation (which she and her husband, Sidney, regarded as natural[78]), it was highly unlikely that men would take women's jobs: "The first assumption is, that in British industry today, men and women are actively competing for the same employment. I doubt whether anyone here has any conception of the infinitesimal extent to which this is true."[79] Most commentators believed, like the factory inspector reporting to the British Association meetings in 1903, that "women will never become engineers, mechanics, stonemasons, builders, miners and so on. And men are not likely to become operative dressmakers, milliners (I know one or two exceptional cases), launderers."[80]

Although female proponents of protection were unified in their opinion that the reality of working-class women's lives justified the need for state protection, they varied in their aims and demands according to their different political allegiances. For example, some middle-class trade union leaders, such as Lady Dilke, who replaced Emma Paterson as the leader of the Women's Protective and Provident League (renamed the Women's Trade Union League in 1889), and Gertrude Tuckwell, deplored all married women's work and hoped that the most radical proposals for a minimum wage would serve to raise male wages, making the work of wives unnecessary.[81] The women's section of the Labour party—the Women's Labour League—was explicit in its support for the family wage system and in its belief that true freedom for working-class wives consisted in their right to stay at home.[82] Clara Collet, a social investigator who worked first for Charles Booth on his massive 1880s survey of London and then, much more unusually, as a civil servant at the Board of Trade, felt that educated middle-class women should be encouraged to contribute to the public world of work and citizenship but that the work of working-class women as wives and mothers was too hard to permit their paid employment. These views were not dissimilar from those of the members of Parliament who expressed the idea that working-class women should be prevented from engaging in paid work because of the probable harm to them and their children. Just as the 1876 Commission of Inquiry into the factory acts contemplated making part-time work compulsory for married women, so the president of the Local Government Board, John Burns, called for legal restrictions of married women's work at the 1906 Conference on Infant Mortality.[83] These ideas, bordering as they did on forcibly driving married women out of the labor market, played to the worst fears of opponents of protective legislation.

The greatest unanimity among female proponents of protective legislation was achieved on the issue of extending the factory and workshop acts. By 1903, even diehard opponents of protection had accepted the value of sanitary inspection of all premises where women worked.[84] In her preface to Beatrice Webb's *Case for the Factory Acts* (1902), Mary Ward, whose conservative politics were diametrically opposed to Webb's Fabian socialism, nevertheless enthusiastically endorsed the campaign for factory legislation as part of natural progress toward a healthy nation and a moralized capitalism. The campaign for greater protection under the acts involved both legislation to cover more occupations, such as laundries, and more workplaces, particularly the home, where women sewed shirts, made matchboxes, and engaged in dozens of other sweated occupations as various as brushmaking and covering tennis balls.

The 1891 factory act tightened the regulation of outworkers following the revelations as to the conditions of sweated labor in workshops made by a Select Committee of Inquiry in 1888[85] and a practical manifestation of the dangers to the population at large from such ill-regulated work in the form of a smallpox outbreak emanating from domestic workshops in Leeds in the same year. In line with the concern about motherhood, the 1891 legislation also included a provision to exclude women from returning to work for four weeks after childbirth, a measure discussed by members of Parliament before the enactment of the 1874 factory act but rejected as unenforceable, while an 1895 act prohibited work with certain toxic substances. The clause providing for (unpaid) maternity leave was passed without debate. Supporters of the measure in Parliament expressed their view that it was not just for the sake of women but, as Lord de Ramsey said, "for the sake of those yet unborn."[86] It was added to the 1891 factory act with Britain's participation in, and agreement on, the resolutions of the Berlin Conference of 1890.[87]

During the 1890s, the newly appointed female factory inspectors added substantially to the collection of evidence as to the need for further extension of the factory acts. Patricia Malcolmson has suggested that the investigations they carried out between 1893 and 1895 were crucial in getting the first measure of regulation applied to laundries in the 1895 act.[88] Large numbers of laundresses (estimates suggested twenty to thirty thousand) had demonstrated in favor of the extension of protective legislation to them in 1891, but the vigorous opposition of egalitarian women's rights supporters stopped the inclusion of laundries in the act of that year. Egalitarians argued that regulation would wipe out the cottage laundry and leave only the steam laundry, which, in line with their assumptions regarding the sexual division of labor, they assumed would remain a male preserve. But after 1891, the broad-based coalition of women trade unionists and social reformers, together with the new women civil servants, swung parliamentary opinion toward implementing regulation in 1895 and again in 1907. During this same period, many male trade unionists in Britain, influenced by their continental counterparts and conferences associated with the Second International, began to press Parliament for an eight-hour day for all workers.

The effectiveness of the factory and workshop acts was a constant cause for concern. Women factory inspectors, who believed strongly in the value of mothers staying at home to look after their children, found case after case of women returning to work immediately after childbirth due to economic necessity. Similarly, social investigators in West Ham in 1907 found that of the 1,786 names of outworkers on the list that local authorities were obliged to keep, it was possible to track down and report on only 520. They concluded that most of the provisions affecting outworkers were effectively dead letters.[89] Managers of workshops employing dressmakers, for example, found it relatively easy to avoid inspectors, as Edith Lytleton's play *Warp and Woof* (1908) sought to bring home to a wider public.

The position of homeworkers in particular was central to the emergence of the campaign to abolish sweated labor, which reached its crescendo in the first decade of the twentieth century with the demand for a minimum wage. A Trades Board Act setting a minimum rate in a limited number of trades was passed in 1909. This measure of state intervention was more controversial than the extension of the factory acts. However, in the climate of the New Liberal reforms of the period 1906–14, when legislation was passed to give old-age pensions in 1908 and national health and unemployment insurance in 1911, and in 1909, when the decision was made to use taxation as a social instrument to pay for social reform, the voice of opponents of protective legislation, who drew on the older tradition of classical political economy, was necessarily muted. Still, the naïve arguments of people like Helen Bosanquet persisted. While not opposed to all aspects of state regulation and inspection, Bosanquet felt that a more lasting solution lay in the establishment of consumer leagues to ensure a fair price for sweated goods, rather than in a fair wages resolution governing the rates of pay offered under government contracts (passed in 1891) or in a minimum wage.[90] Such ideas were easily dismissed by Webb, whose response was cutting and contemptuous: "Even if the consumer made the Quixotic rule of paying the old-fashioned price for everything, he has no ground for hoping or believing that the shopkeeper will pass his bounty onto the wholesale dealer, the wholesale dealer to the manufacturer or the manufacturer to the wage earner."[91]

Commissioners in government investigations into sweating at the end of the 1880s experienced considerable difficulty in defining the phenomenon, agreeing only that sweated workers were usually women and experienced unsanitary working conditions, long hours, and low wages.[92] The widespread view of the commissioners that these were due either to exploitation by "middlemen" or to the reluctance of workers to adopt more modern methods in their work (for example, to use a sewing machine) proved more difficult to substantiate. Again, Webb's analysis, derived from her work for Booth's social survey, proved influential. She insisted that "the sweater is, in fact, the whole nation," for the sweated were "defrauded in every relation of life" by the putter out, the shopkeeper who gave credit, the landlord and the consumer.[93] Investigation by the Women's Trade Union League and more especially by the Women's Industrial Council, an organization founded in 1894 by radical and socialist middle-class women to lobby on behalf of working-class women,[94] revealed both the nature of their labor and the extent to which sweated women workers tended to fall into easily distinguishable categories: wives, whose husbands either did not earn a family wage or were unemployed or sick, and single women, in particular widows, deserted wives, and elderly women.

The National Anti-Sweating League, which was as much a coalition of different political interests as was the group of female proponents of protective legislation, pushed forward the campaign for a minimum wage in the first decade of the twentieth century and argued its case primarily in terms of national efficiency.[95] Goods produced by home-workers carried the risk of infection because they were so often made in unsanitary conditions and their manufacture threatened the physical efficiency of the race because of the strain such work placed on both women and children. In the words of A. G. Gardiner, chairman of the league, sweated trades were not just "an excrescence on the body politic, having no bearing upon its general health, but [were] an organic disease . . . an evil that wasted the whole individual physique . . . a running sore that affected the entire fabric of society, a morass exhaling a miasma that poisoned the healthy elements of industry."[96] The sweated, in short, were "a menace to the communal good." These sentiments were often echoed by female proponents of minimum wage legislation. For example, Constance Smith, a member of the Christian Social Union and later a female factory inspector, wrote of the moral and physical wrecks "to be found among the children of the sweated," who were the natural recruits to "the growing army of the unemployed and unemployable, to fill our workhouses, hospitals, asylums and prisons."[97] The case for wage boards was argued not so much in terms of protecting working-class wives and mothers from husbands or employers but in terms of protecting the nation's health and modernizing its industry.

Few campaigners showed much regard for the needs of individual homeworkers. Webb argued that until sweated women workers enjoyed a minimum level of physical efficiency and leisure they would not be able to act for themselves through trade unions or any other means, thus inferring that protective legislation was a necessary step along the road to the kind of independence advocated by firm opponents to legislation.[98] However, in common with most proponents of minimum wage legislation, Webb based her argument firmly on the needs of nation and industry rather than of the women workers themselves. In this, proponents of protection were no better than egalitarian feminists, who also used working women to their own ends, parading clean and robust pit women before politicians at Westminster in 1886 in an effort to stop any extension of factory legislation and, in 1911, to support the suffrage campaign.

Webb believed that it was sweated women workers' inefficiency that was holding them back from becoming factory workers. Like many commentators since, she failed to recognize the extent to which home-work was an integral part of industrial production. She openly contemplated the idea that large numbers of feeble sweated women workers would find themselves unable to earn the minimum wage and would be pushed out of the labor market. With "inefficient" cheap labor thus disposed of, industries would be forced to modernize their methods of production: "The freedom of the poor widow to work, in her own bed-room, 'all the hours that God made,' and the wife's privilege to supplement a drunken husband's wages by doing work at her own fireside, are in sober truth, being purchased at the price of the exclusion from regular factory employment of thousands of 'independent women.'"[99] The Women's Industrial Council put the case more clearly still. Sweated women workers were an impediment to social progress: "These people are the perplexity of our generation and unless we are to abandon ourselves to despair and to give up all hope of genuine social progress we must call on the state to their protection."[100] Webb deplored Bosanquet's view that education and training, not minimum wage legislation, were the real answers to working women's problems, arguing that this was an appropriate solution for middle-class women but that working women needed protection.[101] But as Bosanquet, for all the naïveté of her economics, recognized, protection *alone* was likely to punish some women by excluding them from the labor market and do little to address the more fundamental issue of their low status in the work force.

◆ ◆

The 1909 Trades Board Act set up wage boards in four trades: tailoring, paper and cardboard box making, chainmaking, and lace finishing, where some four hundred thousand workers, most of them women, were employed.[102] The operation of the trades boards was extended so that by 1920 three million workers were covered by them.

During the 1920s, egalitarian feminists continued to argue through the medium of the Open Door Council—set up for that purpose in 1926—that the legislation had failed to better women's pay and conditions.[103] Their arguments gained force from both the desire of policy-makers to roll back state intervention after World War I and from women's recently gained political voice (women over thirty years old gained the vote in 1918). In particular, when legislation was introduced in 1926 to prohibit women working with lead paint in order to bring

Britain into line with the ILO convention, egalitarian feminists raged against paternalism, arguing that as full political citizens, they should make their own free choice. But this was in the main a debate internal to the organized feminist movement, which was searching for a new focus in the postwar world and many of whose members were conscious of needing to seek an accommodation with trade union women. In 1927, the unceasing hostility of egalitarian feminists who were members of the Open Door Council succeeded in splitting the major postwar feminist organization, the National Union of Societies for Equal Citizenship.[104] Under the leadership of Eleanor Rathbone, noted for her campaign in favor of family allowances, most new feminists within the National Union argued not for the abolition of protective legislation but for its extension to men.

However, a series of independent social investigations by the Ratan Tata Foundation at the London School of Economics showed the Open Door Council's arguments to be not without foundation.[105] Ninety percent of homeworkers in the box trade had never seen an investigating officer, and certainly after 1918 there was a tendency for trades board rates to become a maximum.[106] Furthermore, trades board rates institutionalized sex differentials in payment. Any hope that protective legislation of this sort would prove a stepping stone to women's eventual trades union membership was also doomed to disappointment. Removing trades boards altogether in the manner demanded by the Open Door Council was just as unlikely to promote women's welfare in the labor market as the removal of factory legislation had been in the nineteenth century. Nevertheless, the operation of trades boards served to confirm that the solution to the problems of women's low-paid, low-status position in the labor market lay elsewhere.[107]

By the early twentieth century a majority, male and female, were in favor of protective legislation. But at this, as at previous historical moments, the predominant concern was with protecting women as wives and mothers rather than as workers per se. Crucially, protection at work paralleled the assumption that women would be protected at home by the existence of a family wage. However, as Mary Poovey has pointed out, the other side of protection is control.[108] The debates over protective legislation played an important role in helping to define the limits on women's work, in reinforcing the sexual segregation of labor, and in underscoring the idea that paid labor was primary for men and secondary for women.

In their support of the strategy for protective legislation in Britain, feminists have continued to be divided because of their awareness both of women's needs as mothers and as workers and of the danger that any claim based on difference might be turned back to provide grounds for subordination. Men have tended more to swing between opposition and support according to dictates often quite other than the outcomes for women. The debates over protective legislation in nineteenth- and early twentieth-century Britain were cast in such a way that women were to be considered either the equals of men in the labor market or different from men.[109]

Today we see that such arguments made men the standard in public policy. Women are either the same as men, and therefore should be given equal treatment, or they are different from men, and therefore should be treated differently.[110] The debates over protective legislation in the nineteenth and early twentieth centuries thus began controversies that persist today over the proper nature of women's work, women's sphere, and, more broadly, the relationship between women and the state.

Notes

The authors collaborated on the introduction and conclusion to this essay. Sonya Rose is primarily responsible for the portion of the essay dealing with the period 1820 to 1890; and Jane Lewis is primarily responsible for the portion concerning the period beginning 1890.

1. For an analysis of the contribution of the early debates on factory legislation to the larger discussion of the factory question and the condition of England, see Robert Gray, "The Languages of Factory Reform in Britain, c. 1830–1860," in *The Historical Meanings of Work,* ed. Patrick Joyce (Cambridge: Cambridge University Press, 1987), and Robert Gray, "Medical Men, Industrial Labour and the State in Britain, 1830–1850," *Social History* 16 (Jan. 1991): 19–43.

2. Friedrich Engels was only one of many contemporaries to comment on the implications for family life and gender relations when both married women and young girls worked in factories. See Engels, *The Condition of the Working Class in England,* trans. W. O. Henderson and W. H. Chaloner (1st German ed., 1845; rpt., Oxford: Basil Blackwell, 1958), 159–68.

3. Mariana Valverde has argued that the discourses of moral reform and social science were not contradictory during this period. See Valverde, *The Age of Light, Soap, and Water: Moral Reform in English Canada, 1885–1925* (Toronto: McClelland and Stewart, 1991), 44–47.

4. Problems of enforcing hours legislation rather than a concern about night work per se led lawmakers to set specific times when work would begin and end.

5. See Judy Lown, *Women and Industrialization: Gender at Work in Nineteenth-Century England* (Cambridge: Polity Press, 1990), esp. chap. 4; Sonya O. Rose, *Limited Livelihoods: Gender and Class in Nineteenth-Century England* (Berkeley: University of California Press, 1992), esp. chap. 2; Patrick Joyce, *Work, Society and Politics: The Culture of the Factory in Later Victorian England* (Brighton, U.K.: Harvester Press, 1980), chap. 4.

6. Statistics based on calculations from B. R. Mitchell and Phyllis Deane, *Abstract of British Historical Statistics* (Cambridge: Cambridge University Press, 1962), 60.

7. See Elizabeth Roberts, *A Woman's Place: An Oral History of Working-Class Women, 1890–1940* (Oxford: Basil Blackwell, 1984).

8. See B. L. Hutchins and Amy Harrison, *A History of Factory Legislation* (London: P. S. King, 1907), 43–44. For a good discussion of this history of factory legislation and its impact on the gendering of work, see Robert Gray, "Factory Legislation and the Gendering of Jobs in the North of England, 1830–1860," *Gender and History* 5 (Spring 1993): 56–80. See also Barbara Harrison and Helen Mockett, "Women in the Factory: The State and Factory Legislation in Nineteenth-Century Britain," in *State, Private Life and Political Change*, ed. Lynn Jamieson and Helen Corr (New York: St. Martin's Press, 1990).

9. For example, John Doherty, a cotton spinner and Ten Hours activist, proclaimed at a meeting in Manchester that "men were as much entitled to protection for their labor as masters were for their machines. But men would not apply for it till convinced it was practicable." From *Voice of the People*, Apr. 16, 1831, as quoted in Hutchins and Harrison, *A History of Factory Legislation*, 49.

10. The question of whether or not the reports were exaggerations has been debated ever since. At the time, the mill owners whose establishments were cited in the hearings and in Oastler's published letters and comments defended themselves by charging that the committee was biased. They and their supporters in Parliament attempted to portray factory work as healthy for children. Neil Smelser argued that the Sadler Committee evidence about the brutal conditions under which children were working was an exaggeration of what probably were generally better conditions. See Neil Smelser, *Social Change in the Industrial Revolution: An Application of Theory to the British Cotton Industry* (Chicago: University of Chicago Press, 1959). Robert Gray sees the Sadler Committee as part of the community polemics during these momentous years. See Gray, "Languages of Factory Reform," 143–79.

11. Gray, "Languages of Factory Reform," 150, 154–55.

12. Ibid., 152.

13. Ibid.

14. Smelser, *Social Change*, 283.

15. Richard Oastler, *Letter to the Editor of the Agriculture and Industrial Magazine* (London, 1835), 144–45, as quoted by Smelser, *Social Change*, 284.

16. Quoted in Mariana Valverde, " 'Giving the Female a Domestic Turn': The Social, Legal and Moral Regulation of Women's Work in British Cotton Mills, 1820–1850," *Journal of Social History* 21 (Summer 1988): 626.

17. Ibid.

18. It was not until then that the short-time committees associated with the Ten Hours Movement began to systematically advocate the regulation of women's employment. It was relatively rare for male workers to advocate the complete exclusion of women from a particular trade or industry. In the 1840s and again in the 1880s colliers would mount a concerted effort to have women barred from working in the coal fields. However, it was much less common in the textile trades, although as the century progressed, the argument that men should earn a family wage was increasingly heard. The desire for female exclusion expressed by some male textile operatives in the 1840s was undoubtedly the result of threats by manufacturers to substitute women for men on jobs that were made lighter by improved machinery. At least until midcentury, even skilled male workers expected that the women in their families would be employed. To restrict women's competition, the men usually advocated measures, including protective labor legislation, that would maintain job segregation and male privilege in the factory.

19. Deputation to Sir Robert Peel, "The Ten Hours' Factory Question, a Report addressed to the Short Time Committees of the West Riding of Yorkshire" (1842), reprinted in Patricia Hollis, *Women in Public: The Women's Movement, 1850–1900* (Boston: Allen & Unwin, 1979), 76.

20. They were prodded into doing so by "an independent movement" originating in Manchester that expressed concern about the conditions of women's labor in the mines and urged that all females be barred from working underground. Ivy Pinchbeck, *Women Workers and the Industrial Revolution, 1750–1850* (1930; rpt., London: Virago Press, 1981), 244.

21. For discussions, see Angela V. John, *By the Sweat of Their Brow: Women Workers at Victorian Coal Mines* (London: Routledge, 1984), chaps. 1–2.

22. *Parliamentary Papers*, vol. 16 (1842), 396, as cited in Pinchbeck, *Women Workers*, 263.

23. Jane Humphries, "Protective Legislation, the Capitalist State, and Working Class Men: The Case of the 1842 Mines Regulation Act," *Feminist Review* 7 (1981): 22–23.

24. *Hansard* 63 (June 7, 1842): 1327.

25. Ibid.

26. *Parliamentary Papers*, vol. 17 (1842), 308, as quoted by John, *By the Sweat of Their Brow*, 43.

27. For a discussion of the meanings of "disorder" and their connection to the construction of citizenship in Western societies, see Carole Pateman, *The Disorder of Women: Democracy, Feminism and Political Theory* (Stanford: Stanford University Press, 1989), 17–32.

28. At the third reading of the bill the M.P. for Bradford said, "To the exclusion of women . . . he had not the slightest objection, but just now it would increase the distress of the labouring population." See *Hansard* 64 (July 5, 1842): col. 1003.

29. However, one member of Commons did talk of the dangers of governmental intervention in industrial matters and warned that next they would be "interfering with milliners and pinmakers." *Hansard* 64 (July 5, 1842): col. 1006.

30. *Hansard* 65 (July 25, 1842): col. 583.

31. Hutchins and Harrison, whose history of factory legislation was published in 1907, applauded the passing of legislation to protect women workers, stating: "This is perhaps the most high-handed interference with individuals enacted by the State in the nineteenth century, and it doubtless led the way to the inclusion of women in the much milder Factory Bill of 1844." Hutchins and Harrison, *A History of Factory Legislation,* 82.

32. Lord Ashley introduced an amendment that restricted to ten the hours of work of young persons and women in factories. He proposed that they enter the factory at six in the morning and leave at six at night, with two hours a day being allotted for meals.

33. *Hansard* 65 (July 25, 1842): col. 583.

34. Ibid., col. 1100.

35. Mariana Valverde makes a similar point. See Valverde, " 'Giving the Female a Domestic Turn,' " 628.

36. Dorothy Thompson has argued that Chartists were very active in the strikes, especially in Lancashire. See Thompson, *The Chartists: Popular Politics in the Industrial Revolution* (New York: Pantheon Books, 1984), 282–98.

37. *Hansard* 73 (Mar. 15, 1844): col. 1097.

38. Ibid.

39. *Hansard* 74 (May 3, 1844): col. 611.

40. Ibid., col. 631.

41. Home Minister Graham openly stated in the House of Commons that because of the nature of textile work, restricting women's hours also meant a limit to the hours that men would work. The Webbs attributed this statement to Thomas Ashton. See Sidney Webb and Beatrice Webb, *History of Trade Unionism,* 2d ed. (London: Longmans, Green and Co., 1896), 297.

42. There were demands then and much earlier for an eight-hour day. One of the short-time committees in the 1830s demanded an eight-hour day for men, women, and children.

43. Jane Lewis, "The Working-Class Wife and Mother and State Interven-

tion, 1870–1918," in *Labor and Love: Women's Experience of Home and Family, 1850–1940*, ed. Jane Lewis (Oxford: Basil Blackwell, 1986), esp. 100–101, 103–5. See also Lewis, *The Politics of Motherhood: Child and Maternal Welfare in England, 1900–1939* (London: Croom Helm, 1980).

44. Jane Lewis, *Women in England, 1870–1950: Sexual Divisions and Social Change* (Bloomington: Indiana University Press, 1984), 47.

45. Lewis, "The Working-Class Wife." This development may be interpreted, following Michel Foucault, as the further development of bourgeois society in exercising control by making sex, family, and reproduction the subjects of political discourse. See Foucault, *The History of Sexuality*, vol. 1 (New York: Pantheon Books, 1979), pt. 5. Jacques Donzelot has elaborated on this idea. See Donzelot, *The Policing of Families*, trans. Robert Hurley, 1st American ed. (New York: Pantheon, 1980). Recently, David Levine has situated fertility decline within this development, also drawing on Foucault's ideas. See Levine, "Recombinant Family Formation Strategies," *Journal of Historical Sociology* 2 (1989): 89–115.

46. *Times* (London), June 12, 1873, 6.

47. *Hansard* 221 (Aug. 1874): col. 1547.

48. Rosemary Feurer, "The Meaning of 'Sisterhood': The British Women's Movement and Protective Labor Legislation, 1870–1900," *Victorian Studies* 31 (Winter 1988): 233.

49. See the speech by Asheton Cross in *Hansard* 219 (May 18, 1874): col. 1429. Mundella argued that "women were the slaves of the masters" (*Times* [London], Aug. 5, 1873, 8). Lord Shaftesbury, still active in the movement for factory reform, argued that "women were not free agents; especially those with children as they would submit to anything—any sort of oppression" (*Times* [London], Mar. 27, 1874, 6).

50. Vigilance Association, *Third Annual Report of the Vigilance Association* (1873).

51. Lewis, *The Politics of Motherhood*, 100. Those who took up the issue of domestic violence toward women in the 1870s also tended to treat working-class wives as the victims and to demonize working-class husbands. See Jan Lambertz, "Feminists and the Politics of Wifebeating," in *British Feminism in the Twentieth Century*, ed. Harold L. Smith (Aldershot: Edward Elgar, 1990). In addition, middle-class feminists joined philanthropists and social investigators at the end of the century in problematizing the role of the working-class man as provider and protector.

52. Statement by J. B. Baldwin at the meeting of the Leeds Factory Acts Association, *Leeds Daily News*, June 9, 1873, 3.

53. Quoted in Pinchbeck, *Women Workers and the Industrial Revolution*, 199–200. Also, women evaded the law excluding them from the mines when they were provided with no alternative means of employment. Members of

Parliament reported receiving petitions from areas where there was severe economic hardship. See John, *By the Sweat of Their Brow,* 50–57.

54. In 1871, women fought alongside men in Oldham to secure a reduced work week; and in Leeds, female flax workers were the backbone of a strike for a nine-hour day in 1872. See Rose, *Limited Livelihoods,* chap. 3. Supporters of the nine hours bill claimed that a large majority of working women supported the measure. See Feurer, "The Meaning of 'Sisterhood,'" 237.

55. For a discussion of Emma Paterson and the WPPL, see Teresa Olcott, "Dead Centre: The Women's Trade Union Movement in London, 1874–1914," *The London Journal* 2 (1976): 34–50. Olcott argues that the unions organized by the league were "copies of male craft unions but considerably distorted by the philanthropic and feminist ideals of League members" (35).

56. Quoted in Barbara Drake, *Women in Trade Unions* (London: Labour Research Department, 1920; rpt., 1984), 11.

57. Feurer, "The Meaning of 'Sisterhood,'" 238.

58. Minutes of Evidence Taken before the Commissioners Taken to Inquire into the Factory and Workshops Acts, *Parliamentary Papers,* vol. 30 (1876), 337, C.1443-I.

59. Ibid. Also see Feurer, "The Meaning of 'Sisterhood,'" 241.

60. For a discussion, see Hutchins and Harrison, *A History of Factory Legislation,* 188–89.

61. Report of the Commissioners on the Working of the Factory and Workshop Acts, vol. 1, ix, in *Parliamentary Papers,* vol. 29 (1876), C.1443.

62. George Howell, *The Conflicts of Capital and Labor, Historically and Economically Considered,* 2d ed. (London and New York: Macmillan and Co., 1890), 341.

63. Report of the 11th Trade Union Congress at Bristol, *Women's Union Journal* 3 (1878): 70.

64. Drake, *Women in Trade Unions,* 14.

65. Hutchins and Harrison, *A History of Factory Legislation,* 186. Also see Feurer, "The Meaning of 'Sisterhood,'" 244. To some extent they were right. Broadhurst led a campaign to exclude women from nail and chainmaking, and in those trades in which women and men competed for jobs the men responded by attempting to exclude the women.

66. The classic study of the pit brow women and the efforts to exclude them is by John, *By the Sweat of Their Brow.*

67. Ibid., 142.

68. See ibid.

69. For analyses of this transformation, see Feurer, "The Meaning of 'Sisterhood,'" 247–60; Norbert Soldon, "British Women and Trade Unionism: Opportunities Made and Missed," in *The World of Women's Trade Unionism: Comparative Historical Essays,* ed. Norbert C. Soldon (Westport, Conn:

Greenwood Press, 1985); Hutchins and Harrison, *A History of Factory Legislation,* chap. 9.

70. Feurer, "The Meaning of 'Sisterhood.'"

71. Alfred Marshall, *Official Papers* (London: Macmillan and Co., 1926); L. T. Hobhouse, "The Ethical Basis of Collectivism," *International Journal of Ethics* 8 (Jan. 1898): 137–56. See also Michael Freeden, *The New Liberalism: An Ideology of Social Reform* (Oxford: Clarendon Press, 1978).

72. For example, R. Penn, "Skilled Manual Workers in the Labor Process," in *Degradation of Work? Skill, Deskilling and the Labour Process,* ed. Stephen Wood (London: Hutchinson, 1982); Richard Price, *Labour in British Society* (London: Routledge, 1986), esp. 114–30.

73. Quoted in Webb and Webb, *The History of Trade Unionism,* 297.

74. Hutchins and Harrison, *A History of Factory Legislation,* 197. See also Beatrice Webb, *The Case for the Factory Acts* (London: G. Richards, 1902), and the article by the new head of the Women's Trade Unions League (formerly the Women's Protective and Provident League), Emilia Dilke, "The Industrial Position of Women," *Fortnightly Review* 60 (1893): 499–508.

75. Carole Pateman, "Women, Nature and the Suffrage," *Ethics* 90 (Autumn 1980): 564–75.

76. Jane Lewis, *Women and Social Action in Victorian and Edwardian England* (Aldershot: Edward Elgar, 1991).

77. Jessie Boucherette and Helen Blackburn, *The Condition of Working Women and the Factory Acts* (London: Elliot Stock, 1896).

78. Sidney Webb and Beatrice Webb, *Problems of Modern Industry* (London: Longmans Green & Co., 1898).

79. Beatrice Webb, *Women and the Factory Acts,* Tract no. 67 (London: The Fabian Society, 1896), 10.

80. "That the Economic Position of Women Can Be Best Improved by Legislation," MacDonald Papers, Item 34 (n.d.) British Library of Political and Economic Science.

81. Jenny Morris, *Women Workers and the Sweated Trades: The Origins of Minimum Wage Legislation* (Aldershot: Gower, 1986).

82. Mrs. J. R. MacDonald (wife of the leader of the Labour party), *Wage Earning Mothers* (London: Women's Labor League, n.d.).

83. Report of the Commissioners Appointed to Inquire into the Working of the Factory and Workshop Acts with a View to Their Consolidation and Amendment, lxxviii, *Parliamentary Papers,* vol. 29 (1876): C.1443; and Lewis, *The Politics of Motherhood,* 78.

84. Nora Vynne and Helen Blackburn, *Women under the Factory Acts* (London: Williams and Norgate, 1903).

85. House of Lords Select Committee on Sweating, Second Report, *Parliamentary Papers,* vol. 21 (1888).

86. *Hansard* 356 (July 23, 1891): col. 82.

87. The initial invitation from the German emperor to the British government indicated that the conference would discuss the restriction of female and child labor and a general limitation on the length of the working day. The home secretary responding for Britain said that he would not sanction "direct legislative restriction on the liberty of adult male workmen to work as long as they pleased" but would participate in discussions about matters relating to women and children. The Berlin Conference met in March 1890 and included delegates from the governments of Germany, Austria-Hungary, Belgium, Denmark, Spain, France, Italy, Luxembourg, Switzerland, Portugal, Sweden, and Norway. See copies of correspondence in *Parliamentary Papers*, vol. 31 (1890), 530–31. For discussions of the 1890 Berlin Congress, see the essays in this volume by Sabine Schmitt, " 'All These Forms of Women's Work Which Endanger Public Health and Public Welfare,' " and Ulla Wikander, "Some 'Kept the Flag of Feminist Demands Waving.' "

88. Patricia E. Malcolmson, *English Laundresses: A Social History, 1850–1930* (Urbana: University of Illinois Press, 1986), 60–64.

89. Mona Wilson and Edward G. Howarth, *West Ham: A Study in Social and Industrial Problems* (London: J. M. Dent and Co., 1907).

90. Helen Bosanquet, *The Strength of the People: A Study in Social Economics* (London: Macmillan and Co., 1903).

91. Webb, *The Case for the Factory Acts*, 17.

92. House of Lords, Select Committee on the Sweating System, Third Report, *Parliamentary Papers*, vol. 21 (1889).

93. Beatrice Potter, "How Best to Do Away with the Sweating System" (paper read at the 24th Annual Congress of Cooperative Societies, printed by the Manchester Cooperative Union, Ltd., 1892), London, BLPES Pamphlet Collection.

94. Ellen Mappen, *Helping Women at Work: The Women's Industrial Council, 1889–1914* (London: Hutchinson, 1985).

95. See Duncan Bythell, *The Sweated Trades: Outwork in Nineteenth-Century Britain* (New York: St. Martin's Press, 1978).

96. Clementina Black, *Sweated Industry and the Minimum Wage* (London: Duckworth, 1907), x.

97. Constance Smith, *The Case for Wages Boards* (London: National Anti-Sweating League, 1907), 36.

98. Webb, *Women and the Factory Acts*, 9.

99. Ibid., 14.

100. Frederic J. Bayliss, *British Wages Councils* (Oxford: Basil Blackwell, 1962), 6.

101. Webb, *Women and the Factory Acts*, 5.

102. Sheila Blackburn, "Sweated Labor and the Trades Board Act," *Bulletin*

of the Society of Labor History 53 (Winter 1988): 30–31, has noted that the decision to set a minimum rate for each trade according to what the trade would bear, rather than a national minimum wage, reflected the weakness of labor and socialist voices within the National Anti-Sweating League.

103. Open Door Council, *Restrictive Legislation and the Industrial Woman Worker: A Reply by the Open Door Council to the Statement by the Standing Joint Committee of Women's Industrial Organizations* (London: Open Door Council, 1928), and *Report of a Conference Held in Berlin, 1929* (London: Open Door Council, 1929).

104. Lewis, *Women in England, 1870–1950.*

105. Richard H. Tawney, *The Establishment of Minimum Rates in the Chain Making Industry under the Trades Board Act of 1909* (London: G. Bell and Sons, 1914); Mildred E. Bulkley, *The Establishment of Legal Minimum Rates in the Boxmaking Industry under the Trades Board Act of 1909* (London: G. Bell and Sons, 1915); and V. de Vesselitsky, *The Homeworker and Her Outlook* (London: G. Bell and Sons, 1916).

106. Dorothy Sells, *The British Trades Board System* (London: P. S. King, 1923), and *British Wages Boards: A Study in Industrial Democracy* (Washington, D.C.: The Brookings Institution, 1939).

107. Trades boards, renamed wages councils in 1945, were substantially undermined by the second Thatcher government in 1986 and are slated for abolition.

108. Mary Poovey, *Uneven Developments: The Ideological Work of Gender in Mid-Victorian England* (Chicago: University of Chicago Press, 1988).

109. This does not mean that those arguing for equal treatment thought women and men were or should be the same in all ways. Rather, the terms of the debate, with freedom of contract for autonomous individuals, on the one hand, and women's biological differences from men, on the other, constrained the ways opponents and proponents of protective labor legislation for women argued. For an insightful discussion of the ways that women's movement activists could argue for equal rights in the labor market while still maintaining that women had a special contribution to make because of their differences from men by nature, see Ulla Wikander, "Personal, Historical Notes on Gender Distinctions, *inter alia* about Equality and Difference" (*Lik Het Och Särart*), in Kersti Ullenhag, *"Hundred Flowers Bloom": Essays in Honour of Bo Gustafsson* (Upsala: Acta Universitatis Upsaliensis, 1991). Also see Wikander, "Some 'Kept the Flag of Feminist Demands Waving,'" in this volume.

110. For discussions on this debate, see Joan W. Scott, "Deconstructing Equality-versus-Difference; or, The Uses of Post-Structuralist Theory for Feminism," *Feminist Studies* 14 (Spring 1988): 33–50; Martha Minow, *Making All the Difference: Inclusion, Exclusion, and the American Law* (Ithaca: Cornell University Press, 1990).

· 4 ·

"All These Forms of Women's Work Which Endanger Public Health and Public Welfare"

Protective Labor Legislation for Women in Germany, 1878–1914

Sabine Schmitt

Historians have generally viewed protective labor legislation for women in Imperial Germany as either a laudable achievement of the organized labor movement in its fight for better working conditions or a bourgeois strategy for integrating the working class into the emerging welfare state. Either way, the focus on social order has been understood as an issue of class and disregards notions of gender embedded in social policy. In this chapter I will argue that protective labor legislation was a concept that ordered society along gender lines. Reinforcing differences between men's and women's industrial work, it helped to integrate the socialist labor movement into the construction of the German welfare state on a gendered basis.

During the second half of the nineteenth century, Germans participated in a political debate around the idea that women's wagework should be legally regulated, controlled, and occasionally prohibited. The debate, which labeled regulation as "protection," arose out of a public preoccupation with the social and political consequences of the miserable conditions facing labor in what was a newly industrialized society.

Compared to similar contemporaneous discourses in other countries, the German case bears two particularly prominent features. First, protective labor legislation for women drew a large and ever-growing range of supporters from its inception. After the 1890s virtually no political group opposed it, feminists included. Second, given this near unanimous support, it is striking that Germany lagged behind other countries in enacting protective legislation, due to the government's focus on social insurance policy. Women workers themselves hardly ever actively entered the discussion surrounding this new legal apparatus. They had few opportunities to speak their mind in the debates, and because the laws rarely had any discernible effects on the labor market, they do not seem to have resisted them.[1] It is beyond the scope of this essay to analyze the effects of the legislation on the specific organization of working conditions in particular industries, which I have done elsewhere.[2] Rather, I will show how the discourse on women workers' protection developed in late nineteenth-century Germany and how it introduced the notion of gender into industrializing society.

German industrialization came late but very rapidly in the years between 1850 and 1873. Its consequences—including a high poverty rate, a major upswing in rural-urban migration, a massive rise in the population, overcrowding in towns, and a growing labor movement—came to be perceived as a threat hanging over traditional order. These factors were to instigate a fundamental rethinking of the role of the state in German society. Only a few years after 1871, when free trade (*Gewerbefreiheit*) was achieved, new public forces committed to "social reform" began calling for state intervention into working conditions and the labor contract. With the onset of the Great Depression, which began in 1873 and did not ease up until the mid-1890s, both industry and agriculture also increasingly turned away from liberal principles of the market and sought state intervention on a variety of fronts.

The government under Bismarck responded by introducing in 1883 the world's first compensatory insurance scheme for illness, followed in 1884 by accident insurance, and in 1889 by old-age pensions. The government hoped that these measures would thwart the influence of the growing socialist labor movement; they were accompanied by laws (in force between 1878 and 1890) that outlawed the socialist movement.[3] In the German context Bismarck's policy was not as novel as is often assumed. It built on an old Prussian tradition of state intervention into social issues. Many of its authoritarian and paternalistic provisions were operating under the feudal system.[4] Employers who tended to support Bismarck's insurance policies did so because they believed the policies would counter the appeal of social democracy and because the measures did not interfere directly with working conditions. The labor movement, distrustful of generosity dispensed by the apparati of an authoritarian regime, initially opposed state-orchestrated insurance and argued instead for protective labor legislation.[5]

Today some historians contemplating the crisis in the insurance-based welfare system have reevaluated protective labor legislation, seeing it as a "blocked alternative" to state social insurance, which constituted the main plank in the early formation of the German welfare state. The direct amelioration of working conditions, they contend, might have been more successful than various kinds of compensatory insurance in solving the problem of "industrial pathology."[6] Missing from their assessment is, however, the fact that, like the social insurance programs enacted, attempts to enact protective labor legislation were clearly gendered from the beginning.

In this essay, I scrutinize the extent to which the discourse on protective legislation was gender-specific in its aims and the consequences this bore for the rise of the welfare state in Imperial Germany. I look at the period between the first enactment of such laws in 1878 up to the beginning of World War I, when the German government permitted local authorities to abolish the laws *tout court* to enable full wartime production. My primary focus, however, will be on the early 1890s, when the most important shift in the discourse on protection took place.

◆ ◆

The discourse on protective labor legislation in Germany always referred to men and women workers. But whereas legal protection for adult male workers was always a heavily debated, controversial issue, the idea of women's protection was widely accepted. Together with children and juveniles, women were regarded as somehow deficient workers in need of special provisions. This concept in turn produced the image of the male as the standard worker on the labor market.

German labor legislation followed this concept by first regulating children's work in Prussia in 1839.[7] The protection of women's work was enacted for the first time in 1878,[8] while male workers basically remained "unprotected" until the general eight-hour day was introduced in 1918.

Initially, the most important supporters of women's protection in Germany were the organized labor movement and the bourgeois social reform movement, which included academic, medical, and religious groups.[9] At the center of this latter social reform movement stood the national Association for Social Policy (Verein für Socialpolitik), founded in 1872 and led by so-called academic socialists (*Katheder-sozialisten*), who were primarily professors of political economy. In their search for a "third way" beyond capitalism and communism, they carried out numerous empirical investigations into the terra incognita of working-class life. Members of the women's movement also soon journeyed into this field.[10]

The social reform movement called for state intervention as a solution to "The Social Question" and found support from industrial magnates, administrative officials, and politicians. Its arguments had a strong impact on the rhetoric of the early debates around protective labor legislation and on strategies for translating demands into law. Justifications for protective labor legislation were diverse, depending on whether laws addressed employment of children, women, or men.

The underlying discourse on women's work emanating from reform circles, however, operated on its own terms. In contrast to the demands for a general protection, women's protection never referred primarily to specific working conditions but to women qua women. Its proponents—both in the state and in reform circles—always promoted it as a means of preserving women's "health and morality." In effect, this meant nothing more than safeguarding their physical ability to give birth and their social function as mothers and housewives. These tasks took precedence over women's wagework in the prevailing rhetoric of protection. But because women's labor was indispensable both for industry and the proletarian household economy, the designers of protective labor legislation worked to make possible for women a reconciliation of paid work with familial demands. Thus women's protection was not rhetorically linked to their working conditions, as in the case of men, but rather to their sex. As a result, housework was not treated as work but as part of women's "natural sphere."

In contrast to the importance attached to women's protection in public debate, actual protective legislation bespoke restraint. First, it was applied only to women in industry, a minority among working women. Only 17 percent of working women engaged in industrial production in 1882, compared to 34.8 percent in agriculture and 40.0 percent in domestic service. In 1907, the figures had shifted to 26.9 percent in industry, 27.1 percent in agriculture, and 29 percent in domestic service.[11] Female factory workers were concentrated in textile, garment, and food-processing industries, but even taken together, none of these industrial sectors employed more women than men.[12]

The percentage of married women factory workers was also extremely low: about 13 percent in 1882, rising to 18 percent in 1907.[13] Women with children were especially likely to work irregularly and to combine different types of work. Barbara Franzoi contends: "When women worked in a factory setting, it was often seasonal and intermittent. Women moved in and out of the factory as both industrial demand and personal necessity dictated. Most women who did factory work were young and single; married women chose other ways to earn money. They changed jobs frequently; they combined various kinds of work in agriculture, in domestic service, in factories, and in domestic industry."[14]

Above and beyond its restricted application, protective labor legislation was notoriously poorly enforced. Owing to their vague formulation and the large number of exemptions granted by local authorities, the provisions could be easily circumvented by employers and workers alike. Finally, factory inspectors were so few in number that they had little opportunity to detect violations of the law. Where they did so, the deterrent effect was minimal because the punishments were extremely lenient.[15] The gulf between the declared intentions of protective legislation and its ultimate poor track record cannot be explained by the restricted character of the legislation alone, which did not go much beyond the prevailing status quo in working conditions. Rather, the reasons for the specific construction of protective labor legislation must be sought in the broader ideological concepts of women's work that lay behind it. The symbolic act of protecting women was more important than real interference with women's working conditions. This becomes clear if we take a closer look at the central issues of women's health and morality.

In the nineteenth-century understanding of the terms, "health" and "morality" had quite amorphous meanings, and the boundary separating them remains obscure and porous. Development of health as a concept to be examined in relation to work drew its theoretical foundations from the new scholarly fields of occupational medicine and social hygiene. It was also to play its part in the gendering of social concerns at the close of the century. Revelations about the poor health and fitness of young male conscripts for the military in the early nineteenth century first prompted the restrictions on children's work. Women's protection was, however, borne of rather different concerns. Physicians linked elevated rates of miscarriage and of infant mortality in industrial areas to emerging knowledge about the detrimental effects of certain industrial materials. The proposed restrictions did not, however, refer only to pregnant or nursing women but to any potential mother: her health had to be guarded in order to protect future children.[16] After the turn of the century, these arguments became part of a broader discourse on population policy, fueled by public hysteria about a decline in the birthrate.[17] Beyond this, all sectors of bourgeois social reform marshaled health as an argument for protection of women workers by making women the culprits for poor hygiene and nutrition within the family since the 1870s. Women increasingly became the main targets of public anxiety about health conditions in general, and health reformers made them pivotal in the fight against epidemics and malnutrition.[18]

Morality had its origins in traditional Christian views as well as in the newly developed bourgeois ethics, which imposed on the individual a duty to lead a socially responsible life.[19] On the one hand, its self-appointed defenders problematized women's presence in the factories, doing "male" jobs and working in close proximity to men in crowded workrooms. Particular anxiety collected around women working underground in mines, where work could only mean a "promiscuous mixing of both sexes during rest and work."[20] The guardians of morality also unfailingly saw factories as breeding grounds for boundless sexual intimacies, although it seems clear that sexual harassment had a real presence and justifiably provoked serious debate. On the other hand, women's absence from home in and of itself also threatened morality in this emergent discourse, which cast proletarian women's neglect of children and husbands as the cause of infant mortality, juvenile delinquency, alcoholism, and the rise of social democracy. In this rhetoric, the proletarian family became a bulwark against social upheaval as a whole. Family life by definition discouraged workers from political activity.

The journal of the Catholic social reformers, *Arbeiterwohl,* argued: "Those who want to protect and promote morality, work to strengthen, protect and uphold *family life:* young people must feel *happy* and at home in their *parental homes* and they must find a *morally sound haven* there—through a ban on mothers' factory work!"[21] Rudolf Martin, a speaker (*Referent*) of the Saxon Ministry of the Interior, distilled his views into a single sentence: "Nothing is so social democratic as married women's factory work."[22]

These assumptions found ready acceptance in a range of political factions and broad-based political movements. The most vociferous believers in this chain of connections in the Imperial parliament (the Reichstag) were the Social Democratic party (SPD) and the Catholic Centre party. Having at first wholly opposed industrialization, the Centre party took up a more modest position in the 1890s. Apart from prohibition of work on Sundays for religious reasons, its main demand was the complete exclusion of married women from factory work. Despite a protracted battle, this goal never became law. If any skeptics remained, a wide-ranging official government investigation in 1899 established beyond a doubt that married women in particular worked out of pure economic need.[23] Around the turn of the century, an incipient campaign gave in to the old Centre party demand. At the 1897 International Congress on Protective Labor Legislation in Zurich, Catholic trade union representatives did battle for this goal.[24] Moreover, several new books appeared that echoed this sentiment.[25]

In contrast to many other countries, liberals, socialists, and feminists all accepted protective legislation for women, although their motivations for doing so varied dramatically.[26] All supporters of women's protection agreed that women's need to reconcile their wagework with their housework was a basic problem and formed the root of many other social ills. Many diverse hopes came to rest, then, on the restorative powers of protective labor legislation, and this displaced attention from more fundamental grievances (such as the restrained right to form unions of working-class men and of all women, poor wages, and the housing problem). Even socialists did not expose and criticize this function. The rhetoric of women's health and morality carried the power to unite these diverse interest groups floundering in the face of an industrializing society, their different, even contrary, aims notwithstanding. I will now examine more closely the way in which this broad coalition functioned by looking at the events that led to the enactment of the centrally important and precedent-setting trade code (*Reichsgewerbeordnung*) of 1891.

◆ ◆

The first piece of protective legislation for women workers in Germany was enacted with a revision of the trade code (*Gewerbeordnung*) in 1878. It included prohibition of work for three weeks after childbirth and also underground work in mines. The Federal Council (Bundesrat) had the authority to prohibit women's work (especially at night) in industries deemed "dangerous to health and morality."[27] The council only used this power in a few cases, among them the prohibition of work in the manufacture of condoms, which was considered a case for moral protection.

The forces that had demanded more comprehensive legislation were the Verein für Socialpolitik, the SPD, the Centre party, and some members of the state bureaucracy. Among them was Theodor Lohmann, *Unterstaatssekretär* in the Prussian Ministry of Trade, who had framed a bill that the Federal Council rejected.[28] During the next twelve years there was no opportunity to introduce further protective legislation, for the German government focused exclusively on social insurance policy. Bismarck considered this policy to be the only adequate answer to the influence of socialism, especially in combination with antisocialist laws.

Yet, during the 1880s, all Reichstag parties spoke in favor of protective legislation as a necessary complement to social insurance. There were three basic demands on which all parties could agree: the further restriction of children's work, the prohibition of Sunday work, and the restriction of women's work. Against this, the general maximum working day—which the Conservatives had earlier demanded—now also became a specific socialist goal. The Reichstag parties expressed their agreement by framing a bill in 1887 on the protection of children's, women's, and Sunday work. Addressing women's protection, it included a ban on work for all women at night and on Saturdays and Sundays after 6 p.m., a four-week rest after childbirth, and a ten-hour maximum day for married women.[29]

This concept of workers' protection even found support in the largest and most influential organization of industrial employers, the Centralverband Deutscher Industrieller (CDI). The CDI agreed publicly to protective legislation as long as it did not include male workers and did not differentiate between married and unmarried women workers.[30] Under Bismarck's leadership, the federal government used its constitutional power to reject the Reichstag's proposal twice: in 1888 and again in 1889.

A change in the government's position toward protective legislation finally came in 1890. The new kaiser, Wilhelm II, proclaimed a "New Course" in German social policy as a result of a series of miners' strikes in 1889. These strikes had involved up to a hundred thousand workers. Finally convinced that working conditions cried for intervention, the government proposed a new trade code, which it initiated at the beginning of 1890 with a wide range of public proclamations and activities, including decrees by the kaiser (*Februarerlasse*) and an International Conference on Protective Labor Legislation in Berlin.[31] The New Course included a public agreement to withdraw from Bismarck's repressive strategy and to fulfill the reasonable demands of workers, especially where they might help to avoid unreasonable and excessive demands developed under the influence of socialists and anarchists.[32]

The signal figure of this policy was Freiherr von Berlepsch, who replaced Bismarck as the Prussian minister of trade in February 1890. Bismarck himself resigned the office of chancellor on March 20, 1890, because of disputes about the new social policy. The most concrete outcome of these changes was the new trade code, enacted in June 1891. The new regulation basically mirrored Lohmann's bills of the 1870s and the Reichstag's demands of the 1880s. They limited women's daily working hours to a maximum of eleven (ten on Saturdays) and totally prohibited women's employment between 8:30 P.M. and 5:30 A.M. On Saturdays and the day preceding a holiday, work had to finish at 5:30 P.M. A one-hour break at lunchtime became compulsory, plus half an hour "on request" for women "who had to care for a household." Finally, maternity leave was extended to six weeks after childbirth (or four weeks with a medical certificate).[33]

Historians, past and present, have celebrated the trade code of 1891 as a sign of a real movement in German social policy toward protective legislation. They do not consider the fact that the regulation that was actually enacted had been agreed upon long before in the Reichstag. Moreover, protective legislation for adult workers was gender-based; and, significantly, the New Course finally lost all support when in 1896 Berlepsch tried to introduce maximum hours for adult male workers in bakeries.[34] Therefore, I would argue that the regulations of the 1891 trade code were not an unprecedented compromise achieved after one and a half wearisome years of debate between the different parties of the Reichstag and among various government institutions. Rather, at this stage children's, women's, and Sunday protection was not the main issue at stake but served instead as a handy substitute for broaching topics that were considered more crucial. These were, first of all, the general maximum workday for male workers, or trade union rights and wages. The focus on women also carried with it the advantage that no concrete action needed to be taken on these more controversial topics, even while it provided an opening wedge for state intervention.

Moreover, there were attempts on the political agenda to restrict workers' rights further and thus continue Bismarck's practice of linking social control to social policy. Inside the imperial government and Parliament, many supported the legal restriction of workers' right to form political interest groups and organize strikes. Significantly, they called these measures "employers' protection," presenting them as a counterpart to protective labor legislation.

During the Reichstag's opening debate on the new trade code, the conservative industrialist Freiherr von Stumm hinted at this preexisting all-party agreement when he suggested enacting the whole section on protection "en bloc." He anticipated no opposition.[35] Nevertheless, the Reichstag haggled over protection of women and children for over a year, along with the more controversial issues.[36] Eventually it presented the old clauses on women's and children's protection as a new compromise between all parties, and these formed the brunt of the new code. This strategy allowed the new trade code to appear as a successful resolution, although general working conditions and union rights remained untouched. Social Democrats regarded these measures as insufficient and voted against the bill. Yet they did not question the gender-based cast of the legislation.

Throughout the duration of the New Course in German social policy the only person to resist protection as a principle was Bismarck. Before he was forced to resign in March 1890, he intervened in the debate in many different ways.[37] His opposition toward protective labor legislation for women was mainly based on two arguments. First, he objected to any legal interference with working conditions, seeing it as restricting a worker's chances to act as a free agent on the labor market. This referred only to male workers. Bismarck saw women as the dependents of men, whose ability to sell their wives' and children's work in the labor market would be reduced by women's or children's legal protection.[38] His argument seemed to be purely economic in this context: a forced cut in working hours would provoke a similar cut in wages and thus damage the living conditions of working-class families, no matter who did the wagework. This model ignored statistical inquiries into human productiveness that found resonance with many of Bismarck's contemporaries and proved that productivity did not necessarily increase in line with number of consecutive hours worked.[39]

Bismarck's second argument referred to the fact that the New Course was, above all, intended as a response to the strikes of the preceding year. He pointed out time and again that the miners had not asked for women's and children's protection; they wanted a reduction in their own hours and better wages.[40] Thus, he revealed the ideological character of the New Course, which, while claiming to fulfill the labor movement's demands, actually served to restrict women's work.

The aged chancellor was at odds with the politics of the New Course, not because he was fundamentally opposed to protective labor legislation,[41] but because he was a representative of the openly authoritarian state and was therefore able to speak about real interests and aims. Bismarck never pretended to satisfy workers' demands but blatantly proposed social policy as a means of repression. For their part, proponents of the New Course at least pretended to react to the labor movement's demands by offering a gendered social policy. In contrast to opposition to insurance-based social policies of the 1880s, the Social Democratic party now also supported protective labor legislation.

Still, why did Germany—in contrast to other countries—face so little resistance to the idea and enforcement of protective labor legislation? To begin with, opposition to state interference in the economic sphere had disappeared during the economic crisis prevailing since the 1870s. Thus, while in principle large employers' organizations were always ready to complain about regulations that might destroy their businesses, in practice they accepted the legitimacy of labor protection for women and adjusted accordingly.

We know very little about the women workers eventually affected by the legislation. Among the hundreds of requests and complaints that employees sent to the chancellor or to the Prussian minister of trade,[42] a few letters written by women workers who feared losing their jobs survive. Factory inspectors hardly ever mentioned any contact with women workers in their comprehensive reports and therefore compiled little information about their views on the issue. Yet reading between the lines, it is sometimes possible to see that workers as well as employers found several ways to circumvent the regulations. But how did groups claiming to represent the interests of working women argue the case? In the following sections I will analyze how both German social democracy and all wings of the women's movement became strong advocates of women's special protection.

◆ ◆

From its early years, the organized labor movement in Germany had placed protective labor legislation for women on its agenda. The Social Democratic party's first program, in 1869, included a request for the "restriction of women's work in industrial establishments." The Gotha Program, passed during unification of the party's Lassallean and Marxist wings in 1875, demanded the "prohibition of all women's work that is detrimental to health and morality."[43] Both programs were the product of all-male debates between members who opposed women's wagework and those who considered it an unavoidable element of modern society.[44] The introduction of protective labor legislation for women into the party program clearly signaled a compromise between these two groups.

Early organizations of women workers in fact opposed any special regulation for women's work. Bourgeois feminists had often set up these organizations, and they underscored women's right to gainful employment.[45] One of the most compelling voices of the period was that of Gertrud Guillaume-Schack, founder of the first association of women workers. She strongly opposed protective legislation for women, and when the Reichstag debated such proposals in 1885, she organized protests against them. She joined the SPD in the same year and spoke out in 1887 against the official party position on this issue.[46] Yet the position of socialist-aligned women was not to remain constant or of a piece in the years that followed.

Clara Zetkin, who was soon to become the undisputed leader of German socialist women, also initially opposed women's special protection. At the founding congress of the Second International in 1889, she delivered her famous speech on women's work, taking a clear stand against all kinds of special treatment of women.[47] The speech was apparently well received, yet her position found few takers among the comrades. The resolution on protective labor legislation, which the International eventually passed, included the demand to prohibit women's work in "all industries that are especially detrimental to the female constitution."[48]

Zetkin and the leading socialist women had a change of heart just a few years later. Surprisingly, this shift was never discussed openly and its impulse remains unclear. When the 1890 SPD congress—the first to convene after twelve years of legal proscription under Bismarck—debated a new program, four women delegates continued to demand that the clause about women's special protection be omitted. They sharply queried: "Is industrial work detrimental only to a part of the people, detrimental only to women? Does the whole family suffer less if the man performs his family duties when ill, poisoned, and miserable?"[49] Perhaps significantly, at least three of these four women—Emma Ihrer,

Helma Steinbach, Frau Gundelach, and Louise Blohm—were well-known trade unionists who had been involved in the early attempt to unionize German women.[50] The new party program omitted the issue of women's protection, but this position seems to have been destined for a short life in the party's politics. Prominent leaders such as Karl Kautsky and Eduard Bernstein were still arguing clearly in favor of protective legislation for women that very same year,[51] and during the Reichstag's debate on the new trade code of 1891, the Social Democrats revealed themselves to be firm supporters of such protection.

Between the years 1891 and 1893, Zetkin changed her views in two stages. By 1891 she had stopped opposing women's protection as a general principle, characterizing it as a temporary strategy designed to achieve more general protection for male and female labor alike.[52] Two years later, however, she had come to stress women's categorical difference from men: they were physically and socially weaker. Special protection was therefore necessary to compensate for the disadvantages that women experienced in the labor market. But beyond this, Zetkin denied that a "total equality" between men and women would ever be possible because of biological difference.[53] During the following months, these arguments were put forward time and again in *Die Gleichheit* (the biweekly journal published by Zetkin) and became the official line of the German socialist women.

Only one instance of open opposition to this new orthodoxy reared its head from the socialist ranks. Johanna Löwenherz, a local agitator from the Rhineland, disputed Zetkin on this issue. As a result, Zetkin denied Löwenherz further access to the columns of *Die Gleichheit*.[54] As late as 1896 a party congress again debated protective legislation, and female delegates strongly attacked Löwenherz for her stance.[55] After 1897 she disappeared from SPD accounts. No one from party ranks ever again openly expressed opposition to protective legislation. We can only presume that Löwenherz's fate prompted wavering, more faint-hearted party members to fall in line.

The Löwenherz case also pointed to socialist women's increasing resort to rhetorical weapons aimed at other women. This framing of protection could paradoxically underscore gender difference at work, while giving common purpose to men and women in the party. Any opposition to protective legislation was now exclusively ascribed to the bourgeois women's movement.[56] It is therefore no coincidence that socialist women not only attacked Löwenherz for opposing such legislation but also for being too bourgeois. Indeed, any demand for protective legislation prompted strong attacks against the bourgeois women's movement, which still opposed protective labor legislation for women only. Even when these reviled targets became supporters of such laws a few years later, the women socialists continued to maintain that a wide gulf lay between them on precisely this question and that supporting female protection was fundamentally a "matter of class consciousness."

Why did socialist women maintain this fierce hostility? On one occasion Zetkin implied that such animosity was connected to the fear that ordinary women workers might be confused by the women socialists' turn of mind and "mistake" this shift for capitulation to opposition to women's wagework on principle among the old (male) guard of the labor movement. If women began fearing loss of their jobs, then the position of the bourgeois women's movement might be more attractive to them and their allegiances might be swayed.[57] The dilemma exposes the uncomfortable position in which socialist women found themselves. Caught in a cross fire, they were forced to position themselves somewhere between bourgeois women, who advocated women workers' formal equality, and male opposition to women's employment.

Male opposition also remained an uncomfortable force to be reckoned with in the protection debate; hostility to women's work had considerable staying power inside the organized labor movement. Among the rank and file, an assumption that women were "dirty competitors" and potential "strikebreakers" still prevailed at the turn of the century.[58] Socialist women recommended special protection as a solution. With regulated working conditions, they argued, women could no longer become dirty competitors. Moreover, they argued that special legislation would "blaze the trail" for general protection. Bourgeois society was ready to accept women's protection, they claimed, due to its interest in the further production of "machine fodder and cannon fodder"; bourgeois politicians might later be persuaded to extend the legislation to men.[59]

Thus, following Zetkin, when socialist women shifted gears on protective legislation, they signaled their acceptance of the unspoken compromise made earlier between advocates and opponents of women's wagework within the labor movement. With all parts of the movement fully supporting the compromise, women included, opposition to women's wagework was never again to appear on the official party agenda.

In 1893 the German Social Democrats chose the third congress of the Second International in Zurich as the setting for passing a comprehensive, clear motion in favor of protective labor legislation for women. Louise Kautsky—Karl Kautsky's former wife, who had worked in London as Friedrich Engels's secretary since 1888—proposed the resolution, which began with the obligatory attack on the bourgeois women's movement. The debate that followed, as conveyed through the official minutes, revealed that obstacles in the ranks still hindered full acceptance of such legislation.[60] Some of the criticism took issue with the harsh condemnation of the bourgeois women's movement and some made much of the economic fallout facing "protected" women. Delegates from various countries suggested amending the resolution by including a demand for "equal pay for equal work." Zetkin opposed the new proposal, saying that it did not belong on the agenda and that the legal imposition of a minimum wage was simply utopian.

A large majority eventually passed the original resolution with the equal pay demand added on. The international movement thus did not unequivocally embrace the German position. The two issues attracting the most disagreement were peculiar to Germany. The first was the fact that, because of the German Social Democrats' party policy, the demand for protective labor legislation could not be linked to the claim for equal pay. Fighting for rights under an authoritarian state, SPD leaders had learned only too well to distrust the efficacy of legal tools in making claims for labor. Problems connected to wages should be resolved in the labor market using trade unions, not the state. Yet in mediating women's wages, this proved to be a trap. On the one hand, unions were neither eager nor very successful in organizing women and hence extracting higher wages for them. On the other hand, special protection for women provided yet another justification for employers categorically to pay lower wages to women.

The second German peculiarity revealed here was the intense investment that socialist women had in distinguishing themselves from the bourgeois women's movement and its aims. Protective legislation served as the dividing line. Such a separation allowed socialist women to present themselves as earnest adherents to party principles; it showed them to be reliable party members. According to Jean Quataert's account, this "was the implicit condition for effective participation in the German socialist world." [61] She terms this stance "reluctant feminism": women's issues became above all vehicles for underwriting class unity rather than unifying women across class lines.

The shift in favor of protective legislation for women was a crucial turning point for German socialist women. First, the question of legal protection became more and more a women's topic to the extent that, after 1900, discussions of it were almost exclusively confined to the female preconferences of national party congresses. Second, socialist women always felt pressured to deny that they were pursuing any special interests (*Sonderbestrebungen*).[62] This contradiction between accepting women's need for special protection, on the one hand, and denying their special interests, on the other, greatly restricted the scope of activities risked by the socialist women's movement in Germany. While firmly committed to the success of the labor movement, socialist women could hardly move above and beyond the aims of its male members. Yet their commitment to special protection for women restricted their opportunity to fight for equal rights.

◆ ◆

When organized socialist women declared their support for protective labor legislation for women in the early 1890s, no section of the bourgeois women's movement immediately chose to follow their lead. However, the bourgeois women also failed to mount the kind of fierce opposition to gender-specific protection that had characterized their stance during the 1880s. Bourgeois women's groups steered completely clear of the debates around the trade code in 1891, and they even failed to muster any response to the socialist women's heavy attacks on them, which started in 1891. Yet between 1896 and 1898 some bourgeois women began clearly advocating special protection. They initially demanded female factory inspectors, a topic high up on the wish list of the League of German Women's Associations (Bund Deutscher Frauenvereine), founded in 1894 by thirty-four women's associations as an umbrella organization.[63] However, this did not signal the acceptance of women's protection in principle but sprang instead from an assumption that women workers would derive special benefits from the work of women inspectors. Concerned with women's access to women in authority, bourgeois feminists also began promoting the idea of female physicians and police.

Jeanette Schwerin, a member of the radical wing of the bourgeois movement, was the main force behind this demand. She even set up training courses for future factory inspectors, in anticipation of the day when female inspectors would be permitted.[64] In 1898 she was also successful in getting the BDF's Commission for Female Factory Inspectors renamed the Commission for Protective Labor Legislation for Women. Schwerin's argument shows clearly that up until this point these two issues had not been connected in the German context.[65]

By renaming the commission, the bourgeois women's movement publicly expressed its fledgling support for protective legislation. At the same time, its journals began to take notice of the issue. The campaign to prohibit married women's work provided one incentive for this change of heart. The bourgeois women's journals argued that such attempts were outmoded and advocated "modest" legal protection instead. Their changed viewpoint at least partly suggests that a compromise with extreme conservatives was in the works, including appeasement of women in their own ranks. As Alice Salomon, a pioneer among women in the social work field, put it in 1899, "In Germany principled opposition to protective legislation obviously had no chance."[66] However, they were not yet as friendly to such legislation as their socialist women contemporaries. After an encounter with English antiprotectionists during the International Congress of Women in London in 1899, some bourgeois women voiced renewed doubts about the wisdom of protective legislation.[67]

All parts of the bourgeois women's movement were unanimous in their support for protective legislation when it was linked to promoting motherhood. Concern for mothers found support in protective labor laws, which mandated sufficient rest and care for women workers before and after childbirth. Women from all wings of the movement seemed eager to outdo each other in producing the most far-reaching demands concerning the length of maternity leave as well as adequate financial compensation for lost wages.[68] One-time opponents turned into fierce advocates of women's protection, dropping their earlier differentiation between legal measures for actual mothers and those treating all women as potential mothers. That one did not come without the other appeared to be the new consensus.[69] Motherhood was rapidly becoming a magnetic political pole for many different anxieties and social visions, in part forging unity where little had existed before, but in part also rearticulating sharp divisions through the figure of childbearer.

From its inception in the nineteenth century, the German discourse on women's protection in the workplace centered on motherhood. The first protective law in 1878 dealt with childbirth, and working mothers remained the focus of the debate through World War I. Political initiatives invoking motherhood were able to link many different interests together. "Maternalism," Seth Koven and Sonya Michel rightly suggest, "was and remains an extraordinarily protean ideology capable of drawing together unlikely and often transitory coalitions between people who appeared to speak a common language but had opposing political commitments and views of women."[70] Thus, the centrality of motherhood within the discourse on protective labor legislation for women could join together those who were engaged in pragmatic politics for the improvement of actual mothers' conditions. The aims of others went much further. After the turn of the century, the declining birthrate became a major cause of public consternation and the women's movement was not long in joining the debate on population politics. The emerging eugenics issue became a focal point of discussions, above all in the national League for the Protection of Mothers (Bund für Mutterschutz).[71] Thus, motherhood and its protection accrued many different meanings inside the women's movement, as it did elsewhere on the political spectrum. The sociologist Theresa Wobbe has sketched out these different approaches, concluding that "while social democratic advocates of women's rights discussed protective labor legislation for women and the importance of mothers' work in the framework of class struggle, bourgeois-liberal advocates of women's rights focused on the cultural significance of the 'mother's profession' as a countervailing force in modern industrialized society."[72] A focus on motherhood offered an obvious way for German women to voice their concerns publicly and to circumvent their total exclusion from formal political participation, a ban kept intact until 1908.[73] Seen as an instrumental response to severe political disabilities—among other things—did the motherhood issue in fact enhance bourgeois women's credibility and influence?

Motherhood gave bourgeois women activists a foot in the door of German high politics, but only a narrow and protected view of the room within, its dimensions and possibilities. It is provocative to speculate, as Koven and Michel have, on how a combination of a "strong" state and a "weak" women's movement produces extensive welfare benefits. Nevertheless, this kind of schematic thinking also threatens to erase important, culturally specific differences in how a number of diverse actors mediated state discourse at the turn of the century.

◆ ◆

Although the rhetoric of protection circled around motherhood, it came down heavily on all women, defining their position in society.

Very generally, protective labor legislation for women helped to shape the rising welfare state in Imperial Germany after the shift away from Bismarck's blatantly repressive labor policies. While reinforcing the gendered order of work, it indeed helped to integrate the organized labor movement into bourgeois society. Protection as "the polite way to refer to subordination"[74] confirmed women as the principal wards of the emerging welfare state.

Lacking any political rights and legally subjected to employers and husbands, German women were exposed to a protection that meant, first and foremost, further restrictions on their ability to acquire new jobs in a labor market where they already faced discrimination. Men were reaffirmed as the "normal workers," women as the "deviants" whose employment required special provisions. Even if these measures had few direct effects on working conditions, they arguably legitimized the continuing job segregation that relegated women to subordinate positions and inferior occupations.[75] Alice Kessler-Harris has drawn similar conclusions for the United States: "Protective legislation divided workers into those who could and could not perform certain roles. It therefore bears some of the responsibility for successfully institutionalizing women's secondary labor force position."[76]

Protective labor legislation in Germany, as elsewhere, served to further endorse the family wage model of male breadwinner and female housekeeper-dependent. By taking for granted the need to reconcile waged work and housework, opting for protective legislation (at least in spirit) confirmed that housework was women's "natural" duty. The discourse on women's protection thus played a crucial role in extending bourgeois family ideology to the working class, even while women's incomes remained indispensable for working-class families. Moreover, the rhetoric about protection of women's health and morality as a national task facilitated ever greater legal incursions into working people's lives. This said, protective legislation in Imperial Germany as a whole did not deal concretely with the situation of those women who actually suffered from the "double burden" of employment and child-rearing. It was not a mechanism that could profoundly alter the position of working women, for it did not depart far from the status quo and was easy to circumvent or ignore. Yet the laws constructed a principal difference between male and female workers by giving a new definition to women who toiled as underpaid workers in the labor market and un-paid workers in their families. It perversely labeled them "protected."

Notes

The title of this essay comes from Alice Salomon, "Protective Labour Legislation in Germany," in *The International Congress of Women, 1899,* vol. 6, ed. Isabel Maria Gordon (London: F. Fisher Unwin, 1900), 37.

1. Establishing their attitudes toward the laws would require a detailed investigation of social practices, which is beyond the scope of this essay. See Jean H. Quataert's findings that handloom weavers in Saxony felt negatively about the introduction of gendered social insurance policies ("Workers' Reactions to Social Insurance: The Case of Homeweavers in the Saxon Oberlausitz," *Internationale wissenschaftliche Korrespondenz zur Geschichte der Arbeiterbewegung* 20:1 [1984]: 17–35, and "The Politics of Rural Industrialization: Class, Gender, and Collective Protest in the Saxon Oberlausitz," *Central European History* 20:2 [1987]: 91–124).

2. See Sabine Schmitt, *Der Arbeiterinnenschutz im Deutschen Kaiserreich: Zur Konstruktion der Schutzbedürftigen Arbeiterin* (Stuttgart: Metzler, 1995), chaps. 6–8.

3. For a general overview of the rise of social policy in imperial Germany, see, e.g., Gerhard A. Ritter, *Der Sozialstaat. Entstehung und Entwicklung im internationalen Vergleich* (Munich: Oldenbourg, 1989).

4. See Jürgen Tampke, "Bismarcks Sozialgesetzgebung: Ein wirklicher Durchbruch?" in *Die Entstehung des Wohlfahrtsstaates in Großbritannien und Deutschland 1850–1950,* ed. Wolfgang J. Mommsen (Stuttgart: Klett-Cotta, 1982).

5. See Hans-Peter Ullmann, "Deutsche Unternehmer und Bismarcks Sozialversicherungssystem," in *Die Entstehung des Wohlfahrtsstaates,* ed. Mommsen; Rüdiger Baron, "Weder Zuckerbrot noch Peitsche: Historische Konstitutionsbedingungen des Sozialstaates in Deutschland," in *Gesellschaftliche Beiträge zur Marxschen Theorie,* vol. 12 (Frankfurt a.M.: Suhrkamp, 1979).

6. Hans-Jörg von Berlepsch, *"Neuer Kurs" im Kaiserreich? Die Arbeiterpolitik des Freiherrn von Berlepsch* (Bonn: Verlag Neue Gesellschaft, 1987), 11–14; Lothar Machtan and Hans-Jörg von Berlepsch, "Vorsorge oder Ausgleich— oder beides? Prinzipienfragen staatlicher Sozialpolitik im Deutschen Kaiserreich," *Zeitschrift für Sozialreform* 32 (1986): 257–75, 343–58.

7. The Prussian Fabrikregulativ of 1839, which forbade the employment of children under the age of nine and prescribed a maximum workday of ten hours for juveniles, was the first German protective law. In 1853 the prohibition was extended to children under the age of twelve, and a ban on Sunday work for all was established, at least on paper. With the unification of Germany in 1871, these laws were included in the Imperial Trade Code.

8. The first modest attempts to regulate women's work (*Gesetz zur Abänderung der Gewerbeordnung vom 7.Juli 1878 Reichs-Geseteblatt,* 199–212) in-

cluded a prohibition of work for three weeks after childbirth and also underground work in mines.

9. For a comprehensive history of bourgeois social reform, see Rüdiger vom
Bruch, ed., *Weder Kommunismus noch Kapitalismus: Bürgerliche Sozialreform
in Deutschland vom Vormärz bis zur Ära Adenauer* (Munich: Beck, 1985).

10. Examples of the wide range of empirical investigations conducted on
women's working conditions include: Gertrud Dyhrenfurth, *Die hausindus-
trielle Arbeiterin in der Berliner Blusen-, Unterrock-, Schürzen-und Trikotkon-
fektion* (Leipzig: Duncker & Humblot, 1898); Marie Baum, *Drei Klassen von
Lohnarbeiterinnen in Industries und Handel der Stadt Karlsruhe* (Karlsruhe:
Braun, 1906); Rose Otto, *Über Fabrikarbeit verheirateter Frauen* (Stuttgart:
J. G. Cotta'sche Buchhandlung Nachfolger, 1910).

11. One-tenth of 1 percent of women workers in 1882 and 1.2 percent in 1907
were employed in white-collar work, while 8.1 percent and 15.8 percent, respectively, worked in the tertiary sector performing services (*Dienstleistungen*).
See Angelika Willms-Herget, *Frauenarbeit: Zur Integration der Frauen in den
Arbeitsmarkt* (Frankfurt: Campus, 1985), 128.

12. Ibid., 142.

13. Angelika Willms, *Die Entwicklung der Frauenerwerbstätigkeit im Deutschen Reich: Eine historisch-soziologische Studie* (Nuremberg: Institut für Arbeitsmarkt und Berufsforschung der Bundesanstalt für Arbeit, 1980), 110.

14. Barbara Franzoi, *At the Very Least She Pays the Rent: Women and German
Industrialization, 1871–1914* (Westport, Conn.: Greenwood Press, 1985), 5.

15. The main source for these accounts are the annual reports of factory
inspectors: Reichsamt des Inneren, ed., *Amtliche Mitteilungen aus den Jahresberichten der Mit der Beaufsichtigung der Fabrikenbeirauten Beamten* (Berlin:
Reichsdruckerei, 1879–98) and *Jahresberichte der Gewerbe-Aufsichtsbeamten
und Bergbehörden* (Berlin: Reichsdruckerei, 1899–1914). My own archival research on the administrative district of Düsseldorf confirms their results.

16. The most important early proponent of this was the physician Ludwig
Hirt, who, in addition to his four-volume work on industrial pathology
published in 1871–78, looked for conditions that were especially harmful to
women. See Hirt, *Die gewerbliche Thätigkeit der Frauen vom hygienischen
Standpunkte aus: Mit speciellen Hinweisen auf die an eine Fabrikgesetzgebung zu
stellenden Anforderungen* (Breslau: Hirt, 1873).

17. See Anna A. Bergmann, "Von der 'unbefleckten Empfängnis' zur
'Rationalisierung des Geschlechtslebens,' " in *Rationalität und sinnliche Ver-
nunft*, ed. Christine Kulke (Berlin: Publica, 1985).

18. See Ute Frevert, "The Civilizing Tendency of Hygiene: Working-Class
Women under Medical Control in Imperial Germany," in *German Women in
the Nineteenth Century*, ed. John C. Fout (New York: Holmes & Meier, 1984).

19. See Alfons Labisch, " 'Hygiene ist Moral—Moral ist Hygiene': Soziale

Disziplinierung durch Ärzte und Medizin," in *Soziale Sicherung und soziale Disziplinierung: Beiträge zu einer historischen Theorie der Sozialpolitik,* ed. Christoph Sachße and Florian Tennstedt (Frankfurt a.M.: Suhrkamp, 1986).

20. Adolf Frantz, *Beschäftigung der Frauen und Mädchen bei Bergbau unter Tage* (Beuthen O./S.: Bernhard Wylezol'sche Buchdruckerei, 1869), 31. This study was based on Belgian records, given that hardly any women worked underground in Germany. It became very popular as evidence for what might be expected from further industrialization.

21. (Unsigned), "Bedeutung und Aufgaben der Arbeiterschutzgesetzgebung," *Arbeiterwohl* 7 (1887): 245 (emphasis in original).

22. Rudolf Martin, *Die Ausschließung der verheirateten Frauen aus der Fabrik: Eine Studie an der Textilindustrie* (Tübingen: Laupp, 1897), 59.

23. *Die Beschäftigung verheirateter Frauen in Fabriken: Nach den Jahresberichten der Gewerbe-Aufsichtsbeamten für das Jahr 1899, bearbeitet im Reichsamt des Inneren* (Berlin: R. v. Decker, 1901).

24. See Ulla Wikander, "Some 'Kept the Flag of Feminist Demands Waving,'" in this volume.

25. See, e.g., Martin, *Die Ausschließung;* Ludwig Pohle, *Frauen-Fabrikarbeit und Frauenfrage: Eine prinzipielle Antwort auf die Frage der Ausschließung der verheirateten Frauen aus der Fabrik* (Leipzig: Veit, 1900).

26. For a left-liberal point of view, see, e.g., Karl Baumbach, *Frauenarbeit und Frauenschutz* (Berlin: Leonhard Simion, 1889).

27. *Gesetz zur Abänderung der Gewerbeordnung vom 7. Juli 1878.*

28. Arnold Lohren, *Entwurf eines Fabrik-und Werkstätten-Gesetzes zum Schutz der Frauen-und Kinderarbeit, hergeleitet vom Standpunkt der ausländischen Konkurrenz* (Potsdam, 1877), 70. See Hans Rothfels, *Theodor Lohmann und die Kampfjahre der staatlichen Sozialpolitik, 1871–1905* (Berlin: Mittler, 1927).

29. "Stenographische Berichte der Verhandlungen des Deutschen Reichstags," 7. Legislaturperiode, I. Session 1887, Drucksache No. 233.

30. Henry A. Bueck, *Der Centralverband Deutscher Industrieller 1876–1901,* vol. 3 (Berlin, 1905), 180ff.

31. "*Die Kaiserlichen Erlasse*" (Geheimes Staatsarchiv Preussischer Kulturbesitz Abteilung Merseburg, rep. 120BB VII 1, no. 29, fol. 16ff.); "*Die Protokolle der Internationalen Arbeiterschutzkonferenz*" (Leipzig: Duncker & Humblot, 1890). See Regina Wecker, "Equality for Men?" in this volume.

32. See the Kaiser's "Bemerkungen zur Arbeiterfrage," reprinted in *Fürst Bismarcks Entlassung,* ed. Georg Freiherr von Eppstein (Berlin: Scherl, 1920).

33. *Gesetz zur Abänderung der Gewerbeordnung vom 1. Juni 1891* Reichs-Gesetzblatt, 261–90.

34. See Berlepsch, "*Neuer Kurs,*" 206ff.

35. "Stenographische Berichte . . . ," 19 May 1890, 158.

36. "Stenographische Berichte der Verhandlungen des Deutschen Reichstags," 8. Legislaturperiode, I. Session 1890–92; "Protokolle der VIII. Kommission" (Bundesarchiv Abt. Potsdam, rep. 01.01, no. 490).

37. Ernst Gagliardi, *Bismarcks Entlassung: Erster Teil; Die Innenpolitik* (Tübingen: Mohr, 1927); Georg Freiherr von Eppstein, ed., *Fürst Bismarcks Entlassung* (Berlin: Scherl, 1920).

38. Karl Heinrich v. Boetticher, "Zur Geschichte der Entlassung des Fürsten Bismarck am 20. März 1890," in *Fürst Bismarcks Entlassung*, 37.

39. Anson Rabinbach, *The Human Motor: Energy, Fatigue, and the Origins of Modernity* (New York: Basic Books, 1990), esp. chap. 7.

40. Bismarck to Hohenthal, Jan. 30, 1890, and Bismarck to Rottenburg, Feb. 26, 1890 (Bundesarchiv Abt. Potsdam, rep. 07.01, no. 431, fols. 51ff., 158ff.).

41. He clearly never opposed state intervention in principle, and he demonstrated some sympathy for a general limit on the maximum workday. See, e.g., Rothfels, *Theodor Lohmann*, 87.

42. Bundesarchiv Abt. Potsdam, Reichsamt des Inneren, rep. 15.01, and GStA Merseburg, Ministerium für Handel und Gewerbe, rep. 120BB, contain large quantities of such sources, classified according to industry branches or by the type of regulation they involved.

43. *Protokolle der sozialdemokratischen Arbeiterpartei,* vol. 1: *1869–74* (rpt., Bonn/Bad Godesberg: Verlag Neue Gesellschaft, 1971), 32; ibid., vol. 2: *1875–87,* 45.

44. This difference has been attributed to the Lassallean and the Marxist school. See, e.g., Hilde Lion, *Zur Soziologie der Frauenbewegung* (Berlin: Herbig, 1926), 24–26; Werner Thönessen, *Frauenemanzipation: Politik und Literatur der deutschen Sozialdemokratie zur Frauenbewegung 1863–1933* (Frankfurt a.M.: Europäische Verlagsanstalt, 1969), 13; Richard J. Evans, *Sozialdemokratie und Frauenemanzipation im deutschen Kaiserreich* (Berlin/Bonn: Dietz, 1979), 39. While this is not the place to discuss the ideological background, I consider it to be a much more complex problem that cannot simply be reduced to this controversy.

45. These arguments were put forward forcefully in Louise Otto's well-known book *Das Recht der Frauen auf Erwerb* (Hamburg: Hoffmann & Campe, 1866). For a history of the early women's organizations, see Herrad-Ulrike Bussemer, *Frauenemanzipation und Bildungsbürgertum: Sozialgeschichte der Frauenbewegung in der Reichsgründungszeit* (Weinheim/Basel: Beltz, 1985).

46. *Protokolle der sozialdemokratischen Arbeiterpartei,* vol. 2, 24. A countess, Guillaume-Schack was exiled from Germany in 1886 because of her political activities. Due to her expulsion, she did not turn up again in the German debates. The last report on her activities came from the International Women's Council meeting in 1899, where she spoke fiercely against special protection. See Gordon, *The International Congress of Women, 1899,* 6:56–57.

47. *Kongress-Protokolle der Zweiten Internationale,* vol. 1: *Paris 1889–Amsterdam 1904* (rpt., Berlin: Dietz, 1975), 84.

48. Ibid., 122.

49. *Protokoll über die Verhandlungen des Parteitages der SPD in Halle 1890* (rpt., Berlin: Dietz, 1978), 196.

50. Unfortunately, I have not located any biographical account of Frau Gundelach.

51. Karl Kautsky, *Der Arbeiterschutz, besonders die internationale Arbeiterschutz-Gesetzgebung und der Acht-Stunden-Tag* (Nuremberg: Wörlein, 1890); Eduard Bernstein, "Frauenrechtelei und Arbeiterschutz," *Die Neue Zeit* 9:2 (1890–91): 173–87.

52. Clara Zetkin, "Zur Frage des Arbeiterschutzes für Frauen," *Die Arbeiterin* 1:23–26 (1891).

53. "Das Prinzip der Gleichberechtigung der Frau und der gesetzliche Arbeiterinnenschutz," *Die Gleichheit* 3:19 (1893): 150.

54. Johanna Löwenherz, "Zur Frage des gesetzlichen Arbeiterinnenschutzes," *Die Gleichheit* 3:19 (1893): 147–49. An editorial note immediately and sharply criticized her letter.

55. *Protokoll über die Verhandlungen,* 172.

56. I use the term "bourgeois women's movement"—subdivided into a "radical" and a "moderate" wing since the mid-1890s—because it was used by the women themselves. An extended discussion about how fitting all these terms are is beyond the scope of this essay.

57. Clara Zetkin, "Arbeiterinnenschutz und Frauenrechtelei," *Die Gleichheit* 3:16 (1893): 126.

58. See Gisela Losseff-Tillmanns, *Frauenemanzipation und Gewerkschaften* (Wuppertal: Hammer, 1978).

59. These arguments turned up again and again. See, e.g., "Das Prinzip," 149–51.

60. *Kongress-Protokolle der Zweiten Internationale,* 1:36–37. See Wikander, "Some 'Kept the Flag of Feminist Demands Waving.'"

61. Jean H. Quataert, *Reluctant Feminists in German Social Democracy, 1885–1917* (Princeton: Princeton University Press, 1979), 231.

62. See, e.g., *Protokoll über die Verhandlung des Parteitages der SPD in Hannover 1899* (rpt., Berlin: Dietz, 1980), 289–90.

63. Its membership rose from seventy thousand women in 1900 to two hundred thousand in 1908. The league's founding congress established the Commission for the Employment of Female Factory Inspectors.

64. Helene Lange, "Die Fabrikinspektorin vor dem preußischen Abgeordnetenhaus," *Die Frau* 6:7 (1899): 421–24.

65. *Neue Bahnen* 33:24 (1898): 273.

66. Gordon, *The International Congress of Women, 1899,* 39.

67. Marie Stritt, "Der internationale Frauenkongreß in London," *Die Frau* 6:11 (1899): 641–47; Alice Salomon, "Frauenbewegung und gesetzlicher Arbeiterinnenschutz," *Die Frau* 7 (1900): 212–16.

68. The debate over maternity insurance was mainly set off by Lily Braun, *Die Frauenfrage: Ihre geschichtliche Entwicklung und ihre wirtschaftliche Seite* (Berlin: Hirzel, 1901), esp. 542–53, which was followed by a flood of publications.

69. See Theresa Wobbe, *Gleichheit und Differenz: Politische Strategien von Frauenrechtlerinnen um die Jahrhundertwende* (Frankfurt a.M.: Campus, 1988), 7–21; and Irene Stoehr, " 'Organisierte Mütterlichkeit': Zur Politik der deutschen Frauenbewegung um 1900," in *Frauen suchen ihre Geschichte,* ed. Karin Hausen (Munich: C. H. Beck, 1983).

70. Seth Koven and Sonya Michel, "Womanly Duties: Maternalist Politics and the Origins of Welfare States in France, Germany, Great Britain, and the United States, 1880–1920," *American Historical Review* 95:4 (1990): 1085.

71. Anne Taylor Allen, "Mothers of the New Generation: Adele Schreiber, Helene Stöcker, and the Evolution of a German Idea of Motherhood, 1900–1914," *Signs: Journal of Women in Culture and Society* 10 (1985): 221–49.

72. Theresa Wobbe, "Hausarbeit und Beruf um die Jahrhundertwende. Die Debatte der Frauenbewegungen im Deutschen Kaiserreich," in *Frauenberufe-hausarbeitsnah?* ed. Marion Klewitz, Ulrike Schildmann, and Theresa Wobbe (Pfaffenweiler: Centaurus, 1989), 37.

73. This was also acknowledged by their opponents abroad. See, e.g., Katherine Anthony, *Feminism in Germany and Scandinavia* (New York: Holt, 1915), 115–41.

74. Carol Pateman, "The Patriarchal Welfare State," in *Democracy and the Welfare State,* ed. Amy Gutmann (Princeton: Princeton University Press, 1988), 238.

75. See Angelika Willms, "Modernisierung durch Frauenarbeit? Zum Zusammenhang von wirtschaftlichem Strukturwandel und weiblicher Arbeitsmarktlage in Deutschland, 1882–1939," in *Historische Arbeitsmarktforschung: Entstehung, Entwicklung und Probleme der Vermarktung von Arbeitskraft,* ed. Toni Pierenkemper and Richard Tilly (Göttingen: Vandenhoek & Ruprecht, 1982). Willms contends that in this period the opportunities for entering certain branches became more equal for men and women, but at the same time there was a tendency toward more dissimilarity between occupations and more occupational segregation between married and unmarried women.

76. Alice Kessler-Harris, *Out to Work: A History of Wage-Earning Women in the United States* (Oxford: Oxford University Press, 1982), 181.

· 5 ·

Special Labor Protection for Women in Austria, 1860–1918

Margarete Grandner

A bill presented to the Lower House of Parliament in 1868 by the medical doctor and social reformer Ignaz Roser triggered the protective legislation debate in Austria. Roser's bill called for improving working conditions by reducing and limiting hours for both male and female factory workers. The hour seemed anything but ripe for such proposals: the economy was expanding as never before, and in the new constitutional era launched in 1867, a staunch Liberal majority dominated Parliament. Yet the bill provoked a fair measure of interest.

Following a period of stagnation, Austria witnessed the start of an economic boom in 1867. In the years that followed, lasting through 1873—the so-called *Gründerzeit*—more than 1,000 new stockholding companies were founded, mainly industrial enterprises.[1] Comprehensive figures are not available, but an inquiry organized by the Viennese Chamber of Commerce shows that in 1869–70 a considerable number of women were employed in a wide range of trades in Lower Austria. Women made up the majority of workers in cotton and silk mills, in the production of worsted yarn, trimmings, and lace, in textile finishing and glovemaking, in certain branches of the chemical industry such as the production of candles, soap, perfumes, and inflammable matter, and in paper mills and tobacco factories. Approximately one-third of the work force employed in brick works was female; and in the city of Vienna alone there were approximately 5,000 women among its 19,650 construction workers and 1,200 to 1,500 women and girls among the 3,300 male workers in weaving mills. Industrial work was not restricted to single women either. Among the 3,280 adult female workers in the cotton mills who responded to the Chamber of Commerce survey, 800 were married; approximately one-third of the 2,200 employed in the silk mills were also married, as were nearly half of the 1,803 women employed in brick works.[2]

Hand in hand with the acceleration of industrialization came the threat of social unrest. Feeling uneasy, an influential group of reformer-activists among Liberal politicians began to strategize. Inspired by the active response of English politicians to the threat of rapid industrialization, they reacted to Roser's bill by suggesting that protective measures be applied to children and women only.[3]

Differential treatment of men and women in economic affairs ran counter to certain assumptions embedded in Austrian law. As in most European countries, Austrian women were at a great disadvantage in terms of political rights and family law. Since the enactment of the Civil Code in 1811, however, they enjoyed more formal equality in a range of economic matters in Austria than in any other country in contemporary central or western Europe.[4] The provision of the Civil Code that women were free agents with regard to their property was clearly tailored to the position of the entrepreneurial and middle classes; single or married women's wagework barely figured in the discussions of women's economic rights during the first half of the century. But the Civil Code's general approach encompassed the working classes. Women in Austria were thus entitled to enter into employment contracts as free agents, and wives did not need their husbands' consent to do so.[5]

The state had greatly encouraged female and child labor in textile manufacturing, in particular during its efforts to promote domestic industry in the late eighteenth century.[6] At that time women's and children's menial tasks, which characterized the novel mode of mechanized production, were seen as forming one category of labor separate from men's. Gradually, however, the state began to view children's factory labor less benignly and tried to limit it with protective measures. By contrast, women's working conditions seem to have passed out of sight and out of mind. The Civil Code of 1811 did away with the kind of protection for women that traditional paternalism had implied, and no new measures were substituted thereafter.[7]

Industrial work brought severe dislocations with it. Why, then, the indifference, the invisibility of the women's labor issue? One reason for this apathy may have been that during the first half of the nineteenth century the Austrian state still remained quite indecisive about what to do with labor in general. The Civil Code was overruled by a range of special trade laws and servants' codes that in many cases placed industrial labor under police control and reaffirmed guild regulations.[8] On the one hand, survival of traditional views despite the creation of the Civil Code probably had implications for women in particular. The vast majority of women worked in home industry, domestic service, and agriculture, where the 1811 legislation did not affect traditional labor organization. On the other hand, the Civil Code was, if anything, applicable to textile factories, where women formed an economically indispensable part of the work force. But the subordinated status of most women workers in these establishments made it particularly easy to regard them as some sort of servants.

Indeed, the notion that women and children formed a separate category of the industrial labor force persisted.[9] Traditional views of protection for female workers relied on the assumption that they performed lighter work than men, although these views corresponded less and less with actual working conditions. If the state demonstrated readiness to meddle in labor issues for the sake of military recruitment or to promote education,[10] it apparently lacked any strong, long-term interest in intervening where female factory work was involved.

The Austrian Trade Code of 1859 abolished guild regulations and made the Civil Code generally applicable to labor in industry and trade.[11] It contained remnants of a traditional discourse of protecting women by controlling the kinds of work assigned to them, although it was acknowledged that this provision was void.[12] And in its thrust the Trade Code broke away from any attempt to reinscribe a sexual division of labor.[13] Enumerating the persons subject to its regulations on work, the code included "female laborers who are employed under the same terms of employment" as male white-collar workers, journeymen, and factory workers.[14]

When factory legislation grew into a political issue in the late 1860s, the legal base of equality for women as embodied in the Civil and Trade Codes played an important role in the discussions both inside and outside Parliament. Advocates of special protection for women found themselves attacking women's legal status, while their opponents used the formal equality provided by earlier legislation to argue that women did not need protection.

The Liberal group favoring differential treatment of men and women controlled the parliamentary committee set to report on the question of labor protection. The rhetoric of their report betrayed the authors' awkward legal position. Arguing firmly against interfering with freedom of contract for men, they referred to "adults, that is, male workers, who are free agents."[15] Omitting any special comment, the report allowed women to slip into the category of children and youth, whom the state had "not only the right, but also the duty" to protect. "A glimpse into English conditions" had left no question for these Liberals "that children needed protection against nobody as much as against their parents, and wives against their husbands."[16] According to the Liberal leader Ernst von Plener, all women needed protection—just like young people—"because of their nature . . . and because they are more easily tempted into working beyond the measure of their capacity."[17]

Not surprisingly, employers and Liberal economists took vehement exception to such assertions. Restricting the use of female labor by limits on hours or other special measures ran counter to their interests at the very moment when the boom of the *Gründerzeit* found them eager to recruit more female labor. For them, emancipation came in handy, for it could remove barriers of entry into the labor market. "It is irresponsible," remarked an author in 1872, "to cede an activity to the male sex that had been reserved for it only by prejudice and narrow-minded abuse."[18]

The dispute positioned a state bureaucracy interested in modernizing the economy against a political grouping dependent on its (middle- and upper-class) clientele. Employers could successfully argue that the Austrian economy and especially the textile industry required cheap labor to remain competitive. Insisting that women's work was crucial to keeping down costs resonated well with the state bureaucracy. And they used equal rights for women as the decisive plank in their argument. Countering the Liberals' proposal for special protection, the Ministry of Commerce declared that "adult women doubtlessly [have] the same right to dispose freely of their capacity for work as male workers."[19]

Roser's bill demanding labor protection and the Liberals' proposal for special protection for women and children led to nothing. Both fell victim to the premature end of two consecutive parliamentary sessions. The issue would not die, but the initiative now passed over to the government and the ministerial bureaucracy. Like the Liberals in Parliament, the Liberal government of the 1870s did not see the need for protection for all workers. Unlike the group of MPs mentioned above, however, the government was prone to listen to economic considerations warning against special measures for women as well. The numerous drafts of new labor regulations produced by the bureaucracy from 1869 to 1879 mirror this split of opinion and highlight the importance of the issue. The proposals differed only with regard to whether or not and to what extent they included special protection for women, and the government could not reach a consensus on the issue.[20]

Changing economic conditions in Austria did not disadvantage opponents of special protection. The advent of the Depression in 1873 had witnessed a sharp rise in the number of people out of work. In 1875, Johann Garber, a factory owner, estimated that female unemployment stood at 30 percent.[21] But employers continued to demand the unrestricted availability of cheap female labor. Garber confirmed that it was "perfectly legitimate to expand the field of female employment step by step, and to multiply the army of labor by efficient and industrious female companions for the time when increased demands are made on industry."[22]

In this entrepreneurial discourse, the importance of women to their families still ranked distinctly below their importance to the economy, the latter conveniently framed under the rubric of equal treatment. In 1875 the Ministry of Commerce, for instance, conceded that it was a "well-grounded consideration that by virtue of her fate woman is called upon to take care of the family, to rear a healthy and robust new generation, and that she should not be hampered in this calling by excessive industrial work." Yet despite this, the ministry decided in favor of the "characteristic feature of our time, to promote the participation of the female sex in gainful employment and the creation of a position independent from the support of others, to make barriers fall, which had restricted activities open to the female sex through traditional social views, [and] thus to preserve [that sex's] right of self-determination."[23]

The family argument carried little weight, not least because state authorities recognized that many women in the labor market were not married and could improve their living conditions by working.[24] Attempts to legislate on behalf of pregnant women and new mothers also did not garner enthusiastic support. When, in 1869, the Ministry of Commerce suggested an unpaid maternity leave of six weeks around childbirth, the Ministry of the Interior rejected such a provision "because of the variety of individuals involved and their respective circumstances."[25] None of the subsequent proposals up to 1880 included a maternity leave. Some of them sought special measures for young women between sixteen and eighteen or sixteen and twenty-one rather than for more mature women, wives, or mothers.[26] Through such proposals the government attempted to strike a compromise between the gender-neutral regulations desired by employers and special treatment for all women, which, for instance, a parliamentary resolution again demanded in 1874.[27] But at the same time such compromises, which referred to and attempted to extend child protection, signaled that the protection of young female workers from hazardous working conditions (including moral hazards) was more salient than the protection of women who ran households or raised children. There were no attempts to tailor protection to these latter groups. With Liberal politicians in disarray, ideas of economic liberty and female equality held their ground, mitigating against the first serious attempts to confer special state protections on grown women in the workplace.

◆ ◆

The Liberals lost their parliamentary majority in 1879 in the wake of a prolonged economic depression, and in the same year the last Liberal government fell. The new government of Count Eduard Taaffe, a friend of the emperor, remained in office until 1893. Taaffe's government enjoyed the support of the "Iron Ring," an alliance of various anticentralist, antiliberal, and anticapitalist groupings that now held the majority in Parliament.[28] Charging laissez-faire capitalism with the distress caused by industrialization and the crisis, Catholic social reformers within the Iron Ring—among them several prominent noblemen—turned to social and economic policies that favored traditional crafts over modern industry and corporatist controls over free market competition. These men also brought with them a somewhat nuanced set of gender politics. They deplored the employment of women outside their homes.[29] The image of the well-to-do, middle-class family with separate spheres for men and women was their model for the working classes, idealizing it as the traditional, Christian foundation for society. These Conservative reformers adhered to the belief that "*not* the individual, but rather, the family is the primary element in the economic aspect of human existence." [30]

Like a number of Liberals, Conservatives demanded restrictions on female work. However, these ascendant Conservatives sought special protection not because of women's supposedly weaker physical condition or their social subordination but because of their role as housewives and mothers, a function they assigned to the whole sex, irrespective of differences among women. Lorenz von Stein, professor of political economy at the University of Vienna from 1855 to 1885, even managed to muster a "scientific" explanation for this position:

> If external conditions or her individual nature inwardly compel her, a woman can in the end do *everything* a man can do. . . . But . . . while we do not deny this, it is as certain on the other hand, that a woman, as soon as she really does male things, is only a female form of a man and *a woman no more*. . . . According to the organic conception of goods, a man's economic life task is *production,* a woman's is *consumption,* that of both is *reproduction,* that is, to create property through the proper relation between the consumption and production of values.[31]

Economic considerations continued to leave an imprint on the new regime's policies. With the Conservatives' anti-individualist approach gaining ground, the rhetoric proclaiming women's equal legal status in economic affairs virtually vanished after 1880. Yet neither the Taaffe government nor the Iron Ring could tune out economic arguments against special protection. Immediately after Taaffe came to office, the demand for shorter hours for all women resurfaced in the debates within the bureaucracy but met with resistance from the Ministry of Commerce.[32] Preserving the competitiveness of Austrian industry still ranked distinctly higher for this ministry than did the social policy heralded by the new regime. Inspired mainly by French legislation, the government finally introduced a bill into Parliament in 1880 that aimed to limit hours only for young women between the ages of sixteen and twenty-one and for children up to age ten, and also to prohibit Sunday and holiday work as well as night work for these groups. In addition, the bill included an unpaid maternity leave of six weeks after childbirth.[33] Still, this proposal was highly controversial within the government. Employers in Austria remained interested in ready access to female labor, irrespective of age or marital status. In the eyes of industrial employers, the maturity required for married life—which girls were thought to attain at the age of sixteen—also fully qualified them for wagework.[34] One argument held that married or single, young or old, women could only be employed profitably if they were present on the factory shop floor to assist their male co-workers during *their* working hours. The minister of Commerce himself tried hard to steer his colleagues away from special protection for young women but did not prevail.[35]

An obvious split ran through the government. An interest in fostering economic development seemed incompatible with girding up a preindustrial social order. In this situation the time had come for Parliament to take on the disputes. Count Egbert Belcredi, one of the leaders of the Catholic social reformers in Austria, successfully countered the government proposal with drafts of his own. His strategy was to offer up piecemeal reform that postponed factory legislation. Only in 1883, after the Iron Ring had pushed through its most cherished goals—the protection of small artisans and tradesmen against the dangers of free competition and a law on factory inspectors—did it again begin to consider labor protection.[36]

In 1883 Belcredi presented his draft for a new labor code (later to be known as the *Arbeiterordnung*). This draft limited the hours of both male and female workers over the age of eighteen to sixty per week.[37] In addition, the proposed code reduced hours for young men between sixteen and eighteen and young women between sixteen and twenty-one to ten per day.[38] It prohibited night work for those under the age of eighteen and for all women. Sunday and holiday work was forbidden for all. Finally, the proposal also included an unpaid maternity leave of six weeks after childbirth. All these provisions were to cover factories as well as smaller workshops.[39]

Belcredi's proposal was a remarkable step in that it brought together the protective measures existing in foreign legislation at the time.[40] Nevertheless, a closer look at his plan and the amendments resulting from discussions within the government and Parliament reveals that the Iron Ring was very cautious not to interfere with the vital interests of industry. The draft turned out to be a well-considered prelude to a compromise that both the Catholic reformers and the representatives of economic interests would find acceptable.

The crucial alteration in Belcredi's draft compared to its predecessors was certainly the standardization of working time for all workers. This provision replaced a reduction of hours for women only, and it was in principle accepted by the government without much fuss.[41] Employers themselves voiced a preference for such a measure. Would it not be better, wondered Gustav Pacher von Theinburg, M.P. and textile manufacturer, "if by a reasonable general limitation of working hours the female worker entered and left the workshop at the same time as the male worker" than to exclude women from industrial work altogether through special protection?[42] Such references to the needs of production made the Iron Ring drop Belcredi's provision for young men and women and finally even a special reduction of hours for children between the ages of fourteen and sixteen.[43]

Yet consideration for the economy went further. The Swiss legislation of 1877, which obviously served as Belcredi's inspiration in laying down both a standard work time and prohibition of night work for women, restricted hours to eleven per day, and both provisions applied to factories only. Not surprisingly, the Iron Ring quickly managed to exempt its chief constituents, artisans and small tradesmen, from both provisions.[44] But it also agreed to raise the limitation on working hours in larger enterprises—those with more than twenty employees—to eleven.[45]

Beyond this, Belcredi's draft had already exempted enterprises engaged in continuous production from an hours' limitation, prohibition of Sunday and holiday work, and the night work prohibition for women. The Iron Ring adhered to these exceptions and also created new ones. Following a motion by the Liberal opposition, the parliamentary majority voted, for instance, to exempt the tasks of preparation and cleaning up from limits on standard working time. Austrian legislators once again referred to Swiss legislation to justify this exemption, yet they did not, as the Swiss did, exempt married women from the extra time.[46] As happened in the case of night work, which was unconditionally forbidden for women by Swiss law, Austrian legislators found themselves irresistibly drawn to the argument that the Austrian economy needed female labor with fewer restrictions to remain competitive.

Prohibition of night work was never treated independently of limitations on hours in Austrian legislation.[47] It was regulated for those groups of women (in the 1870s, sixteen- to twenty-one-year-olds) for whom hours were restricted and thus appears to have served as a directive for which part of the working day should be cut. Many employers seem to have been more sympathetic to prohibiting women's night work than to cutting the length of their working day, the former being less difficult to institute.[48] But night work was a standard feature of the textile industry, which employed nearly a hundred thousand women, and this situation prompted Conservative M.P.s and the Taaffe government to move very cautiously.[49] Although they viewed night work as both morally dangerous and detrimental to the welfare of married women workers' families, and sometimes denounced it vehemently,[50] the government proposal of 1880 banned night work only for women under twenty-one whose working hours were also restricted. The prohibition of night work for all women found its way onto the political agenda of the Iron Ring only in 1883 by way of Belcredi's proposal. Belcredi and many of his colleagues in fact thought that this prohibition should be handled flexibly—according to the needs of particular industries.

Finally, economic considerations also left their imprint on maternity leave, the second special provision for women of the Workers' Code. "Out of regard to the conditions of employment and existing practice," the Iron Ring reduced the period in which employers were prohibited from employing new mothers from six weeks to four, as the government had suggested in 1880 and Belcredi in 1883.[51] This provision covered not only large industrial enterprises but small ones as well. While the compulsory restriction on work after childbirth clearly affected the health and employment of the women involved, it was at heart a measure intended to safeguard newborns.[52] In 1885, when the Workers' Code was enacted, maternity leaves were unpaid. Against the backdrop of concern for newborns, in 1888 Austria followed Germany by securing moderate benefits under the Workers' Sickness Insurance Act—involving medical aid and pay—for new mothers during the four weeks they were prohibited from working.[53]

Following passage of the 1885 Factory Law, the Taaffe government immediately used its special powers to grant industries operating with continuous production an exemption from restrictions on working hours. They were able to maintain longer workdays, despite the fact that female employment was quite high in many of these industries, especially textile manufacturing. The Ministry of Commerce hastily issued decrees that permitted night work by women and even young girls in particular branches of the textile industry.[54] Because the prohibition on women's night employment did not apply to small workshops, employers could also evade it by scaling down the size of their production units.[55]

The Conservatives' rhetoric had promised an extraordinarily high measure of special protection for women. The results of their politics were less grandiose.[56] The hours' regulation was an incremental change at best. In many industrial enterprises workers had not, in any event, worked longer than eleven hours. The Workers' Code of 1885 set a standard that fell far short of the goals set by advocates of special protection for women. For example, breaks were not included in the eleven-hour day, but since workers were entitled to 1½ hours, they actually spent 12½ hours in the workplace. And widespread exceptions existed. In contrast to England, which restricted industries with high female employment, in Austria loopholes in labor laws rendered limits on hours and the prohibition of night work inoperative for the very industrial branches in which female employment was high. Conservatives were subjected to protests from employers who insisted that special protection for women would "badly harm the competitiveness of large, thriving industries, which has been gained by many sacrifices and great efforts." That hard-won competitiveness would only be sacrificed in the end "to the advantage of foreign countries."[57]

Austrian factory legislation passed in the 1880s was thus a compromise struck between Conservative ideology and economic interests. Given a choice between the aims of preserving preindustrial forms of production and "saving the working-class family," it was easier to pursue the former. The legislation of 1883 corresponded with small business interests in Austria, then, by rescinding free access to the trades. Moreover, the law of 1885 improved the competitive capacity of smaller businesses in relation to large industry by virtually exempting them from labor protection; the only exceptions were child labor (to some extent) and maternity leave. At the same time, the factory laws that Austrian legislators finally enacted did not fundamentally challenge the status quo ante, and it certainly did not force larger industries that depended on women's labor to adjust in a way that might have hampered their competitiveness.

◆ ◆

In the decades before World War I, gender-specific protective legislation remained caught in limbo as older, mainstream parties took a cooler view of its social promise and the ascending Social Democratic movement scrambled to find gender policies compatible with its labor policies and its base of supporters. The compromise struck between Conservative and economic interests in Austria in 1885 proved to be very stable. One reason why special protection for women workers did not receive a stronger commitment, despite powerful advocates, may have been that Conservatives and employers in Austria viewed the trends in female employment as something remaining within reasonable bounds. While the census returns of 1890 and 1900 are not completely comparable, the overall number of women in wagework seems to have

stagnated during the 1890s. There was, however, a significant redistri-
bution of women in the labor market favoring those industries most
dependent on female labor. In 1890 a quarter of all women employed
in industry, trade, and the service sector were in the textile industry,
but in 1900 the number had risen to 30 percent.[58]

Second, attempts to improve factory legislation fell victim to the
constellation of political power that emerged in Austria in the two decades after 1890. Acrimonious disputes between ethnic groups in particular caused political instability and marginalized social policy considerations. Mass parties made their appearance during this period,
triggering a fundamental realignment and reorientation within Parliament. Large parts of the former Liberal camp dissolved into parties
that pushed nationalistic politics into the foreground. Using aggressive
rhetoric, a new Christian Social party successfully claimed to represent
small property and gradually displaced the aristocratic leadership of the
Conservative camp. Finally, the years after 1890 saw the rise of the Social
Democratic party as the chief political voice of the labor movement.
After the introduction of universal male suffrage in 1896 and universal
equal male suffrage in 1907, the governments appointed by Emperor
Franz Joseph rarely had parliamentary majorities. After Taaffe's fall in
1893, twelve different governments were in power for varying lengths of
time; these resorted more and more to antiparliamentarian rule in the
years before the outbreak of World War I.

In this changing political setting, social reform and factory legislation
gradually became the domain of the Social Democrats. Their ascent
began with the unification of rival labor organizations around a program formulated at the first party congress in Hainfeld in the winter of
1888–89. While using Marxist rhetoric, this program and the actual politics pursued by Social Democrats were reformist at heart. Social Democrats aimed to modernize the Austrian economy and society, which they
viewed as extremely backward. Within this framework, labor protection
and social reform became central arenas for action for the new party.[59]

Austrian Social Democrats followed the lead of the Second International in the early 1890s, which hesitated to accept the gender-specific
factory legislation demanded by (male) bourgeois social reformers. The
Hainfeld Program of the Austrian party called for the eight-hour day
"without clauses or exceptions," Sunday as a day of rest, and prohibition of night work for all workers unless it was necessary for technical
reasons.[60] There was only one special demand for women: a prohibition

on employment in industries that posed a danger to women's health. What Social Democrats actually meant by this clause may be inferred from a statement by Karl Höger, a Social Democratic union leader. At the parliamentary hearing on factory legislation in 1883, he suggested that girls should only be permitted to work in factories after puberty "because a girl of tender years is such a delicate being and is exposed to so many maladies that a man cannot even imagine." Hard physical labor and exposure to toxic substances must be particularly harmful to women during menstruation, he thought, and work around the time of childbirth must be very burdensome for them.[61]

On the one hand, Austrian Social Democrats had good reasons to embrace such a program. Upon their arrival on the political stage, they had to grapple with labor protection as it already existed in Austria. Given this starting point, it made sense for them to push for a further general reduction of hours, as well as for a prohibition of night work encompassing a broader range of employment for both women and men. The Austrian Workers' Code even provided the possibility of banning female employment in industries considered to be particularly detrimental to women's health, but the authorities did not invoke this power.[62]

On the other hand, it is surprising that in the late 1880s and early 1890s, with the Depression not yet over, the Second International—and in its wake, Austrian Social Democrats—did not focus more attention on women's "competitive threat" to men in the labor force. In the 1870s and 1880s Austrian workers' associations and meetings had frequently demanded a "restriction of women's work."[63] By the first party congress in 1888–89, a lone speaker called for such measures, and his call fell on deaf ears.[64] In 1896, the unions came somewhat closer to entertaining the question of male-female competition for jobs, but—in accordance with the International—they demanded equal pay to defuse such tensions, not restriction of female employment.[65] What were the motives for this shift? Were the male leaders of social democracy genuinely committed to the rights of laboring women?

Austrian social democracy, as it emerged in 1888–89, certainly stood for equal rights. Female labor was regarded as an inevitable fact, necessary not only for the survival of many women and working-class families but also for economic progress. Working women thus figured as part of the underprivileged whose emancipation Social Democrats championed. What male leaders of the party and the affiliated unions strongly disliked, however, was particularism.[66] In their eyes, labor had a uniform interest in emancipation, and this view appears to have determined Social Democratic politics vis-à-vis women far more than ideas of equality.

At the party congress in 1888–89 and for a short period afterward the male leadership's perspective exclusively set the tone for this uniform interest. The organizers of the Hainfeld Congress declined to invite the only woman who had been nominated as a delegate, Anna Altmann.[67] They did not think women's issues were worth mentioning. May Day propaganda in 1890 pronounced hearteningly that with the arrival of the eight-hour day, "there will be eight hours left for rest [and] eight hours for education, information and fun," but it remained silent on how women would use this "free time."[68] The labor movement's stance on women at the beginning of the 1890s was challenged soon enough.

To begin with, Social Democratic leaders were well aware that women might have their own opinions with regard to the labor movement's goals. Altmann was excluded from the Hainfeld Congress because organizers thought that women were not yet politicized enough to deserve representation there.[69] Women activists in particular repeatedly demanded that women's working conditions receive more attention, not least because these conditions had a strong influence on male labor. Organizing women, however, posed considerable difficulties for Austrian social democracy.

Until 1918 Austrian law forbade female membership in political organizations. Unions were regarded as nonpolitical, but many of them refused or were reluctant to admit female members. Lacking an alternative, Social Democratic women began to organize themselves by taking advantage of the vague distinction in Austrian law between political and nonpolitical associations.[70] The threat of autonomous women's organizations finally mobilized Social Democratic leaders, and with the consent of women activists they decided in favor of absorbing women workers into existing organizations.[71]

Social Democrats now took pains to intensify agitation among women workers and to assign them to the unions. In 1892 the party started a special newspaper for women, the *Arbeiterinnen-Zeitung,* and the first congress of the Social Democratic unions in 1893 resolved that all affiliated unions were obliged to admit female members. In addition, the unions signaled their intention of establishing a special Federation for Female Hand and Machine Industry, a prerequisite for organizing the mostly unskilled women in "female" trades where hitherto no unions had existed.[72] These efforts by the party and the unions did not mean that female interests gained more importance within these organizations or for their politics. Strong resistance obviously existed when it came to acknowledging special female demands. Only after bitter quarrels did the party agree that women could manage the *Arbeiterinnen-Zeitung.* The unions, which were more important in this process, turned out to be even less cooperative.

After 1893 the plan for a special female union was never discussed again. Male union leaders instead began calling for the unconditional absorption of women into existing, male-dominated federations, where women were expected *"to preserve and promote common interests with male colleagues."*[73] Women had no voice in the Central Commission of the unions because all the large federations—including the union of textile workers—sent only male representatives to it. The unions themselves used almost exclusively male organizers, not only on the top level, but on the regional and local levels as well.

In this period, a gradual acknowledgment that women were part of the labor movement did not change Social Democratic leaders' attitude toward special protection. On the contrary, the party enforced its stance of equal rights and in 1892 added the clause "irrespective of sex" to all planks of its program.[74] Women activists seem to have shared this decision. Adelheid Popp (née Dworschak), the most prominent Austrian Socialist woman at that time, opposed special treatment of female labor at the Third International Socialist Congress held in Zurich in 1893.[75] At the parliamentary hearing on labor legislation in the same year she also spoke against differential treatment of men and women but insisted on a stricter implementation of the existing laws, including the prohibition of night work for women as well.[76] Still, the politics of absorbing women into male organizations without conceding a voice to them proved unsuccessful.

Women activists complained that their renunciation of autonomous female organizations had done harm to the mobilization of women workers.[77] Indeed, there were only 2,216 (4.7 percent) women among the 46,606 union members in 1896, and only 5,370 (4.5 percent) among the 119,050 in 1901. Only between 1 and 2 percent of the female industrial work force was organized in Social Democratic unions in 1898.[78] Male leaders had to admit that organizational efforts so far had been "thoroughly *inadequate*" and that women workers needed more attention.[79] Social Democrats also had a second, perhaps even stronger, motive to move more determinedly on women's issues.

Women's wagework played an important role in the campaigns of the Christian Social party, the Social Democrats' main competitor for lower middle-class and rural working-class votes when suffrage was extended to all men in 1896. The Christian Socials' program demanded that employment of women be banned where "the woman's health and her calling as wife and mother or [her] family life is exposed to danger, or [where it] creates unfair competition to men's work."[80] Contrary to Social Democratic efforts to stress equality of men and women in the labor market, restrictions of women's work sat well with many male workers. They felt threatened by female competition and sought priority for their own family life. "We don't have our wives and daughters to be the factory owners' slaves. Our women belong to us," a weaver and factory worker succinctly stated in 1893.[81] Women's work became a matter of a daily political confrontation that Social Democrats could not afford to avoid.

Social Democratic leaders had to concede more visibility to women's issues. After much stalling, the commission of the unions appointed a women's agitator in 1897.[82] When women activists themselves established a *Frauen-Reichskomité* in 1898, Social Democratic leaders grudgingly accepted this female organization: "The social democratic view may rule out separate agitation among and organization of women; rather, the goal must be to incorporate women workers into unions and female citizens into the political organization. Nevertheless, we cannot do without the *autonomous* activity of female party comrades."[83]

The unions, which — according to Social Democrats' views — played the major role in integrating women workers, were particularly suspicious of autonomous female organizations.[84] Women's sections within individual unions were only introduced in 1903, and these were obliged to act always "in agreement with the leaders of the organization and in close observance of the organization's resolutions." Moreover, the governing bodies of the unions, which were exclusively male in almost all cases, made sure that the women's sections would not discuss only topics of female labor.[85]

Social Democratic leaders acknowledged that women and women's work needed more attention. In 1896 they agreed to organize a hearing on "the working and living conditions of female workers in Vienna" jointly with Liberal reformers and middle-class women's organizations, and also with Christian Social politicians, despite the serious political tensions running among them.[86] Social Democratic leaders nonetheless continued to be critical of special protection for female workers. They took particular pains to distinguish themselves from the Christian Social party and to refrain from a strategy that might impede female employment. "There are two points of view," Leo Verkauf, the party's expert on labor issues, stressed in a public meeting for women workers in 1901: "the system of *exclusionary politics* and the system of *protective politics.* The Christian Socials believe that women's work ought to be forbidden. But we think that—giving full recognition to the necessity and the legitimacy of female work—we should only strive for the protection of life, health and morals of women workers."[87] Using the 1890 census data, Verkauf estimated that approximately one million women in Austria—widows, divorced women, and single women over forty— had to earn their own living, most of them by wagework. In addition, according to Verkauf, a quarter million married women had to contribute to family income by working in factories. The large number of working women could not be replaced: "In 1890," he observed, "there were 185,000 women in the *textile industry.* A complete standstill would result if you eliminated them."[88] Social Democrats were consequently also very cautious about demanding special protective measures for women that might stand in the way of their employment.

Still, with the establishment of the *Frauen-Reichskomité,* special protection for women workers was drawn into discussion within social democracy. Contrary to the position held by Popp in the early 1890s, and like German women who had also changed their minds, Social Democratic women—among them Popp herself—now energetically pushed for special measures. At the party congress held in Brünn in 1899, the *Frauen-Reichskomité* aired its demands for the first time. It wanted the party to agitate not only for the eight-hour day but also for a special reduction of hours for women, especially for a free Saturday afternoon. This would give women time to take care of the household and do family chores that otherwise filled their "day of rest," and— not least—it gave them a chance to take a more active role in the labor movement. Furthermore, Social Democratic women pushed for better regulation of the workplace through a female factory inspectorate and female lay judges for the trade courts.[89] Male leaders of the Social Democratic party and the unions obviously felt very uneasy about such schemes.

The party congress at Brünn quickly brushed the *Frauen-Reichs-komité*'s proposal for special protection aside, leaving it to the male committees of the party. Social Democratic leaders now recognized that women had special concerns and, little by little, gave way in subsequent years to women activists' claims for special protection. However, they were unwilling to abandon their equal treatment position, at least as a principle. In 1901 the party placed the demand to abolish "all laws placing woman in a disadvantage vis-à-vis man in public or civil affairs" in its official program.[90] Characteristically, the demands of the *Frauen-Reichskomité* that Social Democrats were quickest to incorporate in their agenda and most willing to defend were those calling for measures that would help women to enforce and protect their existing rights. As early as 1898 Social Democratic M.P.s posed a parliamentary question calling for female factory inspectors. Female lay judges for the trade courts also figured as an important issue in bills proposed by the party in 1909 and 1911.[91]

The Social Democrats saw fit to adopt the other demands that their women's organization raised again and again, but only if they corresponded to the party's "pragmatic" strategy. While special protection of women qualified as a "realistic" short-term goal, an intermediate step toward more inclusive protection, it did so only within limits. When all efforts for legally reducing hours had proved unsuccessful, the unions finally weighed raising the claim for women (and youth), for then "the ten-hour day will gradually be introduced for the whole industry."[92] In contrast to this stalling cautiousness, Social Democratic women insisted on the eight-hour day as "the most important and main demand for women rather than for men."[93] The unions did not advocate free Saturday afternoons for women, which they assumed required a major reorganization of industrial work and, unrealistically, an attendant reduction of the overall working week, though the party grudgingly agreed in principle in 1912. Male leaders deliberately sidestepped the argument brought forward by women activists that working women needed special consideration. Against this Otto Bauer argued that "with the [slogan] ten-hour day, everything will be said that needs to be said" regarding working hours.[94] Social Democrats did not ask for a sex differentiation with regard to hours in any of the bills for the ten-hour day that they had put on the agenda since 1909, although they were inspired by the introduction of the ten-hour day for women in Germany.[95]

Two further issues serve as good examples for demonstrating the for-

tunes of special protection for female workers in the eyes of those formulating Social Democratic policy: maternity benefits and night work.
In 1903 the *Frauen-Reichskomité* had resolved to push for a sixteen-week
maternity leave plus higher benefits.[96] Because this demand raised the
question of pay for a lengthy period of unemployment, it undermined
the labor movement's concurrent negotiations for a thoroughgoing reform of state social insurance provisions. In order to gain wider support,
the women's organization in the end reduced its demand drastically to
"what [it] believe[d] could be wrested out this Parliament, and that is
a protective period of two weeks before and six weeks after delivery."[97]

The unions and the Social Democratic party took up the maternity
leave demand in this downscaled form for the first time in 1907 and
again in 1909. At this juncture, however, they dropped their traditional
plank of excluding women from "dangerous workshops," asking instead
for measures to protect the health of all workers.[98] The special concern to protect female health had thus crystallized in the protection of
pregnant women and new mothers, who alone should not be allowed
to work. But the Social Democrats also simultaneously reinforced the
strategy of creating equal opportunities for male and female workers by
demanding the same protective measures for both groups.

Finally, the case of night work points to a very similar development
in Social Democratic views: acknowledgment of special demands for
women sensitized men to the shortcomings of protection for themselves. Differentiation by sex thus reinforced general demands. As mentioned above, the Social Democrats' main objective since 1888–89 was
to curtail all night work as far as possible. Austrian legislation prohibited night work for all young persons and for women employed in
larger workshops, but it allowed numerous exemptions. A first step for
the party and the unions, then, was to reject unconditionally any night
work for women and young persons.[99] The existing differentiation between the sexes as encoded in Austrian labor law—reinforced by both
the international Bern agreement of 1906 and Social Democrats' statements on the matter—made it obvious that men's claims for protection
had lost out. Although union leaders felt uneasy about it, the prohibition of night work for men was drawn into the discussion, and the
congress of the unions in 1907 resolved to demand a prohibition of
"*regular* employment of men at night."[100]

On the eve of World War I special protective legislation for women
thus still played a peripheral role in Social Democratic labor policy.

In the late 1880s Social Democrats had proceeded from a stance that relegated female labor to the background. Owing to political exigency and pressure from their own women activists, they were soon forced to devote more attention to it. Their first step was to unionize women workers within existing male organizations; only secondarily did they take special female concerns into account. In 1907 the prominent Social Democrat and leading official of the union of metal workers, Heinrich Beer, admitted it was "a mistake on our [the male] side that when we speak about workers, we do not think of the sex difference at all, but unhesitatingly demand the extension of labor protection to all persons in work."[101]

This concession notwithstanding, special protection for women remained an ambiguous issue for social democracy's leadership. In their eyes economic growth provided a compelling incentive not to take up special protection wholeheartedly. Added to this, women's work still appeared to encroach little on traditionally male jobs in the period before World War I. During the first decade of the twentieth century, female employment grew faster than employment as a whole in industry, trade, and the service sector, but female workers remained clearly concentrated in low-wage employment. The figures for women employed in the textile industry rose from 47 percent in 1900 to 53 percent in 1910, from 18 to 27 percent in the chemical industry, from 19 to 27 percent in retailing and merchandise trade, from 20 to 26 percent in food processing industries, and from 23 to 28 percent in the paper industry. Most of the highly paid male employment sectors were less affected; there, the figure for women remained well below 10 percent in the metalworking and engineering industries, as well as in construction and transport.[102] Finally, Austrian Social Democrats could tap into few alternatives to their stance on female labor. Economic conditions in Austria ruled out the family wages for men that labor in other countries may have considered an alternative to at least married women's work.[103]

◆ ◆

Economic and political equality were unquestionably important issues for Austrian women's movements, which made themselves heard more intensively from the early 1890s onward. Unlike their Social Democratic counterparts, however, these movements seem to have been interested far more in employment opportunities for middle-class women and educational issues than in the conditions of industrial labor.[104] The participation of several women's clubs in organizing a hearing on the working and living conditions of female workers in Vienna in 1896 appears to have been an exceptional event. It was remarkable not least because the women's clubs involved addressed a petition to Parliament on this occasion that closely recorded the complaints brought forward by the women testifying.

Working women could make themselves fully heard for the first time at this hearing;[105] 6 women (and some 36 men) questioned 178 women about their working and living conditions.[106] The women's clubs' petition referred to branches with high female employment where "everything that is otherwise cherished by mankind is placed—in the case of women workers—without defense or protection at the mercy of their employers."[107] In particular, the petition mentioned the exploitation of female apprentices, narrow and limited training that forced women into dead-end jobs, wholly inadequate wages, exaggerated fines for small infractions and overcharging for materials sold by the employers to the women, long hours, unsanitary workshops, and sexual harassment. The women's clubs behind the petition did not demand special protection for female workers to redress grievances. Rather, their demands betrayed close connections to the Social Democrats, who had played an important role in the hearing.[108] They demanded legal measures for more strictly regulating and controlling apprenticeships as well as wages and employers' practices of selling overpriced work materials to their employees. The only special demand for women's work was to ask for the appointment of female factory inspectors, who were expected to scrutinize sanitary conditions of workshops more closely than male inspectors obviously did and to function as women's confidantes in cases of sexual harassment. The petition did not ask for shorter hours or the prohibition of night work in smaller workshops, which Austrian law in fact conceded. Nor did it call for an end to the exemptions that existed for several female industries.[109]

The women's clubs obviously acknowledged women's wagework and tried to improve conditions either through general protective measures or by more adequate supervision of female labor. Their strategy was thus to confirm equal rights and opportunities for working women. Female factory inspectors were only expected to implement existing labor law and civil rights, which—in the case of women—were not respected. During the years that followed, however, activists in the autonomous women's movements found it possible to reconcile their aim of female equality with that of special protection for female labor.

The more radical wing of the women's movements appears to have sympathized with Social Democrats on the protection of women, although there were tensions between them.[110] *Dokumente der Frauen,* the journal published by this group, reported approvingly when the Social Democratic leadership joined in the discussion in 1901 after dragging its feet for so long.[111] The pages of the journal also failed to entertain seriously the notion that women's employment opportunities might be impaired by legal protection.[112] During the last decade before the war, the protection of mothers clearly developed into the main concern of Austrian feminists, and at least some of the more conservative among them went so far as to renounce wagework by mothers.

In 1907 representatives of the women's movements, together with reform-minded male doctors and politicians, founded the Austrian League for Mother Protection. This association opened an information office and a home for unmarried pregnant women. It also sent petitions to Parliament asking that the paid maternity leave as it existed for women in industry and trades be extended to a wider circle and that incentives be given to new mothers in factories to breast-feed their babies.[113] Marianne Hainisch, champion of the more conservative wing and founding member of the League for Mother Protection, went even further. In the 1870s she had assumed that women's work outside the home had positive effects on their families. But by 1911 she wished that "as many women as possible should become housewives." She also believed that "the most advanced persons, inasmuch as they are mentally and morally healthy," shared this wish.[114] In 1909 Camilla Theimer, a feminist writer, stressed the right of women to work as an "equal right for all." Nevertheless, she was highly critical of women's employment in "male jobs" and demanded special labor protection for women, which according to her was rejected "only by extreme feminists in England and France, who must cling dogmatically to their principles." For Theimer, special labor protection meant only a first step toward "special protection of the female sex." "The aim of reasonable social policy," she concluded, "must be to give the woman back to the family, not to drive her out of the home to an ever greater extent."[115]

A similar tension between equality, on the one hand, and the special status of women—and mothers in particular—on the other, even characterized the attitude of Social Democratic women before World War I. Indeed, their rhetoric brought female activists uncomfortably close to reproducing the functionalist ideology employed by more conservative commentators. For instance, Hanny Brentano, a Christian

Social writer, thought that there was a remarkable convergence of view-points.[116] The *Frauen-Reichskomité* was anxious to stress that it wanted "freedom and autonomy in economic and political life." But it saw legal restrictions on the use of female labor as a prerequisite for recon-ciling woman's "natural calling as a mother" with her "social calling as a worker."[117] Thus, for instance, in promoting demands for special pro-tection at the unions' congress in 1907, Emmy Freundlich, a member of the *Frauen-Reichskomité* who was mainly engaged in the Social Demo-cratic Cooperative movement and in child protection, stressed that the goal was "to protect the woman not as a person, but the woman for the sake of her most important function: the woman as mother."[118] On the same occasion Adelheid Popp earned "enthusiastic applause" when she argued that "protection of female workers is protection of mothers and protection of mothers is protection of children. Indeed, protection of the female worker is nothing less than the protection of the entire working class in the next generation."[119]

◆ ◆

In the two decades preceding World War I factory legislation in Austria made little progress.[120] With the rise of social democracy, the knee-jerk panic that had sometimes spurred the opponents of the labor movement into initiating social reform in the 1870s and 1880s turned into rigid defiance against labor's aspirations and all that went with them.[121] The stagnation was also a feature of special protection for women workers, although its supporters grew in number and virtually no one dared oppose the idea in public. Austria acceded only to the international agreement on banning night work, a prohibition already incorporated into its laws at home.[122]

The governments of the 1890s and 1900s were also very slow to use their administrative powers to regulate general working conditions. The Ministry of Commerce issued a decree containing general instructions on the protection of the life and health of workers only twenty years after the law permitting such intervention had been passed. Women's work played an insignificant role in this decree. It recommended sepa-rate lavatories for men and women in larger workshops but did not, for example, deal with female dress among its safety regulations.[123] Three of the five decrees concerning particularly dangerous industries issued after 1905, however, went beyond that. In the construction industry, women in an advanced state of pregnancy were limited to performing easy tasks and strictly forbidden from employment on ladders and at elevators. A decree banned all women and boys from jobs in paintshops and in the printing business that exposed them to white lead, lead paints, or lead type.[124] In the remaining two cases—the paper industry and sugar refineries—the government refrained from any restrictions on female employment, which was comparatively high in both branches, but excluded young persons from sorting rags, an extremely dusty and unhealthy job.[125]

The government proved remarkably quick in introducing female factory inspectors, a measure that did not jeopardize the employment of women and, as shown above, enjoyed particularly wide support. By the turn of the century the Ministry of Commerce had hired a few women to support male factory inspectors, and in 1906 these "assistants" received official status.[126] However, women's lack of political rights made the strategy of improving women's working conditions by introducing female supervision extremely limited at best. Women could not become factory inspectors—that is, state officials—themselves but instead had to rely on the good will of their male superiors for implementing any substantive action. Once more taking recourse in women's equality in economic affairs, the Ministry of Commerce even pondered the eligibility of women for the trade courts. The plan was quickly abandoned, however, for fear of creating a precedent for the political emancipation of women.[127] Dissatisfaction among state authorities about the conditions of female labor was highlighted by the fact that before the war (abortive) plans were drawn up to make "abuse of female and young labor" punishable by penal law.[128]

The appeal of special labor protection for women in Austria grew only when female work threatened to encroach on the domains of male skilled work. For example, in the printing business, where in 1911 women's work was restricted for health reasons, the share of female employment had risen from 15 percent in 1900 to 23 percent of the work force in 1910.[129] In 1912–13, a widespread strike occurred, with the aim of blocking encroachments by unskilled labor; it came to an end when state arbitrators ruled in favor of the male compositors.[130] Finally, during World War I female competition for hitherto male skilled work grew into a problem of great proportions when women took over jobs vacated by drafted men. "Woman ceases to be the producer of certain parts of goods, the production of which is suitable for her physical and occupational capacity," the Social Democratic unions now complained.

"Her work is no longer a complement to the tasks carried out by her male co-worker; rather, she has taken his place and thus rendered him superfluous."[131]

The war not only threatened to transform the labor market thoroughly but also left a decisive mark on the future development of the population. Under these conditions, special protection of working women took on greater importance. Despite a serious overall labor shortage, the Ministry of Commerce immediately withdrew night work permits for women and youth in the textile industry when production there slackened in 1915 and workers began moving into other industries.[132] When the war administration decided in 1917 to subject women to compulsory labor regulations in the armaments industry, women were still permitted to quit their jobs on grounds such as "far advanced pregnancy, nursing [babies], and fulfilling other pressing motherly or familial duties."[133] Using wartime emergency decrees, in 1917 the government extended paid maternity leave to six weeks after childbirth and introduced premiums for nursing mothers for twelve weeks. These measures were among the very few that Parliament transformed into regular laws after it met again in May 1917.[134] In mid-1917 the government promised to introduce after the war a ten-hour day for women and youth and free Saturday afternoons for women. The Social Democrats now began pushing these measures enthusiastically and found a majority in the Lower House to enact them immediately; in the summer of 1918 the government gave in to the pressure.[135]

In 1918, when the Habsburg monarchy dissolved, special protection for women had been on the agenda of Austrian social politics for almost fifty years. During this period the focus of discussions had shifted from equal economic rights for women to women's function in the family, a function potentially demanded of every woman. The strength of conservatism in Austrian society, briefly interrupted by liberalism in the one and a half decades before 1880, blocked the development of visions that transcended more traditional images of womanhood. The bourgeois women's movement in Austria chose not to advance an individual rights argument over the claim that sex-specific protection at the workplace could shore up women's commitments to their families. Social Democrats held fast to an equal rights argument and opposed restrictions of female employment as economically unsound. Nevertheless, labor opted for special female protection if such measures fit in with the agenda of pragmatic politics and if they promised a means of containing competition and de-skilling in traditionally male job sectors.

Carried further by voices in its women's organization, labor in the end also adopted a family ideology to underpin its nascent commitment to "women's protection first."

Notes

1. See Herbert Matis and Karl Bachinger, "Österreichs industrielle Entwicklung," in *Die Habsburgermonarchie, 1848–1918,* vol. 1, ed. Alois Brusatti (Vienna: Verlagder Osterreichischen Akademie der Wissenschaften, 1973), 124.

2. See *Die Arbeits-und Lohnverhältnisse in den Fabriken und Gewerben Nieder-Österreichs* (Erhoben und dargestellt von der nied. österr. Handels-und Gewerbekammer) (Vienna: Leopold Sommer, 1870). The inquiry that the Ministry of Commerce asked the Chamber of Commerce to organize in 1868 produced only rough data, as the Chamber itself acknowledged (ibid., iv–vi).

3. In the late 1860s the Austrian minister of commerce Ignaz von Plener sent his son Ernst, who himself later became a Liberal leader, to Great Britain to study factory legislation. See the account by Ernst von Plener, *Die englische Fabriksgesetzgebung* (Vienna: Gerold's Sohn, 1871). Parliamentary debates on the subject in Austria sometimes echoed the English discussion, particularly the voice of John Stuart Mill.

4. See Marianne Weber, *Ehefrau und Mutter in der Rechtsentwicklung: Eine Einführung* (Tübingen: Mohr, 1907), 342–44. For a similar point of view, see Hermann Conrad, "Die Rechtsstellung der Ehefrau in der Privatrechtsgesetzgebung der Aufklärungszeit," in *Aus Mittelalter und Neuzeit: Gerhard Kallen zum 70.Geburtstag,* ed. Josef Engel and Hans Martin Klinkenberg (Bonn: Hanstein, 1957), 262–64.

5. See Leo Verkauf, "Arbeitsvertrag," in *Österreichisches Staatswörterbuch,* vol. 1, 2d ed., ed. Ernst Mischler and Josef Ulbrich (Vienna: Alfred Holder, 1905), 157.

6. See Gustav Otruba, "Entstehung und soziale Entwicklung der Arbeiterschaft und der Angestellten bis zum Ersten Weltkrieg," in *Österreichs Sozialstrukturen in historischer Sicht,* ed. Erich Zoellner (Vienna: Österreichischor Bundesverlag, Schriften des Instituts für Österreichkunde 36, 1980), 125; and Josef Ehmer, "Frauenarbeit und Arbeiterfamilie in Wien. Vom Vormärz bis 1934," *Geschichte und Gesellschaft* 7 (1981): 444.

7. See Julius Ofner, "Der soziale Gehalt des allgemeinen bürgerlichen Gesetzbuches (ABGB)," in *Festschrift zur Jahrhundertfeier des allgemeinen bürgerlichen Gesetzbuches,* pt. 1 (Vienna: Manz, 1911), 462–63. See also Hugo Herz, *Der gegenwärtige Stand und die Wirksamkeit der Arbeiterschutzgesetzgebung in Österreich* (Leipzig: Deuticke, 1898), 6.

8. See Karl Přibram, "Die juristische Struktur des gewerblichen Arbeitsver-

hältnisses nach österreichischem Recht," *Zeitschrift für das Privat-und öffent-liche Recht der Gegenwart* 31 (1904): 696–98; and Ursula Flossmann, *Öster-reichische Privatrechtsgeschichte* (Vienna: Springer, 1983), 25. Special research into Viennese conditions shows that in the period before 1873 a large part of the working population was still subject to the domestic authority of their employers. See Ehmer, "Frauenarbeit," 445–46.

9. See Ernst Mischler, "Arbeiterschutz," in *Österreichisches Staatswörterbuch,* 1:210 (Hofkanzleidekret, June 11, 1842).

10. That the education of boys was put first is revealed by an ordinance of 1834, which ruled that boys should not be admitted to work in textile factories before the age of twelve, but girls could begin at the age of ten. See Ludwig von Mises, "Zur Geschichte der oesterreichischen Fabriksgesetzgebung," *Zeit-schrift für Volkswirtschaft, Sozialpolitik und Verwaltung* 14 (1905): 240, 245.

11. See Josef Weidenholzer, *Der sorgende Staat: Zur Entwicklung der Sozial-politik von Joseph II. bis Ferdinand Hanusch* (Vienna: Europaverlag, 1985), esp. 107.

12. See Kaiserliches Patent, Dec. 20, 1859, *Reichsgesetzblatt* (hereafter RGBl), no. 227 (hereafter Trade Code), sec. 84. See also Allgemeines Ver-waltungsarchiv (hereafter AVA), Justizministerium (hereafter JM), Post 17, Z.15599, Dec. 12, 1872; *Handausgabe der österreichischen Gesetze und Verord-nungen,* vol. 78, 5th ed., ed. Franz Mueller and Hugo Diwald (Vienna: Hof-und Staatsdruckerei, 1903), 422–23; Viktor Mataja, *Grundriß des Gewerberechts und der Arbeiterversicherung,* vol. 5, subseries 3 (Leipzig: Duncker and Hum-bolt, Grundriss des österreichischen Rechts in systematischer Bearbeitung, 1899), 65–66; and Stefan Licht, *Der gewerbliche Arbeitsvertrag in der Rechts-durchsetzung* (Brünn: Verlag der "Blatter für Selbsterwatung," 1898), 46–47.

13. The Trade Code of 1859 stated explicitly that "sex establishes no differ-ence relevant for admission to trades." See Trade Code, sec. 4. Note that the Trade Code did not explicitly mention the Jews, who had been excluded from a number of trades by former regulations. See *Handausgabe der österreichischen Gesetze und Verordnungen,* vol. 78a, ed. Ottokar Dokupil (Vienna: Hof-und Staatsdruckerei, 1908), 844–45. On the lawmakers' intentions in mentioning sex, see Franz Lakner, *Practisches Handbuch der neuen österreichischen Gewerbe-Ordnung* (Vienna: Leopold Sommer, 1860), 9–10.

14. See Trade Code, sec. 73.

15. "Report of the Parliamentary Committee," no. 208, Abgeordnetenhaus 1869, quoted in Ludwig Brügel, *Soziale Gesetzgebung in Österreich von 1848 bis 1918: Eine geschichtliche Darstellung* (Vienna: Deuticke, 1919), 121.

16. Ibid., 123. It is interesting that the report in this paragraph closely cor-responded to a declaration made by the Viennese Chamber of Commerce of 1868 which aimed to limit hours of children and youth but did not even mention women. Instead of "free agent" the chamber wrote "nonadult." See

Gutächtliche Äusserungen ueber den Entwurf einer neuen Gewerbeordnung: Nach Materien geordnet und herausgegeben im Auftrage des k.k. Handelsministeriums (Vienna: Hof-und Staatsdruckerei, 1879), 134.

17. See *Stenographische Protokolle über die Sitzungen des Hauses der Abgeordneten des österreichischen Reichsrathes* (hereafter StPr), session 8, vol. 3, 3525.

18. Hermann Ritter von Orges, *Die Weltausstellung und die Frauenarbeit* (Vienna, 1872), 18. See also Karl Thomas Richter, *Das Recht der Frauen auf Arbeit und die Organisation der Frauen-Arbeit: Ein Vortrag, gehalten am 10. December 1866 im Frauen-Erwerbs-Verein zu Wien* (Vienna: Pichler's Witwe, 1867) and *Das Recht der Frauen auf Arbeit und die Organisation der Frauenarbeit: Mit einem Anhange; über Ausstellungen der Frauenarbeit; zwei Vorträge gehalten im Frauen-Erwerbs-Verein zu Wien* (Vienna: Pichler's Witwe, 1869).

19. See AVA, JM, Post 11, Z.107, Jan. 4, 1870 (note by the minister of Commerce Ignaz von Plener, Dec. 28, 1869, Z.25531). The comment is printed in Brügel, *Soziale Gesetzgebung*, 70–77; the quotation is in ibid., 75.

20. For a detailed description of the proposals for a new labor law during the 1870s, see Kurt Ebert, *Die Anfänge der modernen Sozialpolitik in Österreich: Die Taaffesche Sozialgesetzgebung für die Arbeiter im Rahmen der Gewerbeordnungsreform, 1879–1885* (Vienna: Verlag der Österreichischen Akademie der Wissenschaften, Studien zur Geschichte der Österreichisch-Ungarischen Monarchie 15, 1975), 58–114, esp. 83–89.

21. See Johann Garber, *Die Frauenarbeit in der Industrie und den Gewerben und die Mittel zur Förderung derselben* (Vienna: Erste Wiener Vereins-Buchdruckerei, 1875), 15. Garber refers to employment numbers estimated for 1873 in Carl Holdhaus and Franz Migerka, *Die Verwendung weiblicher Arbeitskräfte in der Fabriks-Industrie und in einzelnen Zweigen des Verkehrswesens Österreichs: Erläuternder Text zu einer Abtheilung der Ausstellung im Frauen-Pavillon* (Weltausstellung 1873 in Wien) (Brünn: Winiker, 1873), 3.

22. Garber, *Frauenarbeit*, 17.

23. AVA, JM, Post 19, Z.11627, Aug. 20, 1875 (note by the minister of Commerce Chlumetzky, Z.23099, Aug. 9, 1875, Motiven, 79).

24. See ibid., 80.

25. AVA, Ministerium des Innern (hereafter MdI), Praes. Z.49/M.I., minister of the Interior Giskra to minister of Commerce Ignaz von Plener, Jan. 5, 1870.

26. See AVA, JM, Post 17, Z.15599, Dec. 7, 1872 (note by the minister of Commerce Banhans, Praes. Z.1492/H.M., Dec. 3, 1872), and JM, Post 23, Z.14151, Oct. 18, 1878 (note by the minister of Commerce Chlumetzky, Oct. 9, 1878, Z.30821).

27. See StPr, session 8, vol. 3, 3526.

28. See Hans Rosenberg, *Grosse Depression und Bismarckzeit: Wirtschaftsablauf, Gesellschaft und Politik in Mitteleuropa* (Berlin: Walter de Gruyter and

Co., Veröffentlichungen der Historischen Kommission zu Berlin, 1967), 227–52; and William A. Jenks, *Austria under the Iron Ring, 1879–1893* (Charlottesville: University Press of Virginia, 1965).

29. See, e.g., StPr, session 9, vol. 12, 13095 (Count Egbert Belcredi). For a description of these social reformers who maintained close connections to France, see Reinhold Knoll, *Zur Tradition der christlichsozialen Partei: Ihre Früh und Entwicklungsgeschichte bis zu den Reichsratswahlen 1907* (Vienna: Böhlau, Studien zur Geschichte der Österreichisch-Ungarischen Monarchie 13, 1973).

30. See "Die Frauenarbeit als Gegenstand der Fabrikgesetzgebung: Von einem Sachverständigen," *Jahrbuch für Gesetzgebung, Verwaltung und Volkswirthschaft im Deutschen Reich*, N.F. (n.s.) 9 (1885): 461.

31. Lorenz von Stein, *Die Frau auf dem Gebiete der Nationalökonomie* 6th ed. (1st ed., 1875; Stuttgart: Cotta, 1886), 24–25. See also Lorenz von Stein, *Die Frau auf dem socialen Gebiete* (Stuttgart: Cotta, 1880), 94–95, where he vehemently advocated special protection.

32. See Ebert, *Anfänge*, 117. The Ministry of the Interior in particular spoke for special protection.

33. This provision follows the Swiss model. The Swiss Factory Law of 1877 included a prohibition against employing women in factories for a total of eight weeks before and after childbirth; at least six of these weeks had to follow the childbirth.

34. See AVA, JM, ad Z.12000 (petition submitted by the Niederösterreichische Gewerbeverein to the Lower House of Parliament, Dec. 12, 1880).

35. See Ebert, *Anfänge*, 130–32. During the debates within the bureaucracy, maximum daily hours for young persons under the age of sixteen and for young women between sixteen and twenty-one had been raised to twelve. The Committee of Ministers (Ministerrat) rescinded this change (ibid., 137).

36. See Gesetz betreffend die Abänderung und Ergänzung der Gewerbeordnung, Mar. 15, 1883, RGBl, no. 39. See also Gesetz betreffend die Bestellung von Gewerbeinspectoren, June 17, 1883, RGBl, no. 117.

37. At that time Switzerland was the only country to limit working hours. Since 1877 it had restricted hours for men and women who worked in factories to eleven per day.

38. Note that this special provision was redundant if the sixty hours per week for all workers were read as ten hours per day, which was the case throughout the debates. There are no hints as to why Belcredi chose to standardize hours per week rather than hours per day. Theoretically, the standardization of hours per week granted more flexibility.

39. See Ebert, *Anfänge*, 176–77. (The proposal prohibited the employment of children under the age of fourteen; between the ages of fourteen and sixteen, children's hours were restricted to six.)

40. See *Stenographisches Protokoll über die vom 30. April bis inclusive 8. Mai*

1883 im Gewerbeausschusse des Abgeordnetenhauses stattgehabte Enquete über die Arbeitergesetzgebung (Vienna: Hof-und Staatsdruckerei, 1883), 358–59 (Gustav Pacher von Theinburg).

41. See Ebert, *Anfänge*, 179.

42. See Gustav von Pacher, *Zur Reform der Fabriksgesetzgebung in Österreich* (Vienna: Bergmann, 1884), 49–50. See also StPr, session 9, vol. 12, 12845 (the Liberal economist Emil Sax). In 1868, fifteen of the twenty-nine Chambers of Commerce in Austria did not oppose a general standardization of working time, although the restrictions would have had little meaning. See *Gutachten der Handels-und Gewerbekammern über die Regelung der Arbeitszeit in Fabriken: Herausgegeben auf Veranlassung des k.k. Handelsministeriums* (Vienna: Hof-und Staatsdruckerei, 1869). Several chambers had employed Pacher's arguments about child labor (see, e.g., ibid., 21–22).

43. Gesetz betreffend die Abänderung und Ergänzung der Gewerbeordnung, Mar. 8, 1885, RGBl no. 22 (hereafter Workers' Code), sec. 94 and 96b.

44. In addition, the minimum age set for entering a smaller shop was lowered to twelve; hours for children aged twelve to fourteen were reduced to eight. See Workers' Code, sec. 94, par. 1–3.

45. Ibid., sec. 96a.

46. Ibid., sec. 96a, par. 6.

47. See Ernst von Plener, "Gewerbegesetzgebung in Österreich," in *Verhandlungen der dritten Generalversammlung des Vereins für Socialpolitik* (Leipzig: Duncker and Humbolt, Schriften des Vereins für Socialpolitik 11, 1875), 88; and Ebert, *Anfänge*, 86–87, 120, 132, 137.

48. See StPr, session 9, vol. 12, 12874–78; and Pacher, *Fabriksgesetzgebung*, 50.

49. In the parliamentary debates, Leon Ritter von Biliński, a university professor from Lemberg, Galicia, and one of the champions of conservative social reform in Parliament, mentioned that according to government data 346,226 men and 178,261 women were employed in Austrian industry (that is, in factories with more than twenty employees). The textile industry employed 97,307 men and 98,605 women. See StPr, session 9, vol. 12, 12873.

50. For an ingenuous statement, see ibid. (Leon Ritter von Biliński).

51. See Ebert, *Anfänge*, 137, 187, and his note 44; Workers' Code, sec. 94, par. 5.

52. The maternity leave provisions routinely and without exception appeared among the provisions in Austrian factory legislation protecting child labor. See, e.g., AVA, JM, Post 11, Z.107, Jan. 4, 1870; Workers' Code, sec. 94.

53. Law, Mar. 30, 1888, RGBl, no. 33, sec. 6. The benefits amounted to 60 percent of average local wages for female work. The German sickness insurance law was enacted in 1883.

54. See Decrees, May 27, 1885, RGBl, nos. 84–86. For the lobbies de-

manding exemptions from the prohibition of female night work see, e.g., the petition by the Silesian Chamber of Commerce, May 13, 1885, in StPr, session 9, vol. 12, 12891–94, esp. 12893.

55. See Ilse von Arlt, *Die gewerbliche Nachtarbeit der Frauen in Österreich: Bericht erstattet der Internationalen Vereinigung für Arbeiterschutz* (Vienna: Deuticke, Schriften der oesterreichischen Gesellschaft für Arbeiterschutz 1, 1902), 10. Young persons were also prohibited from working at night in smaller shops (Workers' Code, sec. 95).

56. See "Frauenarbeit als Gegenstand der Fabriksgesetzgebung," 466–68.

57. *Gutachtliche Äusserungen*, 111. The case of mines also demonstrates well the compelling weight of economic considerations exerted on the Iron Ring's protective labor legislation. Employers' opportunity to make use of cheap female labor again received special attention. Here hours were restricted to twelve, regardless of sex or age, an arrangement that allowed for two full shifts. The only exemption applied to girls, who were restricted to "lighter" tasks until the age of eighteen, while boys were restricted only to the age of sixteen. The law did not forbid night work, but females were no longer allowed to work underground. To lessen the economic damage this provision would apparently inflict on mining companies, the law granted a five-year transition period. Maternity leave for women employed in mines lasted for six weeks, but the law allowed them to return to work four weeks after delivery with a doctor's consent. See Law, June 21, 1884, RGBl, no. 115. Female employment in mines and the metallurgical industry (*Hüttenwesen*) was rather high in Austria. According to census data, these branches employed 14,000 female workers and day laborers in 1890. Numbers significantly declined during the following two decades to 10,000 in 1900 and 8,000 in 1910. See Birgit Bolognese-Leuchtenmüller, *Bevölkerungsentwicklung und Berufsstruktur, Gesundheits-und Fürsorgewesen in Österreich 1750–1918* (Vienna: Verlag für Geschichte und Politik, Materialien zur Wirtschafts-und Sozialgeschichte 1, 1978), pt. 2, 166.

58. See Bolognese-Leuchtenmüller, *Bevölkerungsentwicklung*, pt. 2, 166–73 (assessment according to my own calculations based on table 58).

59. See Margarete Grandner, "Sozialpolitik und Gewerkschaften: Aspekte der Entwicklung der österreichischen Gewerkschaften 1880 bis 1910," in *"Dass unser Greise nicht mehr betteln gehn!" Sozialdemokratie und Sozialpolitik im Deutschen Reich und in Österreich-Ungarn von 1880 bis 1914,* ed. Helmut Konrad (Vienna: Europaverlag, Veröffentlichungen des Ludwig-Boltzmann-Instituts für Geschichte der Arbeiterbewegung, 1991), 30–34.

60. *Österreichische Parteiprogramme 1868–1966,* ed. Klaus Berchtold (Vienna: Verlag für Greschichte und Politik, 1967), 141 (Hainfeld resolution on protective labor legislation and "social reform," items 2–4).

61. See *Stenographisches Protokoll über die Enquete über die Arbeitergesetzgebung,* 51–52, quotation on 51.

62. See Workers' Code, sec. 94, par. 4.

63. See *Parteiprogramme,* 116 (Neudörfl Program of 1874), 121 (Program of the Wiener Neustaedter Arbeitertag, 1876), 130 (Kautsky-Program of 1882). See also Josef Schwarzinger, *Die neue Gewerbeordnungs-Novelle kritisch beleuchtet* (Vienna: Jacobi, [1879]), 17, 33, 36; as well as "Beilagen" to the StPr, session 9, vol. 11, no. 917. Note that German social democracy's Eisenach Program of 1869, to which Austrian Social Democrats were also committed, demanded restriction on female labor as well (see *Parteiprogramme,* 124).

64. *Verhandlungen des Parteitages der österreichischen Sozialdemokratie in Hainfeld (30./31. Dezember 1888 und 1. Januar 1889),* ed. J. Popp and G. Haefner (Vienna: Bretschneider, 1889), 49 (Anton Weiguny, a tailor and union organizer).

65. See *Protokoll des II. österreichischen Gewerkschaftskongresses, abgehalten vom 25. bis 29. Dezember 1896* (Vienna: Anton Hueber, 1897), 112, 120. It is interesting how the congress changed the wording of this item in order to stress the hierarchy of workers. The Trade Union Commission's draft of the resolution succinctly demanded "the same wages for women's work." After discussion at the congress, the final version read: "Women may not be paid less than men for the same kind of work." After 1896, however, and until World War I, no Trade Union congress demanded equal pay for women.

66. Given the experience of a split in the labor movement in the 1880s that had threatened its very existence and the permanent threat of a new split along ethnic lines, "unity" ranked especially high with Austrian Social Democrats. Taking refuge in a middle position—Austromarxism—they managed to avoid the ideological split over Eduard Bernstein's revisionism in German social democracy. The Austrian party did not disintegrate during World War I, as many Social Democratic parties in Europe did.

67. See Ingrun Lafleur, "Five Socialist Women: Traditionalist Conflicts and Socialist Visions in Austria, 1893–1934," in *Socialist Women: European Socialist Feminism in the Nineteenth and Early Twentieth Centuries,* ed. Marilyn J. Boxer and Jean H. Quataert (New York: Oxford University Press, 1978), 220. See also Gabriella Hauch, "Der diskrete Charme des Nebenwiderspruchs. Zur sozialdemokratischen Frauenbewegung vor 1918," in *Sozialdemokratie und Habsburgerstaat,* vol. 1 of subseries 1, ed. Wolfgang Maderthaner (Vienna: Löcker, Sozialistische Bibliothek, 1988), 101.

68. See Fritz Klenner, *Die österreichischen Gewerkschaften: Vergangenheit und Gegenwartsprobleme,* vol. 1 (Vienna: Verlag des Österreichischen Gewerkschaftsbundes, 1953), 139.

69. See Hauch, "Nebenwiderspruch," 101.

70. Note that the authorities tolerated women's attendance at party congresses.

71. See Hauch, "Nevenwiderspruch," 106.

72. See *Protokoll über die Verhandlungen des I. Gewerkschaftskongresses, abgehalten vom 24. bis 27.Dezember 1893 in Wien (Schwenders Prachtbierhalle)* (Vienna: Vorwärts, 1901), 9, 24.

73. See *Die Gewerkschaft* 7 (July 15, 1895): 4.

74. See Hauch, "Nebenwiderspruch," 106.

75. See the essays by Ulla Wikander, "Some 'Kept the Flag of Feminist Demands Waving,'" and Sabine Schmitt, "'All These Forms of Women's Work Which Endanger Public Health and Public Welfare,'" in this volume. It is interesting that Austrian Social Democratic historiography does not mention this fact or that Popp changed her mind in the subsequent years. Ludwig Brügel, for example, merely mentions that Louise Kautsky spoke about the protection of female workers at the Second International Congress in Zurich in 1893 and that Popp took part in the debate. See Brügel, *Geschichte der österreichischen Sozialdemokratie,* vol. 4 (Vienna: Verlag der Wiener Volksbuchhandlung, 1923), 222. Nor does Popp herself refer to her change of heart in her autobiographical books. See Popp, *Jugend einer Arbeiterin* (Berlin: Dietz, 1983). This edition contains both Popp's *Die Jugendgeschichte einer Arbeiterin* (first published anonymously in Munich in 1909) and her *Erinnerungen: Aus meinen Kindheits-und Mädchenjahren; aus der Agitation und anderes* (first published in Stuttgart in 1915).

76. See *Stenographisches Protokoll der Gewerbe-Enquete im österreichischen Abgeordnetenhause sammt geschichtlicher Einleitung und Anhang: Zusammengestellt von den Referenten Dr. Alfred Ebenhoch und Engelbert Pernerstorfer* (Vienna: Hof-und Staatsdruckerei, 1893), 945–50.

77. See *Arbeiterzeitung* 100 (Apr. 12, 1898) (report on the first Social Democratic Women's Conference, Marie Krasa). See also Hauch, "Nebenwiderspruch," 107.

78. See Klenner, *Gewerkschaften,* 1:283, and *Arbeiterzeitung* 99 (Apr. 10, 1898). There are no numbers available for the membership of female associations that regarded themselves as Social Democratic organizations. As mentioned above, Austrian law forbade direct membership of women in political organizations.

79. *Arbeiterzeitung* 99 (Apr. 10, 1898).

80. *Parteiprogramme,* 170 (1896 Program of the Christian Social Workers' party). See also *Stenographisches Protokoll der Gewerbe-Enquete 1893,* 991 (Leopold Kunschak).

81. *Stenographisches Protokoll der Gewerbe-Enquete 1893,* 1019. Twenty years later Anna Boschek, a prominent unionist, declared with irritation that even Social Democratic activists preferred that their wives did outwork because they expected them to stay at home and run the household. See *Protokoll des Siebenten ordentlichen Kongresses der Gewerkschaften Österreichs, abgehalten vom 6. bis zum 10.Oktober 1913 in Wien* (Vienna: Anton Hueber, 1913), 228.

82. See Julius Deutsch, *Geschichte der österreichischen Gewerkschafts-*

bewegung, vol. 1 (Vienna: Verlag Wiener Volksbuchhandlung, 1929), 316; and *Protokoll des Gewerkschaftskongresses 1896*, 121. Anna Boschek was appointed women's agitator. At the same time the Central Commission appointed an agitator for its Czech membership.

83. *Arbeiterzeitung* 99 (Apr. 10, 1898).

84. See Hauch, "Nebenwiderspruch," 108–9. Female unionists were also critical of establishing a separate women's organization. See *Arbeiterzeitung* 101 (Apr. 13, 1898) (speeches by Lotte Glas and Cilli Lippa).

85. See *Protokoll des vierten Congresses der Gewerkschaften Österreichs, abgehalten vom 8. bis 10.Juni 1903 im Arbeiterheim in Wien* (Vienna: Anton Hueber, 1903), 187.

86. See *Die Arbeits-und Lebensverhältnisse der Wiener Lohnarbeiterinnen: Ergebnisse und stenographisches Protokoll der Enquete über Frauenarbeit* (Vienna: Ignaz Brand, 1897). See also *Verhandlungen des sechsten österreichischen Sozialdemokratischen Parteitages, abgehalten zu Wien vom 6. bis einschließlich 12.Juni 1897 im Saale des Hotel Wimberger; nach dem stenographischen Protokolle* (Vienna: Bretschneider, 1897), 142.

87. See *Arbeiterzeitung* 44 (Feb. 14, 1901).

88. Ibid.

89. See *Verhandlungen des Gesammtparteitages der Sozialdemokratie in Österreich, abgehalten zu Bruenn vom 24. bis 29.September 1899 im "Arbeiterheim". Nach dem stenographischen Protokolle* (Vienna: Bretschneider, 1899), 121–33; and *Protokoll über die Verhandlungen des III. österreichischen Gewerkschafts-Congresses, abgehalten zu Wien vom 11. bis 15.Juni 1900* (Vienna: Anton Hueber, 1900), 210 (motion by Therese Schlesinger).

90. See *Parteiprogramme*, 148 (Viennese Program, item 12).

91. See StPr, session 14, vol. 2, 1139–40; and "Beilagen" to the StPr, session 19, vol. 4, no. 734; session 20, vol. 2, no. 189; session 21, vol. 2, no. 68.

92. See *Protokoll des VI. ordentlichen Gewerkschaftskongresses, abgehalten zu Wien vom 17. bis 22.Oktober 1910* (Vienna: Anton Hueber, n.d.), 320 (Ferdinand Hanusch, then leading official of the union of textile workers and later, in 1918–20, first Social Democratic minister of Social Administration in the Republic of Austria).

93. *Frauenwahlrecht und Arbeiterinnenschutz: Verhandlungen der Dritten sozialdemokratischen Frauenkonferenz in Österreich* (Vienna: Vorwärts, 1908), 37.

94. *Protokoll der Verhandlungen des Parteitages der deutschen sozialdemokratischen Arbeiterpartei in Oesterreich, abgehalten in Wien vom 31.Oktober bis zum 4.November 1912* (Vienna: Bretschneider, 1912), 246.

95. See "Beilagen" to the StPr, session 19, vol. 3, no. 575. (German and Czech) Social Democrats repeatedly moved the same bill in subsequent sessions of Parliament.

96. See *Was fordern die Arbeiterinnen Österreichs? Bericht über die zweite*

Konferenz der sozialdemokratischen Frauen Österreichs, abgehalten zu Wien am 8.November 1903 (Vienna: Ignaz Brand, 1903), 17 (Adelheid Popp). This demand corresponded to a motion of the Social Democrats in the German Reichstag.

97. See *Verhandlungsprotokoll des Fünften ordentlichen Gewerkschaftskongresses Österreichs, abgehalten vom 21. bis inklusive 25. Oktober 1907 im Arbeiterheim Ottakring zu Wien* (Vienna: Anton Huever, n.d.), 187 (Emmy Freundlich), 190–91 (Adelheid Popp). See also *Frauenwahlrecht und Arbeiterinnenschutz*, 43.

98. See *Protokoll der Verhandlungen des Parteitages der deutschen sozialdemokratischen Arbeiterpartei in Österreich, abgehalten in Reichenberg vom 19. bis 24.September 1909* (Vienna: Ignaz Brand, 1909); and *Verhandlungsprotokoll des Gewerkschaftskongresses 1907*, 202. See also Adelheid Popp, *Schutz der Mutter und dem Kinde* (Vienna: Lichtstrahlen series 21, 1910), 28–29.

99. See *Protokoll des Gewerkschaftskongresses 1896*, 112; and *Protokoll über die Verhandlungen des Gesammtparteitages der Sozialdemokratischen Arbeiterpartei in Österreich, abgehalten zu Wien vom 2. bis 6.November 1901* (Vienna: Bretschneider, 1901), 51, 59 (Viennese Program).

100. See *Verhandlungsprotokoll des Gewerkschaftskongresses 1907*, 202. The bakers union had asked the congress to pass a resolution that "regular night work" should be eliminated (ibid., 180); reflecting uneasiness about the economic feasibility of such a demand, in the end the resolution only called on employers not to employ the same men on night shifts on a regular basis.

101. *Verhandlungsprotokoll des Gewerkschaftskongresses 1907*, 200.

102. See Bolognese-Leuchtenmüller, *Bevölkerungsentwicklung*, pt. 2, 166–73 (my own calculations based on table 58).

103. For the United States, e.g., see Olive Banks, *Faces of Feminism: A Study of Feminism as a Social Movement* (Oxford: Robertson, 1986), 105.

104. See Harriet Anderson, *Utopian Feminism: Women's Movements in Fin-de-siècle Vienna* (New Haven: Yale University Press, 1992).

105. No woman was interviewed during the inquiries or hearings on labor legislation conducted by the Ministry of Commerce or Parliament during the 1860s, 1870s, and 1880s. At the parliamentary hearing in 1893, two women were invited: Adelheid Popp, as a representative for the Viennese association of textile workers, and Ottilie Wagner, for the (self-employed) Viennese milliners. See *Stenographisches Protokoll der Gewerbe-Enquete 1893*.

106. It is interesting to note that all female interviewees were listed anonymously (by numbers) in the protocol of the hearing, whereas male workers were addressed by their names, provided they agreed, or else by their initials. A "not negligible" part of the costs to organize the hearing had to be expended on unemployment benefits for women who had been fired for their participation. See *Arbeits-und Lebensverhältnisse*, xv–xvi.

107. StPr, session 11, vol. 19, 24714.

108. Three of the six female interrogators at the hearing represented Social Democratic organizations: Anna Boschek (Commission of the Social Democratic Unions), Adelheid Popp, and Marie Krasa (*Arbeiterinnen-Zeitung*). They were joined by Auguste Fickert and Therese Schlesinger, for the *Ersten österreichischen Frauenvereir*, and the Catholic writer Marie Baronin von Vogelsang. Therese Schlesinger (née Eckstein) left the *Ersten österreichischen Frauenverein* in 1896 to become a prominent Social Democratic women's organizer. See *Die Arbeits-und Lebensverhältnisse*, v–vi, and Anderson, *Utopian Feminism*, 87. Surprisingly, the petition was presented to Parliament by a Young-Czech and a German National M.P., not by an M.P. with close connections to the Social Democrats.

109. See StPr, session 11, vol. 19, 24715–16.

110. See Anderson, *Utopian Feminism*, 86–89.

111. See *Dokumente der Frauen*, 4:740–44.

112. See, e.g., ibid., 1:209–12. The journal reported the affair concerning the female compositors of *La Fronde*, the French feminist newspaper, but drew no conclusions. For the *La Fronde* case, see Mary Lynn Stewart, *Women, Work, and the French State: Labour Protection and Social Patriarchy, 1879–1919* (Kingston: McGill-Queens University Press, 1989), 138–39.

113. See Anderson, *Utopian Feminism*, 112–13. Obviously, women obtained some support by politicians for such demands. In 1914, Michael Hainisch, Marianne's son and from 1920 to 1928 the first federal president of the Austrian republic, together with a representative of the health administration, tried to initiate a bill on nursing rooms in factories. See Brigitte Pellar, "Staatliche Institutionen und gesellschaftliche Interessensgruppen in der Auseinandersetzung um den Stellenwert der Sozialpolitik und um ihre Gestaltung. Das k.k. arbeitsstatistische Amt im Handelsministerium und sein ständiger Arbeitsbeirat, 1898–1917" (Ph.D. diss., University of Vienna, 1982), vol. 3, 816.

114. See Marianne Hainisch, *Die Brodfrage der Frau* (Vienna: Gristel, 1875), esp. 20–21; and Hainisch, *Frauenarbeit* (Vienna: Hugo Heller, Aus der eigenen Werkstatt 1 [Wiener Volksbildungsverein series], 1911), 24.

115. Camilla Theimer, *Frauenarbeit in Österreich* (Vienna: Opitz, 1909), 249–51. For Theimer's role in the Austrian women's movement, see Anderson, *Utopian Feminism*, 20, 210.

116. See Hanny Brentano, *Die Frau in der sozialen Bewegung* (Vienna: "Austria" Franz Doll, Soziale Studien 6, 1911), 10, 12.

117. Emmy Freundlich, *Arbeiterinnenschutz* (Vienna: Ignaz Brand, Lichtstrahlen series 24, 1913), 38–39.

118. *Verhandlungsprotokoll des Gewerkschaftskongresses 1907*, 187. Emmy Freundlich (née Kögler) was among the first women to be elected to Parliament (in 1919) and worked with the League of Nations and the United Nations in the 1920s and 1940s. In 1934 she emigrated to England and later to the United States, where she died in 1948.

119. Ibid., 191.

120. See Emmerich Tálos, *Staatliche Sozialpolitik in Österreich. Rekonstruktion und Analyse* (Vienna: Verlag für Gesellschaftskritik, Österreichische Texte zur Gesellschaftskritik 5, 1981), 94–142.

121. See Everhard Holtmann, "Arbeiterbewegung, Staat und Sozialpolitik in der Spätzeit der Habsburgermonarchie. Strukturelle Bedingungen österreichischer Sozialgesetzgebung zwischen 1890 und 1914," in *Politik und Gesellschaft im alten und neuen Österreich: Festschrift fuer Rudolf Neck zum 60. Geburtstag,* vol. 1, ed. Isabella Ackerl, Walter Hummelberger, and Hans Mommsen (Vienna: Verlag für Geschichte und Politik, 1981), 253–54.

122. See Max Lederer, *Grundriß des österreichischen Sozialrechts,* 2d ed. (Vienna: Österreichische Staatsdruckerei, 1932), 328; Laws, Feb. 2, 1911, RGBl, no. 65, and Dec. 26, 1911, RGBl, no. 237.

123. See Workers' Code, sec. 74; and Decree, Nov. 23, 1905, RGBl, no. 176.

124. See Decrees, Feb. 7, 1907, RGBl, no. 24 (construction); Apr. 15, 1908, RGBl, no. 81 (paint shops); and Aug. 23, 1911, RGBl, no. 169 (printing). An early decree (Jan. 17, 1885, RGBl, no. 8) had dealt with the second spectacular case of industrial poisoning—by phosphorus—in a gender-neutral way. In 1921 Austria acceded to the international agreement on the use of (white and yellow) phosphorus concluded at Bern, Sept. 26, 1906 (announced Sept. 16, 1921, Bundesgesetzblatt no. 519).

125. See Decrees, Aug. 24, 1911, RGBl, no. 172 (sugar); and Sept. 25, 1911, RGBl, no. 199 (paper). The decree on working conditions in the paper industry explicitly mentioned male and female workers.

126. See Decree, May 5, 1906, RGBl, no. 94.

127. See AVA, JM, Post 304/30, Z.11189 and Z.20396 (notes by the Ministry of the Interior, Apr. 15, 1912, Z.10417, and by the Ministry for Public Works, July 8, 1912, Praes. Z.893); AVA, JM, Post 304/39, Z.5543 (protocol of an interministerial consultation, Jan. 20, 1913).

128. See Pellar, Staatliche Institutionen, 3:813–14.

129. See Bolognese-Leuchtenmüller, *Bevölkerungsentwicklung,* pt. 2, 168 (my own calculations based on table 58).

130. See Margarete Grandner, *Kooperative Gewerkschaftspolitik in der Kriegswirtschaft: Die freien Gewerkschaften Österreichs im ersten Weltkrieg* (Vienna: Böhlau, 1992), 34–35. Social Democrats closely watched the implementation of the decree prohibiting women's work with lead in printing shops. See "Anhang" to the StPr, session 21, vol. 13, 195; Sitzung, no. 2, 4681/I.

131. *Die Gewerkschaft* 20 (May 15, 1918): 114.

132. See Grandner, *Kooperative Gewerkschaftspolitik,* 126.

133. See ibid., 281.

134. See "Kaiserliche Verordnungen," Jan. 4, 1917, RGBl, nos. 6 and 7; Law, Nov. 20, 1917, RGBl, no. 457; and Law, Dec. 3, 1917, RGBl, no. 475.

135. See "Beilagen" to the StPr, session 22, vols. 2 and 6, nos. 276 and 1146; StPr, session 22, vol. 3, 4224–26. The end of the war and of the Habsburg monarchy came before the House of Lords could consent to the bill. (Under the conditions prevailing in 1917–18, the House of Lords did not have much choice but to consent.)

· 6 ·

Women or Workers?

The 1889 Labor Law
and the Debate on Protective Legislation
in the Netherlands

Ulla Jansz

Women's wagework in general and protective legislation in particular were hotly debated subjects in the Netherlands at the time of the first feminist wave, especially in the period from 1890 to 1910. Not only were they a bone of contention between socialists and so-called bourgeois feminists, but they were also the issue on which feminists disagreed most among themselves. Because it concerned the sexual division of labor—a burning question at the time—the protective legislation debate enables us to explore the different concepts of gender operating among social reformers, Social Democrats, and feminists of different persuasions—be they communitarian, moderate, or so-called new feminists.

In the first part of this chapter I will trace the path leading up to the 1889 labor law, which, among other things, limited the hours of women working in industrial jobs. By contrast, the law kept its hands off female agricultural and domestic work and all men's work. What were the lawmakers' apparent or professed intentions in creating this measure? Next, I will consider the debates on protective legislation that unfolded among feminists and their socialist friends and foes in the two decades after 1889. What range of contemporary understandings of gender guided the arguments for and against protective legislation? What arguments for and against equality and difference informed the debate?[1] In particular, I will examine images of the ideal future of the family and the sexual division of labor, for it is in these images that we can discern the social definitions of gender that shaped the debates about labor legislation. To which *group* of women did the authors of texts on the subject refer when they used the term "women"? Were these women imagined as married or unmarried, mothers, working-class or middle-class? Or did the authors have an underlying belief that women comprised a unitary or homogeneous social category?

The result of this focus on different gender concepts is that received historiographical dichotomies such as "bourgeois feminists versus socialists," "socialists versus social reformers," and "laissez-faire liberalism versus socialism" dissolve. Moreover, the texts of a surprising number of participants in the debate betray a double standard: according to these authors, middle-class women were conceded a freedom of choice that could not be extended to working-class women. Before focusing on gender ideology, however, certain facts deserve scrutiny. What was the extent of the social problem—women factory workers— that protective legislation was intended to combat?

In 1986 only 34 percent of the total labor force in the Netherlands was female. Of all European Community countries, only Ireland, Spain, and Greece ranked lower, and neighboring countries such as Belgium, the United Kingdom, and France had work forces made up of more than 40 percent women. While this profile of labor has begun to change in the last decade—in 1991 the percentage in the Netherlands had risen to nearly the same as its neighbors Germany and Belgium— Dutch women have traditionally tended to stay home after they married, particularly once they had children. In 1889, more than a century ago, the picture was not much different.

The 1889 census (*Beroepstelling*) reported that 27.3 percent of the total labor force consisted of women. In industrial employment the numbers were even lower: only 12.3 percent was female. Of these 65,668 women working in industry, a mere 29 percent (19,042) were married.[2] Despite these comparatively small numbers, the Dutch Parliament passed a labor law in 1889. With this new law the Netherlands became one of the first countries to introduce special protective legislation for women, the low number of women populating its industries notwithstanding. Consequently, this regulation of women's work must be seen as a result of the fears of the erosion of traditional gender roles that emerged with the beginning of industrialization, rather than as a result of the evils of this process itself. The symbolic value of the legislation is therefore far more important than its actual effects. Furthermore, the

law was ushered in without much discussion. Serious debate was delayed until the 1890s, when feminists began protesting such legislation
and socialists, who supported the law, voiced their suspicions of bourgeois feminist agendas for labor. Discussions became particularly lively
in the first decade of the twentieth century, when the Dutch women's
movement came to occupy a more diverse terrain and different feminist positions on the sexual division of labor became visible.[3]

◆ ◆

Beginning in 1870 a group of Dutch politicians dubbed the "young
liberals" began to challenge the laissez-faire liberalism which, up to that
point, had represented the most powerful school of thought in Dutch
politics and political economy. This new breed of reformers favored a
whole complex of legal measures to improve the material circumstances
of the working class.[4] Their first success was a law in 1874 banning children under age twelve from factory work. The demand for measures
against child labor had cropped up from the 1830s onward in Holland, especially from the ranks of philanthropists and social reformers
concerned about children's health and the lack of provisions for their
education. These voices emanated above all from the textile industry
regions, where child labor was not uncommon.

Industrialization in the Netherlands started late, compared to its
neighbor across the Channel. In 1870 the country remained predominantly agricultural, for industrial takeoff did not occur until the years
between 1890 and 1910. Thus, in midcentury factories were not a common sight in large sections of the country and their social consequences
registered but dimly across Holland. Similarly, trade unions made a delayed appearance; only a few were firmly established before the 1890s.

Industry's late arrival in the Netherlands may well explain why child
labor was not prohibited until 1874. A textile millowner, Samuel Le
Poole, was to play an important role in paving the way for the child
labor law. If the measure was a latecomer compared to such legislation
in Britain, Le Poole had in fact drawn his inspiration from England.
After visits there, he began to advocate similar legislation from 1859 onward. He was the first to introduce these British reforms to the Dutch
public, and they continued to serve as a model for the social reformers
designing later Dutch bills.[5] For example, in an 1860 report to the minister of the Interior, the inspector of steam engine works (*ingenieur voor*

het stoomwezen) advocated the British half-time system (6½ hours a day) for children between ages eight and thirteen. The report proposed a ten-hour day for thirteen- to sixteen-year-olds and for women; on Saturdays, their workday should not extend beyond 4 P.M. Moreover, they should be entirely prohibited from working on Sundays and at night. The restrictions would further "regularity, order, [and] cleanliness" and thus "the happy home life of the workers."[6]

The hygiene expert Dr. S.Sr. Coronel drew attention to the effects of factory work on the health of women and children at approximately the same time. Although Coronel's outrage—like that of other social reformers—was first and foremost directed against child labor, he did not have kind words for women's factory work either. In his opinion, females were by nature less suited for repetitive work than male workers; their health was more vulnerable to the ill effects of industrial tasks. Beyond this he insisted that factory work had detrimental effects on women's morality and on family life.[7]

In 1863 the government reacted to increasing protests against child labor by setting up a state commission consisting of physicians and millowners. After an extensive investigation, the commission recommended in 1869 that no legal prohibition or restriction of child labor be instituted. One of the commission's noteworthy conclusions was that such a law would lead to the replacement of children working in factories with women. Its report pointed out that English investigations had shown that factories undermined the "morality" of girls and women. Moreover, the commission's members reported with relief that married women in the Netherlands did not as a rule work in factories, instead remaining at home to care for their young. There was no point in their minds in replacing one evil with another, as state intervention so often did.[8] At this time, laissez-faire liberalism still dominated Dutch politics.

In the end, public indignation over child labor won the day, overriding all objections to state intervention in industry and even fears that the number of women in factory work would increase. In 1874 the first child labor law was passed; its main achievement was banning factory work for children under twelve. However, proposals for a similar prohibition of child domestic work and agricultural labor, and provisions for compulsory education for all children, were rejected. The law came on the initiative of the young liberal Sam van Houten and it was supported by the recently founded moderate (nonsocialist) general workers' union

(Algemeen Nederlandsch Werklieden Verbond). Acceptance of the law can be read as evidence for growing concern in the Netherlands of the 1870s about "The Social Question."

With this challenge to tradition finally met, social reformers hoped that state intervention in working conditions could soon be expanded, and to this end they paraded foreign examples of legal restrictions on children's and women's work. Indeed, their hopes seemed justified, because from 1874 onward the Department of Justice began investigating the possibilities of extending legislation. The Justice official G. J. T. Beelaerts van Blokland produced draft legislation that relied heavily on Le Poole's suggestion of using the English Ten Hours Bill model for thirteen- to eighteen-year-olds and women as a class; their workday was limited to a maximum of twelve hours, with a two-hour break for meals, and night work and Sunday work were to be banned. Beelaerts argued that "too toilsome and prolonged work by women undermines the prosperity of their families and the future development of the working class. It does so to such an extent that legal precautions are necessary in the interest of society."[9] Regulation of women's labor was all the more necessary, according to Beelaerts, because women would probably replace the children banned from work under the 1874 law.[10]

The young liberal social reformer Arnold Kerdijk pointed out, as Le Poole and Beelaerts had before him, that much could be learned from England, where labor legislation had gotten off the ground much more quickly than in the Netherlands. He also reported extensively on the findings of the British 1876 Commission of Inquiry into the Working of the Factories and Workshops Acts. In his opinion, the Dutch state should take precautions to ensure the health of future workers and the education and morality of its housewives and citizens. Excessively prolonged and unhealthy work undertaken by young persons and women thus needed to be restricted. But first, Kerdijk argued, the state of affairs in the Netherlands should also be investigated to create a sound basis for any legislation.[11]

The reactions of both industrialists and politicians to further labor legislation generally and a possible legal restriction of women's hours in particular were hardly favorable. Even Coronel, while not in favor of women working in factories, insisted that state intervention should at most apply to minors and that women should remain free agents in the labor market.[12] As a result, Beelaerts altered his draft to exclude women.[13] A bill presented to Parliament a few years later, in 1882, by the minister of Justice A. E. J. Modderman also contained restrictions for twelve- to sixteen-year-olds but none for adult women. Two consecutive bills offered up by Modderman's successor, M. W. Baron Du Tour van Bellinchave, likewise steered clear of adult female workers. Regardless, not a single one of these bills got through Parliament; by law they were dropped when Parliament dissolved in 1886 and 1888. Beyond this, it appears that protective legislation was simply not a priority for members of Parliament and ministers in this period, despite the exertions of reformers such as Kerdijk.

The Dutch socialist movement had also begun to develop in the 1880s against this backdrop. These socialists, too, began articulating ideas about legislative controls over women's work. The Sociaal-Democratische Bond (SDB) proposed to improve working conditions by demanding universal suffrage and the eight-hour day. These two measures were formulated in a gender-neutral way, but it is clear from their texts that socialist images of an ideal future were gendered. The "normal working day"—to be obtained directly from employers through class struggle, not by way of legislation—was clearly intended for male workers only. By contrast, the SDB demanded a legal restriction on women's working hours or even a total ban on work detrimental to women's health or morality. According to these socialist speakers, women—the mothers of the future generation—needed protection against these risks. Not far off was the hope and expectation that such legislation would alleviate another perceived ill of women's labor: pressure on men's wages.[14] In this optimistic scenario, the legislation would give men's wages a push upward. Thus, socialist leaders agreed wholeheartedly with liberal reformers on the question of women's labor, even while they remained adversaries on other issues. Ultimately, however, the first restriction of women's working hours came about through the initiative of young liberals, not socialists or trade unionists.

This legislation was a direct consequence of the Parliamentary Inquiry into Factory Work held in 1887 at the prompting of the young liberal M.P. H. Goeman Borgesius. Like some of his contemporaries, Borgesius had already, a decade earlier in 1876, advocated curbing the exploitation of women and children in industrial work. At the time he had argued that, while factory work was not necessarily ill suited for unmarried women, the married woman's place was at home, not on the shop floor.[15] Now he proposed an inquiry into the effects of the 1874 Child Labor Law and into workers' health and safety in factories and workshops. The timing of this latter proposal and the support it received in Parliament were very probably related to the social unrest that flared up in 1886 in response to economic hardships. Borgesius argued that the laissez-faire point of view had generally been abandoned and that the state should intervene to protect the weak, an essential ingredient for the creation of a more harmonious society. The inquiry should establish whether or not employers' self-interest needed to be checked.[16] This argument was characteristic of young liberals such as Borgesius and Kerdijk: the necessity of legislation should always be investigated beforehand.

The Inquiry Commission, consisting of nine M.P.s of varying political persuasions (including Beelaerts, an M.P. since 1883), was commissioned to address two different issues, basically along the lines suggested by Borgesius: Did compelling reasons exist for expanding the provisions of the 1874 law? Were government measures necessary for guaranteeing and improving health and safety provisions? A considerable number of workers (mainly male), employers, and experts (including, for example, factory inspectors) testified before the commission. Published reports of the hearings left a deep impression. Firsthand accounts from industrial workers about their working conditions shocked the reading public. The commission's final report recommended restricting the work hours of women and young people in factories and workshops but not those holding other jobs; it also included a lesser recommendation — reflecting the general sentiments of commission members — that many conditions, including long hours and work on Sundays, should be altered for men as well, but not by way of legislation.

Why restrictions for all women and none for men? The report did not address this question.[17] It seems, on the one hand, that the commission saw legal restrictions for adult male workers as simply beyond the realm of possibilities. On the other hand, one of the featured conclusions of the commission was that married women's factory work was detrimental to their families. Prohibiting female night work and work on Sundays, the commission believed, would better the situation. Paradoxically, the proposed legal restrictions applied to all women, regardless of marital status, while the problem the Inquiry Commission ostensibly wished to solve first and foremost was married women's factory work. The commission had considered recommending a total ban on such work for this class of workers but held back for two reasons. First, married women were clearly sometimes the sole providers for their families. Second, it reasoned—moral panic given full reign—that such a prohibition could encourage formation of illicit sexual relations: couples might decide to cohabit instead of marrying.[18] It appears that the intention here, then, was not to protect women but to protect the iconic working-class family.

Solutions to "The Social Question" offered up by the Inquiry Commission and by the subsequent 1889 labor law were profoundly gendered. According to these architects of labor reform, home life lay at the heart of aspects of the social question, such as child mortality and alcohol abuse. And here they targeted women by limiting their access to factory jobs. (The commissioners had no doubts in their minds that working women drove their husbands to drink.) Thus women were always cast as housewives and mothers, even when they were neither; they were not seen as workers.[19] Legitimate workers were men.

In accordance with the Commission of Inquiry's recommendations, the minister of Justice presented a bill to Parliament in 1888 that limited the working day for young people between twelve and sixteen years and for women generally to eleven hours. These workers were not to be on the job before 5 A.M. or after 7 P.M.; also Sunday work was banned, and the bill made compulsory a one-hour meal break between 11 A.M. and 3 P.M. Moreover, women's work during the four weeks after childbirth was forbidden.[20] (Compensation for the resulting loss of income was not introduced until 1930.) The law applied only to work in factories and larger workshops; agricultural and domestic labor, for example, remained completely unregulated. The first socialist parliamentarian, Ferdinand Domela Nieuwenhuis, who was elected in 1888, was the only M.P. to vote against the 1889 law. It did not go far enough for his taste. He demanded an eight-hour day for men and a six-hour day for women (the two hours less for women would enable them to do the housework before their husbands came home).[21] This never came to fruition. Yet it becomes clear that the official SDB party program statement that "persons of both sexes should have equal rights and duties" was not applied to the combination of housework with paid work, at least not according to Nieuwenhuis. Moreover, in this respect socialists did not differ from their political adversaries, be they laissez-faire liberals or social reformers. All agreed that women did not belong in industry. Factory workers, in a more or less distant ideal future, should be men only. Women were first and foremost (future) housewives and mothers.

The response to this classification protest from any collectivities of women, let alone working women themselves, was at first barely audible. In the years leading up to 1889, the women's movement in the Netherlands was still in its infancy. Women had only begun forming organizations that took on public opinion and targeted government policy for change. Furthermore, in the period from 1878 to 1893, only one periodical was dedicated primarily to the woman question, *De Huisvrouw* (The Housewife). In the course of the 1890s, more feminist periodicals gradually appeared, and, in addition, feminists published articles in various other weekly and monthly journals—including *De Amsterdammer, Sociaal Weekblad, Vragen des Tijds,* and *De Gids*—that attracted a more general readership interested in politics and social reform.

By the middle of the 1890s the Dutch women's movement had gained considerable momentum. In the 1880s, however, this was not yet the case; hence, the labor law bill had met with little resistance from feminists,[22] apart from a handful of articles in *De Huisvrouw* denouncing its provisions. According to editorials in this weekly, the bill went much further than the necessary protections against extremely exploitative labor conditions, for it prevented women who were struggling to make ends meet from earning their living. Why only protect women? Men's health stood no less open to harm through long hours and night work, the journal protested.[23] Yet on the whole the issue provoked little debate; by implication, a broad consensus on the undesirability of women working in factories existed, and all legal restrictions found ready assent. Once the women's movement began to grow in strength, however, feminist protests against the law became more and more vocal.

Although delayed, the controversy about whether or not labor legislation should treat women differently from men attained full flower among feminists in the first decade of the new century. The debate revolved not only around working hours but also around whether or not certain types of women's labor should be prohibited in industries that were considered a particular health risk, such as brickworks and potteries.[24] These issues were entangled with an ongoing and larger debate among politicians and feminists about the desirability of a total prohibition of the employment of married women or, alternatively, of mothers with young children. Working-class women in manual jobs were not the only targets of such prohibition schemes. Female post office employees and teachers in the Netherlands now also faced dismissal upon marriage. The debate on protective legislation and related issues as it developed in the 1890s was not directly connected to the labor law then in effect. It circled more around the advantages and disadvantages of the principle of separate legislation for working women, and of the sexual division of labor in general, rather than on the specific Dutch legislation that had come into force.

◆ ◆

Protective legislation—together with the question of whether priority should be given to limited female suffrage over universal male suffrage, or vice versa—became a major issue on which Social Democrats disagreed with nonsocialist feminists, or so we are led to believe. In reality the opinions on both sides were much more varied.

Feminist protests—in *De Huisvrouw,* for example—were at first mainly directed against left-liberal proponents of social reform. Gradually their targets grew to include trade unions and the socialist movement, both of which were only starting up in the 1880s. From 1896 onward, some prominent members of the newly founded Social Democratic Labor party (SDAP) agitated heavily against this feminist opposition to gender-specific labor legislation. The Social Democratic party's leader, Pieter Jelles Troelstra, and three female members—Cornélie Huygens, Henriëtte Roland Holst, and Henriëtte van der Meij—were the first to launch the attack against what they called "bourgeois feminists." None of them in fact had a working-class background. Their attack was inspired by similar agitation in Germany against nonsocialist feminists; German social democracy served as the model for the tactics and goals of its Dutch counterpart. With very few exceptions, no members of the SDAP seem to have questioned the desirability of special protective legislation for women workers.[25] If consensus on the short-term goal existed, the ideal future was another matter. The composition of the sexual division of labor was to prove particularly controversial.

The group that I will call "socialist feminists" felt that legal protection of women's labor was a defensible step toward protective legislation for both women and men. With protection for men politically far out of reach, they argued, Social Democrats should take what they could get: here, protective legislation for women only. This compromise did not preclude a different goal for the future, when women and men would labor with equal protective provisions inscribed in the law.[26] Beyond this, the position opposed a prohibition of married women's employment, a view resting within a Social Democratic tradition dating from

Friedrich Engels's *Der Ursprung der Familie, des Privateigentums und des Staates* (1884) and August Bebel's *Die Frau und der Sozialismus* (originally published in 1878 under a different title, and much influenced by Engels's work in later editions). In keeping with that tradition, women's employment—regardless of women's marital status—was seen as a progressive development.[27]

So argued *De Proletarische Vrouw* (Proletarian Woman), the journal of the SDAP's women's organization, which was founded in 1905 on a German SPD model. More surprisingly, in his booklet *Woorden van vrouwen* (an important weapon in the SDAP campaign against "bourgeois feminism"[28]), Troelstra also promoted social change that would free women from household chores and thereby ultimately promote equality in women and men's wagework. He argued that women were worse off because they had fewer possibilities for employment, so the changes would surely benefit them.[29] Just thirty pages later, however, Troelstra strongly attacked the feminist movement, arguing that the interests of proletarian women and middle-class feminist women were fundamentally opposed. According to Troelstra, if employment meant emancipation for the latter, the opposite held true for women of the working class. Protective legislation as it stood thus spoke to the interests of working-class women and not to those of middle-class feminists.[30]

Other Social Democrats took a dim view of total equality between women and men even in a remote future. Holst, for example, believed that women were fundamentally different from men, in body and soul; and men were better suited for certain kinds of work, women for others. It was in the interests of working-class women to alleviate their double burden by reducing their work outside the home as far as possible. Holst thus favored legislation that would keep women from working in jobs for which they were "unsuitable by nature."[31] The interests of middle-class women were different yet again: they could afford domestic servants to do the housework. Holst also believed in a future emancipation of women through the socialization of housework. But, according to Holst, this was not possible in the reigning nonsocialist society of the day.[32]

Van der Meij, Holst's sister in socialist feminist arms, did not believe in the socialization of housework, even in the ideal future. Pessimistically, she dubbed it "a castle in the air," at most within the reach of the bourgeoisie. Van der Meij thought that women were economically weaker than men and were thus entitled to more protection from workday exploitation. Because it seemed likely that women would continue to do the housework, they should work shorter hours outside the home than men.[33] In her ideal future, married women would not have to be gainfully employed; they would be able to dedicate all their time to their children. Echoing the Swedish author Ellen Key, whose work enjoyed considerable popularity in the Netherlands at the time, van der Meij criticized feminists for paying too much attention to women's employment instead of motherhood.[34] Yet the vision stopped at working-class women, as she protested vigorously against any prohibition against married women's employment in middle-class professions such as teaching or office work in the civil service.[35]

There was to be no unified Social Democratic take on women's employment. Social Democrats shared a belief that special protective measures for women (such as shorter hours and a ban on women's work in certain dangerous industries) were necessary for the time being. Opinion diverged sharply on the future division of labor, and this bespoke widely divergent conceptions about gender. Some Social Democrats envisioned a future in which working-class mothers did not work outside the home because the compelling economic reasons for doing so would have fallen away. Others expected that once a socialist society had arrived, housework and the rearing of children would be socialized, even while a traditional "natural" division of labor between the sexes continued. A third group of Social Democrats—mainly the founders of the SDAP women's organization—stressed the future equal position of men and women, even if they did not explicitly expect women and men to do the same work.

Barring differences over the future, the socialist women's organization joined together with the bourgeois feminists in protesting the marriage exclusion operating for women in white-collar jobs; they concurred that women in these jobs should decide for themselves how they would arrange life after marriage. Other socialists, too, applied a double standard toward married women, depending on their class position. For them, it was best for working-class women to stay at home: best for the women, their families, and the future generation. Middle-class married women should, however, be free to work. There was no simple binary representation operating here; gender divisions varied with class.

A final striking feature at work in this vision of gender borne by Social Democrats was their near silence on the fact that the shorter working day stipulated by the 1889 law applied to *all* women. Yet the arguments they used to support it applied only to women who had to care for families. Here, marriage and motherhood seemed to serve as the norm for all women, regardless of their age and actual marital status. Ironically, this may be said even of socialist feminists who wanted to close the gap between housework and other kinds of work and who in other senses challenged contemporary gender definitions. This silence, the upshot of this norm, in effect freighted all women with children, if not also husbands and boundless household duties.

For SDAP propagandists, all bourgeois feminists were indistinguishably the same. The well-known feminist Wilhelmina Drucker was often mentioned in this gallery of villains. She opposed special labor legislation for women because she saw it as an obstacle to full economic independence for women, married or not. But, contrary to SDAP propaganda, the majority of feminists outside the SDAP did not share her views. And so a new label was born. A large group of feminists began calling themselves "moderate," to distinguish their ideas from this so-called ultra-feminism.

I will return to these moderate feminists below. First, I will focus on the so-called ultra-feminists. Coined in an internecine political struggle among feminists, the term was and remains problematic. Previous researchers have already suggested that many of the women called "ultra" or even "dogmatic" feminists by their adversaries did not actually adhere to the views ascribed to them.[36] The accusation that these feminists wanted to abolish the family serves as a good illustration; this was in essence advocated by a small, yet compelling group of feminists, among whom Drucker played a prominent part. The label "communitarian feminist" is perhaps more apt in their case, for the most distinguishing feature of their feminism is that they sought to replace the existing familial arrangements, with their attendant sexual division of labor, with communitarian household forms. In their view, this goal could be reached in the not-too-distant future. Domestic labor would cease to be unpaid work done by all women and become an occupation that required proper training. Furthermore, working hours in domestic labor would become comparable with those in other occupations.[37] Most housework would be carried out by the professional domestic workers of the cooperative household, and every individual, woman and man, would do the remainder for herself or himself.

In the 1890s these ideas found their main forum in the pages of the feminist biweekly *Evolutie,* edited by Drucker and Theodora Schook-Haver. After the turn of the century, a larger group of feminists began to voice sympathy with these positions. Perhaps Charlotte Perkins Gilman's *Women and Economics* influenced them; the Dutch translation had appeared in 1900. Gilman's ideas on the importance of economic independence for women and cooperative housework became even more widespread after her lecture tour in Europe in 1904–5.[38] Another influential book containing similar suggestions was *Die Frauenfrage* (1901), by the German Social Democrat Lily Braun, translated into Dutch in 1902. While other Dutch feminists did not write about the cooperative household as the ideal solution for the future, many *did* dispute the assumption that housework was a task assigned to women by nature. They appear to have believed that ever-advancing mechanization and industrialization would eventually be harnessed to tackle all domestic work and essentially dispense with it. In the future, they reckoned, it could be done more easily by individuals for themselves, or perhaps by traditional domestic servants, their burdens greatly reduced.[39]

The communitarian feminists opposed special legal protection for women workers, not because they failed to see the problem of the double burden, but because they sought to alleviate women's household tasks rather than their wagework. Housework was the burden that begged for reform. In a famous 1903 debate between two SDAP members, Marie Rutgers-Hoitsema and Henriëtte Roland Holst, Rutgers-Hoitsema took a rather communitarian stand. In her opinion, the proletariat could not be liberated without the simultaneous emancipation of women, and the emancipation of women was not possible as long as women remained economically dependent on their husbands. But women could only become the equals of men when they were liberated from the slavery of housework.[40] Holst countered this by repeating the argument often heard among Social Democrats: legal protection of working women was necessary for safeguarding their health and that of their offspring.[41] According to some historians, Rutgers-Hoitsema was voicing the opinion held by the majority of the bourgeois women's movement.[42] However, Rutgers-Hoitsema was not only a member of the SDAP at the time but her analysis also bears certain typical Social Democratic traits—an impression confirmed by her references to Bebel and Kautsky.[43]

The main difference between these two socialist women thus lay not in their class background (middle class on both counts), nor in the strength of their political conviction, but in their concept of gender. According to Rutgers-Hoitsema, men and women were certainly different; but, she argued, not only should they have equal rights in the labor market but an equal position in housework. Holst voiced much more ambivalence: on the one hand, she envisaged a socialist family of the future held together not by economic obligations but by moral obligations and affection;[44] on the other hand, she favored perpetuating the division of labor in the family as it had long existed.

This debate seems to indicate that the communitarian feminist solution to the woman question was not so fundamentally different from certain Social Democratic solutions. Both rejected the assumption that wage labor ought to be an exclusively male task. They disagreed primarily on when their ideal division of labor might be realized. It remains unclear, however, whether or not any sexual segregation of labor would survive in this ideal future. Both groups were inspired by the utopian socialist[45] tradition, some by way of Bebel's and Engels's work, others most likely through H. P. G. Quack's *De socialisten*. Others again must have soaked up the promises offered in the writings of Braun and Gilman. However, only very few Social Democrats went as far as the communitarians in challenging the construction of housework as a "natural" female task.

The feminists whom the Social Democrats attacked so vehemently were precisely these congenial communitarians, a familiar phenomenon within the Left, where often more energy was spent on combating the "next-of-kin," who were seen as direct competitors for a small pool of potential supporters. Peculiarly, the socialists paid little attention to the much larger section of the women's movement, those who called themselves "moderate feminists." Nor did they pay attention to the feminist group that began to organize soon after the turn of the century.

From the very beginning of the first feminist wave in the 1860s, many feminists had stood by the conviction that women differed fundamentally from men; for this reason, they argued, women's education desperately needed to be improved. Motherhood was a far too responsible task to be performed by uneducated women. Furthermore, educated women could as housewives and mothers influence their husbands and sons and in this way contribute to a better society and a brighter future. Under the influence of John Stuart Mill's *Subjection of Women* (1869), translated in 1870, the difference argument gradually lost ground in Dutch feminism to arguments that stressed the equality of women and men, their common humanity. The tide turned again beginning in the 1890s, and difference regained its appeal. This was difference with a nuance: now it often appeared in combination with equality arguments,[46] and the feminist tradition that adopted it primarily came to identify "womanliness" as "motherliness."

In keeping with this motherly turn, during the years just after 1900 a group of feminists began calling themselves "new feminists," in opposition to "old" or "ultra" feminists. According to these new feminists, the old feminists denied the laws of nature by propagating economic equality with and economic independence from men. Ironically, the equality feminism they called "old" was in fact of much more recent origin than their own difference feminism, which—some nuances notwithstanding—arguably dated back to the 1860s.

One of the first to formulate a theory of two tendencies within feminism was Ida Heyermans, from 1900 onward the editor of the biweekly *De Vrouw.* Invariably one of the issues that she focused on to indicate clear differences between old and new feminists was special legal protection for women's labor. She herself identified with the new feminism and energetically argued the case for such special legislation. Elisabeth van Dorp and Welmoet Wijnaendts Francken-Dyserinck shared her viewpoint. They took the initiative and engineered a split in the Vereeniging voor Vrouwenkiesrecht (Women's Suffrage Association) in 1906–7 on the grounds that it had become dominated by ultrafeminists.[47] Already back in 1904—issuing a self-fulfilling prophecy— Van Dorp had speculated that the issue of protective legislation and married women's employment would divide the women's movement in the end.[48]

Yet another direction within Dutch feminism can be detected from 1911 onward. Its advocates were Clara Wichmann, W. H. M. Werker, and his wife, Corrie Werker-Beaujon, and they called it "ethical feminism." Their ideas appeared in the weekly *De vrouw in de XXste eeuw* (The Woman in the Twentieth Century) and in a collection of articles, *De vrouw, de vrouwenbeweging en het vrouwenvraagstuk* (The Woman, the Women's Movement and the Woman Question). This group was neither identical to the new feminists nor did they share the same ideas on the woman question. Ethical feminists favored not only the free development of women's womanly faculties but also their economic independence, which new feminists so vehemently opposed. In fact, however, both groups very much favored protective legislation for women.[49] Moreover, in this respect alone did they share a patch of common ground with the Social Democrats. They otherwise differed on many points, most notably on the class struggle doctrine. Their understanding of womanliness as motherliness bears a striking resemblance to the views held by Social Democrats such as Huygens and Holst.

The protests of some feminists such as Drucker and Rutgers-Hoitsema against unequal treatment of women and men before the law could not ultimately prevent the passage of legislation in 1912 limiting the working day for women (and young people) to a maximum of ten hours. Working hours for adult men remained unrestricted except for those in such strenuous occupations as mining and dockwork. Married female factory workers were also forbidden from working Saturday afternoons after 1 P.M. This provision, supported by socialist members of Parliament, was introduced to enable these women to do the housework on the weekend.[50] It is thus nearly impossible to read this simply as an ephemeral way station on the road to general sex-blind laws. Virtually all Dutch political players appear to have inextricably and unapologetically invested protection with a vision of gender. The general debate on labor legislation did not come to an end until after World War I, when the working day for all adults, women and men, was reduced to eight hours by the Arbeidswet of 1919, the very year that Dutch women got the vote.

◆ ◆

There can be no doubt that the architects of the 1889 labor law believed that married women should stay at home, as women generally were already doing in the Netherlands, rather than go to work in factories or workshops. Earlier, lawmakers had expressed some reservations about whether or not women could be subjected to such legal restrictions, but the only member of the Dutch Parliament to vote against the bill was the newly elected and lone socialist member who thought the provision did not go far enough. He, too, wanted women to work shorter hours than men, and for the same reason: women should be able to do the housework properly. Like the other politicians, socialists did not differentiate between married and unmarried women in this respect either. For them workers were male, and females were categorically housewives and mothers, be it then and there or in the future. Protective legislation was formulated accordingly.

A study of the debate on legal restrictions of women's labor in the period between 1895 and 1910 shows that neither a single socialist feminist nor a single bourgeois (or nonsocialist) feminist point of view really existed on the question. Many women whom Social Democrats identified as bourgeois feminists did not in fact advocate the view ascribed to them by their political adversaries. Finally, many nonsocialist feminists appear to have made common cause with a number of Social Democrats on various facets of the woman question, including gender-specific protective legislation. Moreover, arguments about free choice emanating from laissez-faire liberalism played at best a minor role in this debate. The majority of the feminist opponents to special protective legislation for women were not against protective legislation if women and men were protected equally. But labor law was not theirs to remake.

The division of labor between housewife and breadwinner provoked fundamental disagreements in the Netherlands in the late nineteenth and early twentieth centuries. Our understanding of these debates is greatly enhanced if we step beyond the chasm between socialism and bourgeois feminism or laissez-faire liberalism. A gender analysis makes it possible to distinguish between and among feminist ideas on the woman question, and the prejudices of—or deliberate misrepresentations of these ideas by—contemporary socialists and other political adversaries. If some feminists applied the same standards to *all* women, others parted ways where middle-class women tread, wishing to reserve for them the privilege to choose employment after marriage. In the eyes of the latter, "wife" and "worker" were mutually exclusive categories only in the case of working-class women. This was also the dominant Social Democratic position, one taken by socialist feminists as well. But the debates on protective legislation in the Netherlands among these movements provide a fertile source from which to harvest changing and manifold social definitions of women and femininity.

Notes

This essay is based on a paper titled "Gender Constructions in the Dutch Debate on Protective Legislation for Women around 1900," which was presented at the seminar "Gender as a Category of Historical Analysis," held at Groningen University on April 5–6, 1989. Mieke Aerts, Louis Heynsbroek, Els Kloek, Anja Petrakopoulos, Saskia Poldervaart, and Joan Scott provided helpful comments on that paper. Later versions have benefited from discussions with the participants of the research project on protective labor legislation at our conferences in Louvain and Mariefred and from comments by individual members of the group.

1. This focus relates to the second element in the first part of Joan Wallach Scott's gender definition. See *Gender and the Politics of History* (New York: Columbia University Press, 1988), 43.

2. Wantje Fritschy, "De economische ontwikkelingen in Nederland in de 19e eeuw en de vrouwenarbeid," in *Vrouwen, Kiesrecht en Arbeid in Nederland 1889–1919,* ed. Josine Blok et al. (Groningen: SSGN, 1977), 114. As Fritschy points out, these data are not very dependable. But here the main point is that they were the only numbers available to the politicians of the period who discussed protective legislation for women. In the years 1908–9 the first careful survey of married women's factory work was carried out. The total number of female factory workers was put at 43,844 (14.4 percent) in a total adult industrial work force of 304,437. Of these women, only 5,256 (12 percent) were married (including widows and divorced or deserted women—1.7 percent of the total industrial work force). See *Onderzoek naar den fabrieksarbeid van gehuwde vrouwen in Nederland* ('s-Gravenhage: Landsdrukkerij, 1911), 12–13, 26–27.

3. Ulla Jansz, *Denken over sekse in de eerste feministische golf* (Amsterdam: Sara/Van Gennep, 1990), chap. 6.

4. G. Taal, *Liberalen en radicalen in Nederland* (Den Haag: Martinus Nijhoff, 1980), 29–42. See also Siep Stuurman, "Samuel van Houten and Dutch Liberalism, 1860–90," *Journal of the History of Ideas* 50 (1989): 135–52.

5. I. J. Brugmans, *De arbeidende klasse in Nederland in de 19e eeuw 1813–1870,* 8th ed. (Utrecht: Het Spectrum, 1970), 207; A. Postma, *De mislukte pogingen tussen 1874 en 1889 tot verbetering en uitbreiding van de Kinderwet-Van Houten* (Deventer: Kluwer, 1977), 25–32.

6. "Rapport van den ingenieur van het stoomwezen aan Van Heemstra," *Economisch-Historisch Jaarboek* 4 (1918), 33. This inspector was A. A. C. de Vries Robbé.

7. S. Sr. Coronel, *De gezondheidsleer toegepast op de fabrieknijverheid* (Haarlem: Loosjes, 1861), 59–62.

8. *Rapport der commissie belast met het onderzoek naar den toestand der kinderen in fabrieken arbeidende* ('s-Gravenhage: Minister van Binnenlandsche Zaken, 1869–72), 23–24.

9. Memorie van Toelichting bij Ontwerp–1876, as quoted by Postma, *Mislukte pogingen,* 26.

10. Ibid., 23.

11. A. Kerdijk, "De Engelse wetgeving op den kinder-en vrouwenarbeid in fabrieken en werkplaatsen I–IV," *De Economist* 26 (1877), II:949–70, 1024–45, 1077–102; 27 (1878), I:284–301; and A. Kerdijk, "De Wet op den Kinderarbeid," *Vragen des Tijds* 4 (1878), I:93–149. See also Armand Sassen,

"Nadeelige vrijheid en noodzakelijke dwang," *Vragen des Tijds* 4 (1878), I:363–405.

12. S. Sr. Coronel, "In hoever is uitbreiding van de Wet op den Kinderarbeid wenschelijk en uitvoerbaar?" *De Economist* 26 (1877), I:387. See also "Advies van Directeuren der Nederlandsche Maatschappij ter bevordering van Nijverheid over de vraagpunten betreffende wettelijke bepalingen tegen overmatige arbeid van kinderen," *Tijdschrift uitgegeven door de Nederlandsche Maatschappij ter Bevordering van Nijverheid* 40 (1877): 106–7; and G. Bosch, "Kinder-arbeid," *De Economist* 26 (1877), I:204–6.

13. Postma, *Mislukte pogingen*, 34–36.

14. F. Domela Nieuwenhuis, "Internationale arbeidswetgeving," *Vragen des Tijds* 8 (1882), I:276–85; A. H. Gerhard, *Is het algemeende stemrecht eene noodzakelijkheid?* (Groningen: Schut, [1884]), 9–10. See also Fia Dieteren and Ingrid Peeterman, *Vrije vrouwen of werkmansvrouwen? Vrouwen in de Sociaal-Democratische Bond (1879–1894)* (Utrecht: Fishluc, 1984), 49–51.

15. H. Goeman Borgesius, "Stoommachines en volkswelvaart," *Vragen des Tijds* 1 (1876): 20–29.

16. I. J. Brugmans, *Paardenkracht en mensenmacht: Sociaal-economische geschiedenis van Nederland 1795–1940*, 2d ed. ('s-Gravenhage: Nijhoff, 1969), 403–4; Taal, *Liberalen en radicalen*, 119–20.

17. See also Ulla Jansz, "Sociale kwestie en sekse in de politieke geschiedenis: De Arbeidswet van 1889," in *Op het strijdtoneel van de politiek: Twaalfde Jaarboek voor Vrouwengeschiedenis,* ed. Marjan Schwegman et al. (Nijmegen: SUN, 1991).

18. "Verslag der commissie" (Eindverslag), *Een kwaad leven: De arbeidsequête van 1887. Deel III.* (Nijmegen: Link, 1981), 87–88.

19. Marianne Braun, *De prijs van de liefde: De eerste feministische golf, het huwelijksrecht en de vaderlandse geschiedenis* (Amsterdam: Het Spinhuis, 1992), 82–89. See also Scott, *Gender and the Politics of History*, 53–163, and Carole Pateman, *The Sexual Contract* (Cambridge, U.K.: Polity Press, 1988), 125–42.

20. *Handelingen Tweede Kamer* 1888–89, Bijlagen, no. 53.

21. Dieteren and Peeterman, *Vrije vrouwen*, 50–51.

22. The term "feminist" is, strictly speaking, an anachronism here, for it only came into use in the Netherlands in the early 1890s. But from then on it was used widely by persons and groups favoring changes in the position of women and/or in ideas about women.

23. *De Huisvrouw* 18, nos. 31, 33–34, 38–40 (1888–89).

24. I get the impression from the sources I know that trade unionists barely joined in even in this debate.

25. The first prominent SDAP member who did question this policy was Heleen Ankersmit. See Ulla Jansz, "Van wetenschap naar verstrooiing: Een

afgebroken biografisch onderzoek," in *Naar het leven: Feminisme & biografisch onderzoek*, ed. Mieke Aerts et al. (Amsterdam: SUA, 1988), 133–34.

26. Roosje Vos-Stel, *Bijzondere bescherming van vrouwenarbeid* (Groningen: Vredevoogd, [1904]), 10; "Feministen," *De Proletarische Vrouw* 4:23 (1908–9); "De arbeid der gehuwde vrouw," ibid. 5:16 (1909–10); M.W. [Mathilde Wibaut], "Burgerlijke propaganda voor vrouwenkiesrecht," ibid. 6:17 (1910–11).

27. W. Thönnessen, *Frauenemanzipation: Politik und Literatur der Deutschen Sozialdemokratie zur Frauenbewegung 1863–1933*, 2d ed. (Frankfurt a.M.: Europäische Verlagsanstalt, 1976), 37–39; Marilyn J. Boxer and Jean H. Quataert, "The Class and Sex Connection: An Introduction," in *Socialist Women: European Socialist Feminism in the Nineteenth and Early Twentieth Centuries*, ed. Marilyn J. Boxer and Jean H. Quataert (New York: Elsevier, 1978), 10–13.

28. M. Everard, "Het burgerlijk feminisme van de eerste golf: Annette Versluys-Poelman en haar kring," in *De eerste feministische golf: Zesde jaarboek voor vrouwengeschiedenis*, ed. Jeske Reys et al. (Nijmegen: SUN, 1985), 124.

29. P. J. Troelstra, *Woorden van vrouwen* (Amsterdam: Poutsma, 1898), 44–45.

30. Ibid., 74–76.

31. Henriëtte Roland Holst-van der Schalk, *Een woord aan de vrouwen der arbeidende klasse naar aanleiding der Nat. tentoonstelling van vrouwen-arbeid* (Amsterdam: Fortuijn, 1898), 13.

32. Ibid., 14–16.

33. H.v.d.M. [Henriëtte van der Meij], "Misplaatste vrijheidsliefde," *Belang en Recht* 6 (1901–2): 62–64, 72–73.

34. H.v.d.M. [Henriëtte van der Meij], "Misbruikte vrouwenkracht," *Belang en Recht* 3 (1898–99): 21–22 (a review of the Dutch translation of Key's *Missbrukad kvinnokraft*).

35. "Mrs. Charlotte Perkins Gilman te Amsterdam," *Belang en Recht* 9 (1904–5): 92; H.v.d.M. [Henriëtte van der Meij], "Geen inconsequentie," *Sociaal Weekblad* 24 (1910): 305–6.

36. Josine Blok et al., "De vrouwenkiesrechtbeweging in Nederland," in *Vrouwen, kiesrecht en arbeid*, 85–88.

37. For example, Th.S.H. [Th. Schook-Haver], "Ons Huisgezin," *Evolutie* 1 (1893–94), no. 38:2–4, no. 39:2–3, no. 40:3–5; "Koken in het groot," ibid. 2 (1894–95): 17–18; "Coöperatief communisme," ibid. 3 (1895–96): 276–77. The same ideas appear in articles by Margaretha Meyboom: "Onbillijkheid," *Sociaal Weekblad* 8 (1894): 276–77; and "Een proef," ibid., 383–84.

38. For example, B.N. [Betsy Nort], "De economische toestand der vrouw," *De Amsterdammer* 1254 (July 7, 1901); B. Nort, "Gemeenschappelijke keuk-

ens," ibid. 1266–67 (Sept. 29 and Oct. 1, 1901); Martina G. Kramers, "De plaats der vrouw in maatschappij en staat," *De Gids* 71 (1907), III:92–93.

39. For example, H. C. van Loenen de Bordes, "Eene vrouw over de fabrieksarbeid van vrouwen," *De Amsterdammer* 1532 (Nov. 4, 1906).

40. M. W. H. Rutgers-Hoitsema, *Arbeidswetgeving en bizondere bescherming van vrouwenarbeid* (Rotterdam: Masereeuw & Bouten, [1903]), 19–20.

41. H. Roland Holst, "De vrouw, de arbeidswetgeving en de sociaaldemokratie. (Een antwoord aan Mevrouw Rutgers-Hoitsema)," *De Nieuwe Tijd* 8 (1903): 736–37.

42. For example, José Siersema, *Vrouwenarbeid-nachtwerk? Over arbeidswetgeving en emancipatie* (Amsterdam: Pegasus, 1981), 35.

43. Rutgers-Hoitsema, *Arbeidswetgeving*, 44–45.

44. Holst, "De vrouw, de arbeidswetgeving," 729–31.

45. For a critique of the term "utopian socialists," see Saskia Poldervaart, "Feminisme, romantiek, socialisme: Romantiek als bemiddelende factor," *Tijdschrift voor vrouwenstudies* 10 (1989): 39.

46. Nancy Cott finds a comparable combination of equality and difference arguments for American feminism in "Feminist Theory and Feminist Movements: The Past before Us," in *What Is Feminism?* ed. Juliet Mitchell and Ann Oakley (New York: Pantheon, 1986), 51–52; and Joan W. Scott for French feminism in "Deconstructing Equality-versus-Difference; or, The Uses of Poststructuralist Theory for Feminism," *Feminist Studies* 14 (1988): 49–50.

47. "Bij den nieuwen jaargang," *De Vrouw* 11 (1903–4): 1–2; "De moederarbeidster," ibid. 18 (1910–11): 10–12. In 1908 Van Dorp referred to Gertrud Bäumer, *Die Frau in der Kulturbewegung der Gegenwart* (1904), for the new feminism that had discovered woman's real nature. See Marijke Mossink, "Tweeërlei strooming? 'Ethisch' en 'rationalistisch' feminisme tijdens de eerste golf in Nederland," in *Socialisties-Feministiese Teksten 9,* ed. Selma Sevenhuijsen et al. (Baarn: Ambo 1986), 107–12.

48. E. C. van Dorp, "Het internationaal vrouwencongres te Berlijn," *Sociaal Weekblad* 18 (1904): 435.

49. For example, W. H. M. Werker, "Verzet," *De vrouw in de XXste eeuw* 1 (1911–12): 53–54.

50. Braun, *De prijs van de liefde,* 229–31.

· 7 ·

"Lagging Far Behind All Civilized Nations"

The Debate over Protective Labor Legislation for Women in Denmark, 1899–1913

Anna-Birte Ravn

Support for protective legislation regulating women's working hours never gained solid footing in Denmark. Debated several times around 1900 and in the first decades of the twentieth century, such laws .were never enacted. Yet the absence of special protective measures for women, other than maternity leaves, hardly signaled the existence of a Danish labor market erected on egalitarian principles. That market has long rested on thoroughgoing gender segregation, a foundation that remains intact to the present day.[1]

Given this history, how indispensable have protective labor laws for women been as building blocks for the hierarchically gendered construction of the wage labor force? Why was regulation of women's working hours never enacted in Denmark? Why did Denmark, unlike most other industrializing countries, never have a night work prohibition for women workers? What other mechanisms kept that edifice of the gendered labor market standing unshakable and upright? This chapter cannot do full justice to all these questions; it cannot unroll a magnificent master blueprint, revealing every room and corridor in that imposing structure. However, through close analysis of the early Danish debate over protective legislation, it can reveal much about the contours of gender struggles that reinforced the sexual division of labor.

The debate that surfaced in Denmark around the turn of the century was not restricted to women. The Factory Act of 1873, the nation's first protective labor law, did not mention women workers. This act regulated working conditions and limited working hours in factories and workshops with more than five employees for children and young people from the ages of ten to eighteen. It also prohibited the employment of children under ten in such establishments. While the debates leading up to the act's passage touched on the question of protective legislation for women, women did not constitute a central focus of the discussions.[2] Special provisions for women did become central in the debates over later revisions of the act, first between 1899 and 1901 and again between 1911 and 1913. The bills, proposed by a Conservative government in 1899 and a Liberal government in 1911, both contained provisions for limiting women's working hours and for maternity leaves. Yet, despite extensive discussion of women, the factory acts that emerged in 1901 and 1913 focused primarily on general working conditions. Restrictions on working hours applied only to children and young people. While neither act contained any stipulation with regard to the working hours of adult females, both provided for maternity leaves. The acts prohibited women from working for four weeks following childbirth unless a medical doctor testified that the work would not harm mother or child.[3]

The first and most obvious answer to the question of why Parliament did not regulate women's hours or impose a night work prohibition for women can be found in the nature of Danish industrial development. Denmark had few large-scale heavy industries and very few females were in fact employed at night. Industrialization in Denmark is usually dated from around 1850, with a full-blown industrial revolution only taking place in the last decade of the nineteenth century, later than some of Denmark's European neighbors. In 1897 the industrial labor force amounted to approximately 177,000 workers (including homeworkers), of whom 37,000 (21 percent) were women. In 1906 this figure had risen to 207,000 industrial workers, of whom 48,000 (23 percent) were women; approximately 25 percent of the female and 2 percent of the male workers were homeworkers. According to the industrial censuses of 1897 and 1906, some 26 percent of female workers were married women and around 8 percent were widows.[4] In the first decade of the twentieth century only about 300 women worked in factories at night. They held jobs primarily in the textile and printing industries and at glassworks and paperworks.[5]

Given the small numbers involved, it is tempting to conclude that prohibiting female factory work at night was a moot issue, hardly the stuff of major controversy. But such a deduction would be premature. Although no night work prohibition was ever passed, the debate over it and over women's working hours tells us something about how gender was conceived and demarcated. This debate on hours was of signal importance in shaping the Danish labor market of the future. Its significance was evident to the debate's participants. The discussion was therefore never solely about the 300 night workers. Even the most ardent proponents of a night work prohibition for women were willing to make exemptions for them. Rather, the discussion was about the future of thousands of Danish women and men. The failure of Parliament to pass a night work prohibition for women is less important than the delineations and meanings of gender that emerged from the debate. These meanings were integrated, part and parcel, into the future course of daily life and labor in Denmark.

The debate brought into sharp relief the complicated question of women's similarity to or difference from men.[6] Were women and men essentially the same, with identical needs and interests, or were they different? Danish women were enfranchised only in 1915, so these debates occurred within women's organizations and among women organized in various Social Democratic groups. Everywhere the debate was explicitly phrased in these terms, focusing on whether or not women workers were physically and socially weaker than men workers. The different answers provoked by this question meant different legislative answers, even among those who agreed that equality between women and men was the ultimate goal. Putting the debate into these terms also raised the question of women's basic similarity to or difference from each other. Did all women necessarily share overarching common interests and capacities as women? How much room for diversity among women was given credence? Finally, in the interstices of the debate lurked another set of questions regarding the relative salience of gender and class:[7] Was protective labor legislation for women first and foremost a question of the conflictual relationship between women and men, or between women and capital?

In what follows I will first describe the course of protective labor law discussions in the context of Danish party politics. Second, I will sketch out the main arguments offered by female advocates and opponents of such legislation, focusing on the women's movement and the

Social Democratic labor movement, where divisions over the issue crystallized most visibly and most sharply. Finally, I will tie the discussion among these women back to the debate that took place among (male) legislators and assess its impact on the future course of the Danish labor market—indeed, on modern Danish society itself.

◆ ◆

The early parliamentary debate over protective labor legislation for women took place in a political climate of intense class and gender conflict. The Danish government introduced the proposal for revision of the factory act in December 1899 while reeling from two major social confrontations. One had just been resolved a short time before by the so-called 1899 September Settlement between employers' and workers' organizations. After extensive strike activity and a general lockout, employers finally acknowledged workers' right to organize, while workers accepted the right of employers to control the means of production.

Although the conflict about the constitution of the Danish labor market was settled, the Constitutional Battle still raged. It was a battle fought between Conservatives, on one side, and Liberals and Social Democrats, on the other, and it was decisive in determining the future character of the parliamentary system. It was laid to rest by the General Election of 1901, just after the factory act had passed. For the first time the Liberals, who held the majority in the Lower House (the *Folketinget*), were allowed to form the new government, wresting control away from the Conservative upper chamber. To many Liberals, especially the middle-class farmers who formed the backbone of the party, the conflict had essentially been one for individual freedom and majority rule against the last remnants of an authoritarian state and, by analogy, against state power or regulation in any form.

This variant of Danish liberalism formed one backdrop for factory legislation discussions, but, as we shall see, its capacity to set the tone for all Liberal positions was not a foregone conclusion. It is also clear that the issue of special protections for working women was not initially borne into the Danish Parliament as an expression only of indigenous, conservative paternalism. It came at least in part as the cargo of some politicians eager to modernize and industrialize the nation. A ten-hour day and a night work prohibition for women were introduced in the 1899 bill. Before that, discussions about special controls over women's wagework had made only rare appearances in the legislative arena. It seems safe to argue that the basic inspiration for the 1899 proposal came from abroad. Furthermore, once on Danish shores, arguments for protective legislation hardly became the exclusive property of any one party's visions for labor.

Introducing the bill in Parliament (the Rigsdagen) in 1899, Theodor Bramsen, the Conservative minister of the Interior, made several references to laws in other European countries and to international conferences on the subject. Bramsen seemed to have drawn particular inspiration from the Berlin conference of 1890. In fact, his main argument for proposing regulation of women's working hours was that all "cultural states," all "civilized nations," already had this kind of legislation. He argued for the basically conservative rather than socialist character of protective labor laws and implied that they would have the effect of advancing progress, while preserving society by preventing social unrest. While giving a nod to Adam Smith's doctrines of individual freedom, Bramsen argued that one simultaneously had to recognize that human beings did not all have the same capacities and possibilities in life. It was thus in the interest of society to protect the weak from the strong. In a last attempt to retain provisions limiting women's working hours in the 1901 act, the Social Democratic M.P. Jens Jensen reproduced Bramsen's portrait of Denmark as the last backward country of the "civilized world." And when Jens Jensen-Sønderup, minister of the Interior for the reigning Liberal government, introduced the new bill in Parliament in 1911, his main argument was the Danish government's approval of the Bern Convention in 1906.[8] In 1911 Denmark was the only country to have signed the document whose Parliament refused to ratify it. Danish politicians across the political spectrum thus in part laid their concerns about Denmark's image in the Western world on the fulcrum of gendered, domestic social legislation. Yet if their recourse to this fulcrum united them at points, their commitment to using it remained unstable and ambivalent.

That wavering commitment can be seen clearly in men like Gustav Philipsen, leading speaker of the Liberal party, which held a majority in the Lower House of Parliament in 1899 but did not yet rule. In 1899 Philipsen had supported the proposal for protection, albeit somewhat reluctantly. He pointed to female workers' weakness in competition with men and their responsibility for future generations as the main justification for regulation. He discussed at length the problem that the bill as a whole represented an encroachment on individual freedom. Giving his argument a special spin, he asserted that his party had never made the mistakes of Liberal parties in England or Germany, for instance; in clinging to their liberal principles, these parties had long resisted social legislation, with the net result that Conservative parties had come to power. According to Philipsen, the freedom of contract doctrine was old-fashioned and had been abandoned long ago by the modern Danish Liberal party. Such arguments notwithstanding, he pursued the matter halfheartedly and with flagging conviction. In 1912 he advised the Lower House to reject the night work prohibition for women, in accordance with the wishes of women's organizations. Records of parliamentary debates both in the Lower and Upper House (the Landstinget), both in 1899–1901 and 1911–13, reveal that advocates and opponents of female protection cannot be neatly divided up along party or even class lines. Conservatives and Liberals were internally divided over the question and between them could not muster enough votes to carry the special measures. Only Social Democratic M.P.s unanimously supported the extension of protective labor legislation to women.[9] However, the Social Democratic labor movement remained divided over the question of a night work prohibition, with some of their leading female trade unionists—like the bourgeois women's movement—opposing any special regulations of women's working hours. If the positions of male politicians on protective laws defy easy classification, did women speak out on the issue with a more unified voice?

◆ ◆

Danish women were not enfranchised until 1915 and could thus not take part in these parliamentary debates in any direct way. Yet neither bourgeois nor Socialist women's organizations stood idly and silently on the sidelines. In the spring of 1900 they organized three public meetings in Copenhagen to air views on the Factory Bill of 1899. One meeting was organized by the bourgeois women's movement,[10] the Danish Women's Society (Dansk Kvindesamfund), established in 1871.[11] The Women's Progressive Association (Kvindelig Fremskridtsforening), a left-wing group that had split from the society in 1885 and worked in close cooperation with female trade unions, organized a gathering before this. A third meeting came together under the auspices of various female trade unions, including the Women's Branch of the Danish Printers' Union (Dansk Typografforbunds Kvindelige Afdeling), the Union of (Unskilled) Women Workers in Denmark (Kvindeligt Arbejderforbund i Danmark), the Women Tailors' Union (De kvindelige Herreskrædderes Fagforening), and the Women's Dressmakers' Union (Damekonfektionssyerskernes Fagforening).[12] In 1900 approximately one-third, or some five thousand, of women workers in Copenhagen were organized. About one thousand had joined the Women Tailors' Union and about thirteen hundred belonged to the Union of Women Workers in Denmark.[13]

Prominent female and male members of the convening organizations spoke at the meetings, along with male trade union leaders and various M.P.s. All supported the proposal for maternity leaves, and most simultaneously stressed the need for financial compensation. However, opinion divided over the issue of imposing hour regulations on women workers only. Male speakers recommended such measures, while most women present either opposed the idea or expressed grave reservations. At the first meeting, called by the Women's Progressive Association, the organizers proposed a resolution against a night work prohibition but then withdrew their petition to Parliament until the women's trade unions had managed to debate the matter. The Danish Women's Society arranged the next meeting with the primary objective of giving women a platform to voice their views of the factory bill. At the third and final meeting, called by the women's trade unions, the president of the Women Tailors' Union, Andrea Nielsen, offered a resolution stating that women workers accepted the proposed restrictions on women's working hours but only on the condition that protection for all workers would soon be enacted. In addition, the resolution called for financial compensation for women during maternity leaves. The resolution passed unanimously at the meeting and was sent to Parliament.[14]

Later, in 1909, when Parliament was about to revise the Factory Act of 1901, the Danish Women's Society appointed a Standing Committee on the Factory Act and invited female trade unions to join the protest against a night work prohibition only for women. The president of the Women Tailors' Union rejected the invitation, insisting that the restrictions would not affect her members. But the Women's Branch of the Danish Printers' Union and the Union of Women Workers in Denmark joined in.[15] In 1911, when for the second time the factory bill included a night work prohibition for women, the three organizations held a joint protest meeting in Copenhagen, which attracted some twelve hundred people, mainly women. The speakers were all women, and they unanimously rejected prohibition. Those in attendance voted in favor of a

resolution against restrictions on women's working hours, and the resolution was sent to Parliament.[16]

The focal point of public meetings—night work prohibition for
women—was also discussed in journals and newspapers of all political stripes. Mostly women engaged in these debates, both as advocates
and as opponents of prohibition. A few male political economists and
others wrote in favor of the restrictions.[17] All the prominent members
of the Social Democratic party who entered the fray, male and female,
strongly supported prohibition, as did male trade union leaders. As a
whole, however, discussions of the issue within the larger Social Democratic labor movement seem to have been rare,[18] apart from the debates
among female trade unionists.

By contrast, protective labor legislation constituted one of the central issues of the time within the bourgeois women's movement. The
journal of the Danish Women's Society, *Kvinden og Samfundet,* kept a
close watch on the issue during 1899–1901 and 1909–13. With the exception of a few of its prominent male members (one of them being Jens
Jensen-Sønderup), the society stood vehemently opposed to prohibition. Another central issue of the period was political enfranchisement
for women. In the years 1911–13, it appeared almost certain that women
would shortly be enfranchised, and this may well have made politicians
more willing to listen to the views of women's organizations. But the
male politician of the day, opportunistic or not, had many "women's
views" to contend with, many voices to register.

◆ ◆

Although discussions about protective labor legislation for women
were rare within the Social Democratic labor movement, party leaders
made some efforts to communicate their support for such restrictions to
their members. In the earlier debate of 1899–1901 in particular, the party
newspaper, *Social-Demokraten,* published several long articles on the
question by Nina Bang.[19] Along with other Social Democratic women
closely connected to the party leadership, Bang strongly recommended
limitations on women's working hours, and her arguments seem characteristic of other women's views. She wrote the articles with explicit reference and in direct opposition to the opinions expressed by the journal of
the Danish Women's Society. Bang launched an attack on the bourgeois
women's movement, accusing the "upper-class ladies" of maintaining a
doctrine of individual freedom at the expense of working-class women.

In her opinion, women's right to wagework was a claim relevant only to upper-class women; it reflected "a family quarrel within the bourgeoisie."[20] Working-class women had "the right to do all the paid work they could possibly want,"[21] she argued. And so, individual freedom for working-class women only meant "the freedom to be exploited."[22] Denmark was at long last preparing to join the ranks of the "civilized nations" that did not tolerate the boundless exploitation of women.[23]

Bang's arguments in favor of protective legislation paralleled those of her German counterpart, Clara Zetkin.[24] A ten-hour day and a night work prohibition, Bang asserted, were necessary for many reasons. Women constituted a special kind of worker: besides working for wages, they were also mothers. They were in a weaker position in the labor market than men, disadvantaged both physically and in terms of education and the degree to which they were organized. Furthermore, this would always be the case, even in a socialist society. Men were able to defend their own interests by organizing. Women could not do this to the same degree because of motherhood. Thus, Bang argued, the state had to intervene and protect women through special social legislation.[25]

While painting women as a special kind of worker, Bang artfully pushed aside any question of conflict between the interests of male and female workers. Women's obligations as mothers did not imply that they should be confined to domestic tasks, she argued. Like men, women should work for wages, but the two ought to take up different work in the labor market. A sexual division of labor was the most rational way of organizing society, socialist society included. According to Bang, capitalist production had created chaos and anarchy in the division of work, a division characteristic of every orderly society. A new gendered division of labor should be instigated to restore order, one structured according to physical strength.[26] Thus Bang saw no gender conflict inherent in the restriction of women's working hours, and she warned working-class women not to let such an issue come between them and working-class men, for only factory owners would profit from such competition.[27] The question of a night work prohibition was about class conflict alone, female labor pitted against capital. Since night work was an example of extreme exploitation of labor by capital, the solution was obvious: restrictions on women's working hours would benefit the working class, which in this instance happened to be working-class women.

Bang did not question the ultimate goal of equality between women and men. Rather, like Zetkin and others, she saw special legislation for women as a step toward equality; she assumed it would make women stronger in relation both to capital and, by implication, to male workers. From her standpoint, equality between the sexes did not mean they were and should be the same. On the contrary, she was convinced that a rational organization of society had to build on women's and men's different physical strengths and educational opportunities. Because she took the biological and social difference between women and men as her point of departure, Bang ended up casting all women as essentially the same. There was no room for difference or diversity among women in her discourse. Young or old, married or unmarried, with or without children, all women were mothers.

The general meeting of the Danish Federation of Trade Unions (De samvirkende Fagforbund i Danmark) in 1909 seems to be the only occasion at which protective labor legislation for women was discussed at some length by an official body of the labor movement. Here the business manager of the federation, Alfred Christiansen, echoed Bang in strongly recommending a night work prohibition for women. Yet Christiansen seemed more willing to acknowledge that working-class laboring women had varying capacities and levels of endurance. This difference notwithstanding, he went so far as to blame nonlaboring women for leading laboring women into misguided opposition. Women who were able to endure the strains of night work, he believed, should willingly relinquish their jobs in order to make common cause with women who were not strong enough to work at night.[28]

While almost a decade lies between Bang's published statements and Christiansen's pronouncements, their voices can be taken as an accurate register of how Danish protection advocates in the labor movement stated their case and understood the gendering of labor. In propagating restrictions on women's working hours, Bang, representing the Social Democratic party leadership, together with male trade union leaders implicitly constructed women as a homogenous group. They were cast as a special kind of worker but with no special interests to distinguish them from male workers.[29] But could such a position carry the day among other activist women?

◆ ◆

The public meetings mentioned above provided one forum for female opponents of protective labor legislation to speak their minds.

Two international meetings held in Copenhagen both before and after the parliamentary debate on the Factory Act of 1913 offered further opportunities. One was the Second International Socialist Women's Conference, held in conjunction with the Congress of the Second International, the union of mainly European Socialist parties, in August 1910. On this occasion Danish Social Democratic women proposed a resolution calling on the International to use its power to push through a night work prohibition for men as well as for women, thereby rejecting special prohibition for women alone.[30] This had not initially been on the official agenda prepared by Clara Zetkin.[31] A majority of the Danish delegation (thirty-four of thirty-seven delegates) and the Swedish delegation supported the resolution. However, the delegates from fourteen other countries laid it to rest. Delegate Bang also rejected it, informing the conference that the executive committee of the Danish Social Democratic party did not support it.[32]

Zetkin later described the episode as a painful experience, an indicator that the Danish and Swedish Social Democratic women were still enmeshed in an earlier, more primitive stage of development, only to be expected from women at the periphery.[33] In Zetkin's and Bang's view, opposition to a night work prohibition for women revealed a regrettable bourgeois influence on Socialist women.

In Denmark, Socialist and bourgeois women did in fact form a strong coalition in opposition to mainstream party positions. This women's alliance became apparent at the Second Nordic Meeting on the Woman Question, held in Copenhagen in June 1914.[34] Convened at the request of the Danish Women's Society, the meeting was also attended by representatives of Social Democratic women's organizations. The Nordic delegates almost unanimously rejected special legislation for women—except for maternity leaves—and recommended protective labor laws that covered both men and women. Only two Danish women spoke in favor of special legislation for women. One was a factory inspector, Ragna Schou;[35] the other, Andrea Brochman (née Nielsen), representative of the Social Democratic Women's Association (Socialdemokratisk Kvindeforening), an organization closely aligned with the Social Democratic party.[36]

Among the female opponents of a night work prohibition for women, two were particularly outspoken. One was Julie Arenholt,[37] a member of the Danish Women's Society and a factory inspector by profession; the other, Henriette Crone,[38] president of the Women's Branch of the

Danish Printers' Union. Apart from the bourgeois women's movement and the female printers, the Union of Women Workers in Denmark also strongly opposed restrictions on women's working hours. Though leading members of other women's trade unions seem to have had more doubts, all the female trade unionists who were present at the 1900 and 1911 public meetings supported the petitions sent to Parliament.[39]

Calling to mind Bang's accusation that upper-class women maintained the doctrine of individual freedom at the expense of working-class women, it is worth noting that none of the leading female opponents clung to this doctrine. They rejected special legislation not because women would lose individual freedom but because, quite simply, they seemed likely to lose their jobs. Beyond this, a range of basic assumptions lay behind their objections to a night work prohibition. They viewed women, including female workers, as different from each other. Some were mothers, while others were not and never would be. Some were physically weak, while others were as strong as men. They also believed that, like men, women should organize to overcome competition and individual vulnerability in the face of capital.[40] In the later debates of 1911–13 in particular, Arenholt and Crone stressed that a major obstacle to organizing women was the lack of solidarity shown by working-class men who maneuvered to reserve the best jobs for themselves and only halfheartedly supported women's struggles for better education and equal pay. In other words, these female opponents of protection explicitly framed the issue of a night work ban for women as gender conflict. They did not overlook the fact that protective labor legislation also contained elements of class conflict. But because men had transformed the issue into a conflict between the sexes by recommending special legislation for women alone—in Crone's words, "since men of all classes and political convictions have united in order to strike a blow against women"—women of all classes had to unite to fight it.[41]

In general, female opponents of protection argued that night work harmed all workers and should be abolished. However, to abolish it for women alone would worsen women's economic position and underscore gender inequalities in the labor market. Women doing night work in factories were relatively well paid, their working hours and conditions well regulated. Furthermore, these female night workers were in fact well organized. Arenholt, Crone, and others feared that, as a consequence of prohibiting night work, women would be forced to take up other occupations, most likely homework, jobs that were poorly paid, unregulated, or lacking trade union representation.[42] Arenholt and Crone also voiced concern that such a ban might force women out of occupational sectors in which they worked together with men into women-only sectors. Here they did not anchor their argument to a claim that women and men were basically the same. Rather, they pointed to the fact that pay and working conditions for women were better in occupations employing both sexes rather than only females.[43]

In contrast to Bang, other Social Democratic party leaders, and the male trade union leadership, Arenholt, Crone, and others saw equal treatment across the board as a necessary condition for achieving equality between women and men. It is important to note, however, that they did not insist on equal treatment in all situations. Since they acknowledged the diversity of women—some were mothers and others were not—they wholeheartedly supported maternity leave provisions included in the factory acts. In fact, the Danish Women's Society tried to make the four-week maternity leave compulsory, arguing that it should not be possible to shorten the leave even with permission of a medical doctor.[44]

Female opponents of a night work prohibition for women, both representatives of the bourgeois women's movement and the female Social Democratic trade union movement, acknowledged women's diversity. At the same time they insisted that women shared common interests in opposition to men. In debates over the ban they constructed womanhood in complex terms, acknowledging women's diversity while maintaining that women could also share identical goals, such as the right to well-paid work.

◆ ◆

The opponents of a night work prohibition for women won the battle over legislation. No special restrictions on adult females' working hours apart from a four-week maternity leave were incorporated into the Factory Acts of 1901 and 1913, or in later revisions of the acts. Several such attempts failed, including one made by the first Social Democratic government in Denmark, which came to power in 1924. But the question of who won the debate is not so easily answered. Looking at the various debates in Parliament over the years, as well as comparing the internal debates among female opponents of protection with the official statements they issued, suggests what might have been a Pyrrhic victory. In the end, even the opponents of a night work ban for women phrased their arguments in the discourse of special protection advocates, a discourse that spoke in terms of same-versus-different and gender-versus-class.

The "normal" or "maximum" working day constituted the central theme of the parliamentary debate leading up to the 1901 act. Class conflict was the predominant tension in this discourse, gender playing second fiddle. The questions raised included whether or not a ten-hour day and prohibition of women's night work would be the prelude to establishing a normal working day. Would such measures pave the way for an eight-hour day for all workers? In Parliament, bourgeois advocates of protection said that they would not, while opponents insisted they would. In this, Social Democratic M.P.s agreed with their bourgeois adversaries. Social Democrats saw a ban on women's night work as a first step toward a normal working day for all workers. And the fear among bourgeois M.P.s that this would actually come true may have been the main reason why the opponents won the battle. In 1911–13 discussions about a women's night work ban, the tables were turned and gender conflict stood at the center of the discourse. Parliamentarians constructed the debate as a conflict between individual women and a collective national interest in child welfare. Both Conservatives and Liberals, constructing themselves as disinterested representatives of the nation, and Social Democrats, speaking on behalf of the working class, made the abstraction of "benefiting children" their priority and pushed for protective measures. Thus, while the 1899–1901 debate had cast women as workers, it now recast them as mothers.[45]

The reasons behind this transformation from 1899–1901 to 1911–13 are not easily discerned. The general trend in other industrial countries toward accentuating the maternal obligations of working-class women hints at one possible explanation. This trend reached Denmark comparatively late, and in this respect Denmark lagged far behind all "civilized nations." However, any explanation that does not take into account national preconditions for change seems unsatisfactory. It is likely that the clash between workers' and employers' organizations in 1899 had prompted the focus on class in the early 1899–1901 debate. In Parliament, advocates of protective laws played on these tensions, warning that rejection of the legislation would probably lead to even deeper class conflict. Extensive strike activities in fact continued after the turn of the century and on to World War I — the year 1905, for example, saw a major strike in the predominantly female textile industry. Why, then, would gender supersede anxieties around class conflict in the 1911–13 debates?

Perhaps the answer lies in the intensified gender conflict over enfranchisement after the turn of the century. While the struggle for women's political citizenship had stagnated during the 1890s, it gained new force in the first decade of the twentieth century. In 1908 Danish women got the vote in local council elections. However, they were not given the right to vote in parliamentary elections until 1915. This process leading to women's enfranchisement inevitably involved intensified discussions about the meaning of womanhood. It was probably no small coincidence, then, that in 1905 Jensen-Sønderup advised the Danish Women's Society to underscore the difference between women's and men's capacities as a major strategy for laying claim to the vote.[46]

In 1911–13 advocates of a night work prohibition for women workers, including the Social Democratic M.P.s, acknowledged in passing that working women opposed the restrictions but basically ignored their position. The crucial issue for them was women's responsibility for future generations; these took precedence over any "individual interest." Only a few Liberal and Conservative M.P.s who opposed restrictions on women's working hours took this standpoint, because they diverged over whether or not women were first and foremost mothers. Their opposition rested primarily on objections to state intervention in the labor market, either in principle or because they were attuned to employers' desire to block any interference with women's night work.

Opposition was strongest among Liberals with ties to middle-class farming interests; they questioned any kind of state interference in farm work, including work in industries tied to agricultural concerns, such as dairies or corn mills. When only the Social Democrats and one M.P. of the New Liberal party supported the night work ban for women, these opponents began to challenge the maternity leave provisions. They claimed, on the one hand, that pregnancy was not an illness and that agricultural work was healthy, harming neither women nor children. On the other hand, they asserted with perverse, if adroit, logic that farm work was much more strenuous than factory work, suggesting that maternity leaves for factory women were unnecessary. On top of this, they suggested that maternity leave provisions siphoned off taxpayers' money for immoral purposes, for it enabled unmarried factory girls who became mothers to subsist at the expense of decent, married farmers' wives.

In this climate it is obvious that the arguments of female opponents of protective labor legislation for women also shifted over time, changing colors in the later period according to whether they were addressing a predominantly female or a predominantly male audience. The paradox is that the focus on gender in the debates in 1911–13 probably forced these protection opponents to implicitly accept women's difference from men and, by implication, aggregate women's situations, making all women the same. Taking this path meant understating the theme of gender conflict.

The resolution approved at the meeting of women's trade unions and sent to Parliament in March 1900 stated that women workers supported protection of women and children working in factories, as suggested by the Conservative government, "but on the condition that protective legislation for all workers is expected to be enacted shortly, since women would be excluded from various crafts by Section 5 of the present bill."[47] Andrea Nielsen, then president of the Women Tailors' Union, signed the resolution, though she had expressed her doubts at the meeting. She saw the female night work ban as a first step toward prohibition of such work for all workers, yet she admitted that a one-pronged prohibition, just for women, represented an encroachment on women's individual freedom. In the end she herself suggested the resolution as a compromise. In 1914 Nielsen (now Brochman), president of the Social Democratic Women's Association, had cast all lingering doubts aside. She was one of only two women attending the Second Nordic Meeting on the Woman Question who accepted special restrictions on women's working hours.[48] Her transformation may be seen as an example of the more general shift in emphasis from class to gender, irrespective of her new take on the issue.

The most ardent opponents of the night work prohibition for women within the Danish Women's Society and women's trade unions stood firm by their earlier stance on the legislation. The resolution that emerged from the meeting called by the Union of Women Workers, the Copenhagen Branch of the Danish Women's Society, and the Women's Branch of the Danish Printers' Union in March 1911—attended by "women and men of all social classes"—protested against the factory bill's proposed restrictions on women's freedom of contract. The resolution stated:

> Social conditions have increasingly forced woman to support herself and others through her labor. It is not possible to protect her through special prohibitions against the abuse of her labor power. Restric-

tions on her arena of activity will only force her to sell her labor power more cheaply. Therefore, considerations of her health and the health of children, born and unborn, cannot justify special prohibition, since health is not furthered by a depreciation of her economic circumstances.[49]

The phrasing of the resolution shows, first, that while female opponents of protection very clearly sparred with the theme of gender conflict in their internal debates, they played it down in their petition to Parliament. Second, its phrasing shows that these women felt obliged to argue on the premise laid down by the advocates of protection: women were mothers. They did this very elegantly—and wisely—by turning their adversaries' main arguments upside down, stressing that the ones who would suffer most from a special night work ban for women were the children, born and unborn.

By accepting this framework for their arguments, by understating the gender conflict that their own internal debates had expressed so clearly, and by ignoring their own conviction that women were a diverse group, female opponents of protective labor legislation for women implicitly accepted the premises of the advocates. In these terms women were a special kind of worker but with no special interests to distinguish them from men. Women were essentially alike, but without identical interests as women. The general acceptance of these premises has perhaps been as influential as any legislation in shaping the Danish labor market and propelling the gender segregation of modern Danish society.

Notes

I wish to thank all the participants in the research group on "Women's Waged Work and Protective Labor Legislation in Comparative Perspective" for assistance and friendship. I am especially grateful to Ulla Wikander for inviting me to join the group and for making cooperation possible; Alice Kessler-Harris, Jane Lewis, Sabine Schmitt, and Ulla Wikander for constructive criticism and encouragement; and Alice Kessler-Harris and Jane Lewis for help with my English.

1. OECD analyses show that countries like Denmark and Sweden, where women's employment rate equals that of men, have the most strongly segregated labor markets. See *The Integration of Women into the Economy* (Paris: OECD, 1985).

2. See *Tillæg A til Rigsdagstidenden, Lovforslag, Ordentlig Samling 1872–*

73 (Copenhagen, 1873), cols. 1977–2006; *Rigsdagstidende, Forhandlinger paa Landsthinget, Ordentlig Samling 1872–73* (Copenhagen, 1873), cols. 291–322, 421–532, 631–64, 1765–78; *Rigsdagstidende, Forhandlinger paa Folkethinget, Ordentlig Samling 1872–73* (Copenhagen, 1873), cols. 2500–2539, 3847–84, 4833–44, 5344–47; *Tillæg B til Rigsdagstidenden, Udvalgenes Betænkninger, Ordentlig Samling 1872–73* (Copenhagen, 1873), cols. 29–38, 447–52, 1103–6, 1233–34; *Lovtidende for Kongeriget Danmark for Aaret 1873* (Copenhagen, 1873), 249–52.

3. See *Tillæg A til Rigsdagstidenden, Forelagte Lovforslag m.m., 52de ordentlige Samling 1899–1900* (Copenhagen, 1900), cols. 3091–130; *Rigsdagstidende, Forhandlinger paa Folketinget, 52de ordentlige Samling 1899–1900* (Copenhagen, 1899), cols. 1975–82, 2039–174; *Tillæg B til Rigsdagstidenden, Udvalgenes Betænkninger m.m., 52de ordentlige Samling 1899–1900* (Copenhagen, 1900), cols. 2421–70; *Rigsdagstidende, Forhandlinger paa Folketinget, 53de ordentlige Samling 1900–1901* (Copenhagen, 1900), cols. 31–32, 3703–830, 4049–58, 4914–45; *Rigsdagstidende, Forhandlinger paa Landstinget, 53de ordentlige Samling 1900–1901* (Copenhagen, 1901), cols. 1445–523, 1608–33, 1635; *Tillæg B til Rigsdagstidenden, Udvalgenes Betænkninger m.m., 53de ordentlige Samling 1900–1901* (Copenhagen, 1901), cols. 853–938, 2029–36, 2111–12; *Lovtidende for Kongeriget Danmark for Aaret 1901* (Copenhagen, 1901), 317–25; *Tillæg A til Rigsdagstidenden, Forelagte Lovforslag m.m., 63de ordentlige Samling 1910–11* (Copenhagen, 1911), cols. 3271–506; *Rigsdagstidende, Forhandlinger paa Landstinget, 63de ordentlige Samling 1910–11* (Copenhagen, 1911), cols. 402–12, 564–604; *Rigsdagstidende, Forhandlinger paa Landstinget, 64de ordentlige Samling 1911–12* (Copenhagen, 1912), cols. 2066–116, 2229–30; *Tillæg B til Rigsdagstidenden, Udvalgenes Betænkninger m.m., 64de ordentlige Samling 1911–12* (Copenhagen, 1912), cols. 3339–76; *Rigsdagstidende, Forhandlinger paa Folketinget, 65de ordentlige Samling 1912–13* (Copenhagen, 1912), cols. 43–49, 789–845, 5198–239, 5246–53, 5667–72; *Rigsdagstidende, Forhandlinger paa Landstinget, 65de ordentlige Samling 1912–13* (Copenhagen, 1913), cols. 2078–92, 2147–53, 2161–64; *Tillæg B til Rigsdagstidenden, Udvalgenes Betænkninger m.m., 65de ordentlige Samling 1912–13* (Copenhagen, 1913), cols. 1841–54, 2403–506, 2447–48; *Lovtidende for Kongeriget Danmark for Aaret 1913 Afdeling A* (Copenhagen, 1914), 761–82.

The 1901 act stated that public aid during a maternity leave should not have the consequences of poor relief. The 1913 act differed from that of 1901 by making public funding dependent on the mother keeping the baby (unless it was sick or had died). The money would be paid through sickness benefit or charity associations (in Copenhagen) or through relief funds (in other parts of the country). Besides maternity leave there are three minor exceptions to the general gender neutrality of early Danish factory legislation. One is a provision of the so-called Machine Act of 1889 stipulating that adult women were not allowed to clean, oil, or inspect running machines. See *Lovtidende for Kon-geriget Danmark for Aaret 1889* (Copenhagen, 1889), 160–65. When the 1889 law was incorporated into the Factory Act of 1913, the provision was altered, prohibiting women, irrespective of age, from doing this kind of work "unless they wear clothes considered to offer safety protection equal to that of men's clothes, and do not wear their hair loose." The other two exceptions are included in the Factory Act of 1901, which gives the minister of the Interior the authority to permit night work for young male workers (fifteen to eighteen years) but not female workers of the same age, and makes it possible for the Labor Council to prohibit adult women from work that the factory inspectorate considers particularly exhausting and dangerous, or "of such a nature that the carelessness of one worker may cause harm to the other workers." Decisions made based on this last provision could be appealed to the minister of the Interior. In the Factory Act of 1913 the first provision was made gender neutral, while the second was retained in its earlier form.

4. *Danmarks Haandværk og Industri ifølge Tællingen den 12. Juni 1906,* Danmarks Statistik, Statistik Tabelværk, Femte Række, Litra A No. 7 (Copenhagen: Statens Statistike Bureau, 1908), 111–37. See also "Bemærkninger til foranstaaende Lovforslag, 5. Bestemmelser om Hjemmearbejde," *Tillæg A til Rigsdagstidenden, Forelagte Lovforslag m.m., 63de ordentlige Samling 1910–11* (Copenhagen, 1911), cols. 3329–33.

5. "Bemærkninger til foranstaaende Lovforslag, 3. Kvinders Nadarbejde," cols. 3324–28.

6. In my earlier work on the bourgeois women's movement, the Danish Women's Society (Dansk Kvindesamfund), the concept of equality-versus-difference was central to my theoretical framework. I was and still am very inspired by Yvonne Hirdman. See, e.g., Hirdman, "Särart-likhet: Kvinno-rörelsens Scylla och Karybdis?" in *Kvinder, mentalitet, arbejde. Kvindehistorisk forskning i Norden,* ed. Inge Frederiksen and Hilda Rømer (Aarhus: Aarhus Universitetsforlag, 1986). See also Anna-Birte Ravn, "Ligestilling—lighed eller særart," *Årbog for Kvindestudier ved AUC 1987,* Serie om Kvindeforskning no. 25 (Aalborg: Aalborg Universitetsforlag, 1988), 19–39, and "Dansk Kvinde-samfund i Aalborg 1888–1988," in *Historien og erfaringerne som afsæt for visioner om fremtiden,* ed. Helle Algreen-Ussing and Anna-Birte Ravn (Aalborg: Dansk Kvindesamfunds Aalborgkreds, 1988).

I think, however, that Joan W. Scott is right when stating that equality-versus-difference is a false dichotomy and that the true oppositions are equality and inequality, difference and sameness. See Scott, "Deconstructing Equality-versus-Difference; or, The Uses of Poststructuralist Theory for Feminism," *Feminist Studies* 14 (Spring 1988): 33–50, and *Gender and the Politics of History* (New York: Columbia University Press, 1988). See also Anna-Birte Ravn, "Mål og midler i den gamle og den nye kvindebevægelse," *Nyt Forum for Kvinde-*

forskning 9:3 (1989): 8–20, and "Kønsarbejdsdeling-et historisk perspektiv," in *Køn og videnskab,* ed. Ulla Koch, Anette Kolmos, Anna-Birte Ravn, and Birte Siim, Serie om Kvindeforskning no. 27 (Aalborg: Aalborg Universitetsforlag, 1989).

I do not believe that feminist researchers today were responsible for creating this false dichotomy of equality-versus-difference. Historical evidence shows that it has been set up as an impossible choice for women for at least the last hundred years. My point here is that the "true" dichotomy of difference-versus-sameness has been operating in the same way historically. See also Carol Lee Bacchi, *Same Difference: Feminism and Sexual Difference* (Sydney: Allen & Unwin, 1990).

7. Earlier Danish analyses of protective labor legislation for working-class women have focused mostly on the class dimension of this legislation. See, e.g., Birte Broch, *Kvindearbejde og kvindeorganisering: Kvinder i konfektionsindustrien 1890–1914* (Copenhagen: SFAH, 1977); Kirsten Geertsen, *Arbejderkvinder i Danmark 1914–24* (Copenhagen: SFAH, 1977), and *Arbejderkvinder i Danmark: Vilkår og kamp 1924–1939* (Copenhagen: SFAH, 1982); Toni Liversage, *At erobre ordet—Kvinderne og arbejderbevægelsen* (Copenhagen: Tiderne Skifter, 1980). In some analyses gender has been more central. See, e.g., Lise J. Høyrup, "Barselshvile—pligt, ret eller illusion? En undersøgelse af barselslovgivningens betydning for kvinder i industri og håndværk 1901–1933" (Speciale [M.A. thesis], Historisk Institut, Københavns Universitet, 1988); Birthe Mikkelsen, "En undersøgelse af spørgsmålet om den særlige beskyttelse af kvindelige arbejdere, specielt i forbindelse med udformningen af den anden fabrikslov i 1901" (Speciale [M.A. thesis], Historisk Institut, Københavns Universitet, 1975).

8. On the Berlin conference of 1890 and the Bern Convention of 1906, see Ulla Wikander's essay, "Some 'Kept the Flag of Feminist Demands Waving,' " in this volume.

9. The first program of the Danish Social Democratic party, adopted at the so-called Gimle Congress in 1876, was almost an exact copy of the Gotha Program of the German Social Democratic party. One of the exceptions was the proposal to abolish night work for men as well as women. The official policy of the Danish Social Democratic party, as stated in party programs from 1876 to 1913, was that women and men should be treated in the same way. Special legislation for women—except for provisions on maternity leave—was not mentioned in the party programs. The 1888 program included a demand for a "maximum working day" and explicitly stated that "men's and women's work in the various industries should be paid at the same rates." See Hans-Norbert Lahme, ed., *Det danske Socialdemokratis Gimle-kongres 1876* (Odense: Odense Universitetsforlag, 1976); *Det socialistiske Program: En Fremstilling af Socialdemokratiets Principper* (Copenhagen, 1888); *Program og Love vedtagne paa de*

socialdemokratiske Kongresser i Aarhus 1894 og København 1896 (Aarhus, 1896); *Socialdemokratiets Program samt Love for Socialdemokratisk Forbund i Danmark* (Rønne, 1909); *Program og Love for Socialdemokratiet i Danmark, Vedtaget af Kongressen 1913* (Aarhus, 1913).

10. I feel uncomfortable with the description "bourgeois," since many middle-class women such as teachers joined the organization and were, in fact, some of its most active members. I lack a good alternative term, however.

11. The journal of the Danish Women's Society, *Kvinden og Samfundet,* launched a campaign in October 1899 to attract working-class women through articles describing their living and working conditions.

12. The meetings took place on February 10 (the Women's Progressive Association), February 21 (the Danish Women's Society), and March 7 (the women's trade unions). They were covered by *Kvinden og Samfundet* 16:7 (Feb. 13, 1900), 16:9 (Feb. 27, 1900), and 16:12 (Mar. 20, 1900); *Samarbejdet, Organ for Arbejdernes faglige Interesser* 9:4 (Feb. 15, 1900) and 9:6 (Mar. 15, 1900); *Social-Demokraten,* Feb. 10, 22, and Mar. 8, 1900.

13. At the national level only about 20 percent of the female workers were organized in the year 1900, compared to 76 percent of the male workers. See Karin Sandvad, "Den kvindelige fagbevægelse i København 1870–1900," *Årbog for Arbejderbevægelsens Historie 1* (Copenhagen: SFAH/Fremad, 1972), 46–93.

14. *Tillæg B til Rigsdagstidenden, Udvalgenes Betænkninger m.m., 52de ordentlige Samling 1899–1900* (Copenhagen: 1900), cols. 2465–66.

15. *Protokol for Dansk Kvindesamfunds Fabrikslovsudvalg* 1909–12, 1921–26, 1929–[31], Kvindehistorisk Samling, Aarhus. *Forhandlings Protokol for Kvindelig Arbejderforbund i Danmark* [1901–12], Arbejderbevægelsens Bibliotek og Arkiv (hereafter ABA), Copenhagen.

16. *Tillæg B til Rigsdagstidenden, Udvalgenes Betænkninger m.m., 64de ordentlige Samling 1911–12* (Copenhagen, 1912), cols. 3371–72. See also *Kvinden og Samfundet* 27:6 (Mar. 30, 1911).

17. See, e.g., E. Meyer, "Fabrikloven og Kvinderne," *Tilskueren, Maanedsskrift for Litteratur, Samfundsspørgsmaal og almenfattelige videnskabelige Skildringer* 17 (Apr. 1900): 281–90. Emil Meyer was a member of the executive committee of the Danish Women's Society. See also Adolph Jensen, "Kvindens Erhvervsarbejde og Hjemmet" and "Gensvar til Fru Nina Bang," *Tilskueren* 17 (July 1900): 539–46 and (Sept. 1900): 747–54; Frantz Pio, "Fabrikforslaget og Kvinderne," *Politiken,* Mar. 9, 14, and 22, 1900.

18. See the protocols of the Social Democratic party congresses of 1888, 1890, 1892, 1894, 1896, 1898, 1901, 1903, 1906, 1908, 1910, 1913, and the congress protocols of the Danish Federation of Trade Unions.

19. Nina Bang, "De 5 Uger og den frugtsommelige Kvinde," *Social-Demokraten,* Feb. 3, 1900; "De 5 Uger," *Social-Demokraten,* Feb. 8, 1900; "Socialdemokratiet og Beskyttelsen af de kvindel. Arbejdere," *Social-Demokraten,*

Feb. 9, 1900; "Kvinde-Erhvervet. Retten til Arbejde," *Social-Demokraten,* Febr. 18, 1900; "Kvindernes Møde i Aften om Fabrikloven," *Social-Demokraten,* Mar. 7, 1900; and "Kvindesagen og Fabrikloven," *Social-Demokraten,* Mar. 12, 1901. See also "Kvindesagen. Aabent Brev til Fru Dagmar Hjort," *Tilskueren* 16 (July 1899): 575–85; "Kvindesagen. Afsluttende Bemærkninger," ibid. 16 (Aug. 1899): 681–84; "Hjemmets Opløsning," ibid. 17 (Apr. 1900): 323–32; and "Kvindeerhvervet og Hjemmet," ibid. 17 (Aug. 1900): 637–41. Bang became a member of the executive board of the Social Democratic party in 1906. In 1924 she became the first female cabinet minister in Denmark.

20. Bang, "Kvinde-Erhvervet."
21. Ibid.; and Bang, "Kvindernes Møde."
22. Bang, "De 5 Uger" and "Socialdemokratiet og Beskyttelsen."
23. Bang, "Socialdemokratiet og Beskyttelsen."
24. On Clara Zetkin, see the following essays in this volume: Wikander, "Some 'Kept the Flag of Feminist Demands Waving,'" and Sabine Schmitt, "'All These Forms of Women's Work Which Endanger Public Health and Public Welfare.'"
25. Bang, "Socialdemokratiet og Beskyttelsen."
26. Bang, "Kvinde-Erhvervet."
27. Bang, "De 5 Uger" and "Kvinde-Erhvervet."
28. "Fabriksloven og dens Revision," Foredrag af Forretningsfører Alfr. Christiansen ved De Samvirkende Fagforbunds Generalforsamling den 24. April 1909, *Arbejderen, Meddelelsesblad for De samvirkende Fagforbund i Danmark* 5:48–49 (June 1909): 253–76. The discussions at the 1909 general meeting of the Danish Federation of Trade Unions revealed both women and men to be in favor of a night work prohibition for women. Only one woman, Henriette Crone, spoke strongly against it. The federation decided to ask member unions about their demands regarding the new factory act; the executive committee of the federation would then summarize the answers and send them to the Labor Council, which was preparing the new law.
 The executive committee did not ask the trade unions whether a night work ban for women was desirable but whether it could be implemented. Some unions, among them the unions of seamstresses, textile, and tobacco workers, answered in the affirmative. The Union of Women Workers replied that its members in glass factories, dairies, and streetcar companies worked at night, and the Danish Printers' Union answered that while it was possible to prohibit female printers from working at night, it would not benefit the women, and therefore they opposed it. See *Arbejderen* 6:10 (Sept. 1909): 49–60.
29. This point was first made about the German Social Democratic party by Sabine Schmitt. See "'All These Forms of Women's Work Which Endanger Public Health and Public Welfare.'"

30. *Dagsordenens Punkt 4* (Copenhagen, 1910). Socialdemokratiets Arkiv, Kasse 770, Den internationale Kvindekongres i København august 1910, ABA, Copenhagen. The Second International was a league of mainly European Socialist parties, established in 1889. Member parties were found in all European countries, and the German, French, and Austrian parties were especially important for the profile and development of the movement. At its peak, just before World War I, the Second International had approximately 3.5 million members. It was dissolved in 1917.

31. "Anträge und Resolutionen," Zweite Internationale Konferenz sozialistischer Frauen in Kopenhagen, Socialdemokratiets Arkiv, Kasse 770, Den internationale Kvindekongres i København august 1910, ABA, Copenhagen.

32. *Kvinden og Samfundet* 26:15 (Sept. 15, 1910): 171–72; *Politiken,* Aug. 28, 1910; *Social-Demokraten,* Aug. 28, 1910. See also "Bericht aus Dänemark," in *Die Schutzgesetzgebung für Frauenarbeit in den verschiedenen Ländern* (La Haye: Correspondance Internationale, [1912]); Christl Wickert, "Kvinder, valgret og fred. Omkring den internationale socialistiske kvindekonference i København 1910," *Arbejderhistorie, Meddelelser om Forskning i Arbejderbevægelsens Historie* 29 (Oct. 1987): 14–28. The official record of the conference has not been made available.

33. Clara Zetkin, "Die Zweite Internationale Konferenz sozialistischer Frauen zu Kopenhagen," *Die Gleichheit* 20:24 (Aug. 1910): 387–89.

34. *Beretning fra Det 2. Nordiske Kvindesagsmøde i København den 10. og 11. Juni 1914* (Copenhagen: Dansk Kvindesamfund, [1914]). The First Nordic Meeting on the Woman Question was held in Kristiania (Oslo), Norway, in 1902. A resolution against restrictions on adult women's working hours was passed. See *Referat fra Nordisk Kvindesagsmøde afholdt i Kristiania, Norge, 3.–7. Juli 1902* (Oslo: Norsk Kvindesagsforening, 1903).

35. Ragna Schou was a member of the Danish Women's Society. Her recommendation of special legislation is the exception that proves the rule (that female members of the society rejected a night work prohibition).

36. The Social Democratic Women's Association was formed in 1908, with the primary purpose of agitation among female workers. According to Drude Dahlerup, who has analyzed the history of the association from 1908 to 1969, when it was dissolved in the name of equality, Danish Social Democratic women were strongly urged not to diverge from the party line and especially not to express any women's interests that ran contrary to the interests of Social Democratic men. See Dahlerup, "Kvinders organisering i det danske Socialdemokrati 1908–1969," *Meddelelser om Forskning i Arbejderbevægelsens Historie* 13 (Oct. 1979): 5–35. The same point is made, although indirectly, in the report about the Socialist women's movement in Denmark to the Second International Socialist Women's Conference in Copenhagen 1910. See Elisa-

beth Mac, "Die sozialistische Frauenbewegung in Dänemark," in *Berichte an die Zweite Internationale Konferenz sozialistischer Frauen in Kopenhagen am 26. und 27. August 1910* (Stuttgart: Paul Singer, 1910).

37. Julie Arenholt was elected city councillor in Copenhagen in 1909, the first election following women's enfranchisement for local councils in 1908. She became president of the Danish Women's Society in 1918.

38. Henriette Crone was a Social Democratic city councillor in Copenhagen.

39. According to reports from the public meetings in 1900, the following women spoke against or expressed serious doubts about regulations for women's working hours: Johanne Meyer, a leading member of the Women's Progressive Association; Birgitte Berg Nielsen and Anne Bruun, of the Danish Women's Society; Andrea Nielsen, president of the Women Tailors' Union; and Olivia Nielsen, president of the Union of Women Workers in Denmark. Besides Crone and Julie Arenholt, the women speaking against a women-only night work prohibition at the public meeting in 1911 were: Louise Neergaard, a leading member of the Standing Committee on the Factory Act appointed by the Danish Women's Society in 1909; Thora Knudsen, a Social Democratic city councillor in Copenhagen; and Johanne Jensen, president of the Women Glass Workers' Union.

40. To Berg Nielsen the main argument against special legislation was that it would prevent women from building strong organizations. See *Kvinden og Samfundet* 16:9 (Feb. 27, 1900); ibid. 16:10 (Mar. 6, 1900); and ibid. 16:12 (Mar. 20, 1900). See also Julie Arenholt and Henriette Crone, in *Kvinden og Samfundet* 27:6 (Mar. 30, 1911); and Arenholt, in *Beretning fra Det 2. Nordiske Kvindesagsmøde*, 128–32.

41. Arenholt and Crone, in *Kvinden og Samfundet* 27:6 (Mar. 30, 1911).

42. Editorials in *Kvinden og Samfundet* 16:6 (Feb. 6, 1900) and 16:7 (Feb. 13, 1900); Arenholt and Crone, in *Kvinden og Samfundet* 27:6 (Mar. 30, 1911); and Arenholt, in *Beretning fra Det 2. Nordiske Kvindesagsmøde*, 128–32.

43. Arenholt and Crone, in *Kvinden og Samfundet* 27:6 (Mar. 30, 1911).

44. "Beretning fra Udvalget angaaende den kommende Revision af Fabriksloven," *Kvinden og Samfundet* 26:11 (June 15, 1910): 125.

45. For references to the debate in Parliament, see note 3.

46. See Ravn, "Dansk Kvindesamfund i Aalborg 1888–1988," 16. A thorough analysis of the Danish debate over enfranchisement has not been made. On the construction of womanhood in modern Danish society, see Bente Rosenbeck, *Kvindekøn: Den moderne kvindeligheds historie 1880–1980* (Copenhagen: Gyldendal, 1987).

47. See note 14.

48. Brochman, in *Beretning fra Det 2. Nordiske Kvindesagsmøde*, 157–58.

Birde Broch argues that Brochman joined the Social Democratic party line in the early debate. See Broch, *Kvindearbejde og kvindeorganisering,* 156–59. The available sources make it impossible to decide. However, my point is that Brochman's arguments shifted from focusing in 1900 on women as workers to looking at women as primarily mothers in 1914.

49. See note 16.

· 8 ·

The Beginning of a "Masculine Renaissance"

The Debate on the 1909 Prohibition against Women's Night Work in Sweden

Lynn Karlsson

In 1909 Gerda Meyerson, a Swedish liberal reformer, wrote that "during the past decades the influx of women into factories has become so great that it is beginning to arouse alarm." Industry needed women, she continued, "but observers . . . have become more and more disturbed by this situation because the daughters of the working class prefer factory work to domestic chores to such a great extent."[1] Meyerson's statement is typical of sentiments in Sweden and elsewhere at this time. Women's employment in factories was perceived as a disturbing new phenomenon and a growing threat. Ironically, however, Meyerson's observations were mistaken. The fifty thousand women who worked in Swedish factories at the time made up only about 19 percent of the industrial labor force (down from around 30 percent during the 1870s when Sweden began to industrialize). The continued industrial expansion in the decades that followed was concentrated mainly in heavy industry, such as sawmills and metalworking, which employed few women. Instead, the vast majority of working women were employed elsewhere in the early twentieth century: more than half could still be found in agriculture, and domestic service employed nearly one hundred thousand women in 1910. Moreover, large numbers of women (the figures are uncertain) worked at home or in small workshops doing piecework, primarily sewing.[2] Nevertheless, women's employment in industry had begun to draw the attention of authorities and social reformers alike. Many feared for the health and morals of women factory workers and even foresaw the disintegration of family life and society itself as the result of such work.

In Sweden, as in most European countries, restrictive protective legislation designed to regulate women's work in industry was seen as an answer to this perceived threat.[3] Based on assumptions about women's physical and moral weakness, as well as their roles as wives and mothers, adult women became identified with children as being in need of the special protection of the state. While initially reluctant, as the movement for protective laws for women spread internationally at the turn of the century, Sweden too began to introduce legislation to restrict women's industrial employment. However, based as they were on foreign conditions, such laws were often ill suited to the reality of the Swedish labor market, and they became a source of contention. While Swedish legislators felt they were following the lead of more "progressive" European nations, opponents of special protection for women questioned the advisability and necessity of such laws at a time when women were beginning to gain legal and economic equality with men.

One law in particular, the prohibition against women's night work in industry eventually passed by the Swedish Parliament in 1909, became a major political issue in Sweden, arousing intense debate. Trade union and Social Democratic women, with support from organized middle-class feminists — as well as some men with a range of political affiliations — mounted a campaign against such a law. Questioning the assumptions behind gendered protective legislation, they argued that unless a night work ban applied equally to both sexes, it would merely restrict rather than protect women in the labor market. Instead they demanded legislation that would lighten the burden of the working woman: a women's factory inspectorate, the regulation of sweated industry, and maternity insurance. In so doing, Swedish women attempted to balance between an equal rights feminism that demanded full equality with men without regard for women's reproductive role and a feminism represented by the influential Swedish author Ellen Key that accorded women equal value with men on the basis of that role alone.

Opponents of the night work prohibition were nearly successful; the Riksdag rejected it when it was first put to a vote in 1908. However, it was passed the next year by an alliance between the government, liberal reformers, the Social Democratic party leadership, and conservative parliamentarians, each with their own set of interests.[4] For Social Democrats the proposed legislation presented a particular dilemma.

Unlike social democracy in other countries, Swedish social democracy had no articulated policy for the special protection of women before the debate on the night work prohibition. In fact, the male-dominated party had largely ignored the problems facing women workers. However, it quickly joined forces with its political opponents in supporting the ban, despite the opposition of its female members. For liberals and Social Democrats, protective legislation for women came to symbolize a progressive stance, with the state taking on a duty to protect those unable to protect themselves from exploitation in the new industrial marketplace. For conservatives, on the other hand, such laws were a means of reinforcing traditional family values. What united these seemingly opposing viewpoints was a vision of society in upheaval, where women's wagework seemed to threaten established gender relations and norms.

Thus the question of protective laws cut across political affiliations and ideology, shaping new alliances especially among women. What makes the Swedish case unusual is the cooperation that developed between female trade unionists and Social Democrats and the bourgeois women's movement. Only Denmark saw a similar grouping in this period. In this chapter, I will examine the nature of the debate on protective labor legislation in Sweden and outline how opposition against such laws arose, particularly among working-class women.

◆ ◆

From an international perspective, Sweden was slow in adopting legislation to regulate working conditions in industry before the turn of the century.[5] Dominated by conservative agrarian and upper-class interests during the 1870s and 1880s, the Swedish Riksdag showed little interest in pursuing labor regulation. It was not until 1881 that an ordinance limited children's working hours in industry and craft work.[6] Strong resistance from industrial employers induced the government to water down these regulations, and in fact the protection afforded children was minimal.

Demands for more effective protective measures for all workers against dangerous working conditions and lengthy working hours in Sweden's rapidly expanding industrial sector gained strength during the 1880s and 1890s. Initiatives taken by liberals led, for example, to the passage of a law on occupational hazards in 1889. They drew successfully on both humanitarian and tactical arguments: social legislation would defuse the socialist revolutionary threat, a claim that also appealed to social conservatives.

The question of restricting the work of *adult women* in industry was raised officially for the first time by the parliamentary committee appointed in 1875 to formulate the first child labor law. Pointing to English legislation, the committee noted with regret that its instructions were expressly limited to children and that it was thus unable to propose restrictions on the factory work of women as well. The committee wrote that it wished, however, to "take this opportunity to state that in its opinion protection for woman could, without causing any substantial damage to industry, very easily be extended, to the lasting benefit of family life and the future generation."[7]

There was, however, no sense of urgency on the part of the government and the Riksdag regarding such legislation for women, as the treatment of the question in connection with the revision of the child labor law during the 1890s illustrates. Sweden had attended the first international conference on protective legislation held in Berlin in 1890. The following year a parliamentary committee was appointed to revise the child labor law of 1881 and "to consider to what extent the basic principles agreed upon at said conference ought be applied in Sweden."[8] The committee's work eventually resulted in the law of 1900, which regulated the work of children and women in industry. This was the first Swedish legislation to restrict the work of adult women. Along with a prohibition against women working underground in mines and returning to any kind of factory work (unless exempted by a doctor) sooner than four weeks after childbirth, "in accordance with the practice in other countries," the committee also suggested that women under twenty-one be prohibited from doing night work for "hygienic and moral reasons." However, the committee did not adopt the other, more far-reaching resolutions passed by the Berlin conference. These included a prohibition against night work for married women generally and a maximum hours law (eleven hours) for all women.[9]

Thus, the Swedish committee showed great moderation in taking up special legislation for women. The regulations for women's work were characterized as a "regulation of details," which indeed they were. According to the committee's own investigation in 1891, few Swedish women workers returned to work less than four weeks after giving birth, and no women worked underground. At least at this point, the new regulations were primarily expressions of "good will" toward the spirit of protective legislation. The committee saw no need to impose restrictions on the working hours or night work of grown women (or men), as had been done in other countries after the Berlin conference. As the committee put it, relatively few women actually worked in factories in Sweden, and there had been no complaints on this score.[10] Furthermore, when the Riksdag finally passed the new labor law in 1900, the provisions concerning women were watered down even more; the proposed prohibition against night work for women under twenty-one was struck from the government's bill.[11] There was, in other words, little awareness expressed by legislators at this point that women's factory work was a problem, or enough of a problem to warrant setting a precedent of state intervention in the labor market in the controversial area of working hours.[12]

While Swedish protective legislation was modest in European terms, it did signal that a conservative opposition to state intervention in the labor market—at least in the case of women and children—was giving way. Largely under the influence of international trends in legislation and discussions, the idea of restricting the work of adult women in industry gradually began to take root in Sweden around the turn of the century. One sign of this was the country's participation after 1900 in international efforts to promote protective legislation. Sweden sent official delegates to all of the conferences held by the International Association for Protective Labour Legislation after 1901.[13] However, before the night work prohibition, women's work in factories was de facto unregulated. This situation may explain why opposition arose.

◆ ◆

Just as Sweden's legislation was influenced by events occurring abroad, so too was the debate on protective legislation for women. This debate began in earnest among feminists, liberal reformers, and the growing labor movement after the turn of the century.[14] The Fredrika Bremer Förbund (founded in 1884), the major middle-class feminist organization in Sweden, had broached the subject in 1899 in its periodical *Dagny*. In a report from the International Congress of Women held in London the same year, the Swedish delegate Gertrud Adelborg presented *Dagny*'s readers with a relatively detailed description of the debate on this subject, "one of today's most burning questions in many places abroad." She began by pointing out that both opponents and defenders of legislation could summon strong arguments for their positions. Defenders, led by the English Fabian Beatrice Webb, stressed that while women should have equal wages and the same right to employment as men, it was the right and duty of the state to defend women against overexertion for the sake of future generations. However, Adelborg was clearly more impressed by the arguments of opponents of legislation, who were represented by the Finnish delegate Alexandra Gripenberg. Gripenberg argued from the principle of equal and individual rights for women, which in her view protective legislation denied: "The idea of special protective labor legislation for woman is a descendent of the old doctrine that women should have privileges, not rights, that they should be protected instead of having the power to protect themselves, that they are—as the economists say—'a nation's most precious possession' instead of being a part of the nation itself." [15] Adelborg made no comment herself other than to note "with satisfaction" that the question of protective legislation had not yet arisen in Sweden. This, she told her readers, "confirmed what we already knew: that the position of the Swedish woman is in many respects better than in other countries." [16]

When the law regulating the work of women and children was introduced in 1900, the question did arise. Swedish feminists mounted a challenge but only after the fact: by the time the issue was raised in *Dagny*, the Riksdag had already passed the bill. In one article Maria Cederschiöld, one of Sweden's first women journalists and an early feminist,[17] detailed the background to the proposal and described other, more far-reaching foreign legislation, warning that the present proposals were most likely only the beginnings of a more extensive regulation of women's work. She also reported that thousands of women in other countries had become unemployed or pushed into overcrowded, low-paying jobs because of such laws. While Cederschiöld acknowledged that the question was controversial, the tone of the article was academic. The author did not directly challenge the new Swedish legislation for women but merely noted that it was fortunate that the restrictions in Sweden were as limited as they were.[18]

In an article that followed, however, Cederschiöld's contemporary, the feminist Hilda Sachs, presented a direct—and caustic—criticism of the law, questioning the very basis of protective legislation for women only. Sachs too was a journalist and author employed by several of the larger Stockholm newspapers—among other things, as a foreign correspondent in Paris in the late 1890s. She had also participated in the women's rights movement in Sweden from its inception during the 1880s, working actively for women's suffrage and equality with men.[19]

Sachs took the premise of legal equality between the sexes as her starting point. There was, she wrote, no valid reason to prohibit grown women from working in mines as long as they were not also forbidden from "pursuing sports in excess or travelling to the North Pole in a balloon." "It is quite doubtful," she continued, "whether one does adult persons a favor by creating prohibitions of various kind that restrict their freedom when the latter does not intrude upon the rights of others."[20] Sachs also argued from a practical viewpoint. Obviously, she pointed out, she was not advocating that women work in mines, but she was asking whether such work was really more dangerous "for a strong woman than for a strong man or for a weak woman than for a weak man." Furthermore, she declared, work in the mines was hardly more strenuous than many of the other jobs women had always done, such as farm work or brewing. Women, as opposed to children, were also required to support themselves: "as an unmarried woman or widow, always; as a wife, when her husband's wages are insufficient to support the family." It was difficult to understand, she continued, why these women should be denied the right to make a living doing the work that was available in their community.

Finally, Sachs attacked the main rationale for protective legislation, the "biggest trump" of its supporters: that work of this kind is damaging to mother and child. First of all, she wrote, modern science had certainly not proven that the health of the mother was solely responsible for the sound development of children. Had scientific studies of, for example, horse breeding not shown just the opposite? But more important, Sachs questioned how realistic it was to restrict women's work on these grounds:

> These so worthy reasons—a concern for future generations—always strike me with amazement, in that this appeal—no, rather—this demand is always made of those who are poorest. Poor women, who are forced to seek hard and heavy work, are to deny themselves what they can get, if they have a thought of becoming mothers. There is a danger here that the poor woman is going to sit there and starve to death out of pure solicitude for future generations, out of virtuous sacrifice for her unborn children.[21]

For Sachs, women—all women—thus must have the right to work as they wished. They were not exempted by their sex from the responsibility of supporting themselves.

At the opposite pole from Sachs stood Key,[22] an extremely influential writer and lecturer who had been active in Swedish cultural life since the 1890s. She was controversial, arousing opposition among conservatives for her sympathies with the growing socialist movement and her radical ideas on free love and religion. Her relationship to the women's movement was complex. While supporting the economic and legal emancipation of women, she espoused in her book *Missbrukad kvinnokraft* (The Strength of Women Misused), published in 1896, a strict sexual division of labor based on biology and accused feminists who demanded equality with men in the labor market of leading women astray. These were themes that she further developed in her contribution to the debate on the law of 1900, *Barnets århundrade* (The Century of the Child), which appeared in Sweden that same year. While Key was mainly concerned with the need to restrict child labor, her book also included an aggressive attack on feminism and feminist opposition to protective labor legislation.

Key would no doubt have called Sachs one of those "feminists who are a half a century too late," for whom "freedom" still meant "being able to work wherever one wishes for whatever pay one gets," based on the old idea of "abstract rights." In fact, Key wrote, freedom means human dignity, which for a woman involved "bringing forth a people with healthy bodies and souls," a nation's greatest possession.[23] For Key, this "people with healthy bodies and souls" could only be achieved if women devoted themselves to the home and family. A woman of the upper classes who tried to combine a career with motherhood could only become a "dilettante" in both realms. Working-class women, characterized by Key as "amateur workers," risked far more serious consequences: the moral life and good health of both herself and her child, as well as the future of society.

> Woman's unorganized, shoddy, and therefore poorly paid work decreases wages and work opportunities for men; factory work makes a woman unfit to care for a home, unfit for her duties as a mother. In the heat, noise and rush of the factory, nerves are worn down— and with them the finer feelings. . . . These incompetent women render marriage more difficult for the man. . . . The exhausted or in-

competent wife cannot economize with the little the husband earns. Drunkenness and sickness follow.[24]

Key judged women harshly: in the factories they become little more than creatures, incapable and immoral.

No ordinary supporter of protective legislation, Key further developed her radical ideas in *Barnets århundrade* of "woman as the mother of society." Influenced by Nietzsche and new works on eugenics and heredity, she envisioned a transformation of society in which women/mothers would play a central role. Fundamental to her philosophy, therefore, was the idea that it was only as mothers that women could demand equality with men. Women could not free themselves from the "limitations of nature," which was what the misguided "*dogmatici* of feminism" attempted to do in their struggle for equality on the basis of "abstract rights." The latter, Key wrote, considered "the greatest of national questions [a healthy population] as insignificant and woman's natural functions as unimportant, while—on the contrary—it is precisely because of the importance of these functions that woman can support her demands for freedom and rights side by side with men." [25] Key's arguments were clearly "affirmations of difference," to use Joan Scott's phrase.

Key distinguished strongly, however, between traditional motherhood and her new concept of "motherliness." The new mother knows what she is doing. She chooses to have a child and selects the father freely. She is trained for her role as the transformer of society and devotes herself entirely to this "calling." A major problem for Key was of course that women might fall victim to the new principles of individual freedom, of "female egoism" preached by the feminists. However, she was confident that while some women (often feminists in Key's texts) would and should choose celibacy, independence, and careers, motherhood was the goal and "true nature" of most women.

What makes Key so interesting is that she did more than just present an idealized image of motherhood. In her visions of a new society, all members of society were expected to work and support themselves. Moreover, care of home and children would also be considered as work, and mothers would receive support from the state in order to be able to stay at home while their children needed their care. Key's point here was that women would be economically independent, freed from a demeaning dependence on men.[26] This was, however, a new society; in the old, women need to be protected. They worked in factories and shops, Key wrote, for starvation wages, "bled white of their life force, losing their youthful freshness and beauty, their possibilities for happiness . . . as people, as wives and as mothers!" This, too, was the fault of the feminists, "who fail to understand that they themselves have contributed to this evil by continuously urging women on into all sorts of different careers, which thus become overcrowded, which in turn causes the low wages."[27]

The solution for Key was the family wage for men and protective legislation for women. Throughout *Barnets århundrade,* Key therefore presents a variety of arguments for protective laws, citing Webb and other English supporters of legislation. Women could not organize and protect themselves to the same extent as men, and they were particularly susceptible to dangerous working conditions. Women's working hours should thus be limited, they should be prohibited from working with dangerous substances, and married women should only undertake paid work that could be done in the home, which, moreover, should also be regulated.[28] By contrast, Key never really solved the problem of the single woman, whom she said had the right to do as she pleased. She did acknowledge that the unmarried worker and the "poor widow" who was fired because of restrictions on women's work would "become the victims of protective legislation." However, she argued, in nearly evolutionary terms, this was the price one had to pay for the advancement of humanity.[29]

Sachs and Key, who essentially set the boundaries for the continuing debate on protective legislation in Sweden, represent two extremes, with diametrically opposing views of contemporary women, although both claimed the same goal: the emancipation of women. For Sachs this could only be gained by demanding legal equality with men, and she gave voice to an equal rights feminism that was rarely heard in the later debate. Key was a more complex figure. She represented the growing discourse on differences, on the peculiar nature of women, a theme that became more important in the subsequent debate. For Key, this was an emancipatory vision. However, while her view of difference was taken over by supporters of protective legislation, her vision of its radical consequences for women and society was ignored.

◆ ◆

In the years following passage of the 1900 labor law, demands for further legislation to restrict women's work in industry arose on occasion, but there was very little focused activity or public debate on the matter in Sweden until the question of night work prohibition surfaced in 1907.[30] However, the foundations for the coming controversy over this proposal were laid during these years.

The Fredrika Bremer Förbund continued to follow the question of protective legislation limited to women in the pages of *Dagny*, providing information on developments abroad and reports from various international women's conferences dealing with the subject. In 1905 the organization took an explicit stance against such laws.[31] The most important reform to better working conditions for women industrial workers was, in the view of the Förbund, the creation of a female factory inspectorate, a matter that the Riksdag had taken up for the first time in 1902.[32] This was the subject of much discussion in *Dagny* after 1900. Thus feminists continued to reject the idea of regulating the working conditions of women alone.

Support for such legislation did, however, arise among the new generation of social reformers that appeared after the turn of the century in Sweden, best represented by the National Association of Social Work (Centralförbundet för Socialt Arbete). The association was founded in 1903 by a group of upper middle-class, liberal female philanthropists who were active in the fields of social welfare and temperance.[33] Working for such causes as poor relief, social insurance, child welfare, and improved housing for the poor, it drew together many of the leading liberal reformers of the day, both male and female, in a nonsocialist program for social reform. Key was, among others, a great source of inspiration to this group of activists.[34]

Within this group we find the Swedish contemporaries who were most engaged in the question of protective labor laws for women. The organization took an interest in the international movement for such provisions, and its journal, *Social tidskrift*, followed the progress of the International Association for Protective Labour Legislation in formulating a convention against women's night work during these years. Nevertheless, while it supported the idea of special protection for women—referring, for example, to Key—the organization did not work actively for hours legislation or any other restrictive measures to regulate women's factory work in Sweden. Instead, the major concern of the National Association for Social Work was the regulation of cottage industry and piecework, and in 1907 it organized an exhibition to inform the public about the sweated conditions and wages of workers in home industry. While very much aware that it was mainly women who did piecework, primarily in textiles and sewing, writers on the subject did not explicitly use gender in arguing for regulation of this area. The need for protection in the form of inspection, registration, and perhaps a minimum wage was phrased in terms of fairness, decency, and the obligation of the state to aid the poorest and weakest of its citizens.[35]

No initiatives for special protective measures for women workers came from within the Swedish labor movement either, although interest for such legislation had increased abroad within the international labor movement. For example, German Social Democratic policy had swung around in favor of female protection in the 1890s, and far-reaching demands for special legislation for women were raised at the Second International's conference in Zurich in 1893.[36] Yet the Swedish Social Democratic party retained a gender-neutral stance regarding labor legislation. For example, in the party's program formulated at its sixth national conference in 1905, the eight-hour day, the extension of worker protection laws to artisans working in small-scale establishments and to pieceworkers, as well as a prohibition against night work and child labor were called for in general terms, without reference to the sex of the worker.[37] While debating protective labor legislation in general and, more specifically, the eight-hour day (the major demand of the Social Democrats), some speakers emphasized that such reform would be of particular benefit to the woman worker, but no one suggested that this issue should be resolved for women alone.[38]

Nor did the working-class women who, around the turn of the century, began to form separate organizations on a larger scale to promote their own interests within the labor movement demand special protection for women workers.[39] While supporting the demands for regulation of sweated industry as well as for a women's factory inspectorate, organizations such as the Women's Trade Union (Kvinnornas fackförbund, founded in 1902)[40] and the national Social Democratic Women's Conference (founded in 1907), emphasized that the solutions for the problems facing working women were the same as those for men: union organization and political agitation for the Social Democratic party.

As the historian Christina Carlsson has shown, the position taken by the Social Democratic party up to this point did not reflect a conscious stance against protective labor legislation for women but rather revealed that the male-dominated party in general showed little aware-ness of or interest in issues concerning women's wagework.[41] However, when faced with a specific proposal for night work legislation and the need to make policy decisions regarding women's position in the labor market, underlying gender conflicts within the newly formed labor movement rose to the surface and the question split the party in two.

In the early 1900s there was thus little pressure for restrictive mea-sures for women in the labor market in Sweden and very little public debate on the question. Nevertheless, an awareness of the issue had de-veloped, and the international debate both for and against legislation had already gained a hearing in the country and influenced opinion to some degree. When the question of parliamentary legislation in the form of a night work prohibition for women arose, support for the mea-sure was found in all political camps. Opponents countered by arguing that in their view Sweden need not make the same mistakes as other countries; instead, it ought to adopt legislation that applied equally to women and men.

◆ ◆

In 1905, the liberal government that had recently come into power decided, without prior investigation or formal discussion, to approve the proposed convention regarding women's night work that was to be signed in Bern in 1906. A prohibition, it was said, would be of "social and humanitarian benefit" to the country and would cause no eco-nomic damage to Swedish industry or its workers, for the government "assumed" that few women (perhaps five hundred) would be affected by the legislation. This decision was once again an exercise in goodwill on the part of the Swedish government toward international efforts for social reform, not the result of any perceived need for a night work ban in Sweden.[42] The new convention thus gave the government the chance to show its good faith on the question of labor protection inter-nationally and within the country without, however, actually restricting industry and arousing conservative opposition. In 1907 the question was referred to the Committee to Revise the Laws on Worker Protec-tion (appointed in 1905), which was assigned the task of formulating a prohibition against women's night work on the basis of the Bern Con-vention.[43]

Women typographers, aware that they would most probably be hit hardest by a prohibition, became the first to protest against the pro-posed ban. Members of the Typographical Women's Club met with the

committee and expressed their fears that the prohibition would force
Sweden's four to five hundred women typographers out of the industry.
Women in this trade, they argued, were well organized and were guaranteed equal wages and the same working conditions as men; hence,
they were in need of no special protection. Protective legislation just for
women seemed generally suspect to them: far from correcting unsatisfactory social conditions, they argued, legislation of this kind "merely
stood in the way of progress and reduced the value of women's work." A
prohibition against night work, which they favored, should be general
and should apply to both women and men. The club also requested
that the printing industry be exempt from future legislation.[44]

Other Social Democratic and union women supported the typographers. The first Swedish Social Democratic Women's Conference,[45]
held in January 1907, passed a resolution opposing the proposed prohibition. The conference, which described itself as representing the organized women workers of Sweden, had discussed the question of protective legislation for women only and considered such laws, except in the
case of women around the time of childbirth, "not to be advantageous."
Night work, the resolution declared, was dangerous for both men and
women, "but there is no proof that women suffer more from it than
men." A prohibition against women's night work would close relatively
well paying industries to women and increase competition within less
well paying areas, particularly cottage industry, "with its uncontrollable
working hours, often including a greater portion of the night, its often
poor renumeration and . . . unsatisfactory sanitary conditions." In addition, the conference felt that "women should not be excluded by means
of legislation from occupations they themselves have chosen to work
in." Instead, an extension of factory inspection to small workshops and
the establishment of a female factory inspectorate were needed.[46] Calls
for maternity insurance during the obligatory maternity leave were
later added to these demands, as well as a call for general measures to
promote the safety and welfare of all workers, regardless of sex.[47]

Meeting with the parliamentary committee, representatives of the
Fredrika Bremer Förbund also protested against the night work prohibition, both as a matter of principle and on practical grounds. The
Förbund's basic argument against a prohibition was that it violated
women's rights, at least those of single women. Even though a law regulating night work could seem in some respects to be justified, these
women said, it was the firm belief of their organization that "a woman

who had obtained her legal majority should have the right to decide herself how best to use her labor power." [48] While the state may have the right to intervene in the affairs of its citizens for the common good—in this case, for the sake of future generations—"any prospective protective law should be aimed solely at wives and young immature women who have not yet come of age. For these women, perhaps, society, as guardian, can be considered to have the right to legislate." Wives were, as the organization noted, already placed under the guardianship of their husbands. However, older unmarried women and widows were considered to be legally of age and as such ought to have the same rights as men to make their own decisions about work.[49]

In the same vein, the Förbund argued that the women who came under the law's jurisdiction must have some say in the matter. In other countries that had passed night work bans, the women affected had never been consulted. They had, however, protested vigorously, even if in vain and usually after the fact. The organization was anxious that this mistake not be repeated in Sweden, where a wide variety of women had already spoken out against a prohibition. At the very least, the organization felt, any decisions regarding the law should be postponed until a detailed study of women's night work in Sweden—about which little was actually known—had been undertaken.[50] Women factory inspectors should be employed to investigate working conditions for women; if their findings showed a need for regulatory legislation of this kind— a need that, it was noted, had not been felt up to now—the question could be taken up again. However, the Förbund thought that it was "extremely hazardous" to enact laws "on the basis of uncertain assumptions and without knowing for whom or for how many one is legislating." [51]

The organization also pointed out that any labor legislation for women alone would not only infringe on their rights but would "make woman's already heavy and uneven struggle for an honest existence even more burdensome." Women would no longer be able to compete with men for work in industries affected by the law. This, the Förbund noted, was what similar legislation had reaped in other countries. And, the organization continued, while the disappearance of women from industrial night work might seem to be a desirable goal, little was known about the economic and moral consequences for the women concerned. Were a night work prohibition to force women with relatively good jobs, such as typographers, into cottage industry, with its long hours and poor pay, the effect would be far from positive. "Such a law would in many cases lead to much more arduous work and decreased economic remuneration for women—thus even for those who are or will be mothers. For more than one, it would lead to moral ruin." The Förbund concluded by expressing the hope that once an investigation had been completed, the issue would have been made moot through the enactment of an eight-hour day for all.[52]

Such ideologically disparate groups as the bourgeois Fredrika Bremer Förbund and Social Democratic women in the labor movement thus shared a number of arguments against the proposed prohibition. Such a law would be an abrogation of women's rights, at least those of the single woman without children. It would make women less competitive with men, causing many to lose their jobs. Moreover, night work was a danger to the health of both men and women. Banning it for women alone would crowd them into poorly paid jobs in typically "female" areas of employment such as cottage industry (and prostitution, the Fredrika Bremer Förbund threatened), in which case women would be totally unprotected. To these arguments the Förbund added a plea for a thorough investigation of the need for the law in Sweden and of its potential effects.

◆ ◆

These protests deeply impressed the Committee to Revise the Laws on Worker Protection. In its official statement to the government, the committee expressed its doubts regarding the proposal:

> these statements, coming as they do from groups that would be greatly affected by the legislation in question, merit some attention, all the more so since at the present time a growing number of voices are heard urging the removal of those barriers that up to now have blocked woman's attempt to achieve full equality with man, both in public life and in the work place. The legislation stipulated by the convention, however, would lead to considerable changes in those areas of the labor market where up to now woman has been for the most part fully equal to man.[53]

The committee questioned whether or not the well-being of future generations and consideration for women's comparatively weaker physique really demanded "so great a restriction in the freedom to adapt working hours to existing needs that would be the result of the convention's all too narrow limits." It further pointed out that the proposed prohibition would really only affect one branch of industry in Sweden, namely, the printing trade, where women's wages and working hours did not endanger their health and well-being, despite occasional night work. The committee finally all but openly recommended that the proposal be set aside.[54]

Nonetheless, the committee was required to draw up a draft bill for legislation. In so doing, however, it put as broad an interpretation as possible on the Bern accord, attempting to make the legislation "as little of a burden as possible," both for women workers and for industry.[55] Briefly, the proposed legislation required that all women working in mines, factories, crafts, and other industrial activity employing more than ten workers were to have a rest period of eleven consecutive hours per day, including the period between 10 P.M. and 5 A.M. Thus, not only night work but also overtime work after or before the hours stipulated was prohibited for women. The committee defined "industrial activity" very narrowly to mean only work directly involving the production or assembly of goods. Cleaning in a factory at night was, for example, not prohibited. Limited dispensation from the law, allowing a slight reduction of the rest period, could be given for seasonal work or in emergency situations, and industries using perishable raw materials (for example, the canning industry) could be exempted from the prohibition.

In one respect the committee actually went beyond the Bern accord. Opponents of prohibition had argued that it would force women into unregulated work in cottage industry. Taking these arguments seriously, the committee attempted to extend the legislation to this sector as well, so as to offer to women working there whatever protection the night work prohibition might afford. The government, however, later struck this clause from the bill for not adhering to the spirit of the convention, which it maintained was to regulate women's work in industry and not in the home.

◆ ◆

The protests of the women and the parliamentary committee's negative verdict on special female protection had little effect. The conservative government that came to power in 1906 put the proposal to the Riksdag in 1908, arguing that Sweden must maintain its international credibility in the arena of international labor protection. By this time, support for the proposed prohibition had gathered strength in other quarters, and in 1908 an intense debate was carried on in newspapers, pamphlets, and at public meetings. Supporters of the proposed legislation argued their case in a variety of ways. Some insisted that Sweden, having signed the Bern accord, was legally obligated to pass the law. Others maintained that since this was the first real breakthrough in the international effort for worker protection, it was of vital importance for continued work in this area to uphold the convention, even though it was not fully suited to Swedish conditions. Moreover, many asserted, the law would only affect a small number of women and hence would have a limited impact on the female labor market; the figures presented by supporters dropped from 300 to 150 and finally to 17 typographers as the debate progressed, and these, it was alleged, could get jobs on the day shift. However, the most adamant supporters of the regulation of women's work in industry—for whom the ban on night work was just the first step—also justified the prohibition with arguments reminiscent of the themes of home, family, and morals that Ellen Key had evoked earlier. The remarks of Moritz Marcus, a liberal social reformer and member of the National Association for Social Work, sum up this point of view:

> It can by no means be claimed that protective legislation for women conflicts with the demand for equality between man and woman. One does not adopt one-sided legislation, thinking only of women's interests, without consideration for the state, the nation's prosperous development. Woman must be protected since she is physically weaker than man, since she is in greater danger of being brutalized emotionally, and since nature has given her duties as a mother and society, duties as a wife. The state demands that all these peculiarities (*säregenskaper*) be safeguarded against enervation or destruction, for the continued existence of the state itself in many vital respects is bound up with their protection and development. Woman belongs as mother not only to her sex and her class, but to the nation and humanity.[56]

The state consequently had not only the right but also the duty to prevent women from becoming free agents; the nation demanded different contributions of women and men and gave them different tasks to fulfill.

The position taken by the Social Democratic Women's Conference in 1907 seems to have caught the party leadership by surprise. As I noted above, the Social Democratic party had previously not shown any interest in the question of special protection for women, but when faced with the concrete proposal for a night work ban, it joined with the government in supporting the legislation. Accusing the women in its ranks of feminism and antisocialism—of demanding "an equality in the exploitation and destruction of living beings"[57]—party leaders, including some of the leading women, expressed their support in terms similar to those articulated by Marcus. "It is an indisputable fact," one writer stated,

> that woman has a *particular* duty in relation to the welfare of society. How well future generations will fulfill their duties to society is far more dependent on the health and well-being of women than on men. To deny this is to deny one of nature's most unyielding truths. . . . But this, the mission of women, requires that society protect her against the degenerating forces that threaten her, particularly in industry. *Protective legislation for women* is therefore, at least in a capitalist society, a *requirement of social hygiene.*[58]

Party leaders warned that by opposing the proposal—unsatisfactory as it might be—the women were also endangering the future of all such protective labor legislation for men, both in Sweden and internationally.[59] Moreover, the women were undermining party discipline as well as the goals of the international labor movement.

The women responded that the party leadership was not addressing the issues involved; the legislation was misguided and harmful and would put the best-paid workers out of work without protecting the weakest, such as sweated laborers. As one woman put it, the convention had been signed "by diplomats without practical experience . . . while those who would be affected were never heard."[60] The party did, however, have an obligation to listen to them now, as working women whose livelihoods were threatened. The women consistently emphasized that they did not oppose protective legislation as such; they would gladly accept a night work ban for all workers. What they opposed was "this pretense of protection" that handicapped women in the labor market while affording no real protection "for us, as women and as mothers."[61]

Social Democratic women who opposed the legislation joined the Fredrika Bremer Förbund in maintaining that it was wrong to legislate for women without their participation. They made an explicit connection here between the night work prohibition and the ongoing struggle for women's suffrage, which had begun at the turn of the century. When the movement for universal suffrage gathered strength in Sweden during the 1890s, women's political emancipation had—at least osten-

sibly—been included in reformers' demands.[62] However, by the time
the Riksdag took up the issue in earnest after 1900, liberal reformers
and the Social Democratic party had both dropped women's suffrage
from their parliamentary agendas, even though the latter's party program called for the political emancipation of the entire working class.
To demand the vote for women, both groups argued, would indefinitely
delay attainment of the more important cause of male suffrage because
of conservative opposition. Only a few independent M.P.s, such as the
liberal radical and later Social Democrat Carl Lindhagen, continued to
raise this issue in the Riksdag.

In response, middle-class women began a separate campaign for
female suffrage after the turn of the century, forming the National Association for Women's Suffrage in 1903. The Social Democratic women's
movement initially accepted the argument that the interests of the
working class were best served by presenting a united front behind
the demand for "male suffrage first" and showed restraint in criticizing
the party leadership's willingness to compromise on women's suffrage.
It refused any official cooperation with the bourgeois women's movement for suffrage, although it did allow its members to join the National
Association for Women's Suffrage individually.[63] As time went on, however, many Social Democratic women began questioning whether or
not the male leadership actually intended to raise the issue at all. Demands that the party program be honored became more intense and
public, leading to open antagonism within the party.

The question of male suffrage was finally resolved in 1907. The conservative government of Arvid Lindman put forward a proposal that
would give universal male suffrage for elections to the Second Chamber, while certain income requirements were retained for elections to
the First Chamber in order to maintain its aristocratic and conservative
character. The reform was to go into effect in 1909. In a counterproposal
calling for more radical parliamentary reform, the Social Democratic
party leadership, under growing pressure from supporters for women's
suffrage, finally included the demand that the vote be given to both
sexes. It was, however, the government's bill that was voted through
the Riksdag. In 1908, bills were once again put forward demanding suffrage for women as well, but these were unsuccessful.[64]

Thus, when the night work prohibition for women was proposed
to the Riksdag in 1908, the problem of women's suffrage was still very
much alive, and women drew parallels between these two issues.[65] Ten-

sions ran high, in the Social Democratic party in particular. Not only were women still excluded from the political rights now available to working-class men, but they felt they were once more being forced to set aside their own interests for the benefit of the male half of the working class. The women's resentment at being without any direct means of influencing political decisions regarding their lives was strong.[66] And so, toward the end of the public debate in 1909 on night work legislation, the tone of the discussion became quite harsh. Party leaders accused working Social Democratic women of blindly following the leadership of the middle-class feminists, while the women claimed that the question had degenerated into one of "male power," with the Social Democratic members of the Riksdag allying themselves with the conservative government in voting for the law. "Note," one commentator wrote in *Morgonbris,* the periodical of the working-class women's movement, "in what harmony the most angry of political opponents cast their vote."[67]

◆ ◆

The government's bill for a women's night work prohibition was defeated in 1908. In 1909, however, the proposal came up again and was passed. It got through the conservative-dominated First Chamber with a margin of only one vote, but in the Second Chamber it succeeded by a large majority composed mainly of the liberal and Social Democratic factions. The defeat of the bill in 1908 can be attributed mainly to distrust among many conservative Riksdag members for all types of protective labor legislation. It also signaled a lack of interest in the question among the many representatives from rural areas, who remained silent during the 1908 debates. They may have experienced a change of heart in 1909, possibly because the question of Sweden's international reputation played a prominent part in the debates.[68] Sweden's rejection of the law in 1908 had become the object of some disparaging discussion abroad, and at home this was a source of embarrassment.

The debates in the Riksdag show that conventional political labels such as liberal, conservative, or even social democratic are not really relevant for categorizing participants or their views on women or women's work. Social Democrats stood nearly united in their support of the law,[69] but liberals and conservatives were split. On the one hand, opponents of all political persuasions argued against the prohibition to some extent in terms of equality between the sexes. But mostly more practical matters came into play: the law offered little real protection for women and would in fact be to their disadvantage. Furthermore, it seemed simply superfluous for Swedish conditions and women. The parliamentary committee's misgivings carried much weight here, and women's opposition was also a reference point. On the other hand, supporters across the political spectrum argued that night work—and, indeed, all factory work—was dangerous for women. The state had the right and the duty to protect weaker members of society, and it was the obligation of all individuals to put aside their personal interests for the good of all. Even many of those conservatives who normally feared any legislation that threatened to breach the "freedom of contract" said to prevail in the labor market accepted this argument. Both sides noted that the law would in truth affect relatively few women, but each drew different conclusions. Opponents argued that a prohibition was therefore not really necessary, while supporters believed that it would check a growing problem. Social Democrats grounded their support in a tactical argument: a night work prohibition for women was the first step in regulating the working hours of adult men.[70]

◆ ◆

Thus justifications were found for passing the night work prohibition, despite doubts about its necessity and suitability for Swedish conditions. The fact that the law would implement an international convention appears to have been the deciding factor behind its enactment. By protecting its women workers—whether or not they in fact needed or wanted this protection—Sweden would enter into the mainstream of European culture, as several speakers in the Riksdag put it. The conceptions of women workers that earlier led to the formulation of such laws abroad had clearly found resonance among Swedish lawmakers.

Why did the Social Democratic women revolt? Their nearly unified resistance to restrictive labor legislation must indeed be seen as a revolt, a real questioning of party authority. Clearly, much of the reason lay with the female typographers, who quite rightly felt themselves to be directly threatened by the law.[71] However, another important factor is that women's trade union activity and political organization were undergoing a great upswing after 1900. Thus, by the time women's factory work in Sweden was beginning to be defined as a problem and protective legislation as a solution, working women had begun creating alternative options and were articulating their own solutions. By organizing their own trade union or demanding a place in male-dominated unions, as the typographers did, and by becoming active in working-class politics as well as in the campaign for women's suffrage, they showed a new sense of self-awareness that allowed them to question some of the assumptions underlying gendered protective labor legislation.

The women opposing the night work legislation were not defending equality with men in an abstract sense. Few feminists claimed, in the spirit of Hilda Sachs, that all women had the *right* to do whatever they pleased. What women—the single woman, the widow, the woman without means—had was an *obligation* to work, and "as long as this is held to be a social duty, the law cannot in all justice deny her the possibility of doing so."[72] But this does not mean that they were arguing for Ellen Key's "difference." They were arguing difference, to be sure, but their arguments were based on a perception of differences among *women*—married and unmarried, with or without children, doing different kinds of work—and they demanded that this complex reality be taken into account. In *Morgonbris* this position was expressed not as feminism but as humanism:

> The reasons underlying women's antagonism against the law are, quite naturally, primarily of an economic nature. And no matter how much one proclaims the idealistic side of this matter—the agreeable thought of protecting weak women and future generations—we still believe that the demands to protect our means of survival are no less important, even if they cannot be transformed into such nice phrases. And for the unmarried workers, the widows and those women who have to support themselves, the question of survival is the most important of all. . . . This position is not the result of any kind of feminism, but rather, an expression of a purely human urge for survival.[73]

This statement reveals a view of women very different from the Key vision of difference—which in fact meant the sameness of all women— and it differed as well from prevailing gender definitions.

By insisting on the diversity of women and by demanding legislation that would lighten the burden of the working woman (expanded factory inspection, the regulation of sweated trades, maternity insurance that turned the obligatory maternity leave into a benefit rather than a burden), opponents of protective legislation for women were also implicitly insisting upon the autonomy and economic independence of *some* women outside the household setting. This was not necessarily desirable, nor was it a bid for equality. It was, however, a reflection of the reality of many working-class women obliged to support themselves.

The typographers, those most threatened by the proposed legislation, were defending just such economic autonomy and independence. This, too, was a challenge to the prevailing discourse on women's difference that accorded women value only as wives and mothers. I think this helps explain the heat and intensity of Sweden's debate on night work prohibition, which was far out of proportion with its potential effects.

The irony of the debate on the night work ban is that it brings to light the real problems of women workers, the fact that their working conditions in small unmechanized shops or in their homes doing piece-work were subject to less control than men's working conditions. The factory inspectorate, for example, was designed to supervise working conditions in mechanized—male—workshops. The areas where most women worked would not in fact fall under the jurisdiction of the night work prohibition. Cottage industry was explicitly excluded, as we have seen, and in Sweden it was generally left unregulated. The debate on a night work ban revealed the immense gap between the reality and the rhetoric of Swedish women's labor market.

How, then, does one interpret the prohibition and the debate if it scarcely addressed the real problems facing the vast majority of women workers? It quite clearly had a symbolic function. This was a period of upheaval in gender relations, or at least it was perceived to be: much of the imagery in the debate is about *disruption,* of society, of the family, and of relations between the sexes. The legislation helped to "reinstate" a gender balance. As one speaker in the Riksdag put it, the passing of the night work prohibition would signal the beginning of a "mascu-line renaissance."[74] But more than that, it was a way of (re)structuring reality to fit concepts of gender—woman as mother, woman as weaker —by in fact making women weaker through legal means.

Notes

1. Gerda Meyerson, *Kvinnorna i industrin: Anteckningar* (Stockholm: Bok-förlags-Aktiebolaget EOS, 1909), 3–4.

2. Women factory workers were employed primarily in the textile industry, which hired over 60 percent of them. They also worked in the tobacco indus-try, with foodstuffs (brewing, canning), in paper mills, and at printing and bookbinding. See Lynn Karlsson and Ulla Wikander, *Kvinnoarbete och könsse-gregering i svensk industri 1870–1950: Tre uppsatser.* Uppsala Papers in Economic History. Research Report No. 9 (Uppsala: Department of Economic History, 1985), 20ff.

3. I think it is important to distinguish between legislation based on assumptions regarding women's social and reproductive role (such as hours legislation), which I would term "restrictive," and laws based on reproduction itself (maternity leave, etc.).

4. I use the terms "liberal" and "conservative" (always lowercased) in a general sense to denote political ideology as well as party affiliation. The Swedish political party system was relatively unstable at the turn of the century, with liberal and conservative parties splitting and regrouping around different issues, particularly protectionism and universal suffrage. For the purposes of this chapter, it is sufficient to group the non–Social Democratic members of the Riksdag into these broad categories. For a discussion of the development of the political parties in Sweden, see Sten Carlsson, "Partiväsendet i den svenska tvåkammarriksdagen 1867–1970," in *Tvåkammarriksdagen 1867–1970: Ledamöter och valkretsar,* vol. 4, ed. Anders Norberg et al. (Stockholm: Sveriges Riksdag, 1990).

5. The information in this section is based on Hjalmar Sellberg, *Staten och arbetarskyddet 1850–1919: En studie i svensk socialpolitik* (Uppsala: Almqvist & Wiksells Boktryckeri AB, 1950), chaps. 1–2. This is the standard work on protective labor legislation in Sweden. For a discussion of the development of a social policy discourse in Sweden around the turn of the century, see Sven E. Olsson, *Social Policy and Welfare State in Sweden* (Lund: Arkiv Förlag, 1990), chap. 1.

6. The Factory and Crafts Ordinance of 1846 and later the Freedom of Trade Ordinance of 1864 had included some stipulations regarding child labor (children under twelve were prohibited from working in factories and crafts, and night work was prohibited for those younger than eighteen). However, no provisions were made for the enforcement of these regulations, which were generally without effect. In the ordinance of 1881, the working hours of children under fourteen were restricted to six hours and those of fourteen- to eighteen-year-olds to ten hours.

7. *Betänkande angående minderårigas antagande och användande i fabrik, handtverk eller annan handtering, afgifvet af dertill af Kongl. Maj:t förordnande Kommitterade.* (Stockholm: Ivar Hæggströms Boktryckeri, 1877), 87.

8. *Betänkande afgifvet den 11 mars 1892 af komitén för revision af förordningen den 18 november 1881 angående minderåriges användande i arbete vid fabrik, handtverk eller annan handtering m.m.* (Stockholm: Kungl. Boktryckeriet P. A. Norstedt & Söner, 1892), 6.

9. Ibid., 79.

10. Ibid., 153, 164, 179.

11. When called on to examine the committee's proposal, the Royal Board of Trade, strongly influenced by large industrial employers, had in fact struck out all the regulations regarding women on the grounds that they were unnecessary (no women worked in mines), unenforceable (maternity leave), or

ill advised (the night work prohibition—the board failed to understand why morality demanded that women should be denied "honest work," even at night). See *Underdånigt utlåtande af Kongl. Maj:ts och rikets Kommerskollegium och Kongl. Medicinalstyrelsen öfver det betänkande som den 11 mars 1892 afgifvits af komitén för revision af förordningen den 18 november 1881 angående minderåriges användande i arbete vid fabrik, handtverk eller annan handtering m.m.* (Stockholm: K. L. Beckman, 1893), 25, 34–35. The government included the first two provisions to signal its support of the principles of special protection for women established in Berlin (*Riksdagens protokoll 1900:* Prop. 57). See also Sellberg, *Staten*, 129.

12. Bills calling for a maximum hours act for adult workers were proposed in the Riksdag in 1886 and several times during the 1890s by individual members of the liberal left wing. This was one of the major political demands of the growing workers' movement, and an eight-hour day was included in the party program at the first Social Democratic party congress in 1889. In the discussion of one such bill in 1894, conservative opponents to this legislation argued that the state might be forced to pass such a law for children and adult women "in order to protect the weak," but no proposals to this effect were ever presented to the Riksdag (*Riksdagens protokoll 1894:* Första Kammarens Tillfälliga Utskott no. 2, Utlåtande no. 13, 2). See also Sellberg, *Staten*, 116.

13. *Internationella arbetsorganisationen I: Allmän del; Historik-Uppgifter-Verksamhet* (Stockholm: Kungl. Boktryckeriet P. A. Norstedt & Söner, 1928), 1–19.

14. To study the debate I have gone through a number of periodicals and newspapers. The most important sources are Fredrika Bremer Förbundet's periodical *Dagny* (beginning in 1886), *Social tidskrift* (1901), which was a voice for liberals actively working for social reforms, and *Morgonbris* (1904), representing the Social Democratic and union women.

15. Gripenberg, quoted in *Dagny* 12 (1899): 276.

16. Ibid., 278.

17. Maria Cederschiöld (1856–1935) was employed as an expert on foreign affairs by one of Sweden's large daily newspapers. She was a member of several women's organizations and was particularly active in the campaigns for married women's property rights and for women's suffrage. See *Svenska män och kvinnor*, vol. 2 (Stockholm: Albert Bonniers Förlag, 1944), article signed E.Bm. [Eva Bohm].

18. *Dagny* 8 (1900): 171–81.

19. Hilda Engström Sachs (1857–1935) continued to work as a journalist until her retirement in 1920; she published novels and social commentaries as well. Sachs was one of the founders of Sweden's first organization for women's suffrage, in 1902, and sat on the board of the Stockholm section of the Association for Women's Suffrage (Föreningen för kvinnors politiska rösträtt) between 1912 and 1921. After 1921, she was active in the Swedish Women's

Citizens Association (Svenska kvinnors medborgarförbund). See *Svenska män och kvinnor,* vol. 6 (Stockholm: Albert Bonniers Förlag, 1949), article signed T.M. [Thure Månsson]; Ulla Manns, *Women in Sweden: Historical Facts from 1845 to 1921* (Stockholm: Center for Women Researchers and Women's Studies in Stockholm, 1987).

20. *Dagny* 9–10 (1900): 216.

21. Ibid.

22. For a short introduction to Ellen Key (1849–1926) and her works, see Ulf Wittrock, "Ellen Key," in *Svenskt biografiskt lexikon,* vol. 21 (Stockholm: Albert Bonniers Förlag, 1975–77).

23. Ellen Key, *Barnets århundrade* (Stockholm: Albert Bonniers förlag, 1900), 155.

24. Ibid., 103.

25. Ibid., 155–56.

26. Ibid., 105ff.

27. Ibid., 113.

28. Ibid., 152ff.

29. Ibid., 162.

30. As part of bills calling for the revision of the laws on occupational hazards put to the Riksdag in 1902 and 1903, it was proposed that women be prohibited from greasing transmissions or running steam boilers. The question was eventually referred to the 1905 Committee on Occupational Hazards, which rejected this proposal in its final report of 1912. In 1906, Hvita Bandet, the Swedish section of the Women's Christian Temperance Movement, began a campaign seeking to prohibit women from working as stevedores along the coast of northern Sweden. After extensive investigation, in 1916 women under twenty-one were prohibited from doing such work.

31. For example, *Dagny* 17 (1904): 377–83 printed in full the speech made by the Dutch delegate Fru Rutgers-Hoitsema to the 1904 International Women's Conference in Berlin describing in detail the consequences of protective legislation for women workers: in industries such as textiles, where women and men did not compete, a restriction of women's working hours had led to better working conditions. This was encouraging, she noted, but at the same time "it had unfortunately made the general public completely blind to the disadvantages of the system" (380). In branches employing both women and men, such as printing, legislation had caused women to lose their jobs. In 1905, at its yearly meeting, the Förbund clearly rejected protective legislation for women. The point under discussion was What can be done to stop the flood of young women to factory work? Legislation against this was, the organization wrote, "both unwise and without effect." See *Dagny* 2–3 (1905): 41.

32. After extensive investigation, a women's factory inspectorate was created under the new Labor Protection Act of 1912.

33. Among the founders of this organization was Gerda Meyerson.

34. Up to the mid-1920s, this organization had a large impact on the development of government policy in a number of areas such as unemployment policy and poor relief. It numbered several important writers on social and economic issues among its members, and during the early twentieth century many of its male members went on to become leading civil servants in the area of social welfare. For a history of this association and its founders, see Olsson, *Social Policy,* 64–79.

35. *Social tidskrift* 6 (1906): 98ff.; 7 (1907): 547. As the debate on the special protection of women progressed, gendered arguments for legislation regulating sweated industry were adopted. In particular, Moritz Marcus, who carried out an official investigation of conditions in sweated trades in 1908, justified the need for legislation in such terms. However, later proposals for legislation were gender-neutral. See *Betänkande afgivet den 9 december 1909 af den af kungl.maj:t den 20 januari 1905 tillsatta kommittén för revision af lagarna angående skydd mot yrkesfara och angående minderårigas och kvinnors användande till arbete i industriellt yrke m.m.* (Stockholm: Isaac Marcus' Boktryckeri-Aktiebolag, 1909), 24–27, and *Betänkande afgivet den 9 december 1909 af den af kungl.maj:t den 20 januari 1905 tillsatta kommittén för revision af lagarna angående skydd mot yrkesfara och angående minderårigas och kvinnors användande till arbete i industriellt yrke m.m.-Bihang* (Stockholm: Isaac Marcus' Boktryckeri-Aktiebolag, 1909), 313–411.

36. See Ulla Wikander's essay, "Some 'Kept the Flag of Feminist Demands Waving,' " in this volume.

37. *Social tidksrift* 5 (1905): 125.

38. Christina Carlsson, *Kvinnosyn och kvinnopolitik: En studie i svensk socialdemokrati 1880–1910* (Lund: Arkiv Förlag, 1986), 162–66, 172–75, 187.

39. See ibid., 132ff. Women's clubs within the Social Democratic party began forming on the local level during the 1890s.

40. The Women's Trade Union organized primarily seamstresses. In 1904 it began publishing *Morgonbris,* a periodical that addressed women's issues within the labor movement and that the Social Democratic women's organization later took over.

41. Carlsson, *Kvinnosyn,* 172–75. Carlsson suggests that there also may have been tactical reasons for the position of the Social Democratic party on this matter; it was important to emphasize that the adult male worker also must be afforded worker protection. This was particularly true in the case of the normal working day, which was really the only demand for protective legislation on the Social Democratic agenda.

42. The National Archives, *Utrikesdepartementet, 1912 års dossiersystem,* vol. 2327, dossier 30:33, Utrdrag av protokollet öfver finansärenden . . . den 2 december 1905. The government declined to sign the other convention under consideration at Bern—to prohibit the use of phosphorus (which caused poi-

soning among workers) in the match industry—on the grounds that this would severely harm the industry in Sweden. In this case, the government argued, industry's needs outweighed humanitarian considerations.

43. Both the liberal and conservative factions in the Riksdag, as well as employers and the civil service, were represented on the committee.

44. The National Archives, *Konseljakt 35*, undated letter from *Typografiska kvinnoklubben* to Åkerman. See also Elin Johansson, *Typografiska kvinnoklubben 1904–1936* (Stockholm: Typografiska föreningen, 1939), 24, 97. It should be noted that the equal wages guaranteed women handsetters were the minimum wages stipulated in the trade's list of rates. There is evidence that suggests that male typographers in fact earned more than their women colleagues, their wages being supplemented by family allowances, for example. Moreover, employers could assign tasks that were well paid exclusively to men. For a discussion of the gender hierarchy in the printing trade, see Inger Humlesjö, "Förmedling av arbetslöshet? Om kvinnor, 'flickor' och typografer i 1920-talets Stockholm" (ms., Department of Economic History, Uppsala University, 1992).

45. The conference was organized by the Stockholm's Women's Club (Stockholms Allmänna Kvinnoklubb) and the Women's Trade Union. Founded in 1892, the former organization was engaged in both political and union activities and initiated the union activity that eventually led to the establishment of the Women's Trade Union.

46. The National Archives, *Konseljakt 35*, letter of Feb. 1907 fr. Socialdemokratiska kvinnokonferensens Arbetsutskott to Åkerman.

47. *Morgonbris* 3 (1908): 1–2. These demands were made, for example, in a resolution taken at a public meeting held in April 1908 to protest the proposed night work prohibition. The question of maternity insurance to compensate for wages lost during the maternity leave mandated for women working in industry is quite complex. Briefly, the issue arose toward the end of the debate on the night work prohibition as the result of a bill put to the Riksdag in 1908 by the liberal Edvard Wawrinsky calling for an investigation into this matter. The idea of such insurance gained immediate support among feminists, liberals, and the women in the labor movement, and was pointed to as the type of measure that would actually benefit the woman worker. After an investigation, the government did propose an obligatory maternity insurance in 1912. However, this proposal met with a storm of protest from all sides because of how the system was constructed: all women factory workers over the age of fifteen, whether single or married, were to pay premiums, as were their employers. This sum would then be matched by the state. Women protested that this would put the entire burden of parenthood on women and their employers; fathers contributed nothing. Besides protesting the general injustice of such a system, women argued that it would discourage employers from

using female labor. Other opponents feared that the insurance would encourage immorality and illegitimacy. However, what finally defeated the bill was the fact that Sweden had no obligatory workers' insurance at this time, and it was considered unthinkable by many to introduce maternity insurance before this "larger" problem had been solved. In 1912, the Riksdag passed a law providing state subsidies to voluntary insurance schemes. General maternity benefits—that is, not just for factory workers—were introduced in the 1930s, but these were given to mothers only after a means test and did not provide full compensation for lost income. A true maternity insurance for all women, covering hospital costs and compensating for lost income during the now voluntary six-month maternity leave permitted all women workers, was introduced in the 1950s when the question of an obligatory health insurance program was resolved. See Kerstin Abukhanfusa, *Piskan och moroten: Om könens tilldelning av skyldigheter och rättigheter i det svenska socialförsäkringssystemet 1913–1980* (Stockholm: Carlssons förlag, 1987), 158ff.; Elisabeth Elgan, "Fyra uppsatser om kvinnor och moderskap i Sverige och Frankrike under 1900-talets första hälft" (ms., Department of History, Uppsala University, 1991), 1–4; Ann-Sofie Ohlander, "Det osynliga barnet? Kampen om den socialdemokratiska familjepolitiken," in *Socialdemokratins samhälle 1889–1989*, ed. Klaus Misgeld et al. (Stockholm: Tidens förlag, 1989).

48. The National Archives, *Konseljakt 35*, Utdrag af protokollet . . . den 21 oktober 1907, 1.

49. Ibid.

50. The committee subsequently carried out such an investigation, which showed that about three thousand women (5 percent of all women workers in industry), not just five hundred, as was originally assumed by the government, might be affected by the law. For most of these women, night work meant more or less sporadic overtime work in such industries as bookbinding and printing, brewing, knitting, paper mills, and laundries; only about one-third of the women worked at night on a regular basis, in sugar manufacturing, bakeries, and pulp and paper mills. There were, moreover, a little over five hundred women employed in canneries.

51. The National Archives, *Konseljakt 35*, Utdrag af protokollet . . . den 21 oktober 1907, 3.

52. Ibid., 2–3.

53. It should be noted that the committee was *not* generally negative toward labor legislation; rather, it attempted to go quite far in other areas of worker protection.

54. The National Archives, *Konseljakt 35*, Yrkesfarekommittén med förslag till lag . . . 4 november 1907, letter to Konungen.

55. Ibid.

56. M. Marcus, *Svensk arbetarlagstiftning* (Stockholm: Hugo Gebers Förlag, 1907), 24–25.

57. "Kvinnornas nattarbete i industrin," *Social Demokraten*, May 1, 1908.

58. Ibid.

59. The Social Democratic party leader Hjalmar Branting in particular emphasized this point. See, for example, "Det kvinnliga industriella nattarbetet," *Social Demokraten*, May 20, 1908.

60. The speaker was Ruth Gustafsson at the 1908 Social Democratic party congress, according to a newspaper account of that meeting. See "Socialdemokratiska partiets kongress," *Arbetet*, June 10, 1908. This statement was not recounted in the official protocol from the congress. See *Förhandlingarna vid Sveriges socialdemokratiska arbetarepartis sjunde ordinarie kongress i Stockholm 28 maj–5 juni 1908* (Stockholm: A.-B. Arbetarnes Tryckeri, 1908), 240.

61. "Kvinnorna och förbudet mot nattarbete," *Social Demokraten*, May 4, 1908.

62. The following is based on Carlsson, *Kvinnosyn*, 140–61, 200–217; Sten Carlsson, *Svensk historia del 2; Tiden efter 1718* (Stockholm: Läromedelsförlagen, 1961), 460ff.; Kersti Ullenhag, *Industriell utveckling och demokratisering 1862–1921* (Uppsala: Almqvist & Wiksell, 1984), 199–201; Lydia Wahlström, *Den svenska kvinnorörelsen* (Stockholm: P. A. Norstedt och söners förlag, 1933), 58ff.; Erik Timelin, *Ministären Lindman och representationsreformen 1907–1909* (Karlskrona: J. A. Krooks Bokhandel, 1928), 256ff.

63. The dilemma for the Social Democratic women was that the suffrage question was of course as much a matter of class as of gender: what was at issue was whether the right to vote was to be limited by income, by sex, or by both. The National Association for Women's Suffrage demanded that women be given the vote on the same basis as men; hence they could support proposals that only citizens above a certain income level be enfranchised, thus excluding both working-class women and men from the vote. Such a compromise was of course unacceptable for the Social Democratic party, which demanded the vote for all men, and later women, regardless of income. See Carlsson, *Kvinnosyn*, 205–8.

64. Women were in fact not given the vote until 1921.

65. Carlsson, *Kvinnosyn*, 209ff. These gender conflicts within social democracy over protective labor legislation and women's suffrage are the subject of Carlsson's monograph.

66. At a public meeting called in 1908 to discuss the proposal and attended by over four hundred persons, several speakers alluded to the fact that women did not have the vote, and they demanded repeatedly that the night work prohibition be put aside until the question of women's suffrage had been resolved. The same point was made in the final resolution adopted by the meeting. This was an issue that clearly stirred up a lot of bitterness. See, for example, *Social Demokraten*, Apr. 29 and May 1, 1908.

67. *Morgonbris* 5 (1909): 7.

68. Sellberg, *Staten*, 173ff.

69. Carl Lindhagen, a feminist and an extremely independent Social Democrat, submitted bills opposing the proposed legislation and instead proposing a general night work prohibition. He put up a brilliant defense for women's rights, particularly in 1908, which may very well have influenced the outcome of the debate in the Riksdag that year.

70. *Riksdagens protokoll 1908*, F.K. no. 59 and A.K. no. 71; *Riksdagens protokoll 1909*, F.K. no. 28 and A.K. no. 42; and Sellberg, *Staten*, 173ff.

71. Official studies done after the implementation of the law in 1911 show that this occupation eventually became closed to women workers. Inger Humlesjö, Department of Economic History, Uppsala University, is studying the long-term effects of the legislation for women in the printing trade.

72. *Dagny* 12 (1908): 128.

73. *Morgonbris* 3 (1908): 1–2.

74. *Riksdagens protokoll 1909*, A.K. 1909 no. 42, 67. The speaker was Johan C. W. Thyrén, a professor of law and conservative member of the Second Chamber.

· 9 ·

Protection or Equality?

Debates on Protective Legislation in Norway

Gro Hagemann

As long as liberty and equality have figured as central values in our culture, segments of society have asked whether or not and how general civil rights applied to both sexes. Are women to operate in the public sphere on the same conditions as men? Or does being female always entail certain limitations on individual freedom? Since women in our culture are the "other" sex, differing from the male standard in a number of ways, answers to these questions remain problematic.

Labor legislation from the beginning of this century illustrates how the woman question intersected with the shaping of a modern labor market. Like other institutions, the labor market was built on the idea of freedom of individuals to act by themselves, unbound by the restrictions set by ascribed status or privileges. Any idea of protecting workers by law represented a limitation on their freedom to establish themselves in business or to invest capital in labor. The question of affording women special protection added yet another aspect to these discussions, namely, the question of equality among individuals. Do women really have the capacity and the qualities necessary to be treated as independently acting individuals? Or do the differences between men and women require restrictions on women's individual freedom?

These questions were debated in most industrialized countries, including Norway, around the turn of the century. They appeared on political agendas in the 1880s and 1890s as a consequence of industrialization and a growing labor movement. The need for restrictions on children's work in factories was raised first, followed shortly thereafter by the question of special protection for female workers. Conservatives favored labor legislation on social conservative premises and issued a report in 1885 that focused on protecting the social order and stemming implacable class conflict. Social Democrats favored legal regulation as a way of reducing the power of capital. Liberals were divided between a right-wing faction arguing for individual freedom and a social-radical faction that favored labor protection; their disagreement on these issues contributed to the party's breakup in the 1890s.

The debate on special protection for female workers at first did not deal with sexual differences as an explicit issue. This may seem paradoxical. Assumptions about the differences between men and women were so deeply rooted and so widespread, however, that such explicit articulation seemed unnecessary. What was controversial here was not gender but the future course of social policy and the basic relationship between state and individual. For left-wing Liberals, approval of progressive social legislation was the important issue. For right-wing Liberals and Conservatives, opposition to an extensive female protection offered the means to draw a line that would separate them from social radicals.

Not until the bourgeois feminist movement entered into the political arena did special protection for women become an explicit gender question. The group's energetic agitation constituted a major reason for the Norwegian Parliament's rejection of a ban on night work in 1909. Feminist intervention into the debate introduced confusion into traditional political positions. Disagreement on gender issues did not follow older, familiar political divisions, and political parties were divided as a result. New and short-lived alliances were created when some right-wing Liberals appeared on the same side as radical supporters of feminism, while several Conservatives spun out arguments resembling those of the most steadfast Socialists.

The debate was indisputably one in which emotions ran high, with a great number of dramatis personae locked in passionate exchanges. Yet the ferocity of the debate seemed out of proportion to its object of concern. Rare was the woman who worked at night in turn-of-the-century Norway. Nor were there any compelling signs that an increase of their ranks was imminent. The only place where women worked at night to any great extent was in the canning industry of western Norway. There, work went on continously during the fishing season, and everyone agreed that the canning industry would have to be exempted from any prospective prohibitions.

The Norwegian case prompts two obvious questions that will form the subject of this chapter. Why was a ban on women's night work rejected in Norway, in contrast to virtually all other industrialized countries? Why was the debate conducted with such fervor, producing so much ado about next to nothing?

◆ ◆

In accordance with the conservative initiative in 1885, the first Factory Protection Act of Norway, passed in 1892, was a moderate piece of law. The act did not include either general regulation of working hours or explicit restrictions on adult women's working hours. In fact, these issues had not even been on the agenda. The act did forbid women from working in mines or cleaning and oiling machines that were running. Work was also prohibited for six weeks after childbirth. But only young people's working hours were subject to any limitations: factory work was prohibited for children under the age of ten, and working hours were limited until children reached the age of eighteen.

While much public interest focused on children's work, protection of women workers drew only slight and sporadic attention at the time. For instance, the fledgling Norwegian Labor party, founded in 1887, worked out an alternative to the proposed law in 1890, which a mass meeting approved in Kristiania (Oslo). The main demand of the Labor proposal was the eight-hour day. However, special regulation of married women's working hours also was part of the proposed law: "Workers under the age of 18—male and female—and married women of all ages should not work more than 6 hours a day and should not be occupied at night."[1]

A draft bill far more radical than the 1892 law found its way to Parliament in 1901; it proposed extending restrictions on young people's working hours to include adult female workers. The man behind the proposal was Johan Castberg, a member of the left wing of the Liberal party. In the decade following passage of the 1892 act, social questions had become pressing issues in the realm of high politics. Accelerated by the spread of protective legislation abroad and by the growth of the domestic labor movement, Liberals and Conservatives alike devoted more attention to such matters.

The debate mirrored the general situation in the country. Struggle for a parliamentary system brought about a change in the political regime in 1884, when the Liberal party came to power. Until 1905, when the union between Norway and Sweden came to an end, a period of constitutional and national upheaval ensued. The vital popular and national movement that brought the Liberal party to power in 1884 encompassed wide differences, however, and was too loosely structured to survive the acute political crisis that ensued. The political situation became unstable, the Liberal party divided, and the government changed hands repeatedly.[2] Among its members the Liberal party counted labor politicians and probably as many employers as the Conservatives.

The future direction of social policy became one of the main political disputes in the 1890s. Moved by fears of social radicalism as well as by the desire to gain working men's votes, both Liberals and Conservatives devoted attention to social questions. The Liberals imposed direct taxation on income and property, replacing duties on imported consumer goods. They introduced national labor insurance and the eight-hour day, as well as a more radical factory law (in 1901). In part these initiatives stemmed from the watchful eye Liberals kept on trends in other northern and central European countries; they were eager to be "modern." Conservatives largely opposed such schemes, as did members of the right wing of the Liberal party. Although these groups favored some social legislation, they resisted the extensive changes proposed. Stemming social radicalism became one of their most urgent political priorities.[3]

Among legislators, female protection was not initially a question of gender. It was part of the broader controversy around social issues to which potential solutions have been somewhat hapazardly stuck together by men armed with international precedents and eager to keep their fingers on the pulse of the times. Left-wing Liberals wished to introduce extensive regulation of the working day for all, including a ban on night work for women. They were also eager to emulate the most advanced social legislation from abroad. Conservative party members were in favor of more moderate regulation as a way to protect the family and social order. Right-wing Liberals clung to the comforts of a detached laissez-faire stance and wanted regulation to be kept as limited as possible, be it for men, women, or children.

The discussion going on outside the halls of Parliament turned female protection into a gender issue. After establishing the Norwegian Feminist Association (Norsk Kvinnesaksforening) in 1884—roughly parallel to bourgeois feminism elsewhere—feminists became active participants in public political discussions. General conditions enhanced their influence. Broadly supported within the political and cultural elite, moderate feminist ideas derived legitimacy from the strength of lower middle-class freeholders and small farmers among whom women occupied relatively free and independent positions. Also, from the 1870s on, the radical ideas of Henrik Ibsen and others had put the emancipation of women on the public agenda. Finally, the small group of feminists had close connections with the inner circles of the ruling Liberal party, sharing ideological convictions and personal alliances with its leaders. In contrast, antifeminists tended to be associated with the former political elite, whose disrepute after their political defeat in 1884 they also shared. As the involvement of feminists in the labor protection debate increased from the turn of the century onward, the debate took on a different character.

The Storting (Norwegian Parliament) never actually discussed the 1901 proposal. In fact, protective legislation did not appear on the parliamentary agenda until 1909, with a watered-down version of the 1901 proposal. After stormy sessions in the Storting, a small majority of deputies rejected any limits on working hours for women and for adult workers generally. For children and young people working hours remained limited: work was prohibited entirely for children under the age of ten, restricted to six hours a day for those between the ages of ten and fourteen, and restricted to ten hours a day for those between fourteen and eighteen. Blocked by the votes of Conservatives and a considerable number of Liberals, a ban on night work for women failed to pass. In turning back night work restrictions, Parliament refused to ratify the international Bern Convention of 1906.[4] The result was to be decisive for Norway's stand on female protection during the decades that followed. According to the Liberals, rejection of the Bern Convention placed Norway outside the community of "civilized nations." Such warnings notwithstanding, the night work convention was never to be ratified.

Norway's position is best viewed against the international legislative landscape. Ample evidence exists that Norwegians essentially imported their concept of protective legislation from abroad. Legislators and administrators on the national level generally gave high priority to adjusting to standards set by international organizations. On the whole, protection as such enjoyed a broad popular base in the country. All these factors make Norway's repeated rejection of night work prohibition for women quite striking. Where did the reluctance lie?

A partial explanation rests in Norway's economic situation at the turn of the century. Having industrialized comparatively late, Norway had only scant experience with factory work. While industrialization had picked up, factory workers remained few in number. The vast majority of working women were employed not as factory labor but as servants, seamstresses, or cleaning women outside the industrial sector. Of all women engaged in waged labor in Kristiania, the industrial center of the country in 1900, only 12 percent were factory workers.[5] Only the printing industry operated with night work for women, and the female compositors numbered no more than a few hundred. Except for the canning industry of western Norway, the legislation would have affected few women.

From an economic point of view, prohibiting night work for women was at best a marginal problem. In fact, neither employers nor workers showed much interest in the question. The Employers' Federation (Norsk Arbeidsgiverforening) objected to such a ban on principle, affirming its members' liberal convictions. The trade union movement remained virtually mute on the question. Concern among unionized women was evident, most of it mobilized by the Socialist women's movement, which had made support of female protection a major pursuit. But for most organized working-class women, factory work was no more than a temporary occupation in the years before marriage. What activism there was by working-class women was generally ignored by the male-dominated labor movement.

The political situation in Norway shed further light on the reluctance to institute a night work ban. The process of modernization was being conducted by a large class of small freeholders, including a peasantry that was mostly free and equal. During the nineteenth century this lower middle class was closely associated and identified with a nationalist movement and progressive democratic development. The convergence of nationalism and democracy was a distinctive feature of the political climate in nineteenth-century Norway, at least as long as the union with Sweden was maintained.[6] On the one hand, liberal ideas had a strong hold inside the ruling classes and the growing bourgeoisie. On the other hand, the old economic, political, and cultural elite was weak and conservative ideas were not very influential in the political arena. Modern ideas such as feminism, general education, and humane working conditions, then, all met with less resistance than elsewhere. Support for such impulses became even more favorable in the political climate that arose around the turn of the century, set in motion by the shift to a parliamentary system in 1884 and the fight for dissolution of the union with Sweden in 1905.

◆ ◆

As a result of this political situation, conditions in Norway were highly favorable for feminists seeking to exert influence on the political discourse. They set their opposition to the 1901 proposal in motion in 1902. That summer feminists from the Scandinavian countries gathered in Kristiania, and protective legislation occupied a prime spot on the agenda. The Danish Parliament, the Folketing, had recently rejected a proposal to ban night work for women, and feminists from neighboring countries felt inspired by this success. Delegates at the meeting adopted a resolution that declared their opposition to any night work prohibition.

When the 1906 Bern Convention demanded prohibition of women's night work, it added fuel to the growing fire. Norway's bourgeois feminists began a concerted campaign against the idea of a ban. They ran mass meetings, issued statements to the Storting, and sent articles to newspapers arguing the virtues of their position. A variety of other women's associations added their support to the resolutions produced at feminist meetings. Most of these groups were united in the Norwegian Council of Women, established in 1904 as a division of the International Council of Women and presided over by a prominent feminist, Gina Krog. Opinions on protective legislation differed among members of the national branch as they did in the international council, and the organization did not take a formal position on the question. Nevertheless, Krog's strong opinion on the matter worked to spread the debate to parts of the women's movement that had shown little interest in feminism or social policy.

Efforts made by bourgeois women to persuade women in the labor movement to join them in opposing a ban on night work, however, were in vain. Unlike their sisters elsewhere in Scandinavia, Socialist women in Norway were virtually unanimous in their support for female protection. Beginning in 1901, women, like trade unions and political clubs, had their own group within the Labor party. They arranged mass meetings and issued public statements denouncing the impoverished version of "equality" that they complained was being forced on them by wrongheaded bourgeois women.

A handful of working-class women parted ways with the Socialist mainstream on this question. Female compositors in the printing industry drew on their own experience with night work to enter the debate. They had experienced the cost of female protection: male printing workers had used it to squeeze them out of their jobs. Accordingly, they took a firm stance on the "interests of working-class women," opposing night work prohibition and other resolutions targeting women's working hours.[7] They were joined by a group of women from a mining district in the northern part of the country, the *skeidersker,* who protested because their jobs, too, were in danger. The mining director explicitly announced that with a ban on night work for women the *skeiding* would be taken over by men.

The various groups of women involved in the debate took diametrically different positions. Bourgeois feminists argued from what they held to be fundamental principles of citizenship. Protecting working women, they believed, meant treating them as minors and declaring them incapable of managing their own affairs. For women as well as men, economic freedom was a fundamental right; regulation, if necessary, should include both sexes equally. The arguments marshaled by working-class women were of a more practical nature. Their everyday experience of long working hours and poor working conditions attuned them to the benefits of protection. Since the majority worked in sectors dominated by women, the effect of female protection would be no different than that of general protection. The female compositors and *skeidersker* constituted an exception in this respect. However, the arguments of working-class women also relied on fundamental principles: their main concerns were the health and living conditions of the working-class family. As women they considered this to be their primary responsibility; and they held individual rights to be a matter of secondary importance.

If working-class women were marginal in the debate, bourgeois feminists wielded considerable influence. Allied with the political elite, their star was on the rise. Beginning in 1885, when a separate movement for female suffrage began, they made the enfranchisement of women their top priority. Their first victory came in 1901, when women with a certain minimum income were granted the right to vote in local elections. In 1907 women were also granted the right to vote in parliamentary elections, revealing Norwegian legislators for once as impervious to masculinist examples set elsewhere in Europe.

Women were given the vote in 1907 in part because of their role in the dramatic national events of 1905, which brought to an end the ninety-year-old union with Sweden. The union had been established after the Napoleonic Wars in 1814, when the settlement between the great powers forced Denmark to give away the province of Norway. Sweden was forced to accept the Liberal Norwegian constitution and Parliament, which meant great independence within the union and created much tension between the Swedish king and the Storting. The conflict came to a climax in 1884, when a parliamentary system was installed that seriously weakened the power of the king. After the turn of the century the situation came to a head once more and nearly brought the two countries to war before a peaceful solution was finally found in 1905.

As dissolution of the Norwegian-Swedish union became imminent, several feminists were heard in the nationalist movement. In 1896 they organized women's volunteer groups to provide medical services in the event of war against Sweden.[8] When the union drew to an end in 1905, they put both their nationalist commitments and feminist aims on show on a grand scale. Excluded from the general plebiscite on continuation of the union, they arranged for their own popular vote. Some three hundred thousand women signed a petition to the Storting demanding dissolution of the union. This number was close to half of Norway's adult female population at the time and almost reached the number of women qualified to vote in local elections.

The national enthusiasm following the 1905 events made the climate favorable for feminism. In 1907 the Storting agreed to grant women with a minimum income of their own the right to vote in parliamentary elections, and it was clear to all that women were a political constituency that could no longer be overlooked. When the 1909 Factory Law was debated, women were poised to participate in the general election for the first time. Some legislators engaged in that debate argued that the decision on prohibiting night work ought to be made by the women themselves; they wanted the decision to be put off until the next session of the Storting, when the members would represent the female electorate. This was not done, but it was clear that everyone assumed women would wield influence in the impending election.

The opposition raised by bourgeois feminists against special protection for women came to dominate the public discussion on the new factory law. Both Socialists, who were represented in the Storting from 1903 on, and social radicals in the Liberal party expected a great deal from the impending law. But their priorities did not specifically encompass women. Rather, they wanted the law's provisions to incorporate artisanal labor and to provide for all workers the framework for a normal working day. Both goals were highly controversial, involving important interest groupings and stirring up much agitation among workers and employers. Nevertheless, the feminist issue overshadowed the whole debate on general protection. When the bill finally went through its reading in the Storting, the result was rather disappointing. Only small amendments were made to the 1892 law, which was still in force. No "normal day" was accepted for adults; neither was coverage extended to other kinds of labor. Night work prohibition for women was rejected, as was the 1906 Bern Convention. Other special protection for women remained unchanged, with one important exception: a female factory inspector would be appointed on the national level, and women would be represented in every local factory inspectorate as well.

◆ ◆

More than anyone else, the feminists emerged as the victors after the 1909 decision. Not only did they win the battle but they came to set the terms of future debate on female protection. From 1909 onward, this was no longer to be a debate within the framework of seemingly gender-neutral social policy. By putting expanded female protection on the public agenda, feminists had brought new dimensions to the debate on social policy and exposed the problem of gender difference embedded in the concept of protection. From now on, *feminism* was an issue that could not be overlooked. Traditional political dividing lines grew fuzzy. Right-wing Liberals who usually advocated laissez faire positions balked at the idea of equality between the sexes. Some radicals even assigned women's emancipation a higher priority than the idea of protection, which Norwegian bourgeois feminists had constructed as its antithesis.

In the years that followed, left-wing Liberal parliamentarians made attempts to reverse the 1909 rejection of the Bern Convention. A new proposal was presented in 1914, and female protection received thoroughgoing scrutiny. Apart from a ban on night work, a proposal excluding women from work that was considered dangerous for medical or moral reasons was put forward. The 1914 proposal was a radical piece of work drawn up by Johan Castberg, who was now minister of Social Affairs. However, the proposal never gathered support; nor did the Storting give it serious consideration. In the end it produced only one concrete result: a standard working day of ten hours. After thirty years of debate, this provision was hardly considered controversial. Other elements in Castberg's proposal—among them, extensive female protection—were too far-reaching to gather much political support. Moreover, the coalition that did support the proposal was fragile. No single political group had the strength and resolution to carry through another stormy debate over the issue. The Conservative block was in favor of maintaining the status quo, the Socialists were still too weak, and the left-wing Liberals in power were eager to close their ranks.

Another twenty years passed before a full-blown protective labor law was proposed, in 1935, only one week before the Labor government came into power. Although it represented a significant compromise with their priorities, the Socialists presented the bill in the Storting. Unlike their Liberal predecessors, they possessed both the decisiveness and the political support to carry it through. The new Employment Protective Act, which passed into law in 1936, included important reforms. Its reach was greatly extended; hence its new name. Only state administration, shipping, farming, and fishing were exempted from the legislation. In addition, more importance was attached to preventing workplace accidents and creating healthy working conditions. Regulation of working hours was extended by requiring employers to provide nine days of vacation for their employees each year, a provision that several tariff agreements already included. From the labor movement's point of view, protection against arbitrary dismissals constituted the most important provision. This meant limits on employers' control, the need for which had been pressing during the postwar economic crisis.

Once more the subject of female protection unleashed a heated debate. While given high priority by the Socialists, the 1936 act did not include a ban on night work for women workers. Again feminists led the opposition against international pressure to provide special protection for women. In contrast to the situation twenty-five years earlier, however, many more women from the labor movement joined them. To be sure, staunch advocates of female protection were still found in the ranks of Social Democratic women. Among women active in trade unions, however, opposition to female protection was on the increase. This paralleled the changing political attitudes of many Socialist women toward other parts of the prevailing Labor policy. Since the late 1920s both the Labor party and the Norwegian Federation of Trade Unions had worked to exclude married women from wagework. In a period of high unemployment, such restrictions found broad support among male trade unionists.[9] Among Socialist women this was a very touchy issue, for such social policy seemed to clash with their interests as working women. Their opposition to bourgeois feminism ran deep, as did their loyalty to the leaders of the Labor party and the trade unions. Despite the tug of these alliances, they found the courage to oppose these men openly and made protective legislation a gender issue in the party as well.

The Employment Protective Act imposed no special restrictions on women and in fact removed two older stipulations. Women were no longer excluded from underground work in mines, and—if suitably clothed—they were also allowed to clean and oil machines in operation. The conditions of many women were also materially improved by extending maternity provisions. In addition to the six weeks of obligatory leave after delivery, women could now also take six weeks off before giving birth. They were granted some compensation from the state, the right to return to their jobs after maternity leave, and the right to a break from work to breastfeed their children. Except for the maternity period, working women were subject to no more protection than were working men. At least formally, they were treated as equals.

The 1936 act marked the end of the battle over female protection in Norway. The events leading up to it tell the story of the problem and its resolution within the context of Norwegian legislation. On the one hand, adult women were included in an extensive health and safety protection system for all workers. On the other hand, they were subject to special protection during maternity. Protective legislation was not, however, the only aspect of the law that dealt with women's participation in the labor market. Another cluster of legislation that made the problem even more obvious was developing simultaneously. From the mid-nineteenth century on, equal rights legislation gradually opened to women the economic opportunities available to men. Formal access to trades and crafts opened up in the 1860s, as the guild regulations were definitively laid to rest. Married women attained control over their income and property in 1888. Positions in the Civil Service and academic professions gradually opened to women from the 1880s onward. The year 1912 marked a temporary end to an intensive period of reforms in this field, in which women obtained the right to hold all offices except in the church ministry and the military. None of these reforms came without resistance. However, compared to many countries, the strong Liberal tradition and a weak upper class made the path less difficult.

Norwegian lawmakers thus grappled with gender questions in a range of ways, trying to figure out how male-female differences could be adapted to a modern labor market. In the decades around the turn of the century, the labor market opened up for women in some fields, while barriers were added in others. Of course protective and equal rights legislation did not necessarily advocate principles that were incompatible. Though relying on different arguments, these principles were not mutually exclusive, for each type of legislation tended to deal with women from separate social groups. The factory workers covered by protective legislation did not have much in common with the well-educated female applicants to the Civil Service.

Equal rights legislation had a dual purpose. In part it dealt with the problem of "women not provided for," meaning the increasing number of women who did not opt for marriage. Equal rights laws aimed at giving these women alternative channels of support. The Storting also gradually passed legislation with a female elite in mind—women with exceptional talents or career ambitions. In its Norwegian formulation, protective legislation did not impinge on either of these groups but dealt with the real or anticipated problems of working-class households, focusing on women as mothers, wives, and housewives.

It would be misleading, however, to regard these two kinds of legislation mainly as two sets of regulations coexisting peacefully. On the contrary, as the Norwegian debate on protective legislation indicated, these regulations also entailed some inevitable clash among opposing principles. Opposition to protective legislation was consistently articulated using the argument of equal rights. The case for protective legislation, by contrast, hinged on conjuring up the goodwill and competence of an interventionist state to protect workers' welfare. The underlying principles assumed different ways of working with and within the modern labor market. The questions remained, How were traditional gender differences to be handled within a modern context?

◆ ◆

The debate on gender in the labor market came to establish special protection for women and emancipation as opposing, incompatible principles. For women this meant an inextricable dilemma, for they could not have both. If they wanted to be equal, they had to renounce all special treatment on the basis of sex. If, on the contrary, they wanted protection, equality was what they had to relinquish. This opposition underlay the arguments of all participants in the debate. Protective and equal rights legislation, then, would seem to express different principles in defining gender within the modern labor market. A closer look at the more general aspects of the debate can help us to establish whether or not the participants indeed disagreed in their understanding of gender.

Two different positions can be identified in the parliamentary debate. Proponents of equal rights argued that the principle of equality was confirmed when women were granted citizenship status. By extension, they also wanted women to be treated as equals in the labor market. Advocates of special protection for women only supported reforms that granted equal rights for women provided more serious social problems did not result. Medical authorities were marshaled to underscore that freedom and equality for women on the labor market were at best secondary concerns in the face of certain harmful and dangerous occupations. "Abstract theories," Johan Castberg stated in 1914, "cannot prevent the legislator from protecting female workers and through this, future generations." [10] Like other legislators, then, he presupposed that women possessed certain characteristics that separated them from the "human" (i.e., male) norm. Did differences between the two positions really imply irreconcilable conceptions of gender?

Protective legislation assumed gender difference, which constituted the primary justification for special protection of women and were delineated by the special characteristics of women. First, women's constitution was purportedly weaker than men's, physically as well as mentally. Second, women were seen as living out a different social destiny than men. Advocates of protective legislation seized on these arguments and translated them into a panoply of concrete industrial prohibitions. They maintained that women were unsuited for work that entailed continuous standing, sitting, or moving their legs; work that included lifting heavy objects, carrying, and like exertions; or work involving dust, smoke, steam, or high temperatures. [11] The scope of this project was enormous: a range of almost unimaginably complex and variegated tasks called for in industrial production were thus encoded as "male" and "female." While politicians were not explicit on this score, it sometimes appeared as if they considered all industrial work "unnatural" and therefore unsuitable for women. Such statements were explicitly made by some local unions, which proposed that women and young people be excluded from all work on running machinery. [12]

Equal rights legislation, by contrast, took as its anchor the equality of men and women in civil rights. Norwegian legislators in fact wanted to open the entire Civil Service to women in 1912. In his proposal to the Storting in 1911, the minister of Law stated that the exceptions made for the military service and the church ministry should be seen as a temporary state of affairs. He assumed that there were no longer any reasons to exclude women from any offices, unless the physical demands involved were excessive.[13] The idea found backing among Liberals both from the left and right wings. However, consideration for the natural differences between men and women was a major reason why many Conservatives opposed the proposal. A member of the Storting from the Conservative party argued against "the endeavor in our time to blur the natural distinction in individual characteristics existing between men and women."[14]

Yet all this does not imply that the legislators did not recognize gender differences. The argument that parliamentarians seized on arguably demonstrates that even advocates of equal rights saw women as weaker in body and in mind, lacking stamina and resoluteness, more steered by their emotions, and more susceptible to illness. Indeed, creating equal opportunity to *apply* for posts was never intended as the creation of equal opportunities for women to *acquire* those positions. Most legislators seemed to agree that women's extreme sensitivity would make them inappropriate as judges. What was seen as the female tendency toward "irresoluteness" made them poorly qualified for other positions of major responsibility as well. Women's physical and psychological weakness also made them less suitable to be district medical officers.[15] Even equal rights legislators—for all their high-minded generosity— seemed to accept the gendered character of jobs.

These legislators had also shared with advocates of female protection conceptions of the special social destiny of women. They never considered woman's participation in public life as her main role in society. Rather, her role included motherhood and responsibility for meeting the needs of the entire family. For all legislators, the pull of this destiny on women was quite incompatible with wage labor, be it in industry or the Civil Service. Protective legislators considered all women to be mothers, real or potential; their responsibility for raising future generations was inherent. Taking care of women's health, then, involved far more than protecting individuals. As one legislator put it in 1922: "It is part of our responsibilities to our own future as a nation to watch over women and their ability to renew and protect the strength of the nation."[16] Beyond this, proponents of equal rights also seemed to assume a fixed gendered order in the family that the law should not and could not encroach upon. Only a few radical feminists argued that a woman and a man had the same destiny, namely, "to be a human being."[17] Most legislators were of a quite different mind. They considered it to be in the interests of women as well as Norwegian society to recruit only a small number of women into the Civil Service. Such opportunities—afforded by the lifting of occupational bars—were intended very narrowly, for exceptionally talented women only or those who could not marry. The majority were still expected to fulfill their destiny as mothers and housewives, or to accept their position in the gendered hierarchy at work.[18]

While Storting legislators disagreed on the legal formulas for women's labor market participation, their concepts of gender and gendered work were basically the same. The arguments they employed seemed to indicate that every job had a gendered character. To do a certain type of work required skills and talents adapted to gendered qualities. Of course, their ideas were not all identical. Advocates of protective legislation articulated their attitudes toward gender more explicitly. They also more consistently refused to contemplate even incremental changes in gender relations. And they were less ready to entertain ideas about individual variation among the female sex. Such prospects were vigorously rebuffed as impossible, undesirable, and, not least of all, unnatural.

◆ ◆

What primarily divided the legislators, then, was not their way of defining gender and what it stood for; they shared the same basic ideas about gender differences and gender. Their main quarrel lay in their convictions about the context in which gender operated. These assumptions also hinged on how legislators interpreted their mandates as representatives of the state. Their views on the relationship between state and individual, and between state and family, offer important clues about their interpretation of the mandate. What authority gave them the right to interfere with the freedom of the individual and the autonomy of the family?

Despite disagreements among them and different attitudes toward specific laws, all legislators shared the assumption that legislation should ensure a certain freedom of contract in the public arena. They also shared a tradition that understood the internal affairs of the family to lie outside the control of the state and outside the mandate of legislators. The dualism between private and public placed the relations of the family under other laws than those made by the state. As matters of the private sphere, they were subject to other arrangements, such as the unwritten "gender contract" regulating the relationship between men and women outside the public sphere. Both in theory and reality this contract differed from the free social contract by including relationships of dependency and subordination[19]—relationships that were considered "natural" and beyond the reach of legislation. The exception, of course, was legislation that defined the very institution of the family.

Even for the most consistent Liberal, however, these principles could not be applied with absolute purity. Circumstances arose when the freedom of the individual and the autonomy of the family had to yield to other considerations. The difficulty was that little agreement existed as to when this became necessary and desirable. The answers depended on legislators' conceptions of society and of their own role and mandate to step in.

The equal rights legislator advocated the rule of law. He saw his authority as limited vis-à-vis individuals and families. He also represented a state with a very circumscribed self-interest. His mandate was to guarantee the freedom and liberty of individuals, to ensure that the rules of justice prevailed. Women had become citizens, and to the legislator women's legal inequality was a social injustice. These legislators also most consistently defended the legal autonomy of the family. If for them the sexual contract was no concern of the state, it was hardly irrelevant to the social order as based on a particular gendered order, one taken for granted and apparently timeless. The possibility that married women could hold positions in the state was unimaginable for most legislators. For them, fulfilling duties as a housewife seemed incompatible with working as a civil servant.

Advocates of equal rights conveyed an ambiguous message to women. On the one hand, they bestowed civil rights on women, including the freedom to enter into social contracts. On the other hand, women remained bound to a sexual contract outside the public sphere, a contract based on a presumed natural order that defined the female as subordinate to the male. This implied both responsibilities and dependence, and clearly gnawed away at women's free citizenship. By implication, women who wanted to use their human rights in a certain sense had to abandon their "female destiny."

The advocates of protective legislation represented a state with a broader mandate and more active interests. "The main principle of this law is to prevent workers from chosing the work they want to," one M.P. stated during the debate on the employment protection bill in 1936.[20] In these terms, no clear distinction was drawn between state and society; the concepts were used more or less synonymously. By implication, the interests of the state were automatically identical with the interests of the majority of its citizens. Consideration for society/state took precedence over consideration for the individual.

The dualism between private and public—the sexual and the social contracts—lay beneath the definition of labor as formulated by the advocates of protective legislation. Work done outside the public sphere or labor market was perceived as nonlabor. In fact, one of the implicit aims of protective legislation seems to have been putting in place a strict separation between public labor and private nonlabor. Both labor movement activists and Liberal reformers considered this distinction crucial for thinking about the modern organization of work. More explicitly than the equal rights legislators, they also concerned themselves with the institution of the family itself. The sexual contract and the well-being of family members could not be entrusted solely to the law of nature. On the contrary, these men viewed freedom of the social contract as a threat to contractual relations *within* the family. Faced with the deep inroads made by industrial capitalism, they construed state intervention as necessary to protect the gendered order of the family and even to take over certain functions that the family was no longer able to meet by itself.

Protective legislators' argument in favor of the "normal" workday illustrates well their way of thinking. Their demands were based explicitly on consideration for the family. The worker was to have the opportunity to take part in family life, but this certainly did not have identical meanings for men and for women. For male workers it meant recreation, rest, and the services of women; for female workers it meant more work. Not stated explicitly, the implications nevertheless seem obvious, as a statement made by Castberg in his 1914 proposal would indicate. The working day should start no earlier, he judged, "than the time required for food to be prepared, which the wives usually do, and enjoyed quietly before the worker leaves the home." The statement leaves us with no doubt that the worker is a man, and that family life for married female workers was synonymous with the large expanse of work and care falling to "women's destiny."[21]

Such interventionist legislation seems to have been aimed at keeping the gendered order intact, as market forces threatened its dissolution. This also involved a responsibility for protective functions that the family no longer seemed able to tackle alone. Stepping in for the father, the state had to underwrite the health and future of its children and youth. As a good husband, the state also had to protect the wife and control her activities in the public world. Given their inability to watch out for their own best interests, both young persons and women had to accept certain limitations on their individual freedom. These limitations were in complete concord with the familial structures imposed by the Law of Nature.

Young (male) persons were in some respects accorded more individual rights than were adult women. In contrast to women, male children and youth only needed protection for a limited time, for they were prospective citizens and workers in the full sense. Thus, for instance, exemptions for dangerous work could be granted to male youth when it was deemed necessary for their technical training and skills. For women, all such exemptions were out of the question.[22]

Protective legislation did imply some limitations on the freedom of contract for every worker, even for men, though for women the limitations were always of a different order. General protection based on a male norm aimed at cementing individual rights. By contrast, female protection was supposed to ensure the maintenance of women's subordination in the gendered order. According to the sexual contract, the possibilities of children, youth, and adult men for claiming individual rights presupposed subordination of the individual citizenship of women.

The message emanating from protective legislators was resoundingly clear. They took into consideration what they understood to be the real situation of working-class men and women and strove to ease the burdens of their daily lives. From this perspective the demand for equal opportunities seemed nothing more than "abstract ideas coming from middle-class women with no experience of working-class reality."[23] Faced with the destuctiveness of modern capitalism, limitations on individual freedom seemed a cheap price to pay, even if it meant consigning women to the position of second-class citizens.

◆ ◆

The strength of the bourgeois feminists was a major reason why the ban on women's night work was rejected in Norway, in contrast to virtually all other industrialized countries. However, this was hardly the only reason why special protection of women remained so limited in Norway and was done away with in 1936. This course was also due to a strong Liberal tradition on the right wing of the political scale. More than Conservatives, these Liberals established the premises for right-wing policy in Norway. They gave their support to equal rights principles and thereby contributed to gender-neutral legislation on labor conditions as well. The statute, then, was the product of an odd alliance between strong Liberal forces within the political system and influential feminists acting outside it.

Weakly rooted in appreciable practical problems, the ban on night work had above all a symbolic character. There was no evident correlation between the great emotions invested in the debate and the hypothetical practical consequences of such regulations. Its proponents made great efforts to limit and regulate a type of work that barely existed, and the regulation thus seemed superfluous. Women's nocturnal labors became a symbol in the ongoing debates about social politics in general and about gender politics. Depending on the position of those engaged in the debate, night work came to represent a breakdown of social order, exploitation of the workers, or freedom of the individual. A concrete social problem was not at issue here but rather general political principles. This might be said as well of other European debates on women's nocturnal labor.

This controversy did not arise, however, out of fundamentally different ideas on gender. A broad consensus existed as to how sexual differences and gender relations were understood, as well as a consensus as to the desirability of maintaining the established gender order. The difficult question was how to adapt this order to a modern institution like the labor market. How far should modern principles of citizenship and individual rights apply to human beings of the female sex? Which should carry more weight: the individual rights of women or the welfare of working-class families? In their answers to such questions, most of those involved in the debate found themselves in one of two positions. One position accorded full legal citizenship to women, but to make use of her rights, a woman had to renounce some of her "female destiny" and thereby her claim to an unproblematic gender identity. The other position focused on the gender differences revealed through the everyday experience of working-class families and married women, even as it assumed that a woman was inextricably locked into the characteristics ascribed to her sex.

The dilemma revealed by the debates on female protection expresses a more general one within modern culture. In broad terms, the controversy is based on the tension between freedom and equality. The principle of equal rights, argued for by Liberals and feminists, was based on the idea of freedom of the individual. They advocated universal rights and interests exceeding particularities created by gender, class, or local conditions. The arguments used by the social radicals and Socialists, by contrast, took difference as a starting point and social justice as the goal. Legal regulations were to compensate for existing inequalities between employers and employees, and between men and women. The debates reflected controversies among those who wanted the state to advance the possibilities of each individual and those who wanted the state to reduce individual and social differences.

A statute bearing evidence of two different principles was worked out through the tense debate on women's night work in 1909. This solution came about as the result of historical conditions and the political situation in Norway. Around the turn of the century, conditions were most favorable for a solution to the problem of difference that took into account both the principle of equal rights and the need for protection of working people. The compromise was to affect Norwegian legislation in the following decades as well. The Employment Protective Act of 1936 was based on a combination of social radicalism and equal rights. On the one hand, social radicals and Socialists achieved an extensive general protection of working people. In their efforts they were helped by the models offered by other European countries and by egalitarian traditions at home. On the other hand, the strength of bourgeois feminists and right-wing Liberals ensured that the law also accepted the idea of equality between men and women.

Notes

1. *Stortingets forhandlinger 1890*, document no. 105 (Kristiania, 1890), 4.

2. The Liberal party (Venstre) and the Conservative party (Høyre) were both founded in 1884 during the dramatic political events that resulted in a parliamentary system. The Liberal party was divided in 1889 between a left wing, which stayed in the Liberal party (Rene Venstre,) and a right wing,

which was later integrated into the Conservative party. In 1906 a more radical group also left the Liberal party and founded their own Social-Radical party (Arbeiderdemokratene).

3. Rolf Danielsen, *Det norske Stortings historie*, vol. 2 (Oslo: Gyldendal, 1964).

4. Gro Hagemann, "Særbeskyttelse av kvinner-arbeidervern eller diskriminering. Striden om forbud mot nattarbeid for kvinner med hovedvekt på diskusjonen i Norge til og med stortingsdebatten i 1909" (master's thesis [*hovedoppgave*], University of Oslo, 1973).

5. Official statistics of Norway, *Census of the Kingdom of Norway 1900*, V. "Folkemængde fordelt efter livsstilling" (Kristiania, 1900).

6. Francis Sejersted, *Demokratisk kapitalisme* (Oslo: Universitetsforlaget, 1993), 172.

7. Ingrid Andersgaard, "Striden mellom settersker og typografer i trykkeriene i Kristiania, 1870-årene-1907" (Ph.D. diss., University of Tromsø, 1975).

8. This association (Norske Kvinners Sanitetsforening) was later to become one of the largest women's organizations in Norway, providing nonprofessional care and service for the sick and convalescent.

9. Elisabeth Lønnå, "LO, DNA og striden om gifte kvinner i mellomkrigstida" (Ph.D. diss., University of Oslo, 1975).

10. *Stortingets forhandlinger*, proposition to the Odelsting, no. 35 (Kristiania, 1914), 118.

11. Ibid., 120.

12. "Innstilling til lov om arbeidervern fra komiteflertallet" (1922), 196; appendix to *Stortingets forhandlinger*, proposition to the Odelsting, no. 31 (Oslo, 1935).

13. *Stortingets forhandlinger*, proposition to the Odelsting, no. 1 (Kristiania, 1911).

14. Debate in the Odelsting on women's access to Civil Service, *Stortingets forhandlinger*, Tidende O (Kristiania, 1912), 2.

15. *Stortingets forhandlinger*, proposition to the Odelsting, no. 18 (Kristiania, 1911).

16. "Innstilling til lov om arbeidervern fra komiteflertallet" (1922), 192; appendix to *Stortingets forhandlinger*, proposition to the Odelsting, no. 31 (Oslo, 1935).

17. Ragna Nielsen from the Norwegian Feminist Association in the discussion on the education of girls in 1896. See "Betænkning af en komite for behandling av spørgsmaal vedrørende pigeskolen," *Stortingets forhandlinger*, information to the Odelsting, no. 1 (Kristiania, 1896), 341–42.

18. Hagerup Bull (Conservatives) debate in the Odelsting on women's ac-

cess to Civil Service. See *Stortingets forhandlinger,* Tidende O (Kristiania, 1912), 6.

19. Carole Pateman argues that the contract between men and women, the sexual contract, is a necessary condition for the social contract. In contrast to the latter, however, the sexual contract is not based on liberty and equality. Pateman also emphasizes that the dualism between private and public is based on separation as well as mutual dependency. See *The Sexual Contract* (Cambridge, U.K.: Polity Press, 1988).

20. Report from the debate in the Odelsting on the Employment Protective Act, *Stortingets forhandlinger,* Tidende O (Oslo, 1936), 246.

21. *Stortingets forhandlinger,* proposition to the Odelsting, no. 35 (Kristiania, 1914), 136.

22. Report from the debate in the Odelsting on the Employment Protective Act, *Stortingets forhandlinger,* Tidende O (Oslo, 1936), 139.

23. Magnus Johansen (Labor) debate in the Odelsting on the Employment Protective Act, *Stortingets forhandlinger 1936,* Tidende O (Oslo, 1936), 254.

· 10 ·

"To the Most Weak and Needy"
Women's Protective Labor Legislation in Greece

Efi Avdela

Industrialization occurred in Greece later than in many other western European countries, giving a unique cast to Greece's history of protection for women industrial workers. An examination of the issue of protective legislation therefore offers a window on the variety of approaches taken during industrial development and state building at the turn of the century.

In this chapter, I analyze the process leading up to the adoption of gendered protective labor laws in Greece and the sometimes elusive stakes that were involved in debates on such legislation. I lay out the different views contemporaries expressed on the protection of women workers and explore the evolution of their views from the end of the nineteenth century to World War II. I also seek to identify the general trends and main arguments for and against protectionist laws and to consider the ways in which such legislation became a factor in the social construction of gender. Examining different positions and their transformation over time, I aim to demonstrate that discussions of such legislation took place in the context of a much larger debate concerning women's wagework.

Laws protecting women workers, adopted in Greece as part of labor legislation that covered a wide range of issues concerning industrial and manufacturing labor, marked the intervention of the state in the contractual arrangement of labor and in the labor market. Implemented over a period of twenty years, from the early 1910s up to the late 1920s, this legislation included regulating weekly days off, hours of work, the health and safety of workers, wages, trade unions, and the settlement of disputes between workers and employees. It also established a Labor Inspectorate.

Although Greek labor legislation always considered women's and children's protection jointly, here I shall concentrate almost exclusively on the former. My main argument is that in Greece, laws protecting women workers—as well as labor laws in general—had less to do with popular social demands than with the expanding role of the state, and they were more particularly linked to the reform policies of the Liberal government of the second decade of this century. By including legislation on female labor, these policies reproduced the dominant configuration of gender in the course of a transition from rural patriarchy to a more industrial framework.

In the first part of this chapter, covering the period from the late nineteenth century to World War I, I discuss women's labor as an aspect of "The Social Question" as it emerged in the context of militant nationalism. Socially sensitive reformers and the first Greek feminists brought the social and moral aspects of the exploitation of women workers to public attention. Reformist discourse described women as "mothers of the nation" and used this definition to demand their protection. The measure, which I analyze in the second part of the chapter, was legally enacted by the Liberal government in 1912. Legislators explicitly argued for the adoption of protective laws to safeguard men's positions in the labor market together with women's role as mothers and wives.

The third and fourth parts of this essay cover the interwar period, which was dominated by the influx of hundreds of thousands of refugees from Asia Minor and Eastern Thrace and was characterized by political instability and social unrest. The interwar years were marked by the parliamentary ratification of the International Labor Conventions in 1920, a move that aimed to consolidate the international position of the Greek state. During the same period, rapid industrial growth set the conditions for the systematic organization of the labor and feminist movements. Both of these new social forces joined the ongoing debate concerning women workers' protection by blaming the government for failing to enforce the relevant legislation. As I will show, the limited interest taken by Greek trade unions in the issue of women workers' protection and the weak enforcement of protective laws were due to two factors: the premature implementation of labor laws before there had been any significant development of industrial relations; and

the late and highly politicized organization of the Greek labor movement. As different strands of feminism emerged in interwar Greece,
their positions on the issue also proved to be sharply divided, for they
rested on diverging assumptions about womanhood.

The terms of the debate in Greece seem to have been constructed
in implicit dialogue with other European countries. At the same time
they stand at a considerable remove from the actual conditions that
women workers experienced in workaday factory jobs. Evaluating the
nature of the debates therefore demands some scrutiny of the evolv-
ing characteristics of women's industrial work. The temporary nature
of women's industrial work, its early and basic segregation from men's
work, and its dispersal throughout a multitude of small workshops not
only inhibited the implementation of protective laws but also provided
evidence that enables us to understand the discursive foundation of
protective legislation, as well as to calculate the historical accuracy of
the arguments put forward in this debate.

Completely absent at this stage of historical research in Greece are
the voices of women workers themselves. This silence makes it impossible for us to gauge these women's attitudes toward the regulations that
were discussed in Parliament and in the press, and sometimes imposed
on their productive activities.

◆ ◆

Industrialization did not spread in Greece at the accelerated rates
experienced in many other European countries. Greece remained predominantly rural throughout the nineteenth century. The first, if short-
lived, wave of industrialization occurred in the late 1860s under the impact of developing urbanization and the influx of Greek capital from the
Diaspora. While women and children were employed in the first textile
manufacturing factories as early as the 1860s, their numbers remained
small until the 1920s. According to the 1870 census, only 5,735 women
and 22,665 men, representing 1.2 and 4.9 percent of the working population respectively, were employed as production workers. Yet these figures give only a vague picture. In this as well as the subsequent censuses
of the nineteenth century, agricultural laborers, artisans, and occasionally even servants were grouped under the category "worker." Therefore
we cannot gauge the number of women workers with much accuracy
before the beginning of the twentieth century. We know, however, that
in 1873–75 women represented one-fourth of the relatively small group

of the country's industrial work force (that is, those employed in the few factories with steam-powered machinery). We know, too, that throughout the nineteenth century women were almost exclusively employed in the cloth, silk, and garment manufacturing industries, where they represented the majority of the labor force. Finally, according to the 1907 census, women made up 16 percent of all industry workers, who in turn constituted a mere 18.3 percent of the working population.[1]

Historians have calculated a wage profile for this manufacturing and industrial work force. During the 1870s in the main cities of Greece, men received an average of 2.00–3.00 drachmas a day, women, 1.00–1.50, and children, 0.20–1.00 for a twelve-hour day of relatively unskilled work. These rates, which showed limited variations throughout the century, compared favorably to those of rural workers and were the result mainly of a shortage of labor, particularly of permanent industrial workers.[2] One can discern here an important feature of Greek culture that explains many aspects of the issues discussed here: the reluctance of Greek males to engage in permanent industrial work. Men's yearning for household autonomy along with the predominance of small-holdings in the rural economy seem to account for the creation of a temporary and therefore unskilled labor force that since the 1880s has turned toward overseas emigration.

Women's working conditions in Greece attracted attention from the very beginning, not least because of the significant work force participation of females under the age of eighteen who were employed mainly in the new textile factories of Hermoupolis, on the island of Syros, and in Piraeus, the port of Athens. Greek reformers and advocates of modernization, as well as the country's first feminists, stressed the need for legislation that would protect women's health and guarantee that their maternal function would not be impaired. These discussions paid close attention to descriptions of women's wagework recorded in other European countries. In Greece, these accounts stirred up anxiety about women going out to work and signaled the decadence of Europe. Homework for women thus seemed far more desirable. In 1877, "the evident shift of Athenian industry toward female labor" prompted intervention by the attorney general as information circulated that this new trend constituted nothing less than an "assault on public morals." He declared that "if, supposedly, woman's freedom to work is indeed one of the most sacred human rights, it does not follow that abuse of this freedom should be subject to no restraints."[3] This moralistic approach, inherently contradictory and indicative of the fragile tolerance for women's capacity to enter the labor contract, colored attitudes toward the protection of Greek women workers from the very beginning.

One must bear in mind the context in which these developments were taking place. In the last quarter of the nineteenth century, ethnic Greek investors, discouraged by the political situation in the Ottoman Empire, brought large amounts of capital into Greece. In the sphere of Greek politics, this period was also marked by the first coherent, yet still unsuccessful, attempts toward the fulfilment of the country's nationalist goal: to enlarge its frontiers and integrate parts of the Ottoman Empire that were inhabited by a large section of the Greek population. Institutional reform and industrial development were thought to be the necessary conditions for the realization of this irredentist vision, known as the "Great Idea." [4] Yet the first wave of industrialization did not extend beyond the late 1880s, and before the turn of the century the defeat of the nationalist policy led the country into a new phase of stagnation that would last up to the 1910s.

The last two decades of the century also saw the consolidation of the bourgeois ideal of separate spheres and of the ideology of domesticity among the developing urban middle classes. These ideas assigned women a predominant role as mothers and nurturers of the nation's future patriots. Even the educated and middle-class Greek women who first raised the issue of women's rights in education and work subscribed to this ideal. [5] Anything that would inhibit women's role as mothers and educators was considered a threat not only to women's interests but also to the common national interest. It is in this historical context that the Greek debates on women workers and their protection belong.

To speak of a "debate" on these issues at this stage strains credibility. Neither the need for such protection nor women's wagework in principle were controversial. In fact, women's presence in Greek factories was never seriously questioned; for some, it even constituted a sign of progress or, barring that, an inevitable socioeconomic development. The limited labor supply in the largest towns often pushed employers to advertise female industrial jobs in glowing terms. Other contemporaries, however, put emphasis on the poor working and living conditions of women workers. The journalist Evgenia Zografou's pioneering research on the working conditions and daily life of women workers in Athens and Piraeus is a rare document for its time. In 1898, the year in which Zografou published her findings, she addressed a proposed law restricting women's access to work and regulating their working hours and sanitary conditions at work. Despite the support of several deputies, this first parliamentary debate on the adoption of protective measures for women's industrial work did not lead to any concrete measures.[6] Protective legislation already approved in other countries often served as a model both in parliamentary debates and the press.[7] This hardly comes as a surprise, given that throughout the nineteenth century Greek legislation drew extensively on foreign, primarily French, laws.

Most people concerned with social problems at this time justified special female protection by pointing out women's physical weakness and voiced a belief in the necessity of safeguarding women from exploitation. They discussed what seemed to be a new social phenomenon, stressing the dangers it could represent for the well-being of future mothers and their children and urging the state to undertake their protection for the sake of the nation's future. But they rarely proposed any specific measures.

This attitude was, however, denounced as hypocritical by Kallirroi Parren, the leading feminist of the time, a former teacher, and the founder of the first Greek feminist journal, *The Ladies' Newspaper*. From 1887 onward, for almost thirty years, Parren and a close-knit group of women advocated women's rights in education, work, and the family. The widely circulated weekly was written exclusively by them. Considered by Greek historians to be the first feminists, despite the fact that they never used this term themselves, these women demanded the emancipation of their sex from the constraints of the past. Their analysis of women's place in Greek society assumed natural differences, predispositions between men and women, and the separation of social life into private and public spheres, and it led them to demand an "equality in difference." Yet they steered clear of the sensitive issue of political rights for women. In this context, they fought against any aspect of what they considered to be injustice toward women. They also closely followed the developments of international feminism.[8]

In her newspaper, Parren repeatedly undertook to demonstrate the inconsistencies inherent in discourses about women's physical and moral weakness, thus inhibiting the adoption of protective measures for women factory workers. She argued that "when women are on the brink of being recognized even in a small way as capable beings and when they are about to be granted minimum privileges, their weakness is put forward as a handicap."[9] Thus, since women were clearly considered the weakest of all, their need for specific protective laws should be accepted without question. Noting that the state as well as private interest groups had abandoned women workers to exploitation without providing the protection that their physical weakness obviously demanded, she observed with irony that not one "of our strict moralists" ever thought of opposing women's factory work, which industrialists preferred "for women's natural skills and their docile character, but most of all because their daily wages are much lower than men's."[10] Parren concluded that for state and society the exploitation of women's labor power was above all putting their reproductive function in jeopardy: "The young girl or young woman of today who is sick and anemic and suffers from organic disorders because of the nature of her work, which saps her strength, shall either never become a mother or will give birth to weak and sickly children, children better suited for the hospital than for the army barracks."[11]

Such reactions were as limited as the phenomenon that generated them. The controversies about women's wage labor in France, Britain, or the United States during the second half of the nineteenth century emerged from a level of development that Greek society had not yet reached. In nineteenth-century Greece, a traditional society in transition, social conditions differed from those prevailing in countries for which this was the century of industrialization. At the turn of the century, Greece was still a predominantly rural society whose efforts at innovation and industrial relations seemed to be at a stalemate and whose limited opportunities drove considerable numbers of its male workers to emigrate.[12] This said, it seems remarkable that for a country whose intellectuals closely followed every twist and turn of developments in Europe, some aspects of these conflicts seem to have provoked little discussion, particularly the arguments against the protectionist logic and claims generated in other countries by socialist women and feminists.

These remarks also apply to the Greek trade unionists' stand on the subject. The labor movement in Greece organized itself late and with difficulty following the limited and short-lived first wave of industrialization. The first unions, which were called "working centers," only appeared at the end of the 1900s. These were local associations of workers' unions from different, mainly skilled trades and were established in the main Greek towns. Preceding the organization of the labor movement at a national level, these associations—which brought together exclusively male workers—were often highly politicized and aimed, usually with limited success, at organizing male workers and at propagating class solidarity, as well as supporting the demands of the various trades.

Women industrial workers, limited in number and restricted to particular industries, do not appear to have been a serious source of concern for Greek male workers, be it either as potential competition or as comrades. The first references to the protection of women's labor surfaced from the newly formed small socialist groups in the 1890s; still, they devoted little attention to this demand, presenting it primarily as one component of a long-term global agenda for a socialist program for the future of labor rather than as a response to a concrete situation in Greece.[13]

The rise of Eleftherios Venizelos's Liberal party to power in 1910 after the 1909 military coup of Goudi gave an unprecedented impetus to efforts to organize Greek workers, for Venizelos's labor policy was the backbone of his strategy for institutional reform and national completion.[14] He promoted labor legislation and facilitated the organization of workers for two reasons: first, to rationalize relations between capital and labor to promote industrial development; and second, to gain the support of the working masses for his nationalist policy. Prominent Liberals participated in efforts to organize workers who would agree to support the government's labor policy and participate in the debates about labor legislation. The foundation of the Working Center of Athens in 1910 as a federation of the city's trades unions—as well as of several unions from other parts of the country—should be seen as an outcome of such efforts. Working centers from all over the country were required to present their amendments to the labor bills submitted to Parliament. Thus, in 1911 the Working Center of Athens presented a memorandum to Parliament concerning the working and living conditions of those in the different industrial and manufacturing sectors, and it also proposed relevant legislative measures. Demands to prohibit women's night work, to regulate housework, and to protect motherhood figure in the long list of labor laws that the center submitted to legislators.[15] These efforts seem to have emerged from male workers' perceptions of appropriate roles rather than from any need to correct an existing problem. The center's memorandum took the existence of protective legislation for women and children in other countries as sufficient justification for its introduction into Greek society and assumed further debate was not necessary.[16]

Before the 1920s, unions rarely returned to the subject of protection for women's labor. In questioning this silence on women, we must take into account the nature of Greek workers' unions in general, as well as the particular type and structure of their members' occupations. Industrial work and, especially, work in large factories was still extremely limited in Greece. Workers often combined casual and seasonal manufacturing jobs with agricultural labor. Most contemporary unions were "corporations" of craftsmen or artisans working in exclusively male trades. For example, the six corporations of the Working Center of Piraeus, which in 1912 presented a memorandum on the working conditions in their trades and a list of demands to the Supreme Labor Council, were stokers, sailors, carpenters, pasta production workers, and coal and wheat workers.[17] Unionized workers came, then, from trades where competition between men and women was rare. By contrast, the great bulk of nonunionized labor consisted of casual workers, newcomers from the countryside about to emigrate, or artisans working in family-based enterprises.

The nature of women's industrial labor in Greece during this first period was another factor that molded male workers' attitudes toward female workers. In the 1870s, women were almost exclusively employed in the few new textile factories of Piraeus and Hermoupolis, the main industrial towns of the period, where they made up the majority of the work force. Though we do not know their precise distribution in other branches of industry before 1920, their participation in nontextile sectors seems to have remained limited, even after a large part of the male population was conscripted into the army during the war years 1912–22.[18] Some trade union leaders believed this factor gave a major push to women's entry into factories and workshops,[19] but there is no evidence of major retooling of factories for armaments production, nor of male unemployment due to female factory labor. Women were employed mainly by a few industrial branches: the textile, paper, tobacco, and chemical industries. This remained the case even when other aspects of the situation changed dramatically with the arrival of 1.5 million ethnic Greek refugees following the Greek defeat in the Greco-Turkish war in 1922, the exchange of ethnic populations between Greece and Turkey in 1923, and, finally, as a result of Greece's interwar industrial development. But by then—as we shall see—the issue of protecting women's industrial work faced a very different context.

◆ ◆

The Liberal government of Eleftherios Venizelos adopted the first legislative measures for the protection of female workers. Historians regard Venizelos as the political leader of an upcoming, "enlightened" Greek bourgeoisie. His reform program aimed to establish an institutional framework for facilitating the bourgeois transformation of Greek society, modernizing the structure of administration, and laying the basis for a welfare state.[20]

The first parliamentary provisions protecting women's work appeared in 1910 in Law 3524 on mineral mines. This law forbade "young girls and women in general" from working at night in the mineral mines and in the metal industry;[21] it was followed in 1912 by Law 4029 on the labor of women and minors, which regulated women's industrial labor according to the European model, and by a number of subsequent amendments. The latter act regulated women's and children's employment not only in the industrial and manufacturing sector but also in smaller workshops, mines of all kinds, construction work, transport services, commercial establishments, hotels, coffeehouses, and restaurants. In addition to stipulating that women could not be employed in such places at night or on Sundays, or in certain heavy and unhealthy jobs, it fixed their working hours at a maximum of ten per day. Provision was also made for compulsory unpaid leave of four weeks before and four weeks after childbirth. A special inspection service was established to enforce the law, although legislators did not at the time consider female factory inspectors necessary for such a task.[22]

The commission that introduced the bill to Parliament justified its adoption by pointing out the necessity of reducing "the excessive use" of children and adolescents as well as women, "which is detrimental to adult workers, many of whom are condemned to inactivity as a result of the competition from their children and wives."[23] The law, it argued, would encourage the preference for employing "adult workers" in the new industries. The commission presented this intervention in the labor market as the first stage in protecting all workers whose working conditions had been affected by mechanization. Protection would only temporarily be limited to those described as "the most weak and needy."

Writers of the report evidently felt compelled to set forth in detail the case for protecting children, invoking the damage to their physical and mental health caused by hard work and lack of education. However, they made do with only a few lines about protecting women: "Working women are . . . in an exceptional position, on the one hand, because of their weaker physical constitution compared to that of men, their greater sensitivity, and their maternity and, on the other hand, because of their particular place in the family with respect to household management and responsibility for the children's education. This is why it is necessary for the state to provide special protection to women as well."[24]

The main object of this protection, then, was not so much to put an end to women's exploitation as to ensure the maintenance of their social functions, seen to derive from the female nature itself. At the same time, these protective laws seemed to underwrite men's priority in finding work in the labor market. There was no need for Greek legislators to conceal the positive effects they believed women's protection would have on men's working conditions, as was the case in England and France; no need either for elaborate arguments about whether or not women were "free agents."[25] Women were bluntly declared intruders into the labor market and accused of being liable to generate male unemployment. The legislators explicitly described protection measures as a means of prevention, despite the lack of any concrete evidence that such a threat existed. The assumptions underlying their arguments were obvious: men as breadwinners and heads of households were by right and nature the primary beneficiaries of labor market opportunities; if women were to be driven into wagework, it should not compete with their household and maternal duties. Limited industrialization thus made it possible for Greek legislators to articulate arguments that elsewhere were concealed under humanitarian concerns. The Greek case supports the assertion of the historian Joan Scott that "since its first appearance . . . protective legislation was not approved in order to improve working conditions in the industry, but to provide a specific solution to the problem of women's and children's work."[26]

Greece's protective legislation was not the result of pressure from the labor movement; rather, it was part of the Liberal party's labor policy.[27] Yet during this early period, Greek labor laws and protective legislation were influenced by concerns similar to those of other European governments. Recent research has shown that even before parliamentary proposals for protection emerged, Venizelos recognized "the existence of social rivalries and tensions, which could only be defused through the timely satisfaction of justified interests of the working masses."[28] However, government policy on labor legislation, as inspired by the liberal reformist ideology characterizing Venizelism through 1920, aimed at neither satisfying specific demands nor defusing particular social tensions: the demands that the weak and unorganized labor movement could formulate were limited, and the social tensions could not yet represent a threat to social order. Rather, its purpose was to extend the field of the state's preventive intervention, mainly in the increasingly important area of the relations between capital and the labor force, and to gain the workers' electoral support.

It is also clear that most socialists at the time were not taken in by the limited goals of this policy and its failure to protect workers adequately. They were either too weak to oppose it successfully or supported it merely to promote movement in the direction of what they believed to be the workers' interests. Here, the virulent criticisms made by Nicos Giannios, leader of the small Socialist Center of Athens, are revealing. Giannios railed against what he called "state socialism," meaning not just the labor legislation itself but also the role adopted by the Working Center of Athens, which essentially lent support to the new government policy. Other socialist workers, however, such as the predominantly Jewish and well-organized Socialist Federation of Workers of Thessaloniki, relied on government labor policy to make their demands accepted by employers and to intensify their organizational efforts.[29] The advent of World War I and the "National Schism" between Venizelists and royalists over the position of Greece in the conflict accelerated the labor organization process until the General Workers Confederation of Greece was founded in 1918.[30]

Greek labor legislation in 1912 largely copied that of other countries; its rationale as well as its timing followed a similar logic, although circumstances and the explicit objectives of this legislative activity were somewhat different. One can hardly speak of a significant delay in Greece concerning women's protection, however, for the corresponding laws were only approved in 1891 in Germany, in 1892 in France, and in 1912 in Russia.[31] In the Greek case, it is clear that the limited demand for women's specific protection and its legislative adoption in 1912 was neither the result of the actual extent and concentrations of women's industrial labor nor of conflicts over the evolution of the sexual division of labor.

Laws regulating women's industrial work should be understood as part of state policy in Greece. The adoption of these laws reflected an attempt to enact institutional reform. Assumptions identifying women with the household and maternity—and a focus on their weakness—provided fertile, if traditional, ground for pursuing this goal. Thus, arguments supporting women's protection attribute a particularity to women and give priority to men in the labor market on the basis of their respective natures. In confirming a widely accepted notion of femininity and masculinity, they reproduced dominant gender constructs.

Unanimous agreement on the need for working women's protection went virtually unquestioned until the 1920s. By then the stakes in women's wagework and female protection had changed. Nevertheless, the success of a range of labor laws as preventive measures for maintaining either the social or the "natural" order depended on the extent of their enforcement. Yet it was at this level of implementation that many problems appear to have been insuperable, as is evident from the first reports of factory inspectors and as was confirmed repeatedly in later years. The particularly fragmented structure of the labor market in Greece, as well as the chronic inadequacy of the Labor Inspectorate, rendered the enforcement of protective laws ineffective. Thus, the laws do not seem to have been a decisive factor in the development of female wagework during the following years. On the one hand, employers often blatantly ignored labor legislation with the silent complicity of the police. On the other hand, women were often reluctant to make use of protective measures, either because they feared retribution and could not afford to lose their jobs or because they worked in family-based enterprises. In the interwar years, and as the general strategy with which the state tried to control social tensions changed from a labor policy to more coercive methods, the application of labor laws was to become the major focus of both workers' demands and the debates on women's protection. ◆ ◆

In the first two decades of the century the labor question was widely debated in Greece. Again, contemporary Greek social investigators approached the experience of other countries with curiosity. Progressive thinkers emphasized the role that labor legislation could play in regulating social conflicts generally. While positively inclined toward the recent organization of the labor movement—specifically the General Workers Confederation of Greece (GSEE)—they were also keenly vigilant for signs of the dangers of its possible radicalization in the face of the recent Russian revolution. Intervention by the state was therefore considered indispensable, and it became all the more certain that

> no civilized state today will leave the drawing up of work contracts to the will of the parties involved alone. This would be contrary to the liberal spirit [*sic*] of our times, which is [all the more] strongly grounded in ethics. This state role is all the more obvious because a large part of the work contract has already been regulated beforehand by the compulsory provisions of public law. It is clear that this protection is accorded to those who need it most, that is, minors and women.[32]

The Greek government could congratulate itself on its promptness in meeting these international concerns as early as 1912. Historians even believe that the liberal reforms introduced by the Venizelos goverment may have inhibited the emergence of a strong socialist movement such as those appearing in other Balkan countries.[33] Yet the apparent failure of Venizelos's political strategy to win the allegiance of workers to nationalist goals left its mark on his labor policy. The new labor organization at a national level emerged in Greece in the context of the Third International, whose growing influence was to mold it deeply. The founding of the Socialist Labor Party of Greece (SEKE) soon followed that of the General Workers Confederation of Greece, and the determination of socialists to impose the "correct line" on the trade unions resulted in early and lasting divisions within the Greek labor movement. With the start of the Greco-Turkish war in 1919, the government's concerns shifted toward securing the alliance of European powers to its nationalist policy. Greece's international image became all the more important.

Following the end of World War I, labor legislation became more institutionalized internationally. Greece was the first country to approve the international labor conventions that were adopted during the first International Labor Conference by the ILO held in Washington, D.C., in 1919. As early as 1920 the Greek Parliament ratified the conventions prohibiting women's night work, introduced paid maternity leave before and after childbirth, and limited the working day to eight hours.[34] In the first case, a new law enacted in 1920 incorporated the provisions of the older law of 1912 and enlarged the scope of protection provided by the convention to include the nonindustrial enterprises listed in the old law. It specified the duration of "night hours"—from 9 P.M. to 5 A.M.—and tightened exemptions made for the ban. The law stipulated, however, that night work was permitted for women working in enterprises employing only members of one and the same family. In the case of maternity protection, another 1920 law extended maternity leave to six weeks before and six weeks after childbirth, providing for an allowance fixed by the state and suitable for maintaining the mother and child in good health. In practice, the cost of maternity allowances during this period was transferred to industry and hardly compensated for wage losses.[35] For the first time the government also entrusted female factory inspectors with enforcing these measures.[36]

The defeat of the Liberal party a few months later and the rise to power of the royalist Popular party had a deep effect on the enforcement of labor laws. On the one hand, the new government had to face difficulties linked to the war, and its relations with international organizations were less than cordial. On the other hand, the state of emergency created by the Asia Minor disaster in 1922 and the exchange of ethnic populations between Greece and Turkey in 1923 forced the war governments to postpone the implementation of labor legislation to facilitate the expansion of industry and the establishment of new enterprises.[37]

Evidence indicates that labor legislation generally and laws concerning the labor of women and children in particular were not enforced during the entire interwar period. Successive reports of the female labor inspectors confirm that employers systematically violated provisions relating to women's work and that women workers ignored them too. The problem became even more acute with the massive influx of refugees, many of whom found jobs in the developing industrial and manufacturing sectors.[38]

The multitude of small family enterprises employing from one to five workers typified Greek industrial development of the period and added to the problem of enforcing the laws. Since these businesses were scattered all over Athens and the port of Piraeus, primarily, it was difficult to keep tabs on them and to determine whether they were conforming to labor stipulations prohibiting night work or whether they were making maternity leaves available. Furthermore, one quarter of industrial firms functioned on a seasonal basis, closing down from three to six months during the year.[39] Two other factors made the problem seemingly insoluble: the Labor Inspectorate proved inadequate to the task, lacking sufficient personnel and funding; and labor inspection enforcement was burdened with the seemingly limited interest in labor laws shown in practice by both workers and employers. Evidence for the latter phenomenon—which a recent study calls "the lack of reciprocity" between the institutional adoption of labor legislation and its use by those concerned[40]—soon multiplied in the reports of the Labor Inspectorate.

The structure of the labor market in Greece during the interwar years played a crucial role in this lack of reciprocity. As recent research indicates, Greece suffered from an oversupply of unskilled labor, yet it could not meet the chronic demand for skilled workers. The resulting industrial development relied heavily on intensive use of labor but could not evade a costly labor force. At the same time, the bulk of workers in urban areas experienced migration, unemployment, and poverty. While historians debate the link between wage levels and industrial development in the case of Greece, they do not seem to disagree that,

> in the final analysis, wage labor in industry did not constitute a permanent situation [in interwar Greece]. Rather it was an alternative for the small artisan in periods of crisis, for the small farmer during the "dead" periods of the agricultural cycle or for the woman before her marriage. All this in the context of a society that was characterized by the multiple activities of its members and where in most cases the worker and the artisan were no more than the two sides of the same coin.[41]

Women's labor in industry and manufacturing seems to have conformed to this picture. During the entire interwar period, women workers remained concentrated in a limited number of industrial branches—textile, paper, tobacco, and chemical—and were in the main employed as unskilled workers, be it in the production process directly or in a large number of auxiliary tasks varying according to the trade. The largest factories, where the division of labor was most advanced, preferred women's labor,[42] for women represented a young and mobile labor force, sharply differentiated from male workers by the jobs they performed as well as by their much lower wages. But women were also found in innumerable small family enterprises and in the expanding homeworking sector.

The reports of the Labor Inspectorate reveal a clear picture of women workers in the interwar years: the majority were very young (50 percent were between the ages of ten and nineteen), had very little formal education, and often had one or more dependent family members. After

1922, one-third of the women's labor force consisted of refugees, many of them half or full orphans. Married women workers were rare, and they mostly held skilled jobs, mainly in weaving, where they received wages on a piecework basis. From 1913 to 1935, women workers' wages generally amounted to 22.3 to 58.6 percent of the average male wages.[43] Their daily working hours far exceeded the eight-hour limit stipulated by the law, and sanitary conditions in the factories were reportedly appalling. In many cases women's wages were so low that children also had to work for a family to make ends meet. As the inspector Anna Makropoulou noted: "The enforcement of the law which prohibits the recruiting of minors under 14 in the factories always runs square into the absence of any state and social welfare measures. . . . 72 percent of the children are orphans and their small wages are indispensible for the family budget. . . . Sometimes it is even the family's only income."[44]

Recent research indicates that most of the children working in industry and the manufacturing sector during this period were girls; in fact, a large part of the child industrial work force consisted of female labor. Girls were predominantly employed by the large textile factories for unskilled and low-paid tasks, while boys opted for small workshops where they could get an unofficial apprenticeship in skilled—preferably artisanal—work.[45]

Women's participation in the industrial and manufacturing labor force increased from 16 percent in 1907 to 20 percent in 1920, and from 23.2 percent in 1928 to 26.8 percent in 1951. Accelerated industrialization and the mass influx of refugees from Asia Minor and Eastern Thrace were important factors in women's increased participation in this sector during the 1920s: 36.2 percent of women workers in 1928 were refugees compared with 23.8 percent of male workers.[46] Men tended to engage only temporarily in wage labor, preferring to earn their living by self-employment rather than by entering a wage contract. For example, in 1928, unskilled, seasonal, and employed male workers outnumbered industrial workers by 120 percent.[47]

Although the number of women in Greek industry increased in the 1920s, the country did not experience much male-female job competition or openly articulated hostility from trade unions toward women's industrial work, as was evident elsewhere in Europe.[48] With the exception of the tobacco industry, women's work did not appear to represent a threat to men's work, not least because a large part of this work was performed within the framework of family-organized production units, thus reproducing a sexual division of labor that corresponded to the traditional family hierarchies. Sex segregation in the various industrial sectors, small, family-based workshops, and extensive homework is the key to understanding the lack of male hostility toward women's industrial work in Greece.

This fact may also explain the limited interest of trade unions in both the issue of women's work and its protection. Trade unions initially included women's protection in their demands, but they never made it a major issue. In principle, both the GSEE and the SEKE had adopted a favorable attitude toward women's work and supported women's political and social equality from the moment they formed. More specifically, the participants in the first congress of the SEKE—all men—included in their resolutions demands concerning a prohibition on night work for women and children and free medical care for working mothers, as well as women's right to vote, political and social equality of the sexes, and abolition of all laws discriminating against women.[49] Yet all indicators seem to suggest that these commitments were not particularly important to organized male workers. The trade unions were often reluctant to admit women as members, and efforts to organize them—repeatedly acknowledged by their leaders as an urgent necessity—produced few results. Beyond this, enforcement and extension of the law prohibiting night work for women and minors appeared among trade union demands at first without reference to equal pay for equal work. This last issue was simply added to the long list of demands formulated in the interwar period by the GSEE and the SEKE, which became the Communist Party of Greece (KKE) after 1924. Along with the protection of women and children, equal pay for equal work joined the protection of childbirth in this list, without further comment.[50] The political confrontations between communists, reformists, and conservatives that tore apart the Greek trade union movement in the 1920s and split the GSEE do not seem to have had any effect on attitudes toward women's work.

During the entire interwar period, which was characterized by political instability, successive military interventions, and the buildup of anticommunism as a state ideology, both trade unionists and reformers discussed women's industrial work solely in terms of the state's failure to enforce protective legislation. Criticism of employers who failed to adhere to the laws was blunted by the state's inability to enforce them. Liberals—again in power after 1928—who defended the extension of state intervention in the workplace also adopted this view. For them, the issue of women workers' protection was "so exhausted . . . that it would be tedious to reiterate the negative effects of unlimited freedom as applied to this work force [i.e., children and women] yet again." [51]

Criticism concentrated mainly on the consequences of defective enforcement and the severe continued exploitation of the female labor force. Some authors affirmed that the absence of such protection would not only lead to a general crisis in marriage but also to the reduction of male wages. They increasingly turned to the rhetoric of female job competition and predicted that the rivalry between the sexes would grow, in spite of the lack of evidence for such competition. They seem to have relied on the experience of other European countries during the same period, although they never made direct reference to the European experience. Others saw protection as a necessary condition for the preservation of the family, stressing women's delicate health. Underlying these arguments was also the fear that the greater involvement of women in the labor market would cause the loss of their "femininity" as well as facilitate the emergence of a movement for their emancipation. [52]

While the steady increase of women in the industrial labor force was generally accepted, commentators treated women's protection in an abstract and impressionistic manner, never referring concretely to the conditions that women faced at work. [53] Early reports of the Labor Inspectorate pointed out with great precision the characteristics of women's labor that rendered the enforcement of protective legislation impossible and prevented any real competition between male and female workers. Since Greece adopted protective legislation before its industrial sector matured, the laws provided a preventive regulatory mechanism that maintained and consolidated sexual divisions in industrial labor.

◆ ◆

The long-standing, unanimous approval of protective legislation began to crumble in the years 1920–30, challenged by a growing feminist movement fighting for political, economic, and institutional equality for women. Greek feminists were not united on this issue, however, and their divisions resembled the divergent views of various international feminist organizations on protective legislation. The Council of Greek Women, the League for Women's Rights during the interwar years, and the Socialist Association of Women represented three strands of the Greek feminist movement that historians have classified as conservative, radical, and socialist respectively. From their differing feminist understandings and strategies, these groups adopted varying standpoints on the issue of women's labor protection.[54]

The most radical and important (in strength as well as impact) feminist strand of those years came in the form of the League for Woman's Rights (Syndesmos gia ta dikaiomata tis gynaikas), which, as the Greek section of the International Woman Suffrage Alliance, chose to shift its stance in line with the larger alliance. The demand for women's labor protection formed part of the first program of the Greek League in 1920 but was eliminated after the alliance decided at its 1923 congress in Rome that such measures were adverse to women's interests. From this time on, the League for Woman's Rights opposed any protective measure only for women, seeing any discrimination based on sex as intrinsically opposed to the principle of equality and as an obstacle to women's emancipation. The league also welcomed the formation of the International Open Door Council in 1926, provoking the anger of Greek socialist women.[55]

The other two strands of the Greek feminist movement favored protective legislation. For the Council of Greek Women, which was affiliated with the International Council of Women, women's "natural" weakness and their long-lived social inferiority demanded both protection and gradual emancipation. For the small Socialist Association of Women, which was affiliated with the Socialist International of Women, only the advent of socialism would guarantee the political and social emancipation of women; in the meantime, however, women workers' ongoing exploitation, which impeded their reproductive role, was adequate justification for special protective legislation, which had been won through hard struggle by the labor movement.[56]

These divergences provoked a long debate between the two camps similar to that which divided feminists in other countries.[57] In fact, the League for Women's Rights remained isolated in its defense of total equality between the sexes in the labor market, for both conservatives and socialists favored protective legislation. Yet the Greek version of this debate entailed certain peculiarities. Each organization followed the cue given by the international organization to which it belonged, resulting in a national confrontation that came to center most heatedly not on women's industrial labor but on their employment in the Civil Service. While the League for Women's Rights and the Socialist Association of Women debated the principle of special protection for women workers, they rarely included concrete examples from the Greek situation in their arguments. The absence of demands voiced by women workers themselves helps to explain this silence. However, in 1928, when a group of Greek women teachers used women's physical weakness and their reproductive roles as the basis for demanding married women's right to early retirement after fifteen years of public service, the debate was refocused on the Greek situation. As more women civil servants adopted this demand, which the civil servants' associations also favored, the feminist arguments for or against it came to reproduce the diverging positions on protective legislation. It was on this matter that the league's opposition to any demand based on women's presumed nature and their physical and moral weakness was most vehement.[58] The league's analysis of women's protection thus represents a unique attempt to question the position that women's nature dictated their social roles, an assumption that had long gone unchallenged. In claiming universal human rights for women, the league's notion of gender was no longer structured around the concept of difference but around equality.

Independent of their differences on the issue of women's protection, both trade unionists and feminists defended the principle of equal pay for equal work and demanded the establishment of a minimum wage that would be the same for male and female workers. Yet this common stand never extended beyond principled declarations. The trade unions' demand for equal wages for men and women was listed along with their demand for women's protection, but it was never more than an elusive quest. Feminists of all stripes expressed only occasional concern over women's industrial labor, and they never criticized the contradictory demands emanating from trade unions, with their simultaneous call for women's protection and for equality.[59] Women workers themselves remained wholly unorganized, and we have no real record of these women that effectively and collectively registers protest about the specific problems they faced at work because of their sex. Both the unanimity and the elusiveness of the demand for equal pay bring to mind Alice Kessler-Harris's remark that "the capacity of the phrase to reflect both individual aspiration and family norms accounts both for its appeal as a slogan and for its failure as a political goal."[60]

At any rate, wage equality in Greece would have been impossible in practice, for, contrary to feminist expectations, toward the end of the interwar period the establishment of a minimum wage for all categories of workers legally confirmed the inferior value attached to women's work. The 1935 law on collective bargaining agreements, which provided for variations in wages for the same profession according to different criteria, sex being one of them, was put into practice during the Metaxas dictatorship after 1936.[61] Thus, by adopting the same considerations as protective legislation with respect to women's "natural" weakness, collective bargaining agreements definitively institutionalized and consolidated the existing sexual division of labor.

Within this framework, women's increasing presence in the labor market did not challenge the hierarchy of the sexual division of labor, the logic of which was easily adapted to an extensive range of salaried jobs. The primary ties of women workers to the family received reinforcement at every turn, making the maintenance of this priority—through protective measures in the workplace—obvious and "natural."

◆ ◆

The early adoption of labor legislation in Greece—preceding organization of the labor movement and the country's industrial takeoff—influenced the subsequent debate on Greek women's wagework in general. The specific nature of Greece's late industrialization did not allow for the emergence of job competition between men and women or for any confrontation in the organized discourses emanating from trade unions and from feminists with regard to women workers' best interests. The trade unions demanded protection of women workers as a matter of principle but paid scant attention to the issue, while feminists concentrated on women clerks rather than women workers in general. In contrast to France and England, arguments favoring the protection of women and children first with an eye to extending such measures to the whole working class did not develop in Greece.[62] Although legislators invoked such arguments in 1912, they were simply paying lip service to the language of protection. The main object of this first law on women's work was manifestly something else: the maintenance of male primacy in the labor market as well as the safeguarding of women's place in the family, both allegedly endangered by industrial development and the "excessive use" of women and children in industry.[63]

Further research might demonstrate that the discrepancy between discourse and experience in the protectionist debate in Greece lies in the cultural values that organized the social basis of work rather than in working-class demands. In the Greek case, at least, the definitions of gender inherent in protective legislation reflected the reshaping of patriarchal and household values within the context of the state's struggle to modernize. New boundaries of gender sought to guarantee the maintenance of the sexual division of labor in the face of challenges generated by industrial development.

Notes

I have benefited greatly from the comments of the editors and from Jan Lambertz on earlier drafts of this chapter, as well as from discussions with Angelica Psarra and Akis Papataxiarchis.

1. Evangelos Makris, "O oikonomikos energos plithysmos kai i apascholisis aftou," *Statistikai meletai 1821–1971: I statistiki kata ta 150 eti apo tis Palingenesias tis Ellados* (Athens: National Center for Social Studies, 1972), 113–212; Christina Agriantoni, *Oi aparches tis ekviomichanisis stin Ellada ton 190 aiona* (Athens: Foundation for Research and Culture of the Commercial Bank of Greece, 1986). For a general overview of women's industrial work in Greece in the nineteenth and twentieth centuries, see Efi Avdela, *Dimosioi ypalliloi genous thilykou: Katamerismos tis ergasias kata fyla ston dimosio tomea, 1908–1955* (Athens: Foundation for Research and Culture of the Commercial Bank of Greece, 1990), 16–59.

2. Agriantoni, *Oi aparches,* 197, 289–92.

3. "Ithiko-viomichaniki tis gynaikos epopsis," *Oikonomiki Epitheorisis* 53 (1877): 196.

4. Richard Clogg, *A Short History of Modern Greece* (Cambridge: Cambridge University Press, 1979), 90–93; Douglas Dakin, *The Unification of Greece, 1770–1923* (London: Ernest Benn, 1972), 140–48.

5. Eleni Varikas, "Gender and National Identity in Fin de Siècle Greece," *Gender and History* 5:2 (1993): 269–83.

6. Evgenia Zografou, "Pos doulevoun oi gynaikes mas," *Dimosievmata* (Athens, 1903), 32–64 (a series of articles originally published in the journal *Acropolis* in 1898). See Panayota Tsopela-Saliba, "Le profil de l'ouvrière dans l'industrie et l'artisanat en Grèce 1870–1922" (diss., DEA diploma, University Paris I-Panthéon-Sorbonne, 1989), 50–51.

7. See "I ergasia en tois ergostasiois," *Oikonomiki Epitheorisis* 70 (1878): 477–80, which analyzes the Swiss law of 1878. French legislation of 1893 was proposed as a model during the parliamentary debates in 1898.

8. On Kallirroi Parren and her involvement in *The Ladies' Newspaper,* see Eleni Varikas, *I exegersi ton kyrion: I genesi mias feministikis synidisis stin Ellada, 1833–1907* (Athens: Foundation for Research and Culture of the Commercial Bank of Greece, 1987).

9. [Kallirroi Parren], "Dystycheis ergatides," *Efimeris ton Kyrion* 4:191 (Dec. 9, 1890): 2.

10. Ibid., 2–3.

11. Ibid., 3.

12. Historians have calculated that from 1900 to 1920 some 369,632 emigrants (predominantly male) left rural Greece, chiefly for the United States. Emigration is believed to have sapped the Greek economy of cheap labor and kept wages high. See Michalis Riginos, *Paragogikes domes kai ergatika imeromisthia stin Ellada 1909–1936: Viomichania-Viotechnia* (Athens: Foundation for Research and Culture of the Commercial Bank of Greece, 1987), 68–70.

13. See the proclamation of the Central Socialist Group of Stavros Kallergis for the May Day celebration in 1893, where a limit to women's and children's working hours was demanded (Michalis Dimitriou, *To elliniko sosialistiko kinima: 1. Apo tous outopistes stous marxistes* [Athens: Plethron, 1985], 142).

14. George T. Mavrogordatos, *Stillborn Republic: Social Coalitions and Party Strategies in Greece, 1922–1936* (Berkeley: University of California Press, 1983).

15. *Oi ergates tis Ellados pros tin Diplin Voulin ton Ellinon* (Athens: Annex of the "Workers' Journal," 1911). Because the national assemblies elected in 1910 and 1911 were revisionary assemblies, they each were comprised of double the normal number of deputies and were called "Double Parliaments."

16. No specific reference is made to the Bern Convention of 1906, which Greece did not ratify until after World War II. See André Andréadès, *La législation ouvrière en Grèce* (Geneva,: 1922), 24.

17. *Oi ergatai tou Peiraios pros to Anotuton Symvoulion tis Ergasias* (Piraeus: Workers' Center, 1912). The Supreme Council of Work was created in 1911 and affiliated with the Ministry of National Economy. It consisted in equal numbers of deputies, civil servants, professors of economics, and representatives of employers and workers. Its mission was to study any question concerning the relations between employers and workers, to propose measures for the improvement of working and living conditions of the working masses, and to advise on parliamentary bills and decrees concerning labor issues. See Andréadès, *La législation,* 15.

18. This was a decade of constant state of war for Greece: the Balkan wars of 1912–13; World War I, with Greece intervening on the side of the Allies in 1917; the Ukraine expedition in 1918; and the Asia Minor war of 1919–22. See Dakin, *The Unification of Greece,* 190–245.

19. Avraam Benaroya, *H proti stadiodromia tou ellinikou proletariatou* (1932; rpt., Athens: Olkos, 1975), 212.

20. On the modernizing role of Venizelos's governments during this and the following periods, see *Venizelismos kai astikos eksynchronismos,* ed. George T. Mavrogordatos and Christos Hatziiossif (Irakleion: Crete University Press, 1988).

21. Giorgos Lixouriotis, "Prostateftikos nomothetikos paremvatismos kai i emfanisi tou ergatikou dikaiou stin Ellada: I periptosi tis paidikis ergasias," in ibid., 206.

22. See *Efimeris tis Kyverniseos* 46 (Feb. 7, 1912); and Ypourgeion Ethnikis Oikonomias-Tmima E' Ergasias, *Ergasia Gynaikon kai Anilikon: Nomos, V. Diatagmata, Engyklioi* (Athens: National Press, 1919).

23. "Ekthesis tis epitropis tis Voulis epi tou nomoschediou peri ergasias gynaikon kai anilikon," *Parartima Efimeridos Syzitiseon tis II Diplis Anatheoritikis Voulis,* fascicle II (Athens: National Press, 1912), 533.

24. Ibid., 535.

25. Sonya O. Rose, *Limited Livelihoods: Gender and Class in Nineteenth-Century England* (London: Routledge, 1992), 50–75; and Mary Lynn Stewart, *Women, Work, and the French State: Labour Protection and Social Patriarchy, 1879–1919* (Kingston: McGill-Queen's University Press, 1989), 59–67.

26. Joan Scott, "La travailleuse," in *Histoire des femmes en Occident,* vol. 4: *Le XIXe siècle,* ed. Geneviève Fraisse and Michelle Perrot (Paris: Plon, 1991), 440. See also Nicole Arnaud-Duc, "Les contradictions du droit," ibid., 94–98.

27. The labor legislation of the years 1911–12 also included provisions for a weekly (Sunday) holiday, an eight-hour daily work limit, health and safety measures for workers, wage rates, the settlement of disputes between workers and employers, and the creation of a labor and social welfare department in the Ministry of National Economy. See Georgios Leontaritis, "To elliniko ergatiko kinima kai to astiko kratos 1910–20," in *Meletimata gyro apo to Venizelo kai tin epochi tou,* ed. Thanos Veremis and Odysseas Drimitracopoulos (Athens: Philippotis, 1979).

28. Leontaritis, "To elliniko ergatiko kinima," 52.

29. Nicos Giannios, *O sosialismos tou kratous* (Athens: Socialist Center Press, 1914). On Giannios and the Socialist Centre of Athens, see Panayiotis Noutsos, *H sosialistiki skepsi stin Ellada apo to 1875 os to 1974,* vol. 2, pt. 1 (Athens: Gnosi Publications, 1991), 292–95. On the Socialist Federation of Workers and its role in organizing the Greek labor movement after the Balkan wars of 1912–13, and the annexation of Macedonia to the Greek state, see Benaroya, *H proti stadiodromia.* For a case illustrating the legitimacy the government's labor policy provided for workers' demands, see Efi Avdela, "Socialism of the 'Others': Class Struggle, Ethnic Conflict, and Gender Identities in Post-Ottoman Thessaloniki" (ms., 1993, author's files).

30. George B. Leon, *The Greek Socialist Movement and the First World War: The Road to Unity* (Boulder, Colo.: East European Quarterly, 1976).

31. On the first protectionist laws in Britain (1844, 1895), see Louise Tilly and Joan Scott, *Women, Work, and Family* (New York: Holt, Rinehart and Winston, 1978), 173; Jane Rendall, *Women in an Industrializing Society: England, 1750–1880* (Oxford: Basil Blackwell, 1990), 60–62; and Jane Lewis and Sonya O. Rose's essay, "Let England Blush," in this volume. For France (1892), see Stewart, *Women, Work, and the French State.* For Germany (1891), see Werner Thönnessen, *The Emancipation of Women: The Rise and Decline*

of the Women's Movement in the German Social Democracy, 1863–1933 (London: Pluto Press, 1973), 43; and Sabine Schmitt's essay, " 'All These Forms of Women's Work Which Endanger Public Health and Public Welfare,' " in this volume. For Russia (1912, 1917), see Sheila Rowbotham, *Women, Resistance, and Revolution* (London: Pelican Books, 1975), 139.

32. Heinrich Herkner and Dimitris Kalitsounakis, *To ergatikon zitima* (Athens: Eleftheroudakis and Bart, 1919), 201–2. This Greek edition of the well-known German liberal's work was revised by Herkner and translated and completed (with chapters about Greece) by Kalitsounakis, one of the most important Greek liberal thinkers of the period.

33. Clogg, *A Short History of Modern Greece,* 101.

34. Law 2275 on women's night work, Law 2274 on the protection of maternity, and Law 2269 on the duration of work, June 24–July 1, 1920, *Efimeris tis Kyverniseos* 145 (July 1, 1920): 1366–72.

35. Only with the creation of the Institute of Social Security, set up in 1934 (though not put into operation until 1937), were all women workers provided with maternity leaves of six weeks before and six weeks after childbirth, during which they were paid an allowance amounting to one-third their daily wage. The cost of the allowance was borne by the Institute of Social Security, from mandatory contributions by workers and employers. See Yfypourgeion Ergasias, *Nomos 6298 peri koinonikon asfaliseon* (Athens: National Press, 1938), 37.

36. For a comparison of the laws of 1911–12 and 1920, see Andréadès, *La législation,* 24–25. See also Ypourgeion Ethnikis Oikonomias-Tmima Ergasias kai Koinonokis Pronoias, *Ergatiki kai koinoniki nomothesia,* ed. K. G. Pasagiannis (Athens: National Press, 1919). The publication date notwithstanding, this work includes the entire labor legislation of 1910–20.

37. See Anthony Liakos, "Problems on the Formation of the Greek Working Class," *Études Balkaniques* 2 (1988): 51.

38. "Genikai ektheseis ton Epitheoriton Ergasias tou etous 1913," *Deltion tou Ypourgeiou Ethnikis Oikonomias,* II. Ergasia kai Pronoia, fascicle 4 (Dec. 1914); Ypourgeion Ethnikis Oikonomias-Diefthynsis Ergasias, *Ektheseis tou prosopikou epitheoriseos ergasias epi tis efarmogis ton ergatikon nomon, etos 1921* (Athens: National Press, 1923); Ypourgeion Ethnikis Oikonomias-Epitheorisis Ergasias, *Ektheseis kai pepragmena somatos epitheoriseos ergasias epi tis efarmogis ton ergatikon nomon kai ton synthikon ergasias en Elladi kata to 1931* (Athens: National Press, 1934). See also the ILO report, "Les conditions du travail des salariés de l'industrie et du commerce et leurs conséquences du point de vue sanitaire," Archives of E. Venizelos, Benaki Museum, Athens, fascicle 28, document 81 [1928]; also Bureau International du Travail, *Les problèmes du travail en Grèce* (Geneva: Bureau International du Travail, 1949).

39. Liakos, "Problems," 47.

40. Antonis Liakos, *Ergasia kai politiki stin Ellada tou Mesopolemou: To*

Diethyes Grateion Ergasiaskai i anadysi ton koinonikon thesmon (Athens: Foundation for Research and Culture of the Commercial Bank of Greece, 1993).

41. Riginos, *Paragogikes domes,* 252. See also Liakos, "Problems," 43–54, and Stathis N. Tsotsoros, *H syngrotisi tou viomichanikou kefalaiou stin Ellada (1898–1939),* vol. 1 (Athens: Cultural Foundation of the National Bank of Greece, 1993), 141–43.

42. Riginos, *Paragogikes domes,* 30–39.

43. Ibid., 49, 64. A shortage of male and female skilled labor and wage differences between trades relativize the notion of the average wage in the case of Greece. See Liakos, "Problems."

44. Anna Makropoulou, "I gynaika stin ergasia: Pos ergazetai i Ellinida se pende megales viomichanies," *O Agonas tis Gynaikas* 70 (1928): 5–6.

45. Michalis Riginos, "Morfes paidikis ergasias sti viomichania kai ti viotechnia, 190s–200s aionas" (ms., 1989, author's files), 37, 39–42, 44, 49. Most contemporary texts dealing with children's labor nonetheless refer to working children as if they were self-evidently male.

46. Geniki Statistiki Ypiresia tis Ellados, *Statistika apotelesmata tis apografis tou plythismou tis Ellados tis 15–16 Maiou 1928,* vol. 3A (Athens: National Press, 1937), 54.

47. Liakos, "Problems," 49.

48. See Renate Bridenthal, "Something Old, Something New: Women between the Two World Wars," in *Becoming Visible: Women in European History,* ed. Renate Bridenthal and Claudia Koonz (Boston: Houghton Mifflin, 1977), 430.

49. *To proto synedrio tou SEKE: Ta praktika* (Athens: Edition of the Central Committee of the Communist Party of Greece, 1982), 138–42. The proceedings of the first congresses of the GSEE have not survived.

50. *KKE: Episima keimena,* vol. 2: *1925–1928* (Athens: Synchroni Epochi, 1974), 220–21.

51. Spyros Koronis, *I ergatiki politiki ton eton 1909–1918* (Athens: Papazissis, 1944), 46.

52. For these arguments, see Avdela, *Dimosioi ypalliloi,* 50–53.

53. This seems to be a constant feature of the debate on working women's protection, not specific to Greece. See Stewart, *Women, Work, and the French State,* 4.

54. On the different strands of the Greek feminist movement of the interwar years, the differences among Greek feminist organizations with regard to the protection of women's labor, and the debate of the same issue on the international level, see Efi Avdela and Angelica Psarra, "Introduction," *O feminismos stin Ellada tou Mesopolemou: Mia anthologia* (Athens: Gnosi Publications, 1985).

55. Ibid., 80, 82–83. On the International Open Door Council, see

Thönnessen, *The Emancipation,* 148–50, and Jane Lewis, *Women in England, 1870–1950* (Bloomington: Indiana University Press, 1984), 104, 188. For a contemporary socialist critique of this organization's activities, see "La Protection des Ouvrières et les Tendances de la 'Porte Ouverte' devant l'Internationale des Femmes Socialistes" (pamphlet, *Propagande et Documentation* 2:1 [Spring 1930]).

56. Avdela and Psarra, *O feminismos,* 77–89.

57. On the beginnings of this debate in France, see Laurence Klejman and Florence Rochefort, *L'égalité en marche: Le féminisme sous la Troisième République* (Paris: Presses de la Fondation Nationale des Sciences Politiques/Des Femmes, 1989).

58. See Avdela, *Dimosioi ypalliloi,* 143–44, 193–204.

59. The journal of the League for Woman's Rights, *O Agonas tis Gynaikas,* is the only feminist publication of the period that systematically published information on women workers and, in particular, the detailed reports of the Labor Inspectorate on women's work in different industrial and manufacturing branches in Athens and Piraeus for the years 1924–30. Scattered references can also be found in *Socialist Life,* the bulletin of the Socialist Association of Women (1928–35).

60. Alice Kessler-Harris, *A Woman's Wage: Historical Meanings and Social Consequences* (Lexington: University Press of Kentucky, 1990), 84–85.

61. "Law on Collective Bargaining Agreements," Nov. 16–21, 1935; Dimitrios G. Portolos, *I rythmisis tis ergasias dia syllogikon symvaseon kai to dikaion aftis* (Athens, 1939). Metaxas's dictatorship showed a particular interest in labor issues as a means of extracting workers from communist influence.

62. See Stewart, *Women, Work, and the French State;* Lewis, *Women in England;* Rendall, *Women in an Industrializing Society.*

63. See Circular Letter no. 31, Sept. 17, 1913, concerning the application of Law 4029 (1912), "The Aim of the Law," in Ypourgeion Ethnikis Oikonomias, *Ergasia Gynaikon kai Anilikon,* 37–38.

· 11 ·

A Paradise for Working Men but Not Working Women

Women's Wagework and Protective Legislation in Australia, 1890–1914

Renate Howe

> Australia may be, and probably is, the working man's paradise, but it is far from a celestial condition for working and business girls.
>
> —Jessie Ackerman, *Australia from a Woman's Point of View*

This observation by a visiting American journalist on the position of Australian wage-earning women in 1913 may seem surprising given the country's reputation for advanced industrial legislation at this time and the fact that Australian women were among the first in the world to gain the franchise.[1] A central focus of this chapter is the contradiction between the innovative nature of protective legislation affecting Australian women workers, as well as its importance as a model for other countries, and the highly gendered labor market that had emerged by World War I with women in a relatively powerless position in the labor movement. I will argue that protective legislation facilitated this gender segregation, which is still a marked feature of the Australian work force in comparison with other Organization for Economic and Co-operative Development (OECD) countries.

In a comparative study of protective legislation for women workers, it is important to emphasize the different social and industrial context in which protective legislation developed in Australia compared with Europe, Britain, and the United States. Australia and New Zealand were settler societies. In the nineteenth and early twentieth centuries Australians liked to view themselves as "the coming nation, the redeemers of their European legacy who were able to realize the potential of that parent civilization because they had escaped its constraints and were accordingly freer, more equal, less cynical, better able to invent the future."[2] The construct of Australasia as a social laboratory was especially strong at the time of the federation of the colonies to form the Commonwealth of Australia in 1901 and was popularized in a book by W. Pember Reeves, then New Zealand high commissioner in London. *State Experiments in Australia and New Zealand* (1902) listed women's suffrage, land legislation, infant life protection, and labor relations as areas in which the colonies had enacted legislation ahead of other countries.[3]

Such legislation provided the context for debate on protective legislation in Australia. Compared with labor movements in other countries, the early Australian labor movement had a positive view of the potential of the state to bring about a new economic and social order, as well as the opportunity to implement that order. Political labor parties were formed in the 1890s with the purpose of achieving favorable social and industrial legislation and were successful in electing members to colonial parliaments and to the Commonwealth Parliament, where the first Australian Labor party took office in 1904. Given this electoral success, few within the labor movement regarded the state as oppressive or questioned the political focus on state activity.[4]

The Australian experience of protective legislation was thus markedly different from the other countries discussed in this book. In Australia, protective legislation for women workers was introduced earlier, was more comprehensive, and was part of a wider industrial and social legislative context.

Two phases can be identified in the Australian response to women working in manufacturing industries. The first phase, in the 1880s and 1890s, coincided with the development of industry in the capital cities of the eastern colonies of Sydney, Melbourne, and Adelaide; outside these capital cities, the work force remained male-dominated, concentrated in the pastoral, mining, and transport industries. The high point of female manufacturing employment in Australia came before World War I. In 1911 women made up approximately 40 percent of the Australian work force, and in the census of that year the proportion of women employed in manufacturing (28.42 percent) for the first time exceeded women employed in domestic occupations (26.80 percent).

Compared with America, Britain, and the industrialized countries of Europe, the numbers of Australian women in factory employment were neither large nor drawn from an immigrant work force.[5] Melbourne was the center of manufacturing industry, fostered by the Victorian government through a system of protective tariffs. These labor-intensive, import-substituting industries — especially clothing, footwear, and food — depended on low-paid women workers, who comprised approximately half of Victoria's industrial work force.

Victoria was not only the center of manufacturing in Australia but also the leader in factory legislation, reflecting the colony's liberal reformist tradition. Most early colonial legislation drew on British models, with the first Victorian Factory and Shops Act of 1873 mirroring British legislation. A Royal Commission hearing in 1882 led to the amendment of the act in 1885 and again in 1890. These acts set up a factory inspectorate and required minimal industrial and safety conditions in workshops employing six or more persons; they also limited the hours women and juveniles could work. The 1885 act was introduced by Alfred Deakin (later prime minister of Australia), who proudly described it as "the first social legislation of its kind in the Australian colonies."[6]

Similar legislation passed in South Australia (1894), New South Wales and Queensland (1896), and Western Australia (1897) established an inspectorate, regulated working conditions, and banned night work for women and children. Concern over the increase in women's industrial employment was a major reason for these factory acts, yet they were ineffective in dealing with small and home-based workshops, where the worst conditions affecting women workers prevailed.

The situation of outworkers became a public issue during the Depression of the 1890s, which was especially severe in Melbourne and led to an influx of underpaid workers into the clothing and footwear industries. The antisweating campaign of the 1890s was the most intense period in the first phase of debate about women industrial workers. This emotional campaign in Melbourne was led by a coalition of middle-class reformers, especially churchmen. It drew some support from male union leaders in the sweated industries, although the Victorian Trades Hall Council expressed little official interest. Melbourne's active women's suffrage societies supported, but did not play a leading role in, the antisweating movement, while the voices of working women, whose unions had been decimated by the depression, were hardly heard at all.

The antisweating debates focused on the assumption that women workers needed protection from unscrupulous employers. Women's working conditions were portrayed as matters of public debate, as moral and social rather than industrial issues. The solution to women's exploitation therefore was found not, as with men, in negotiations between women workers and employers but in protective legislation, seen as a "charitable intervention by the state on behalf of the innocent and helpless." When the chief secretary, following a parliamentary inquiry into sweating, introduced yet another Factory and Shops Bill into the Victorian Parliament in 1895, he stated that the aim of the legislation was to protect women and children "who cannot help themselves," compared to men who were "able to organize and unite."[7] When finally passed, the Factories and Shops Act of 1896 consolidated earlier legislation and introduced new protective measures. Although the only gender-specific reference in the act was to hours of work, the intention of the legislation was to reduce the number of women outworkers and to regulate the underpayment of women workers in sweated industries through the introduction of a minimum wage. The definition of a factory was changed from a place employing six persons to one employing four, in order to bring smaller workshops under inspection requirements. The act also introduced a stipulation that outworkers be registered and that a description of the work performed and the prices paid for that work be kept by the employer. Women and juvenile outworkers were also subject to the same limitation on working hours as inside workers—a forty-eight-hour week, no more than ten hours on any one day, and no work after nine o'clock at night.

As can be seen from other chapters in this book, provisions of the act were little different from protective legislation for women workers either enacted or proposed in other countries. What was different was that the act was widely accepted, even by employers. The reluctance of Victorian employers at this time to contest protective legislation in the courts on the basis of infringement of freedom of contract contrasted with the situation in America, for example. In 1893 the Illinois legislature passed a bill to limit the hours of work for women and juveniles and to introduce factory inspection. In the larger, more advanced American economy, capital used political power and the judicial system to defend the principle of freedom of contract, and in 1895 the Illinois Supreme Court upheld an appeal, financed by the National Manufacturers' Association, ruling that an eight-hour day infringed the Constitution. In Victoria, employers in the sweated industries were themselves the beneficiaries of colonial protective philosophy, especially from the system of tariffs on imported goods designed to foster industry. This dependence on the government for protective tariffs meant that the Victorian Chamber of Manufacturers did not join other employers in vehement opposition to the bill.[8]

The most controversial aspect of the 1896 Factory Act was the setting up, on a trial basis, of boards to "determine the lowest price or rate" in the sweated trades for full- or part-time workers producing "any particular article of clothing or wearing apparel or furniture, or for bread making or baking." These special boards, generally known as wages boards, were appointed to fix wages and piece rates for persons employed either in or outside a factory in the named trades. The boards were to consist of not more than ten or less than six members, half being elected by employers and half by the employees, with an independent chair. Board determinations had legal status, and an employee could sue for wages at the agreed-upon rate. When the act was proclaimed, Harrison Ord, the chief inspector of factories and shops, described it as "probably the most advanced Factories and Shops Act in the world."[9]

The idea of having an enforceable minimum wage to prevent the underpayment of women workers was not new but had not elsewhere been translated into legislation. The British factory acts protected working conditions and hours of work but not wage rates. Ernest Aves, an official of the British Board of Trade, visited Victoria in 1906 to investigate the workings of what was generally known as the Wages Boards Act. He believed the inclusion of the power to set minimum wages resulted directly from colonial determination to resist the spread of sweating "and if necessary, to pass measures framed to avoid the repetition in a new land of at least this particular form of old-world trouble."[10]

Although the dominant discourse of the antisweating campaign had been one of preventing the exploitation of women and child outworkers, concern over the effect of this exploitation on male wage rates was never far below the surface. The protection of male industrial workers from the competition of women was as much the issue as was the protection of women workers from exploitation by greedy capitalists. The importance of wages in this "workingman's paradise" was fundamental to the aspirations of the male colonial labor movement. Although the wages boards were initially introduced into Victoria's 1896 bill to protect women's wages, an amendment by Labor members while the bill was still in committee extended the provisions of the legislation to male workers. The amendment had the backing of the Victorian Trades Hall Council, as manufacturing unions perceived the value of a minimum wage especially after a recent strike in the boot and shoe industry had failed to achieve gains in piecework payments. This last-minute extension of the wages boards to cover men reinforces the general point made about protective legislation for women by Ray Strachey in *The Cause:* that "it enabled men to secure for themselves, behind the women's petticoats, protection which public opinion was not yet ripe for conferring on men."[11] The inclusion of men also indicates the positive view of industrial legislation held by the predominantly male Australian labor movement. It should be noted, however, that widespread opposition from male-dominated labor organizations in other countries inhibited legislation that would provide minimum wages for women. In the United States, for example, unions preferred collective agreements as the means of wage setting; and in Britain, where the Trade Union agreement ruled, there was resistance to the centralized arbitration and wage-fixing tribunals (often poorly distinguished in this early period) that were developing in Australasia.

The number of industries covered by wages boards was increased when the legislation was amended in 1903. By 1906, ten years after the passage of the initial act, two-thirds of the manufacturing industries of the state, employing approximately half of the female work force, were covered by wages boards, which had become a dominating influence on the industrial position of Victoria's women.[12]

How beneficial, then, was the legislation for working women in Victoria? In 1901, three-quarters of the women in the manufacturing work force were employed in apparel and textile industries, so the effect of the wages boards on these industries was of paramount importance. The Clothing Board was established to regulate employment in the manufacture of men's and boys' clothing, where the more skilled and organized tailors were employed. Its first determination took nine months to draw up and "filled thirty-five pages of closely printed foolscap."[13] The minimum wage for men was fixed at forty-five shillings per week; for women, only twenty shillings. An exhaustive schedule of piece rates was issued, set to be a little higher than the equivalent daily and weekly rates.

The board covering shirtmaking, a badly sweated trade, did not arrive at a determination until January 1898. It stipulated a minimum of four pence an hour for women in factories, amounting to a wage of sixteen shillings for the legal limit of forty-eight working hours per week. Piecework rates corresponded to the weekly wage rate. The first Underclothing Board covered the white work industry, which "had been in a wretched condition, and was looked upon amongst needlewomen as little better than a refuge for the destitute."[14] Unable to agree on wage rates, its members resigned. A second board appointed in 1898 did not make a determination until 1899, fixing the wage at the same rate as in shirtmaking (four pence an hour). Members of the board could not agree on piecework rates, however, and left it to employers to set rates that would enable an "average" hand to earn the sixteen-shilling-per-week minimum wage. Many employers took advantage of this flexible situation, and in 1900 the average weekly wage paid to women in the underclothing industry was only twelve shillings, seven pence.

The minimum rates set by the wages boards confirmed women's wages at a rate at least 50 percent below men's wages. However, these rates were considerably higher than earlier rates, especially for women factory workers, who also benefited from the standardization of the forty-eight-hour week. A comparison of wages in those industries covered by wages boards and those not found women's wages to be higher where board determinations were in force, although even those higher rates were often hardly sufficient for a woman to support herself.[15] The act's impact as far as hours were concerned was also mixed, consolidating the forty-eight-hour week for women but making the more lucrative overtime payment (generally time-and-a-quarter) available only to men because of the limitations on women's working hours.

Supporters of wages boards claimed that outwork in the men's and boy's clothing industry was all but eliminated by the boards' determinations. Employers, "finding they could get work done cheaper by the time-workers in the factories, ceased to give it out. The more fortunate of the piece-workers were taken on as factory hands at the new and improved wage. Most of the others lost their work altogether."[16] The reduction of homework in the men and boy's clothing industry also diminished employment opportunities for married women who were solely responsible for dependents or whose husbands were unemployed, sick, or in casual employment. The effect on these households was to make them reliant on haphazard colonial charity. Thus, the income needs of women with dependents largely became a welfare rather than an industrial issue.

The wages boards helped to preserve and extend gender segregation of the work force, especially in the clothing trades. Board determinations ensured that cutting remained a relatively well paid, high status male occupation and that pressing also was reserved for men; sewing, however, was confirmed as an unskilled female occupation.[17] Even where there was job competition, the gendering of skills was achieved through equal pay provisions. When demands for equal pay came before the wages boards, labor representatives invariably couched their arguments in terms of equity. But their clear intention was to exclude women, as men were generally favored by employers who were forced to pay men and women the same wages. Equal pay applications resulted in some of the most controversial determinations of the early wages boards. Decisions granting equal pay for female steam pressers (1901) and cutters (1909), for example, effectively reinforced the male monopolies of these occupations.

The feminist historian Jenny Lee concludes that "it is inconceivable that the trade unions could have managed by industrial action to reestablish the boundaries between men's, women's and boy's work as swiftly and decisively as they did with the assistance of the state" and that overall wages boards "entrenched and codified disparities within the working class."[18] A study of women workers and the New Zealand Arbitration Court also concludes that "awards were not framed with the interests of women workers as the foremost concern. . . . male workers wanted to protect their jobs, the skilled status of their work, and their rates of pay from the threat posed by cheap female labor." As in Australia, both the Arbitration Court and male workers used provisions for equal pay as a means to exclude women and to categorize certain jobs as "men's work."[19] A similar use of equal pay provisions is described by Alice Kessler-Harris in her work on protective legislation in the United States.[20]

These disadvantages notwithstanding, most women workers continued to support protective legislation as a safeguard against further exploitation. Ernest Aves stated in his report on the wages boards that "especially those formed in the women's trades are greatly valued and widely believed in, and a chief explanation of this must, I think, be found, not so much in any demonstrable and lasting effects that they have had on the individual earnings of women as in the increased feeling of security that they give, and in the belief that they make treatment more uniformly fair."[21] One woman who had represented workers on wages boards pointed out that another advantage of the boards was certainty: "previously if the money was short and a protest was made, the reply would be 'price cut down' and there was nothing more to be said. All this has changed." [22] The wages boards also prevented the accumulation of small grievances, such as the continual and arbitrary reductions in piecework rates that infuriated women workers whose meager incomes were substantially affected by the smallest movement. In the end, the wages boards restricted women to low-paying, low-status positions in the manufacturing work force even as they provided a safety net on which most working women could rely.

The Victorian Wages Boards Act was regarded as the most successful of the early Australian industrial acts. Ten years after the introduction of these boards in Victoria, a similar act was passed in South Australia and then in Tasmania, in 1910. The highly legalistic New South Wales Industrial and Arbitration Act of 1901, which had little influence on women workers, was also modified in 1910 to incorporate aspects of the wages board model.

This model also attracted the attention of the revamped Women's Trade Union Leagues (WTUL) in America and Britain, which were seeking legislative solutions to the underpayment of women wageworkers. In 1906, while visiting Hull-House during an overseas tour, the Australian journalist Alice Henry was recruited to work for the American Women's Trade Union League. Margaret Robbins, later president of the WTUL, employed Henry because of her knowledge of Australian industrial legislation, which was "to the rest of the world so novel and thrilling." Henry publicized Australian legislation through the WTUL paper *Life and Labor,* which was then edited with the help of a fellow Australian, Stella Franklin. [23] Trades boards, including some aspects of the Victorian model, were introduced into the clothing industry in New York and Chicago after widespread strikes in 1909–12.

The Victorian legislation was subject as well to the scrutiny of British visitors, including Sidney and Beatrice Webb, Keir Hardie, and Margaret and Ramsay MacDonald. As in America, it was the WTUL that pushed the Victorian 1896 act as a model for minimum wage-fixing legislation for women in Britain. The act was initially publicized by Lady Dilke, president of the league, who was kept informed of the legislation and its administration by Alfred Deakin. However, the most committed protagonists of the legislation in Britain were Mary Macarthur, secretary of the league, and Clementina Black, secretary of the Women's Industrial Council, which had undertaken numerous studies of sweating in British industries. Black believed that the Victorian legislation, which she called "the first systematic effort to grapple with the grave evil of sweating," was an important experiment in social reform.[24] Acknowledging the infinitely larger and more complex female industrial work force in Britain, she argued that the Wages Boards Act nonetheless provided a useful model to protect women working in low-paying industries, and it was in fact used as the basis of the British Trades Board Act of 1909.

A later evaluation of the British Trades Board Act found that, as in Australia, the boards provided a safety net but delivered low wage rates. "The wages fixed were far from extravagant — indeed in many cases they were not sufficient for healthy maintenance. The great point of trades board regulation was that its action was preventive. Some degree of security was attained in the industries concerned, and a stop was put to the downward tendency that seems inevitable in unorganized trades."[25]

By this time, the Australian debate about protecting working women had taken a new direction. The discourses that accompanied the 1896 Wages Boards Act had been emotive ones about preventing the old-world evil of sweating and protecting women from exploitation as outworkers and young women from exploitation in factories. At the time of the federation of colonies into the Commonwealth of Australia, there were more nationalistic discourses concerning women's rights and obligations in a new country in which the terms of women's participation in domestic and paid work was central. A strident pronatalism developed as the commonwealth sought a larger and more active population for nation building. Preoccupation with the quantity and quality of Australian children inevitably followed.

The equation of motherhood with women's citizenship focused attention on the effect of factory employment on women as mothers and potential mothers. The change in the nature of the debate about women's employment is illustrated by comparison of the 1895 parliamentary inquiry into sweating in Victoria and the 1911–12 Royal Commission on Female and Juvenile Labor in Factories and Shops in New South Wales. Evidence offered to the former was dominated by social reformers and to the latter by doctors, while the dominant concerns moved from protecting women workers from exploitation (1895) to protecting them as future mothers (1911–12). A. B. Piddington, who conducted the 1911–12 Royal Commission, saw the investigation as involving "the stem itself of progress in the Commonwealth, viz: the increase in the population, particularly native-born, and the maintenance and improvement of good health, physique, and moral type in that increase." The commission also provided a list of the problems of factory work for married women: (1) it encouraged them to practice prevention (contraception); (2) it involved the risk of miscarriage; (3) it necessarily meant the abandonment of breastfeeding for women with children, which would lead to an increase in infant mortality; (4) women's energy went toward making money in the factory, to the neglect of the home; (5) it encouraged idleness and extravagance in men; (6) it placed unmarried girls under the often unhealthy influence of married women.[26]

The commission's report called for new protective measures for working women to be added to the existing restrictions in New South Wales in the areas of overtime, night work, lifting heavy weights, and working no sooner than four weeks after childbirth. It also urged that women should not be employed in factories until the age of sixteen, when their bodies and minds had the maturity to cope with factory life, adding that the time between leaving school and gaining employment could be spent receiving instruction in health, hygiene, physiology, and domestic science. To dissuade married women from working, the commission recommended that they should only be allowed to work if they were the sole or chief support of the family. It suggested too that a married woman's situation be examined by a magistrate before a work permit was issued. This draconian requirement was considered necessary because "it is obviously inconsistent with the normal duties of a married woman's life that she should give up the whole of a working week to factory employment."[27]

Although few of the royal commission's recommendations were translated into legislation, other gender-specific amendments to the various Australian factory acts were passed during this period. In Victoria, for example, eighteen amendments between 1896 and 1912 further regulated working hours for women and juveniles, who were no longer allowed to work more than five hours without a break. Many of the amendments were aimed at young women: for example, females under sixteen could not work between 6 A.M. and 6 P.M., nor could they lift weights over twenty-five pounds; and females under eighteen could not work as typesetters or in wet spinning.

The concern of the New South Wales Royal Commission was that factory employment should not be attractive enough to entice married women away from the home. Its efforts were supported by the new

Commonwealth Court of Conciliation and Arbitration, established in 1905. In extending the growing Australian tradition of centralized wage fixing to the introduction of a family or basic wage, the court attempted to make it economically possible for married working-class women with children to stay at home. The principle was affirmed in 1907 when Justice Henry Bourne Higgins, in hearing a case involving the Sunshine Harvester Company (agricultural implement makers), set a minimum or basic wage of forty-two shillings per week for all adult male workers. He argued that the company should pay this wage in return for the protective tariffs introduced by the Commonwealth government. Higgins made his ruling after soliciting evidence on working-class household budgets and determining that this was the minimum amount needed for a decent standard of living for a workman, his wife, and three children.[28]

The Harvester judgment went beyond the Victorian wages boards legislation in moving the determination of wages away from a relationship to productivity and skill and toward the concept of need. In an article in the *Harvard Law Review,* the justice described the determination as "a new province for law and order." However, this new province did not consider women's wages at all. When the court did consider women's wages in 1912 and again in 1919, they were set at 54 percent of the adult male's basic wage. The devaluing of women's wages thus reinforced the view that women's earnings were supplementary to those of the male breadwinner in a patriarchal family structure.

The Harvester judgment and subsequent wage decisions by the Commonwealth Conciliation and Arbitration Court further structured a divided and hierarchical work force. Eleanor Rathbone, an English reformer and member of Parliament, commented that the Australian family wage "prevents the full development of the productive capacities of women workers by making it impossible for them to compete in the labor market with men on terms that are at once free and fair."[29] The family wage benefitted the single adult male who was paid the same rate as the married adult male, but self-supporting single women were not treated equally. The domination of the suburban lifestyle, dependent on women's unpaid domestic work, combined with the family wage to encourage married women with children to stay at home. As a result, participation rates of married women in the work force remained low in Australia even during World War I, when they rose in other countries.

The growing women's movement in Australia was more central to this phase of the debate about women's paid work than it had been in the 1890s. The claim made in other countries that protective legislation was forced on disfranchised women could not be made in Australia. At the time of federation, white women over twenty-one years of age were granted suffrage and the right to stand for public office. One of the earliest women candidates, Vida Goldstein of the Women's Political Association in Victoria, was a candidate for the Senate in the 1903 election. Her platform was described as "a mixture of social nationalism and feminism" and included demands for equal pay for equal work, a minimum wage for women workers and support for conciliation and arbitration.[30] Middle-class feminists in New South Wales and Victoria argued for independent women candidates or a mobilization of women's vote irrespective of party, while other women voiced their belief that support for and involvement in the male political parties was the best political strategy for working women. Winning the vote fostered class and gender tensions, and many Labor party women regarded the nonparty Women's Political Association in Victoria and the Woman's Political Educational League in New South Wales (begun by suffrage leader Rose Scott) as "anti-Labor and anti-working class."[31]

As Alice Henry's biographer has observed, "the woman movement in Australia, albeit primarily a middle-class one, was geared towards social reform, and the suffrage movement was in large part motivated by a desire to alleviate the conditions of working women."[32] Despite conflicts on political strategy, both the nonparty feminist organizations and the women's groups within the Labor party supported protective legislation for women workers. Although not successful in electing women to Parliament, the feminist and working-class political organizations formed by women after federation followed the male labor movement in their confidence that through the vote they could work "as a leaven" to influence the state to create a new social order for women and children. Henry wrote from America in 1912, after the Biennial Convention of the General Federation of Women's Clubs declared "out of order" a resolution endorsing political equality, that the protective work they were "trying to do with so much expense of time and effort is accomplished in Australia by the direct suffrage of women." She listed the measures that could be traced to women's suffrage as "Australian state and federal legislation such as prematernity acts, acts raising the age of consent, family maintenance acts, acts improving children's conditions by extending juvenile courts, limiting hours of work, providing better inspection, and forbidding the sale to children of drink, drugs and doubtful literature." [33] In 1911, Goldstein informed a gathering of British women suffragists at the Royal Albert Hall, in London, that "all the social reform legislation for which Australia is noted has been vigorously supported by women voters." [34]

The different social and legislative context of the Australian debate meant that protective legislation was not as contested a strategy as in other countries. The split between labor and feminist groups after federation was not over the need for protective legislation but over the most effective political strategy to achieve such legislation. Even in relation to the family wage, Justice Higgins's biographer notes that "there were few feminists ready to take Higgins to task, particularly as his awards, in raising wages for men (and, indeed, women) appeared to benefit all concerned." [35] Both Henry and Goldstein (who claimed to have assisted in establishing Higgins's family budget) welcomed the Harvester judgment. In publicizing the "living wage" concept in America, Henry wrote of the "practical unanimity" of Australians "in favour of a humane standard of living for all as an admirable and patriotic end," [36] an indication of the extent to which Australian feminists accepted women's domestic role in the family.

Kate Dwyer and Lillian Locke, the first women organizers appointed in 1903 by the Labor parties in New South Wales and Victoria, respectively, wanted better conditions for women as wage earners, but they also believed that women's most important roles were as wives, mothers, and homemakers. Dwyer, as a member of the New South Wales Royal Commission of 1911–12, strongly supported protective measures for women outworkers, and her questions during hearings focused on working conditions and sex discrimination in the workplace. There is no evidence however, that she was critical of the commission's concerns about the moral dangers of factory work. [37] Locke argued that "capitalism was breaking up the home—socialism did not mean breaking up the home" and affirmed her support for the family wage. She equated socialism with "domestic feminism": her ideal was the politically active suburban woman, although she warned that "no woman could be so much interested in a budget speech or an electoral Bill to forget to put the chops on." [38]

Both Locke and Dwyer were middle-class women who had assumed leadership roles in the labor movement through their involvement in suffrage organizations. Along with the feminist separatists, such as

Scott and Goldstein, with whom they had worked for women's suffrage, Locke and Dwyer supported the idea of protective legislation for
women, recognizing that it reinforced "the dictum that women have a
special place and singular requirements which were within the parameters of the family and home."[39]

Working women themselves were more concerned with their economic position and were increasingly aware that protective legislation
was not delivering economic equality in the industrial area. In Victoria,
the wages boards had encouraged the industrial organization of women,
whereas in New South Wales women workers were restricted in their access to the legalistic, trade union–dominated Arbitration Court.[40] The
chief female factory inspector in Victoria acted as secretary to wages
boards determining awards in industries with a predominantly female
work force, and in the clothing industry, women representatives of both
factory and outworkers could present cases at these hearings. Although
a woman need not be a representative of a union to be represented
at a hearing, the wages boards led to the reinvigoration of the Tailoresses Union, while new unions were formed to represent shirtmakers,
collarmakers, and white workers. By the end of 1912, female workers
were represented by an estimated thirty-one unions functioning either
as independents or as the female sections of existing male-dominated
organizations.

The development of women's industrial activities led to the organization of a Victorian Labor Women's Political Conference at the Trades
Hall in June 1909 and the election of a woman representative to the
Victorian Trades Hall Council Organizing Committee. Tensions over
the equal pay issue, not only between women and men but also among
women workers, threatened these advances. Issues of gender and class
are not easy to unravel in the conflicts sparked by a surprising determination of the Commercial Clerks' Wages Board in August 1912 to
give equal pay to female clerks and typists, a determination based on
work value rather than the intention to exclude women. Employers immediately appealed the decision—an appeal that was not opposed by
the Melbourne Trades Hall Council. When the Conference of Working
Women was subsequently convened in October 1912 to press for equal
pay, the audience created an uproar when the clothing union organizer
Sara Lewis moved that: "a Bill providing that women should receive
equal pay should be introduced into the State parliament and that the
elimination of the word 'sex' from the Factories Act be asked for."[41]

Still, a substantial number of women in the labor movement did not support equal pay as an industrial strategy. Unskilled women who had experienced the discriminatory effects of past wages boards were wary of equal pay, while more-skilled women feared the effects of equal pay on their wage margins. Some women workers were simply unwilling to pursue such a divisive issue at this time.[42]

Male trade unionists in the protected manufacturing industries were opposed to equal pay, which they believed would threaten the viability of industries that depended on a low-paid female work force. This resistance and the subsequent decision by the Victorian Labor party to disband its Women's Organizing Committee (after arguments about selecting women parliamentary candidates) were deliberate frustrations of feminist aims of representation and autonomy by an entrenched male-dominated labor movement. The most effective women political and industrial organizers in Victoria were increasingly critical of the low wages and lack of implementation of awards under the wages boards, as well as the failure of the Labor party to endorse women candidates for winnable seats in the federal elections of 1906 and 1907. The Melbourne historian Patricia Grimshaw writes that while the male labor movement supported women's enfranchisement, its political and industrial actions were designed to preserve and extend its own dominance. "Socialist feminists sought that democratic comradeship of equals, which labor men in other contexts acknowledged, not a prioritization of the interests of male workers over women's."[43]

In the male-dominated historiography of the Australian labor movement, the development of protective legislation, arbitration, and the basic or minimum wage have been interpreted as outstanding achievements. Feminist historians have questioned this interpretation and argue that the history of women's experience of industrial legislation has not been one to celebrate, as women were denied economic justice in the workplace via low wage rates and gendered segregation of the work force. For some feminists, the living wage, whatever the humanitarian ideals that inspired it, was "an albatross" that "supported and condoned the severe exploitation of women."[44]

The dominant "new country" and "social laboratory" ethos in Australia during this period influenced the nature of and response to protective legislation for women wageworkers. The protective role of the state was more widely accepted than in America, Britain, or Europe and led to early legislation restricting the hours and working conditions of women in manufacturing industries and, in Victoria, the introduction of a minimum wage in industries where women workers predominated. This social and industrial context meant that protective legislation was not as divisive an issue among Australian feminists as it was in other countries. In Australia, the women's movement looked to the state to protect working women within the context of the protection of all workers, and it had not campaigned for women alone. However, the strength of an Australian masculine ethos, the strident pronatalism of the early commonwealth, and the introduction of the family wage combined to discourage married women from entering the paid work force and to marginalize women who worked for wages. It is not surprising, then, that Australia probably was "the working *man's* paradise."

Notes

1. Women's franchise bills were passed in the colonies of South Australia (1894) and Western Australia (1899). When the colonies of Victoria, New South Wales, South Australia, Queensland, Western Australia, and Tasmania federated in 1901, all white Australian women over the age of twenty-one were given the vote and the right to run for public office.

2. Stuart Macintyre, "The Meanings of the Clever Country," *Australian Universities' Review* 34:1 (1991): 34.

3. W. Pember Reeves, *State Experiments in Australia and New Zealand,* 2 vols. (Australia: Macmillan, 1969).

4. Stuart Macintyre and Richard Mitchell, eds., *Foundations of Arbitration: The Effects of State Compulsory Arbitration, 1890–1914* (Melbourne: Oxford University Press, 1989).

5. The census of 1891 estimated 109,261 women worked in factories. The female factory worker in Melbourne and Sydney was usually young (under twenty-five years of age), single, and Australian-born, with parents of English, Irish, or Scottish origin. In Sydney, they were mainly drawn from an influx of young women from rural areas; in Melbourne, from the daughters of gold rush immigrants. For changing women's employment patterns during the period 1901–47, see Beverley Kingston, *My Wife, My Daughter and Poor Mary Ann: Women and Work in Australia* (Australia: Nelson, 1975), 61.

6. Quoted in J. A. La Nauze, *Alfred Deakin: A Biography* (Melbourne: Melbourne University Press, 1965), 83.

7. John Rickard, *Class and Politics: New South Wales, Victoria and the Early Commonwealth, 1890–1910* (Canberra: Australian National University Press, 1976), 94–100.

8. See ibid., 89.

9. "Report of the Chief Inspector of Factories for 1896," *Victorian Parliamentary Papers,* 1897–98, vol. 2, 7.

10. "Report to Secretary of State on Wages Boards and Industrial, Conciliation and Arbitration Acts of Australia and New Zealand," *British Parliamentary Papers,* vol. 71 (HMSO, 1908), 76. For a discussion of the extension of the wages boards to cover male workers, see Rickard, *Class and Politics,* 88–103.

11. Ray Strachey, *The Cause: A Short History of the Women's Movement in Great Britain* (1927; rpt., London: Virago, 1978), 82.

12. "Report to Secretary of State on Wages Boards," 59.

13. Ibid.

14. Ibid.

15. Jenny Lee, "A Redivision of Labor: Victoria's Wages Board in Action, 1896–1903," *Historical Studies* 22 (Apr. 1987): 58.

16. Ibid., 55.

17. Raelene Frances, "No More Amazons: Gender and Work Process in the Victorian Clothing Trades, 1890–1939," *Labor History* 50 (May 1986): 99–101.

18. Lee, "A Redivision of Labor," 61.

19. Stephen Robertson, "Women Workers and the New Zealand Arbitration Court, 1894–1920," in *Women, Work and the Labor Movement in Australia and Aotearou/New Zealand,* ed. Raelene Frances and Bruce Scates (Sydney: Australian Society of Labour History, 1992), 33.

20. Alice Kessler-Harris, *A Woman's Wage: Historical Meanings and Social Consequences* (Lexington: University Press of Kentucky, 1990), chap. 2.

21. "Report to Secretary of State on Wages Boards," 76.

22. Ibid. See also Robertson, "Woman Workers," 32, which identifies the popularity of employment subject to awards with women, to the uniformity and improved conditions delivered by arbitration awards.

23. See Diane Kirby, *Alice Henry: The Power of Pen and Voice* (Melbourne: Cambridge University Press, 1991).

24. *Labor Laws for Women in Australia and New Zealand* (London: Women's Industrial Council, 1906).

25. B. L. Hutchins, "The Present Position of Women Industrial Workers," *Economic Journal* 31 (Dec. 1921): 463.

26. "Report of Royal Commission of Inquiry into the Hours and General Conditions of Employment of Female and Juvenile Labor in Factories and Shops and the Effect on Such Employees," New South Wales, *Parliamentary Papers,* vol. 2 (session 1911–12), 1142. Kingston, in *My Wife, My Daughter,* discusses in detail the 1910 Royal Commission (63–73). See also Edna Ryan and Anne Conlan, *Gentle Invaders: Australian Women at Work* (Melbourne: Penguin, 1975), 49.

27. "Report of Royal Commission into Conditions of Employment," 1182.

28. Macintyre and Mitchell, *Foundations;* John Rickard, *H. B. Higgins: The Rebel as Judge* (Sydney: George Allen and Unwin, 1984), 170–204.

29. Eleanor F. Rathbone, "The New South Wales Scheme for the Grading of Wages according to Family Needs," *Economic Journal* 30 (Dec. 1920): 552. The influence of the Arbitration Court in gendering occupations is documented in Penny Ryan and Tim Rowse, "Women, Arbitration and the Family," in *Women at Work,* ed. Ann Curthoys, Susan Eade, and Peter Spearritt (Sydney: Australian Society for the Study of Labor History, 1975): 15–30.

30. Betty Searle, *Silk and Calico: Class, Gender and the Vote* (Sydney: Hale and Iremonger, 1988), 13ff. See also Audrey Oldfield, *Woman Suffrage in Australia: A Gift or a Struggle* (Melbourne: Cambridge University Press, 1992), 145–63.

31. Judith A. Allen, *Rose Scott: Vision and Revision in Feminism* (Melbourne: Oxford University Press, 1994).

32. Kirkby, *Alice Henry,* esp. chap. 2.

33. Alice Henry, "Labor Legislation in Australia," *Outlook,* Feb. 8, 1908.

34. Vida Goldstein, "Before and since Woman Suffrage," *Votes for Women,* Sept. 1911, 3.

35. Rickard, *H. B. Higgins,* 176–77.

36. Henry, "Labor Legislation in Australia."

37. See Kingston, *My Wife, My Daughter;* Ryan and Conlan, *Gentle Invaders,* 73–76.

38. Quoted in Searle, *Silk and Calico,* 50.

39. Ibid., 16–17.

40. See Ryan and Conlan, *Gentle Invaders,* 57.

41. Melanie Raymond, "Labor Pains: Women in Unions and the Labor Party in Victoria, 1903–1918," *Lilith,* 1988, 7.

42. See Melanie Nolan, "Sex or Class? The Politics of the Earliest Equal Pay Campaign in Victoria," in *Women, Work and the Labor Movement,* ed. Frances and Scates.

43. Patricia Grimshaw, "Equals and Comrades of Men? *Tocsin* and the Woman Question" (paper delivered at Labor History Conference, July 1991), 13.

44. Ryan and Conlan, *Gentle Invaders,* chap. 4.

· 12 ·

The Paradox of Motherhood
Night Work Restrictions in the United States

Alice Kessler-Harris

Among Western industrial countries, the United States was a late-comer to maternal protection. It did not pass national legislation to protect women's jobs in the weeks before and after childbirth until 1993. With the exception of New York, where a provision for paid job leaves and medical insurance for pregnant working women was discussed and then defeated in 1919, the states have also largely ignored the issue of maternity leaves for most private-sector workers.

Considering that concern for the welfare of mothers has dominated the discussion of protection for women workers in the United States, the absence of maternity leaves, which constitute the backbone of pro-tective labor legislation in most other countries, is puzzling. In the early twentieth century, when the search for protection became a legis-lative priority, advocates of maximum hours, night work regulation, and safety and health measures rooted their arguments in the need to protect the family roles of women. At the same time, independent of the workplace, reformers struggled to address high levels of infant mor-tality through clinics for pregnant women and young children, and they argued successfully for mothers' pensions that would permit some mothers of small children to stay out of the work force.[1] Yet neither in this early period nor until very recently has maternal protection for women in the workplace ever seriously entered the U.S. legislative agenda.[2]

The silence about maternity legislation can hardly be explained as a function of the peculiarities of American labor legislation, which, until the 1930s, was rooted in gender differences. Gender-neutral legislation, offering minimal protections to industrial workers without regard to their sex, did not emerge in the United States until the late 1930s. Before that, with few exceptions, protective labor legislation was designed for women only. The exceptions involved the working conditions of federal and some state and municipal employees, as well as workers whose health and safety affected public well-being. The hours of railway workers, for example, were reduced by federal law, and those of miners were reduced by many states because of the danger that exhausted workers might hurt passengers or other workers. However, in a precedent-setting 1905 case the U. S. Supreme Court refused to allow New York State to regulate the hours of bakers because there was nothing intrinsically unhealthful in allowing bakers to work as long as they wished.[3]

While this case and others effectively stymied gender-neutral laws, legislation specific to women progressed rapidly. Between 1908 and 1920 an astonishingly wide array of laws emerged from state after state. Thirty-nine of the forty-eight states regulated hours for women; thirteen states and the District of Columbia passed minimum wage laws; sixteen states passed laws that expressly forbade night work for women. Because the progress of this legislation varied from state to state and because its impact has been well documented, I will not summarize it here.[4] Rather, I want to focus on the larger meaning of this body of legislation by looking at the case of night work laws.

License for the several states to regulate women's right to work under conditions of their own choosing derived from the U. S. Supreme Court's decision in the 1908 case of *Muller* v. *Oregon*. There the Court sharply distinguished between what was appropriate for men and what was desirable for women. Arguing that the state had an interest in women's present and future roles as actual mothers and as "mothers of the race," the Court upheld Oregon's effort to reduce the hours of women workers.[5] It thereby inscribed into precedent the notion that women, all of whom could be viewed as potential mothers, constituted a separate class and a proper subject for legislative action. For the next three decades, the basis of American protective legislation resided in women's capacity to become mothers. But no effort was made to address one of the central issues of motherhood: the difficulty of giving birth and of holding down a job at the same time. In sharp contrast to the frequent discussions of maternal and infant health, concern for maternity leaves for wage-earning women rarely entered the agendas of state legislators or female reformers.

Part of the explanation for this curious gap may lie in how the debate over protective legislation was constructed in the United States. First, in contrast to most other countries, the debate was not primarily the province either of political parties or of the labor movement. No socialist or social democratic party was powerful enough to dominate the debate; neither of the leading parties (Republican or Democratic) took on the issues as a national cause; and the struggling trade union movement was too weak to provide leadership. For most of the first two decades of the twentieth century, the dominant American Federation of Labor resisted efforts to legislate on behalf of men and acquiesced reluctantly and ambivalently to efforts to legislate for women. Trade union leaders believed that the only real protection for workers derived from effective organization, and they convinced themselves that if male workers were unionized and earned a family wage, women would not have to work at all. In the meantime, union leaders offered lukewarm support for the efforts of groups like the Women's Trade Union League and the National Consumers' League to pass legislation for women only.

The failure of political and working-class leadership left the legislative initiative in the hands of a loose coalition of mostly female reformers. For the most part, the campaign for protective legislation was led on a state-by-state basis by middle-class women who possessed a vision of family as traditional as that of trade union men. Recent discussions of Florence Kelley and the National Consumers' League suggest that the political coalitions they formed to campaign for reduced hours, night work laws, and minimum wages for women led the drive to regulate women's paid labor.[6] Their efforts derived from concern for family life, and their strategies were shaped by the constraints of the legislative and judicial systems rather than by the agendas of poor working women.[7]

A second critical factor in the U.S. experience was the role of the courts. The legal debate over protective labor legislation intersected two discussions in U.S. law. The first, from the perspective of labor, was the conflict between the doctrine of freedom of contract and that of the police power of the state. By the late nineteenth century it had become pretty much settled law that the courts would not interfere with a worker's "individual right" to negotiate with an employer. This doctrine, known as "freedom of contract," held that every citizen had the right to decide when and under what circumstances he or she would work. Since, in the judgment of the courts, a practical equality existed between employer and employee, legislation that would impinge on the contractual relation was held unconstitutional. The state could intervene by regulating hours, wages, and working conditions only when it perceived the public interest or the general welfare to be at stake. In practice, court interpretations deprived even well-intentioned lawmakers of the opportunity to legislate for workers, except when the health of the worker was threatened in such a way as to damage public well-being. The police power of the state could thus be used to limit freedom of contract only in special circumstances.

Because she belonged to a class of people who could become mothers, a female worker turned out to be a special circumstance. From the perspective of family law, the state perceived, and the courts upheld, a primary interest in the family. They had, by the end of the nineteenth century, constructed an image of married women as individuals entitled to limited citizenship rights. Yet this class of citizens had particular claims on the courts by virtue of its role in preserving family life.[8] The entry of large numbers of women into the industrial labor force compelled legislatures and the courts to consider how women could simultaneously exercise the freedom of contract implicit in citizenship and demand the protection of the police power of the state to preserve their own health and that of their present and future families. At the heart of this debate lay the meaning of womanhood itself.

As in most other countries, debates over social legislation took place in the ferment surrounding a rapid industrialization process. Many commentators have noted the absence of feudal and other obligatory constraints and the particularly predatory nature of U.S. capitalism at the end of the nineteenth century. This period has been labeled the "age of the robber baron," due to the rapid consolidation of capital, the speed of industrial mergers, and the concentration of major production industries. Historians have commented on the Darwinian rationalizations adopted by leaders of industry and on such notions as the "gospel of wealth" to justify unapologetic and increasingly sharp divisions between rich and poor. A massive influx of immigrants (some 20 million from foreign countries, and some 11 million from rural to urban areas in the United States between 1870 and 1920) made industrial workers particularly vulnerable. The process and its ideological justifications led to deteriorating working and living conditions for all workers and created special concerns about whether or not family life among the least skilled and most vulnerable might deteriorate to the point where the poor would no longer be trained to participate in the labor force. These concerns were exacerbated by the increasing numbers of women drawn into wage labor. By 1900, women constituted 25 percent of industrial workers. Though relatively few married women were employed (perhaps 6 percent) in 1900, they represented about 15 percent of all women workers.

Political, judicial, and economic parameters together heavily influenced the nature of the discourse on protective labor legislation. This discourse, which ultimately shaped visions of what was possible in the legislative sphere, created the paradoxical situation in which the idea of motherhood became the object of protection in the workplace, while women who became mothers derived no job protection at all.

The debate around prohibiting night work, which began in the United States in the late nineteenth century, provides a useful illustration of how this paradox came about. As part of the movement for shorter hours, the debate over night work added complexity to an already difficult issue. Historically, the debate emerged from discussion regarding maximum hours. Restricting night work was a heuristic device designed to encourage employers to obey the shorter hours legislation just beginning to emerge and to facilitate its enforcement.[9] Contemporary reformers understood that their efforts to reduce the daily hours of women wage-earners would be stymied if women worked split shifts or if they took a second job. To solve the problem, reformers called for prohibiting night work altogether. Their efforts quickly found justification in a range of arguments about the importance of family and the humane effects of shorter hours. Like arguments against the long working day, those formulated to prohibit women's work at night frequently confronted the equally salient issue of male night work. Though reformers were often sympathetic to laws that might have prohibited night work for men as well as women, legal precedent and a hostile judiciary vitiated this possibility. Thus, the moral effort to ensure that no one would work at night confronted the legal conviction that the work of adults could not be regulated. To resolve this standoff required exaggerating gender differences and placing the qualities of women, not social justice for workers, in the forefront of the debate.

At the time of the Bern conference in 1906 (to which the United

States did not send delegates because the individual states were empowered to legislate working conditions), only four of the forty-eight states had laws restricting the employment of women at night.[10] In one of these (New York), the state's highest court would declare night work laws unconstitutional in 1907. The Bern conference's resolution restricting women's night work seems to have had little effect on U.S. legislation.[11] No other states even attempted to restrict night work until after the U.S. Supreme Court declared in 1908 that women were in effect wards of the state, whose prior interest in their health and mothering capacity permitted intervention.[12] In the aftermath of this decision, several states included the regulation of night work among their laws restricting women's work. But even by 1918, only twelve states had such laws, as compared with the forty-two that had adopted maximum hour laws for women workers.[13]

The debate over night work for women heated up in the years following World War I, and in the early 1920s four new states (New Jersey, North Dakota, Washington, and California) passed restrictive night work laws.[14] Two other states moved in the opposite direction: Maryland and New Hampshire explicitly acknowledged women's right to hold night jobs by limiting to eight hours the length of time a woman could work at night. In 1924, the U.S. Supreme Court decisively upheld the constitutionality of legislation that restricted night work for women but not for men, but state legislatures did not respond. The total number of states regulating women's night work remained at sixteen—only one-third of all the states.

Even that number exaggerates the kinds of protection women could expect. The laws varied dramatically from state to state as to the hours during which restrictions applied and the industries covered and exempted. For example, Indiana, Massachusetts, and Pennsylvania covered only manufacturing plants; South Carolina covered only retail stores; Ohio regulated night work for female ticket sellers; and Washington singled out elevator operators.[15] Even states with stringent regulations permitted exceptions: nurses, hotel workers, and those employed at seasonal agricultural and cannery labor were most frequently allowed to work at night. But other states, in no discernible pattern, thought it unnecessary to restrict the hours of women employed, for example, as domestics, actors and performers, or cloakroom attendants. Some exempted store workers for the two weeks before Christmas; others refused to restrict women who worked in small towns no matter what their occupation.[16] Most regulations prohibited work from 10 P.M. until 6 A.M. Massachusetts denied textile mills the right to employ women from 6 P.M. until 6 A.M. but allowed other businesses to utilize women during the evening hours. Some rural states with almost no industrial workers, such as North Dakota and Nebraska, passed restrictive night work laws, while heavily industrialized states like Illinois refused to do so. The Women's Bureau of the Department of Labor, surveying with some dismay this chaotic array of legislation in 1924, concluded that night work legislation was "found not only in a much smaller number of States than is legislation limiting the daily and weekly hours of work[,] but in many States which have both types of legislation, the night-work laws cover a much smaller group of industries or occupations."[17]

The wide array of laws, and the refusal of many states to adopt them, may reflect the fact that relatively few women earned their livings at night. A 1928 Women's Bureau study of twelve states found that on the average slightly more than 2 percent of all female wage earners worked during the night hours.[18] Mississippi, the state with the highest percentage, counted 6.4 percent of its working women in night jobs; Alabama, South Carolina, and Virginia each had between 4 and 5 percent. The heavy concentration of night work in these southern states can be traced to the textile mills, which employed 40 percent of all night workers (87 percent of whom were employed in Alabama, Georgia, Mississippi, South Carolina, and Tennessee).

If night work was confined to a relatively small group of women, these women were crucially placed. Among the night workers, as the Women's Bureau noted, "all but a negligible proportion were in the years of development or of highest childbearing capacity, the years precisely when all the characteristic injuries of night work are most disastrous."[19] Of the women who worked at night, some 75 percent were between the ages of twenty and forty; and an equal percentage were mothers of young children. Other studies confirmed these figures. In Passaic, New Jersey, ninety-six of a sample group of one hundred night-working women surveyed in 1919 were married; ninety-two of them had children; only five were widowed or did not live with or have husbands.[20]

These figures stand in sharp contrast to the female work force as a whole in 1920, less than 15 percent of which was married,[21] and probably no more than one-third of whom were mothers of small children.

The problem, then, was that night work confronted a reluctant legislative and court system with what to do about working mothers. This phenomenon shaped the debate, structuring perceptions of the work force as a whole and leading to a formulation of gender distinctions that encouraged both the continuing exclusion of males from legislative protection and legislative silences about women who became mothers during their working years.

An examination of the rhetoric of the debate around night work that occurred in the late nineteenth and early twentieth centuries appears to explain how this happened. The debate locates itself in three areas: in the effort to modify harsh working conditions for all workers, regardless of sex; in the creation and precise definition of an idealized version of women (a universal woman); and in the problem of how to regulate competition in the labor force. These are neither uncontested nor mutually exclusive; arguments for all three are sometimes made by the same person in the same sentence. Commentators also frequently acknowledged disagreement when offering their own strongly felt opinions. But distinguishing them allows us to see how ideas play themselves out in ways that produce regulation and reflect a particular construction of gender.   ◆ ◆

Since the discussion of night work arose from an effort to restrict the role of capital and to humanize its uses in the treatment of all workers, night work legislation, like other protective legislation, initially was meant to incorporate an apparently gender-neutral concept of workers. Eliminating night work was necessary to increase the possibility of leisure, to allow full family lives, to provide access to education, and to encourage effective participation in political citizenship. These arguments continued through the first decades of the twentieth century.

Night work, it was argued, was not good for any worker. Thus, the secretary of the male Bakery and Confectionery Workers International Union used the following language to condemn it. Night work, he suggested, was "one of the greatest evils against humanity." Its deleterious effect on bakers "makes them dissatisfied and warps and spoils their dispositions because they are prevented from enjoying proper rest which they can not get during the day. Furthermore they are prevented from sharing in the joys of family life or the opportunities of educating themselves for a better station in life." [22] Note that the deleterious consequences are said to detract only from the lives of individuals, not specifically men alone. Contrast this with the language used in Josephine Goldmark's influential 1912 study, *Fatigue and Efficiency,* which identified the negative features of night work in gender-neutral terms. The "characteristic and invariable effects" of night work, she argued, were "the loss of sleep and sunlight," with its "inevitable physiological deficits." But, she continued, the evil effects of night work on everyone's health produced in women the additional problems of "loss of appetite, headache, anaemia, and weakness of the female functions."[23] With few exceptions, advocates of night work legislation turned arguments for its abolition into special pleadings for women. A typical article in the *American Journal of Public Health* would begin by asserting, "I am not in favor of night work for anybody," and then turn to the particular ill effects of night work on women.[24]

Failing to establish effective legal grounds for regulating capital's ability to buy labor, reformers turned to women as examples of what the state might appropriately do and sometimes offered them up as the vanguard of state activity. This discussion was inevitably influenced by the sharpening conflict over definitions of womanhood. Calling attention to the problem of night work for women in particular presented the issue as a social problem that could and did require state intervention, for the state, as many reformers pointed out, did not hesitate to exercise its police power when public health was at stake. This strategy at first stumbled on the roadblock of freedom of contract—defined as a right of citizenship.

While even the most ardent reformers hesitated to infringe on the citizenship rights of men, those of women proved to be much more vulnerable. When the issue first emerged in the landmark case of *Ritchie* v. *The People,* the court held that "if one man is denied the right to contract under the law as he has hitherto done under the law, and as others are still allowed to do by the law, he is deprived of both liberty and property." It struck down an effort to regulate women's hours as a "purely arbitrary restriction upon the fundamental right of the citizen to control his or her own time and faculties."[25] But within five years, women's citizenship rights came under pressure. In 1905, Pennsylvania's highest court allowed the state to regulate women's hours, asserting that "the fact that both parties are of full age and competent to contract does not necessarily deprive the state of the power to interfere when the parties do not stand upon an equality, or when the public health demands that one party to the contract shall be protected against himself." The state, the court added presciently, "retains an interest in his welfare, however reckless he may be."[26] The male adjective aside, we should not let this warning to womankind go unheeded. Later events were to sustain the court's notion that women's citizenship rights were vulnerable to legislative and judicial determinations about the public health, with or without the consent of the women involved. What was at issue, then, was not whether women needed the protection but whether to sustain state intervention required a modification of women's rights.

The slow pace of legislative activity, especially around night work legislation, tells us something about the skepticism with which this interpretation was initially viewed. In reviewing New York State's early attempts to put night work clauses into legislation, the economic historian Elizabeth Faulkner Baker notes that "there was quiet question in the minds of New York labor officials from the start as to the right of the legislature to prohibit *adult* women from working at night." As late as 1906, the state's labor commissioner argued that

> there is no present necessity in this state for the prohibition of night work by adult women. On the other hand, if enforced, it would deprive some mature working women, employed at night only, at skilled trades, for short hours and for high wages, of all means of support. And the prohibition in its application to factories only seems rather one-sided when we consider that probably the hardest occupations of women, those of hotel laundresses and cleaners, are not limited as to hours in any way.[27]

Because protective labor legislation relied on a special effort to restrict the citizenship rights of one class of people, the hope that it would serve as a vanguard—an example that would be followed by regulations for all workers—seemed doomed before it began. The discourse over night work quickly transformed what might have been a general struggle into a woman's issue, constructing contrasting pictures of gendered citizenship rights, organizational capacity, and natural and social circumstances.

◆ ◆

How this happened can best be explained by looking at the rhetoric that formed the core of the debate over a period of more than two decades. Taken as a whole, the rhetoric creates a concept of an ideal, or universal, woman. To make the case for special legislation for women required riding roughshod over class, race, and ethnic distinctions and ignoring questions of life cycles and personal choice. The debate situated all women within a single framework defined as "natural" and located within childbearing and childrearing functions. It sought to portray a world in which these attributes dominated—and therefore justified the sacrifice of all others. The words of the New York State court that in 1914 articulated the standard for all other night work decisions drew on and extended the decision in *Muller* v. *Oregon.* Night work in factories, as contrasted with day labor, wrote the court, "substantially affects and impairs the physical condition of women and prevents them from discharging in a healthful and satisfactory manner the peculiar functions which have been imposed upon them by nature." The court offered little sympathy to the many women who did not exercise these functions, suggesting that such differences among women did not tempt it to modify the decision. Moreover, the court acknowledged that "this statute in its universal application to all factories will inflict unnecessary hardships on a great many women who neither ask nor require its provisions by depriving them of an opportunity to earn a livelihood by perfectly healthful labor although performed during some of the hours of the night." [28] But, the court insisted, such women should turn to the legislature, not the courts, for relief, for the prerogative of defining public welfare lay in legislative hands.

If this decision did not repeat the language of the public debate, it and the 1908 U.S. Supreme Court decision that sealed approval of all such restrictions certainly reaffirmed what would by the mid-1920s become a prevailing theme. That debate, firmly rooted in the traditional family and in women's place within it, identified women in terms of their family roles and articulated the expectation that they would reproduce. The debate was conducted as if all women were mothers or potential mothers. The evil effects of night work, on both men and women, receded in the face of its consequences for those who would bear or care for children. Rather, legislatures attempted to persuade the courts that women's health in particular required state intervention. Drawing heavily on the research utilized by successful European advocates of night work prohibitions, American supporters painted a distressing picture. Their language invoked the female's "delicate organism" and cited at length the injuries to women's reproductive systems, menstrual cycles, and general vitality that the state had a special interest in guarding. Inevitably, women's physical capacities were described as being far less than those of men. "No-one doubts," wrote the judge who issued the opinion in *The People* v. *Schweinler* (1914), "that as regards bodily strength and endurance [a woman] is inferior. . . . As healthy mothers are essential to vigorous offspring," he continued, "the physical well-being of women becomes an object of public interest and care in order to preserve the strength and vigor of the race."[29]

Advocates did not fail to add, nor courts to take notice of, the social burdens imposed on women by household tasks. Women's double day, suggested Frances Perkins, then the Industrial Commissioner of New York State, provided the rationale for protection. "Night work," she argued, "bears with special severity on women who under these conditions tend to work all night and discharge family and home duties most of the day."[30] Louis Brandeis and Josephine Goldmark, in their brief to the court hearing the New York State case on night work legislation, wrote that "Women who work in factories are not thereby relieved from household duties—from cooking, washing, cleaning and looking after their families,"[31] and the court concurred. Housework, it noted in its favorable ruling, filled "most of the day" for those who worked at night.[32]

These arguments were not uncontested. Medical opinion differed as to the effect of night work on the menstrual cycle,[33] and many experts testified to the disadvantages of long hours, long periods of standing, and the stress of responding to machines. Attempts to place the discussion in the framework of poor working conditions in general proved successful in only two states that limited night work to eight hours, rather than banning it altogether.

In general, however, the effects of poverty and malnutrition and the debility caused by overwork were identified as the peculiarly gendered consequences of night work. Infant mortality and higher morbidity rates for working women were widely laid at its door. "It goes without saying," Brandeis and Goldmark dismissively wrote in their New York State brief, "that many other factors besides the mother's employment contribute to a high infant mortality, such as poverty, inadequate attendance at birth, wrong feeding, bad sanitation, and the like."[34] Though studies conducted by the U.S. Children's Bureau confirmed European research that demonstrated an overwhelming relationship between infant mortality and father's wages, arguments that an increase in male wages might solve some of the problems of malnutrition and long hours fell on deaf ears.

The possibilities inherent in higher wages for men (which would have required a different kind of regulation) were rarely pursued by investigators who preferred instead to depict the horror inherent in night work for women. In the textile mills of Passaic, New Jersey, night-working women were described as "weary, tousled . . . . half dressed, trying to snatch an hour of sleep after [a] long night of work in the mill." Their children were "aimless" and "neglected," the tragedy of their lot reflected in their "woebegone and wistful faces."[35] A government investigation described the children of night workers as "pitiable drifts and strays deprived of anchorage."[36] The homes of these women night workers were "as dismal and neglected as similar homes were found by investigators abroad."[37] Implicitly these descriptions blamed poor health, household disorder, and neglected children on the problems of night work, exonerating the role of desperate poverty. These descriptions also encouraged an image of women who deprived their families of domestic comforts, negating a healthy moral as well as physical environment. "Young women who work at night," wrote Goldmark in 1912, "are deprived of all the restraining influences of home life." And when the mother of a family "spends the night or evening in work, disorder is almost unavoidable, and the comfort of the men as well as of the children dependent upon her ministrations, is lost."[38]

The unspoken text that appealed to the legislative instinct was the helplessness of women engaged in night work. What kinds of women would abandon their homes and children to such depravity? The literature described them as foreigners: "Poles, Hungarians and Russians," women who "speak little English" and were "always willing to work overtime." They were also "poor negro women" employed as substitutes for boys; or they were the "lintheads" of the southern textile industry.[39]

The language used to describe women's night-time experiences affirmed their helplessness. Louise Kindig, the twenty-three-year-old woman who tested the constitutionality of New York State's night work law in 1913 was described as "a frail girl" who "represented hundreds of working women who, night after night are employed in the factories and workshops of New York." Like other such women, Kindig was "forced to go outside for meals at midnight"[40] and was "turned into the streets at a late hour of night or at early dawn."[41] Women night workers were "ignorant women" who could "scarcely be expected to realize the dangers not only to their own health, but to that of the next generation from such inhuman usage."[42]

❖ ❖

This message was eagerly, even anxiously perpetuated by male and female reformers for whom protective labor legislation, and particularly restrictions on night work, seemed to respond to a need to regulate a

chaotic labor market. Here the emphasis shifted to the need to protect
the male provider role, both in its economic aspects and in its social
assumptions of patriarchal entitlements. Employers, union men, and
reformers, as well as some wage-earning women, debated efforts to restrict night work and sometimes unilaterally limited women's ability
to work at night as a function of implicit understandings about who
should support the family and what constituted an appropriate job.
The discussions here reflect and affirm a sense of entitlement on the
part of males that turns women's refusal to submit to regulation into
selfish acts that threaten to undermine the family.

Assumptions about male roles may explain why so few women
worked at night to begin with—partly out of their own expectations
and partly out of what the Women's Bureau described in 1928 as "an astonishingly strong feeling among employers in industry against the employment of women at night, irrespective of legal regulation."[43] These
feelings, affirmed by union men, were not independent of generally
shared assumptions about female roles. Lurid sketches of opportunities
for immoral behavior inherent in female work at night, accusations that
unscrupulous employers fed their female workers "liquor and narcotics
to overcome exhaustion," and the conviction that the bad character of
some night workers would infect even decent women—all these con-
spired to construct an image of night work that negated the possibilities
of respectable family life.[44]

Opponents of night work restrictions adopted the same language
but gave it a different twist. Conceding that family life was the most
important issue at stake in whether or not legislation should be passed,
they constructed images of sturdy, self-supporting women who used
the extra income they could earn at night to support families in modest comfort. They repeated such stories as that of the female elevator
operator whose family situation deteriorated when she lost her relatively comfortable job only to end up as a poorly paid charwoman.
They circulated hardship stories of skilled women printers who could
no longer keep their families after they lost their night jobs. Waitresses
who could not work at night when the tips were highest complained
that the hatcheck girls and cabaret singers, who were exempted from
the law, were less likely to have children and families in need.[45]

The language of male prerogative and of family values translated directly into the work force. Elizabeth Faulkner Baker, in a thoughtful
discussion of the problem, noted that both sides of the argument under-

stood that if legislation passed, then "men will always be preferred . . . leaving women to earn a scanty living out of the left-over jobs—a part of the luckless mass of underpaid, unskilled and unorganized workers who toil long and hope little."[46] Such job segregation would inevitably follow night-work restrictions because whole categories of jobs would be removed from female competition.

Perhaps more significant in the long run, the explicit rejection by unionized men of the need for protective legislation was sustained and supported by a false perception of the role of trade unions that played off images of women's weaknesses. One popular magazine, for example, advocated night-work restrictions for women because "working women and girls, less able to organize for self protection need, if they are to fulfill the functions of motherhood, to be protected against the exploitation of their physical and mental life by a greedy and inhuman industrialism."[47] In 1907, perhaps 12 percent of America's urban male workers belonged to unions—a figure that rose to nearly 20 percent during World War I and then declined again in the 1920s. Not until the mass-organizing drives of the mid-1930s did the proportion of organized men in industry reach even 25 percent. Still, advocates of night work insisted that women needed the protection of laws to offset a protection already negotiated by men. Frances Perkins, for example, noted that women who were poorly organized could not be expected to reproduce the experience of men who had "in many instances created excellent industrial conditions for themselves without legislation and through the medium of the trade union and the strike."[48]

Distinguishing men from women in this way preserved benefits for the relatively few, mostly skilled men who were union members—a boon to which working men were not insensitive. For example, when New York's unionized female printers, deprived of their night jobs under state law in 1914, petitioned the legislature for relief, they were opposed by a significant proportion of the membership of their own union. When in 1921 an exception was made in women's favor, union men and foremen placed obstacles in the paths of their return to their old jobs.[49] Despite a Women's Bureau finding that streetcar conducting was healthful outdoor work, the New York State legislature refused to grant an exemption when male workers fought against it. As a result, 83 percent of New York City's female streetcar conductors lost their jobs.

A rhetoric that obscured male needs and took its stance from questionable depictions of the character and lives of women concealed some of the larger issues of the debate. Though reformers frequently raised questions about the efficiency of running factories late at night, such questions did not enter the agenda until the discussion broadened in the 1930s. Rather, manufacturers thought about the problem in terms of control of the work force, constructing images of women that accorded with their own and with community perceptions of present and future labor force needs. Generally, it was easier to play the sexes off against each other than to exclude one sex or the other. "Night work for women," concluded Agnes de Lima, "is fostered by the low wage scale for men, coupled with a comparatively high wage level for women which tempts them to enter the industry." [50]

◆ ◆

This very cursory, tentative examination of the rhetoric surrounding night work legislation in the United States reveals a public culture in which men and women differ dramatically in their possession of citizenship rights. Night work, equally evil for men and women, was regulated only for women (albeit ambivalently) because their claims to citizenship rights were subject to public perceptions of appropriate behavior for females in family life. Such perceptions inhered in women's role in social reproduction and in the characteristics of person and physique assumed to be necessary to fulfill that role. Assumptions about women's roles and attributions to them of qualities that inhibited their capacity to function effectively in the work force turned the debate over night work into a discussion of women's functions. In the face of this onslaught against women's physical stamina and character, other alternatives such as nurseries for children, minimum wages for men, and police patrols for dangerous streets became invisible. The shape of the debate, framed in terms of settled assumptions about motherhood and domesticity, contributed to the passage of laws that exacerbated differences between men and women. Rooting legislation in this manner did more than characterize and disadvantage women; it discredited protective legislation for men. The unspoken message that legislation was necessary for the weak and inferior implied that only the weak and inferior would seek it. Mature adult males could be left to the mercy of an unencumbered capitalism.

Equally important, the particular construction of citizenship that facilitated legislation for women was rooted in the states' right to protect motherhood and family roles, not in a woman's right to protect her job. The discourse that made such a division possible created a vision of motherhood that precluded an amalgam of wagework and mothering in the public mind and therefore mitigated against maternity leaves to protect jobs and instead supported maternal protections that saved babies. A rhetoric that reduced women who worked to inadequate mothers left little room for policies that might allow mothers more rights at work. Instead, it encouraged ways of removing mothers from the work force through such devices as mothers' pensions.

What emerged in the late nineteenth and early twentieth century was at best a limited and hard-fought consensus on social reproduction and women's place in it. But it was costly. To assert woman's primary roles as childbearer and childrearer meant subsuming her role as provider. The result was that women's individual rights as citizens were regulated on behalf of motherhood. The powerful images invoked in the debate enabled the public to accept the loss of economic rights for women in favor of the states' desire to protect the rights of all women to be mothers. Consistent with the judicial antagonism against economic rights for all workers, as well as with the preferences of American industry, the courts did not protect the rights of women as workers. Instead, they offered women, conceived in terms of motherhood, the right not to work at all, setting up a contradiction between motherhood and work that made asking for maternity legislation all but inconceivable.

Notes

1. Joanne Goodwin, "An American Experiment in Paid Motherhood: The Implementation of Mothers' Pensions in Early Twentieth Century Chicago," *Gender and History* 4 (Autumn 1992): 323–42; Molly Ladd-Taylor, *Raising a Baby the Government Way: Mothers' Letters to the Children's Bureau, 1915–1932* (New Brunswick: Rutgers University Press, 1986), and *Mother-Work: Women, Child Welfare, and the State, 1890–1930* (Urbana: University of Illinois Press, 1994); and Theda Skocpol, *Protecting Soldiers and Mothers: The Political Origins of Social Policy in the United States* (Cambridge: Harvard University Press, 1993).

2. New York State provides perhaps the only exception to this. For a discussion of the New York legislative debates of 1917–19, when a maternity benefit proposal went down to defeat, see Beatrix Hoffman, "Insuring Maternity: Women Reformers and the New York Health Insurance Campaign, 1916–20" (ms. in author's possession).

3. The case is *Lochner* v. *New York,* 198 U.S. 45 (1905). A good discussion of law in relation to American workers can be found in William Forbath, *Law and the Shaping of the American Labor Movement* (Cambridge: Harvard University Press, 1991). The standard discussion of law in relation to gender is in Leo Kanowitz, *Sex Roles in Law and Society: Cases and Materials* (Albuquerque: University of New Mexico Press, 1973).

4. A summary and discussion of this legislation can be found in Alice Kessler-Harris, *Out to Work: A History of Wage-earning Women in the United States* (New York: Oxford University Press, 1982), chap. 7. See also Judith Baer, *The Chains of Protection: The Judicial Response to Women's Labor Legislation* (Westport, Conn.: Greenwood Press, 1978).

5. *Muller* v. *Oregon,* 208 U.S. 412 (1908).

6. Skocpol, *Protecting Soldiers and Mothers;* Kathryn Kish Sklar, *Florence Kelley and the Nation's Work: The Rise of Women's Political Culture, 1830–1900* (New Haven: Yale University Press, 1995).

7. Vivien Hart, *Bound by Our Constitution: Women, Workers, and the Minimum Wage* (Princeton: Princeton University Press, 1994), suggests that the shaping strategy was a desire to avoid the constraints of rigid judicial interpretation of the U.S. Constitution.

8. Michael Grossberg, *Governing the Hearth: Law and the Family in Nineteenth-Century America* (Chapel Hill: University of North Carolina Press, 1985), 300.

9. See, for example, discussions of New York and Massachusetts in Clara M. Beyer, *History of Labor Legislation for Women in Three States,* Bulletin of the Women's Bureau, No. 66 (Washington, D.C.: Government Printing Office, 1929), and Elizabeth Faulkner Baker, *Protective Labor Legislation, with Special Reference to Women in the State of New York* (New York: Columbia University Press, 1925), 236.

10. These were Massachusetts (1890), Indiana (1894), Nebraska (1898), and New York (1903). See Mary D. Hopkins, *The Employment of Women at Night,* Bulletin of the Women's Bureau, No. 64 (Washington, D.C.: Government Printing Office, 1928), 2.

11. There is certainly evidence, however, that American reformers and legislators were aware of it. For example, when the New York State law came under judicial scrutiny in 1913–14, *The Survey,* an important outlet for the reform community, reported that in drafting the original law, members of a Factory Investigation Commission had "availed themselves of the recorded experience of the fourteen European nations who in 1906 met in Bern, Switzerland, to sign an international treaty prohibiting night work for women in industrial establishments" ("Progress of the New York Women's Night Work Case," 32 [June 12, 1914]: 169). The 1906 Bern Convention shows up frequently in the

literature of reformers who refer to it as a mark of civilization. For example, *The Survey* frequently compared the lack of night work laws in the United States with those in Europe: "This tardy progress is in striking contrast to the action of the fourteen civilized countries of Europe which have, since 1906, by international treaty prohibited the night work of women" ("Night Work Law Tested in New York State," 31 [Dec. 24, 1913]: 343). Similar references can be found in the editorial pages of *The Charities and the Commons,* for example, in contrasting "the European movement towards total prohibition of women's nightwork in industrial establishments—representatives of all the civilized governments, having met twice during the past two years to draw up international agreements on the subject—and the indifference to such protection in this country" ("Night Work: Women and the New York Courts," 17 [Dec. 1906]: 183).

12. Nancy Erickson sees this decision as less dramatic than is typically the case ("*Muller* v. *Oregon* Reconsidered: The Origins of a Sex-based Doctrine of Liberty of Contract," *Labor History* 30 [Spring 1989]: 230–31).

13. *State Laws Affecting Working Women,* Bulletin of the Women's Bureau, No. 40 (Washington, D.C.: Government Printing Office, 1924), 5.

14. Hopkins, *The Employment of Women at Night,* 4.

15. *State Laws Affecting Working Women,* 5.

16. "Regulation of Women's Working Hours in the United States," *American Labor Legislation Review* 8 (Dec. 1918): 345–54.

17. *State Laws Affecting Working Women,* 5.

18. Hopkins, *The Employment of Women at Night,* 6, acknowledges the possibility of an undercount.

19. Ibid., 10.

20. Agnes de Lima, *Night Working Mothers in Textile Mills: Passaic, New Jersey* (National Consumer's League and the Consumer's League of New Jersey, Dec. 1920), 8. Another study of forty-six women revealed that forty-two of them were under school age. See Mary E. McDowell, "Mothers and Night Work," *The Survey* 39 (Dec. 22, 1917): 335.

21. African-American women are a significant exception. Since the vast majority of them were excluded from industrial work and were occupied in domestic service and agricultural work, they would, in any event, not have been covered by this legislation. See U.S. Department of Labor, *Negro Women in Industry,* Bulletin of the Women's Bureau, No. 20 (Washington, D.C.: Government Printing Office, 1922).

22. Charles Iffland, "Reasons Why Night Work Should Be Abolished in Bakeries," *American Federationist* 26 (May 1919): 408.

23. Josephine Goldmark, *Fatigue and Efficiency: A Study in Industry* (New York: Charities Publication Committee, 1912), 266.

24. Emery Hayhurst, M.D., "Medical Argument against Night Work Especially for Women Employees," *American Journal of Public Health* 9 (1919): 367.

25. 155 Ill. 98 (1895), 105.

26. 15 PA Superior Court, 5 (1900), 17; and see *People* v. *Williams*, 184 N.Y. 131 (1907).

27. Baker, *Protective Labor Legislation,* 236–37. Part of the difficulty here was the insistence of the courts on dealing with "women and children" as if they had unified interests and needs.

28. *People* v. *Schweinler Press,* 214 N.Y. 395 (1915), 400, 409.

29. Ibid., 401, 402.

30. Francis Perkins, "Do Women in Industry Need Special Protection?" *The Survey* 55 (Feb. 15 1926): 531.

31. "A Summary of the 'Facts of Knowledge' Submitted on Behalf of the People," in National Consumer's League, *The Case against Night Work for Women* (New York: National Consumer's League, 1914), A10.

32. *People* v. *Schweinler Press,* 403.

33. Elizabeth Faulkner Baker, "Do Women in Industry Need Special Protection?" *The Survey* 55 (Feb. 15, 1926): 583.

34. "A Summary of the 'Facts of Knowledge,'" A10.

35. De Lima, *Night Working Mothers in Textile Mills,* 5.

36. *The Cotton Textile Industry,* vol. 1 of *Report on Condition of Women and Child Wage Earners in the United States,* S. Doc. 645, 61st Cong., 2d Sess. (Washington, D.C.: Government Printing Office, 1910), 289, 293.

37. Goldmark, *Fatigue and Efficiency,* 275.

38. Ibid., 267.

39. De Lima, *Night Working Mothers in Textile Mills,* 5; *Wage-earning Women in Stores and Factories,* vol. 5 of *Report on Condition of Women and Child Wage Earners in the United States,* 214; Goldmark, *Fatigue and Efficiency,* 275.

40. "Night Work Law Tested in New York State," 343.

41. *Annual Report of the Consumers' League of New York* (1906), 19, cited in Baker, "Do Women in Industry Need Special Protection?" 239.

42. "Progress of the New York Women's Night Work Case," 169.

43. *Summary: The Effects of Labor Legislation on the Employment Opportunities of Women,* Bulletin of the Women's Bureau, No. 68 (Washington, D.C.: Government Printing Office, 1928), 15.

44. See Hopkins, *The Employment of Women at Night,* 57. For a discussion of glass workers and decent women, see "Fighting Women's Night Work in Rhode Island," *The Survey* 36 (Feb. 13, 1916): 48.

45. Rheta Childe Dorr, "Should There Be Labor Laws for Women? No," *Good Housekeeping* 81 (Sept. 1925): 52ff.

46. Baker, "Do Women in Industry Need Special Protection?" 531.

47. "Night Work: Women and the New York Courts," 183.

48. Perkins, "Do Women in Industry Need Special Protection?" 530.

49. Baker, "Do Women in Industry Need Special Protection?" 532; Beyer, *History of Labor Legislation for Women.*

50. De Lima, *Night Working Mothers in Textile Mills,* 16.

Selected Readings

Abukhanfusa, Kerstin. *Piskan och moroten: Om könens tilldelning av skyldigheter och rättigheter i det svenska socialförsäkringssystemet 1913–1980*. Stockholm: Carlssons Förlag, 1987.

Avdela, Efi. "To antifatico periechomeno tis koinonikis prostasias: i nomothesia gia tin ergasia ton gynaikon sti viomichania (1905–2005 aionas)." *Ta Istorika* 11 (1989): 339–60.

———. *Dimosioi ypalliloi genous thilykou: Katamerismos tis ergasias kata fyla ston dimosio tomea, 1908–1955*. Athens: Foundation for Research and Culture of the Commercial Bank of Greece, 1990.

Baer, Judith A. *The Chains of Protection: The Judicial Response to Women's Labor Legislation*. Westport, Conn.: Greenwood Press, 1978.

Ballestrero, Maria Vittoria. *Dalla tutela alla parità: La legislazione italiana sul lavoro delle donne*. Bologna: il Mulino, 1979.

Banks, Olive. *Faces of Feminism*. New York: St. Martin's Press, 1982.

Berry, Mary Frances. *The Politics of Parenthood: Child Care, Women's Rights, and the Myth of the Good Mother*. New York: Viking, 1993.

Bock, Gisela, and Pat Thane, eds. *Maternity and Gender Policies: Women and the Rise of the European Welfare States*. London: Routledge, 1991.

Boris, Eileen. *Home to Work: Motherhood and the Politics of Industrial Homework in the United States*. Cambridge: Cambridge University Press, 1994.

Boxer, Marilyn J. "Protective Legislation and Home Industry: The Marginalization of Women Workers in Late Nineteenth–Early Twentieth Century France." *Journal of Social History* 20 (1986): 45–65.

———. "Foyer or Factory: Working-Class Women in Nineteenth-Century France." In *Proceedings* of the Second Annual Meeting of the Western Society for French History. Ed. Brison D. Gooch. College Station: Texas A&M Press, 1975. Pp. 192–203.

Braun, Kathrin. *Gewerbeordnung und Geschlechtertrennung: Klasse, Geschlecht und Staat in der frühen Arbeitsschutzgesetzgebung*. Baden-Baden: Nomos, 1993.

Braun, Marianne. *De prijs van de liefde: De eerste feministische golf, het huwe-*

lijksrecht en de vaderlandse geschiedenis. Amsterdam: Het Spinhuis, 1992. Chapters 4, 5, and 10.

Broch, Birte. *Kvindearbejde og kvindeorganisering: Kvinder i konfektionsindustrien 1890–1914.* Copenhagen: SFAH, 1977.

Bumiller, Kristin. "Victims in the Shadow of the Law: A Critique of the Model of Legal Protection." *Signs: Journal of Women in Culture and Society* 12:3 (Spring 1987): 421–39.

Carlsson, Christina. *Kvinnosyn och kvinnopolitik: En studie i svensk socialdemokrati 1880–1910.* Lund: Arkiv Förlag, 1986.

Coyle, Angela. "The Protection Racket?" *Feminist Review* 4 (1980): 1–14.

Creigton, W. B. *Working Women and the Law.* London: Hansell, 1979.

Eastman, Crystal. "There Is No Protection without Equality." In *On Women and Revolution.* Ed. Blanche Wiesen Cook. New York: Oxford University Press, 1978. Pp. 154–231.

Ebert, Kurt. *Die Anfänge der modernen Sozialpolitik in Österreich: Die Taaffesche Sozialgesetzgebung für die Arbeiter im Rahmen der Gewerbeordnungsreform (1879–1885).* Vienna: Studien zur Geschichte der Österreichisch-Ungarischen Monarchie 15, 1975.

Ellerkamp, Marlene. *Industriearbeit, Krankheit and Geschlecht: Zu den sozialen Kosten der Industrialisierung; Bremer Textilarbeiterinnen 1870–1914.* Göttingen: Vandenhoek, 1991.

Feurer, Rosemary. "The Meaning of 'Sisterhood': The British Women's Movement and Protective Labor Legislation, 1870–1900." *Victorian Studies* 31 (Winter 1988): 233–60.

Francis, Raelene. *The Politics of Work: Gender and Labour in Victoria, 1880–1939.* Melbourne: Cambridge University Press, 1992.

Franzoi, Barbara. *At the Very Least She Pays the Rent: Women and German Industrialization, 1871–1914.* Westport, Conn.: Greenwood Press, 1985. Chapter 3.

Geertsen, Kirsten. *Arbejderkvinder i Danmark 1914–1924.* Copenhagen: SFAH, 1977.

Gray, Robert. "Factory Legislation and the Gendering of Jobs in the North of England." *Gender and History* 5 (Spring 1993): 56–80.

Hagemann, Gro. "Saervern av kvinner—arbeidervern eller diskriminering?" In *Kvinner selv . . . Sju bidrag till norsk kvinnehistorie.* Ed. Ida Blom and Gro Hagemann. Oslo: Aschehoug, 1982. Pp. 95–121.

Harrison, Barbara, and Helen Mockett. "Women in the Factory: The State and Factory Legislation in Nineteenth-Century Britain." In *State, Private Life and Political Change.* Ed. Lynn Jamieson and Helen Corr. New York: St. Martin's Press, 1990. Pp. 137–62.

Hause, Steven C., and Anne R. Kenney. *Women's Suffrage and Social Politics in the French Third Republic.* Princeton: Princeton University Press, 1984.

Hilden, Patricia Penn. *Women, Work, and Politics: Belgium, 1830–1914.* Oxford: Clarendon Press, 1993.

————. *Working Women and Socialist Politics in France, 1880–1914: A Regional Study.* Oxford: Clarendon Press, 1986.

Hill, Anne Corinne. "Protection of Women Workers and the Courts: A Legal Case History." *Feminist Studies* 5 (1979): 2.

Hoff, Joan. *Law, Gender, and Injustice: A Legal History of U.S. Women.* New York: New York University Press, 1991.

Horst, D. A. J. van der, H. F. de Jong, and J. C. M. Luybregts. "Vrouwen en arbeidswetten: De effectiviteit van arbeidswetgeving voor vrouwen in Nederland, toegespitst op ziekenverpleging, kledingindustrie en steenbakkerijen, 1889–1940." In *Van particuliere naar openbare zorg, en terug? Sociale politiek in Nederland sinds 1880.* Ed. W. P. Blockmans and L. A. van der Valk. Amsterdam: NEHA, 1992. Pp. 139–59.

Høyrup, Lise J. "Barselshvile—pligt, ret eller illusion? En undersøgelse af barselslovgivningens betydning for kvinder i industri og håndværk 1901–1933." M.A. thesis, Historisk Institut, Københavns Universitet, Speciale, Copenhagen, 1988.

Humphries, Jane. "Protective Legislation, the Capitalist State, and Working Class Men: The Case of the 1842 Mines Regulation Act." *Feminist Review* 7 (Spring 1981): 1–34.

Jansz, Ulla. "Sociale kwestie en sekse in de politieke geschiedenis: De Arbeidswet van 1889." In *Op het strijdtoneel van de politiek: Twaalfde Jaarboek voor Vrouwengeschiedenis.* Ed. Marjan Schwegman et al. Nijmegen: SUN, 1991. Pp. 70–90.

Jenson, Jane. "Paradigms and Political Discourse: Protective Legislation in France and the United States before 1914." *Canadian Journal of Political Science/Revue canadienne de science politique* 22 (June 1989): 235–58.

————. "Representations of Gender: Policies to 'Protect' Women Workers and Infants in France and the United States before 1914." In *Women, the State, and Welfare.* Ed. Linda Gordon. Madison: University of Wisconsin Press, 1990. Pp. 152–77.

Kessler-Harris, Alice. *Out to Work: A History of Wage-earning Women in the United States.* New York: Oxford University Press, 1982.

————. *A Woman's Wage: Historical Meanings and Social Consequences.* Lexington: University Press of Kentucky, 1990.

Kingmans, Magdaleen. "De wetgeving op de vrouwenarbeid." In *Vrouwen, Kiesrecht en Arbeid in Nederland 1889–1919.* Ed. Josine Block et al. Groningen: SSGN, 1977. Pp. 187–214.

Kirkby, Diane. " 'The Wage-earning Woman and the State': The National Women's Trade Union League and Protective Labor Legislation, 1903–1923." *Labor History* 28 (1987): 54–74.

Klejman, Laurence, and Florence Rochefort. *L'égalité en marche: Le féminisme sous la Troisième République.* Paris: Presses de la Fondation Nationale des Sciences Politiques—des Femmes, 1989.

Lake, Marilyn. "The Independence of Women and the Brotherhood of Man: Debates in the Labor Movement over Equal Pay and Motherhood Endowment in the 1920s." *Labour History* 63 (1992): 1–17.

Lehrer, Susan. *Origins of Protective Labor Legislation for Women, 1905–1925.* Albany: SUNY Press, 1987.

Leira, Arnlaug. *Welfare States and Working Mothers: The Scandanavian Experience.* Cambridge: Cambridge University Press, 1992.

Levine, Philippa. "Consistent Contradictions: Prostitution and Protective Labor Legislation in Nineteenth Century England." *Social History* 19:1 (1994): 17–35.

Liversage, Toni. *At erobre ordet—Kvinderne og arbejderbevægelsen.* Copenhagen: Tiderne Skifter, 1980.

Macintyre, Stuart, and Richard Mitchell, eds. *Foundations of Arbitration: The Origins and Effects of State Compulsory Arbitration, 1890–1914.* Melbourne: Oxford University Press, 1989.

Mappen, Ellen. "Strategists for Change: Social Feminist Approaches to the Problems of Women's Work." In *Unequal Opportunities: Women's Employment in England, 1800–1918.* Ed. Angela V. John. Oxford: Basil Blackwell, 1986. Pp. 235–59.

McDougall, Mary Lynn. "Protecting Infants: The French Campaign for Maternity Leaves, 1890s–1913." *French Historical Studies* 13 (1983): 79–105.

McFeely, Mary Drake. *Lady Inspectors: The Campaign for a Better Workplace, 1893–1921.* Oxford: Basil Blackwell, 1988.

Münz, Rainer, and Gerda Neyer. "Frauenarbeit und Mutterschutz in Österreich: Ein historischer Überblick." In *Frauenarbeit, Karenzurlaub und berufliche Wiedereingliederung.* No. 30. Ed. Rainer Münz, Gerda Neyer, and Monika Pelz. Linz: Arbeitsmarktpolitik, 1986. Pp. 13–76.

Nielsen, Ruth. "Special Protective Legislation for Women in Nordic Countries." *International Labour Review* 119 (1980): 39–49.

Ohlander, Ann-Sofie. "Det osynliga barnet? Kampen om den socialdemokratiska familjepolitiken." In *Socialdemokratins samhälle 1889–1989.* Ed. Klaus Misgeld et al. Stockholm: Tidens Förlag, 1987. Pp. 170–90.

Olsson, Sven E. *Social Policy and Welfare State in Sweden.* 2d ed. Lund: Arkiv Förlag, 1993.

Oostendorp, Mirjam. "'Een openbare parade van veile vrouwen': Politieke debatten in Nederland over zedelijkheid en arbeid aan het einde van de negentiende eeuw." In *Op het strijdtoneel van de politiek: Twaalfde Jaarboek voor Vrouwengeschiedenis.* Ed. Marjan Schwegman et al. Nijmegen: SUN, 1991. Pp. 49–69.

Pederson, Susan. *Family, Dependence, and the Origins of the Welfare State: Britain and France, 1914–1945*. New York: Cambridge University Press, 1993.

Postma, A. *De mislukte pogingen tussen 1874 en 1889 tot verbetering en uitbreiding van de Kinderwet-Van Houten*. Deventer: Kluwer, 1977.

Quataert, Jean H. "A Source Analysis in German Women's History: Factory Inspectors' Reports and the Shaping of Working-Class Lives, 1878–1914." *Central European History* 16 (1983): 99–121.

Rose, Sonya O. *Limited Livelihoods: Gender and Class in Nineteenth-Century England*. London: Routledge, 1992.

Sachs, Albie, and Joan Hoff-Wilson. *Sexism and the Law: A Study of Male Beliefs and Legal Bias in Britain and the United States*. New York: Free Press, 1978.

Sarvasy, Wendy. "Beyond the Difference versus Equality Policy Debate: Post-suffrage Feminism, Citizenship, and the Quest for a Feminist Welfare State." *Signs: Journal of Women in Culture and Society* 17:2 (Winter 1992): 329–62.

Schmidt, Dorothea. "Wenn der Staat die Arbeitszeit regelt . . . Die Geschichte der Arbeiterschutzgesetzgebung für Frauen im Kaiserreich und ihre Verwirklichung in Bremen." *Leviathan* 12 (1984): 50–84.

Sellberg, Hjalmar. *Staten och arbetarskyddet 1850–1919: En studie i svensk socialpolitik*. Uppsala: Almqvist & Wiksells Boktryckeri AB, 1950.

Shanley, Mary Lyndon. *Women's Rights, Feminism, and Politics in the United States*. Washington, D.C.: American Political Science Association, 1986.

Siersema, José. *Vrouwenarbeid—nachtwerk? Over arbeidswetgeving en emancipatie*. Amsterdam: Pegasus, 1981.

Skocpol, Theda. *Protecting Soldiers and Mothers: The Political Origins of Social Policy in the United States*. Cambridge: Belknap Press of Harvard University Press, 1992.

Stewart, Mary Lynn. *Women, Work, and the French State: Labour Protection and Social Patriarchy, 1879–1919*. Kingston: McGill-Queen's University Press, 1989.

Stone, Judith. *The Search for Social Peace: Reform Legislation in France, 1890–1914*. Albany: SUNY Press, 1985.

Vogel, Lise. *Mothers on the Job: Maternity Policy in the United States Workplace*. New Brunswick: Rutgers University Press, 1993.

Wikander, Ulla. "International Women's Congresses, 1878–1914: The Controversy over Equality and Special Labour Legislation." In *Rethinking Change: Current Swedish Feminist Research*. Ed. Maud L. Edwards et al. Uppsala: Ord & Form/HSFR, 1992. Pp. 11–36.

Willms-Herget, Angelika. *Frauenarbeit: Zur Integration der Frauen in den Arbeitsmarkt*. Frankfurt a.M.: Campus, 1985.

Contributors

EFI AVDELA, an assistant professor of history at the University of Thessaloniki, Greece, is the author of several articles on gender and work as well as two books, one on women civil servants (*Demosioi hypalliloi genous thilykou: Katamerismos tis ergasias kata fyla ston dimosio tomea stin Ellada, 1908–1955* [1990]) and another, with Angelica Psarra, on the Greek feminist movement of the interwar period (*O feminismos stin Ellada tou Mesopolemou: Mia Anthologia* [1985]). She is currently engaged in research and writing on gender, class, and ethnicity in the construction of identities among workers in twentieth-century Greece, especially in the tobacco industry.

MARGARETE GRANDNER, an assistant professor in the Department of History, University of Vienna, has published several articles and a book, *Kooperative Gewerkschaftspolitik in der Kriegswirtschaft* (1992), on the history of trade unions and social politics in Austria, and with David Sood and Mary Jo Haynes has edited *Frauen in Österreich: Beiträge zu ihrer Situation im 19. und 20. Jahrhundert* (1993), which is forthcoming in English as *Austrian Women in the Nineteenth and Twentieth Centuries: Cross-Disciplinary Perspectives*. She is now studying the impact of the introduction of sickness insurance on the health care system.

GRO HAGEMANN is a senior researcher at the Institute for Social Research in Oslo and a professor of women's research at the University of Oslo. She has published in the area of gender and industrialization and is the author of *Skolefolk: Lørernes historie i Norge* (1992) and *Kjønn og industrialisering* (1994).

RENATE HOWE, an associate professor of Australian studies at Deakin University, Victoria, Australia, is the author of *New Houses for Old: Fifty Years of Public Housing in Victoria, 1938–88* (1988), the editor of a special issue of the *Journal of Australian Studies* entitled "Women and the State: Australian Perspectives" (1994), and the coauthor, with Shurlee Swain, of *Disposal and Punishment: The History of Single Mothers and Their Children* (1995). Her current work focuses on international networks of women reformers and the role of Australian women.

ULLA JANSZ is an assistant professor of feminist history at the Universiteit voor Humanistiek, Utrecht, the Netherlands. Her publications, mostly on the history of Dutch feminism, include *Denken over sekse in de eerste feministische golf* (1990). She is currently working on the relationship between feminism and humanism in Dutch history.

LYNN KARLSSON, a doctoral candidate in economic history at Uppsala University, Sweden, is completing her thesis on the history of protective legislation for women. She is the coauthor, with Ulla Wikander, of "Om teknik, arbetsdelning och ideologi som formare av Kvinnors—och mäns—arbetsvillkor," in *Historisk Tidskrift* 1 (1987).

ALICE KESSLER-HARRIS is a professor of history and the director of the Women's Studies Program at Rutgers University, New Brunswick, New Jersey. The author of *Out to Work: A History of Wage-earning Women in the United States* (1982) and *A Woman's Wage: Historical Meanings and Social Consequences* (1990), she is currently working on a book about women's economic citizenship.

JANE LEWIS is a professor of social policy in the Department of Social Sciences and Administration at the London School of Economics. Among her many sociological and historical books on women are *Women in Britain since 1945* (1992) and an edited collection entitled *Women and Social Policies in Europe* (1993). She is completing a study of the relationship between the state, the voluntary sector, and social work in the late nineteenth and twentieth centuries.

ANNA-BIRTE RAVN is a senior lecturer in women's studies at the Feminist Research Center in Aalborg (FREIA), Department of Development and Planning, Aalborg University, Denmark. She has published many articles on Danish women's movements and on women's work in agriculture and industry and coedited a special issue of *Women's Studies International Forum* entitled "Images from Women in a Changing Europe" (vol. 17, 1994). Her current project analyzes the relationship between gender and class in Danish women's history.

SONYA O. ROSE is a professor of history and sociology at the University of Michigan, Ann Arbor. Her publications on women and social conditions in England during the nineteenth century include *Limited Livelihoods: Gender and Class in Nineteenth-Century England* (1992). She is currently involved in a project on gender and race in World War II Britain.

SABINE SCHMITT completed her doctoral examinations at the Technische Universität Berlin, Germany, in 1994. Her dissertation was published in 1995 under the title *Der Arbeiterinnenschutz im Deutschen Kaiserreich: Zur Konstruktion der Schutzbedürftigen Arbeiterin.*

REGINA WECKER has taught women's history at the Universities of Bern and Zurich and at the Free University of Berlin. She is now an assistant professor of women's and gender history at the University of Basel. Her main publications have been on women's labor and on legal history and include *Zwischen Ökonomie und Ideologie: Arbeit im Lebenszusammenhang von Frauen in Kanton Basel-Stacht, 1870–1910* (1995). She directs a research project on protective labor legislation in Switzerland in the twentieth century.

ULLA WIKANDER is a docent in economic history at the University of Uppsala. An early student of multinational corporations, she published *Kreuger's Match Monopolies, 1925–30: Case Studies in Market Control through Public Monopolies* in 1980. More recently, she has explored the relations between men's and women's work in the Swedish pottery industry, the subject of *Kvinnors och mäns arbeten: Gustavsberg 1880–1980, Genusarbetsdelning och arbetets degradering vid en porslinsfabrik* (1988). She is now writing a book about the debates at international congresses on women's work and women's nature.

Index

accident insurance, 126
Adelborg, Gertrud, 239–40
Alabama, women's night work in, 343
Algemeen Nederlansch Werklieden Verbond, 192
Altmann, Anna, 163
American Federation of Labor, 339
American Journal of Public Health, 345
Amsterdam, Congress of the Second Socialist International (1904), 55
Amsterdammer, De, 196
Ankersmit, Heleen, 207–8n25
Anthony, Susan B., 61n86
Arbeidswet of 1919, Dutch, 204
Arbeiterinnen-Zeitung (newspaper), 163, 164
Arbeiterwohl (journal), 130
Arbeitordnung, Austrian, 157
Arenholt, Julie, 52, 220–22
Ashley, Lord, 98–100
Association for Social Policy (Verein für Social-politik), 128, 132
Association of Industrialists (Handels-und Gewerbeverein), Swiss, 69, 70
Australia: industrialization of, 319–20; minimum wage in, 8, 322–27, 329; pronatalism in, 327, 334; protective labor legislation for children in, 321; protective labor legislation for women in, 4, 5, 13, 18, 318–36; regulation of working hours in, 321, 324, 328; social reform in, 327, 330–31; wages boards in, 322–27, 332; women's morality in, 321; women's night work laws in, 320, 328; workers' safety in, 320
Austria: industrialization of, 151; maternalism in, 11; maternity leaves in, 154–55, 156, 157, 159, 168, 171, 174; protective labor legislation for children in, 6, 153, 155; protective labor legislation for women in, 12, 17, 150–87; regulation of working hours in, 8, 9, 150, 157–60, 161, 163, 167, 174; social insurance in, 159, 168; social reform in, 161, 172; Trade Code of 1859 in, 152; unemployment in, 154; women's clubs in, 170; women's health in, 162, 165; women's night work in, 156, 157, 158–59, 161, 168, 172, 174; Workers' Code of 1885 in, 159, 162
Aves, Ernest, 322, 325

Baker, Elizabeth Faulkner, 346, 350–51
Bakery and Confectionery Workers International Union, U.S., 344
Bang, Nina, 217–19, 220, 221, 222
Basel: Congress of the Second Socialist International (1912), 55; International Congress on Protective Labor Legislation (1913), 31, 55
Baudelaire, Charles-Pierre, 15
Bauer, Otto, 167
Bebel, August, 40, 41, 43, 198, 201, 202
Beelaerts van Blokland, G. J. T., 192, 194
Beer, Heinrich, 169
Belcredi, Count Egbert, 157–59
Belgium, women's night work laws in, 53
Bélilon, Camille, 48
Bellinchave, M. W. Baron Du Tour van, 193
Berlepsch, Freiherr von, 133
Berlin: International Congress on Protective Labor Legislation (Der Internationalen Arbeiterschutzkonferenz, 1890), 12, 17, 31, 34–36, 51, 54, 76, 111, 133, 214, 238; Der Internationale Frauen-Kongress in Berlin (1904), 49–50, 56, 261n31; Der Internationale Kongress für Frauenwerke und Frauenbestrebungen (1896), 56
Bern: conference (1913), 15; International Congress on Protective Labor Legislation (Conference Diplomatique pour la Protection Ouvrière, 1906), 17, 31, 51, 55, 341–42, 354–55n11; Ninth International Economic History Congress (1986), 20; proposed congress in 1890 in, 76

Bern Convention of 1906, 17, 51, 53–54, 168, 186n124, 214, 247, 251, 252, 271, 273, 276, 313n16

Bernstein, Eduard, 137, 181n66

Biliński, Leon Ritter von, 179n49

Bismarck, Otto von, 34–35, 126, 132, 133, 134–35, 136, 143

Black, Clementina, 326–27

Blackburn, Helen, 109

Blatch, Harriot Eaton Stanton, 48–49

Blohm, Louise, 137

Bonnevial, Marie, 39, 42–43, 44–45, 49, 88n59

Booth, Charles, 109, 112

Borgesius, H. Goeman, 193–94

Bosanquet, Helen, 112, 114

Boschek, Anna, 182n81, 182–83n82, 185n108

Boucherette, Jessie, 109

Bramson, Theodor, 214

Brandeis, Louis, 348

Branting, Hjalmar, 265n59

Braun, Lily, 39, 40, 42, 149n68, 201, 202

Brentano, Hanny, 171–72

Broadhurst, Henry, 106

Brochman, Andrea Nielsen, 216, 220, 225, 233n39

Brussels: Congrès Féministe International de Bruxelles (1897), 43, 45–46, 56; Congrès Féministe International de Bruxelles (1912), 56; Congress of the Second Socialist International (1891), 34, 55; International Congress on Protective Labor Legislation (Congrès International de Législation du Travail, 1897), 31, 54, 62n104

Bruun, Anne, 233n39

BSF. *See* Bund Schweizerischer Frauenvereine (BSF)

Bundesgesetz betreffend die Arbeit in den Fabriken (Federal Law on Work in Factories) (Switzerland, 1877), 63, 68–69, 72, 78, 178n33

Bund Schweizerischer Frauenvereine (BSF), 79, 83

Burns, John, 110

Burrows, Mrs. Herbert, 61n88

California: protective labor legislation for women in, 2–3, 9; women's night work laws in, 342

Carlsson, Christina, 246

Case for the Factory Acts (Webb), 110

Castberg, Johan, 269, 276–77, 280, 284

Caté, Marcel, 51

Catholic Centre party, German, 131, 132

Catholic church: in Austria, 11, 157; and elimination of women's work, 39–40, 130; in France, 19, 25n8; in Germany, 130; in Switzerland, 38–39; and workers' protection, 76

Catholic Union Feminine Civique et Sociale (France), 19

Catholic Workers' Organization, Swiss, 38–39

Cause, The (Strachey), 323

Cederschiöld, Maria, 240, 260n14

Centralverband Deutscher Industrieller (CDI), 132

Century of the Child, The (*Barnets århundrade*) (Key), 54, 242–43, 244

Chicago, World's Congress of Representative Women (1893), 55

Child Labor Law of 1874 (Netherlands), 193

Children's Bureau, U.S., 18, 348

Christiansen, Alfred, 219

Christian Social party, Austrian, 161, 165, 166

Civil Code (*Zivilgesetzbuch*), Swiss, 72

Civil Code of 1811 (Austria), 151–52

Claeys, Emilie, 37

Clothing Board, Australian, 324

Collet, Clara, 109

Commercial Clerks' Wages Board, Australian, 332

Commission for Women's Work, 39

Commission of Inquiry into the Working of the Factories and Workshops Acts, British (1876), 192

Committee to Revise the Laws on Worker Protection, Swedish, 247, 250–51

Commonwealth Court of Conciliation and Arbitration, Australian, 329, 332

Communist Party of Greece (KKE), 307

communitarian feminism, Dutch, 200–203

Comte, August, 15

Conference of Working Women (1912), 332

Conference on Infant Mortality (1906), 110

Congrès Féministe International (Paris, 1896), 43, 44, 55

Congrès Féministe International de Bruxelles (Brussels, 1897), 43, 45–46, 56

Congrès Féministe International de Bruxelles (Brussels, 1912), 56

Congrès Français et International du Droit des Femmes (Paris, 1889), 44, 55

Congrès Général des Sociétés Féministes, 32

Congrès Général des Sociétés Féministes (Paris, 1892), 32, 43, 44, 55

Congrès International de la Condition et des Droits des Femmes (Paris, 1900), 49, 56

Congrès International des Oeuvres et Institutions Féminines (Paris, 1889), 55

Congrès International des Oeuvres et Institutions Féminines (Paris, 1900), 49, 56

Congrès International du Droit des Femmes (Paris, 1878), 32, 55

Congresses of the Second Socialist International: description of, 31–32, 33–34, 36–38, 51–52; list of, 55

Congress for Female Suffrage (Paris, 1927), 81

Congress of the Second Socialist International (Amsterdam, 1904), 55

Congress of the Second Socialist International (Basel, 1912), 55

Congress of the Second Socialist International (Brussels, 1891), 34, 55

Congress of the Second Socialist International (Congrès International Ouvrier Socialiste) (Paris, 1889), 33–34, 55, 76, 136

Congress of the Second Socialist International (Copenhagen, 1910), 51–52, 55, 220

Congress of the Second Socialist International (London, 1896), 55

Congress of the Second Socialist International (Paris, 1900), 55

Congress of the Second Socialist International (Stuttgart, 1907), 55

Congress of the Second Socialist International (Zurich, 1893), 34, 36–38, 55, 138–39, 164, 182n75, 246

Conservative party, Norwegian, 269–70, 277, 281

Contagious Diseases Act (Great Britain), 104

Copenhagen: Congress of the Second Socialist International (1910), 51–52, 55, 220; Second International Socialist Women's Conference (1910), 52, 232–33n36; Second Nordic Meeting on the Woman Question (1914), 220, 225

Coronel, Dr. S. Sr., 191, 192

Cotton Factory Times, 108

Council of Greek Women, 308, 309

Court of Justice of the European Communities, ruling on night work restrictions, 2

Crone, Henriette, 220–22, 231n28

Cross, Asheton, 104

Dagny, 50, 239, 240, 245, 260n14

Danish Federation of Trade Unions (De samvirkende Fagforbund i Danmark), 219

Danish Printers' Union (Dansk Typografforbunds Kvidelige Afdeling), Women's Branch of, 215, 216, 220–21, 225, 231n28

Danish Women's Society (Dansk Kvindesamfund), 215, 216, 217, 220, 222, 224, 225, 228n6

Deakin, Alfred, 320, 326

Decurtins, Dr. Caspar, 38, 41, 42, 75–76, 77

de Lima, Agnes, 352

Denmark: failure to ratify Bern conventions, 51, 214; industrialization of, 211; maternity leaves in, 210, 216, 220, 222, 227–28n3; protective labor legislation for children in, 211; protective labor legislation for women in, 9–10, 12, 210–34; regulation of working hours in, 8, 17, 210, 211, 212, 213, 214, 216–17, 218, 221, 223; social democracy in, 15, 215, 217–19, 220; women's night work laws in, 53, 210, 211, 212, 213, 215, 216–17, 218, 219, 220, 221, 222, 223, 224, 225–26, 273

Deraismes, Maria, 44

de Ramsey, Lord, 110

Devon, earl of, 98–99

Dilke, Lady, 109, 326

Disraeli, Benjamin, 102

Dixième Congrès International des Femmes— Oeuvres et Institutions Féminine—Droits des Femmes (Paris, 1913), 32, 53, 56

Doherty, John, 117n9

Dokumente der Frauen, 171

Drucker, Wilhelmina, 45, 200, 201, 204

Dworschak, Adelheid. *See* Popp, Adelheid Dworschak

Dwyer, Kate, 331–32

egalitarianism, 14, 109, 111

Eigenart ("peculiarity"), 47, 54

eight-hour day, movement for, 33, 42, 76, 111, 119n42, 127, 161, 163, 167, 193, 195, 204, 223, 246, 250, 260n12, 269, 270, 303, 321

Employers' Federation (Norsk Arbeidsgiverforening), Norwegian, 272

Employment Protective Act of 1936 (Norway), 277, 278, 284, 287

Engels, Friedrich, 6, 41, 91, 139, 198, 202

England. *See* Great Britain

Englishwoman's Review, 109

equality/difference ("peculiarity") question, 1–2, 10, 13, 23, 33, 47, 54, 83, 137, 188, 202–3, 209n46, 212, 218–19, 225, 228–29n6, 243, 252, 257

equal pay for equal work, 37–38, 42, 45, 139, 307, 310, 325, 332–33

Equal Rights Amendment, Swiss, 81

ethical feminism, Dutch, 203–4

European Community Directive 76/207/CEE, article 5 (1976), 2

Evolutie, 201

Fabrikregulativ of 1839, Prussian, 144n7

Factories (Health of Women etc.) Bill, British, 102

Factory Act of 1873 (Denmark), and revisions (1901, 1909, 1913), 211, 213, 215, 216, 217, 220, 222, 227–28n3

Factory Acts Reform Association, British, 101, 102

Factory and Crafts Ordinance of 1846 (Sweden), 259n6

Factory and Shops Act of 1873 (Victoria, Australia), and amendments (1885, 1890, 1896, 1903), 320, 321–23, 324

Factory and Workshops Consolidation Act of 1878 (Great Britain), 105

Factory Law of 1885 (Austria), 159

Factory Protection Act of 1892 (Norway), 269, 276

family wage, for men, 11, 12, 13, 22, 93, 109, 143, 329, 331, 334, 339

Fatigue and Efficiency (Goldmark), 345

Favon, Georges, 75

Fawcett, Henry, 104, 106

Fawcett, Millicent, 104

Federation for Female Hand and Machine Industry, Austrian, 163

Federation of Trade Unions, Norwegian, 277

feminism, reluctant, 139

feminist movement, 14, 32, 33, 42–43, 45–46, 49, 52, 53, 115, 126, 136, 171, 188, 196, 197, 200–204, 236, 239–44, 270–71, 273–76, 291, 292, 295, 308–11, 330–31, 334

Feurer, Rosemary, 107

Fickert, Auguste, 185n108

Finland: ratification of Bern conventions, 51; social democracy in, 15; women's night work laws in, 53

First Nordic Meeting on the Woman Question (Kristiania, 1902), 232n34, 273

France: concept of motherhood in, 35; pronatalism in, 11, 19; protective labor legislation for children in, 6; women's night work laws in, 2, 14, 20, 44, 51, 53

Franz Joseph (emperor), 161

Francken-Dyserinck, Welmoet Wijnaendts, 203

Franklin, Stella, 326

Franzoi, Barbara, 129

Frauenfrage, Die (Braun), 201

Frauen-Reichskomité, 165, 166–67, 168, 172

Frau und der Sozialismus, Die (Bebel), 198

Fray, Mrs. (of Leicestershire Stitchers and Seamers Association), 105

Fredrika Bremer Förbund, 239, 245, 248–50, 253

Freedom of Trade Ordinance of 1864 (Sweden), 259n6

Freundlich, Emmy Kögler, 172, 185n118

Frey, Emil, 74–75

Fronde, la, 185n112

Garber, Johann, 154

Gardiner, A. G., 113

gendered division of labor: in Australia, 318; in Denmark, 210, 218; in Germany, 125, 126; in Great Britain, 91; in Greece, 305–7, 308, 311–12; in the Netherlands, 188, 197, 205; in Norway, 279–82, 286; support for, 4, 38, 45, 46–47, 49, 53, 54; in Switzerland, 64, 68, 72, 82

General Federation of Women's Clubs, Australian, 330

General Workers Confederation of Greece (GSEE), 301, 302, 303, 307

Georgia, women's night work in, 343

Germany: industrialization of, 126; infant mortality in, 130; maternalism in, 141–42; maternity leave in, 133; protective labor legislation for children in, 127, 130, 132, 134; protective labor legislation for women in, 7, 12, 34–35, 46, 125–49; regulation of working hours in, 9, 127, 133, 167; social insurance policy in, 126–27, 132, 159; social reform in, 126, 127–28, 130, 246; trade code of 1891 in, 131, 133–34, 137, 140; trade code revision of 1878 in, 131–32; women's health and morality in, 128, 129–31, 136, 143; women's night work laws in, 132

Geschlecht und Charakter (Sex and Character) (Weininger), 15

Giannios, Nicos, 301
Gids, De, 196
Gilman, Charlotte Perkins, 201, 202
Gimle Congress (1876), 229–30n9
Gleichheit, Die, 137
Goegg, Marie, 87n30
Goldmark, Josephine, 345, 348, 349
Goldstein, Vida, 330, 331, 332
Gouttes de Lait (France), 11
Graham, Sir James, 101
Gray, Robert, 96
Great Britain: concern about morality in, 92–
    93, 96; cult of domesticity in, 93, 97, 98, 99,
    100, 104, 106; infant mortality in, 102–3;
    maternalism in, 102; maternity leave in, 94,
    110; minimum wage in, 94, 109, 111, 113, 326;
    protective labor legislation for children in,
    6, 95, 96–97; protective labor legislation for
    women in, 5–6, 8, 10, 12, 17, 18–19, 91–124;
    regulation of working hours in, 92, 95–101,
    108, 111; "schools for mothers" in, 11; women
    as "mothers of the race" in, 93, 102; women's
    night work laws in, 53
Greece: ideology of domesticity in, 294; in-
    dustrialization of, 290, 291, 292–93, 294,
    298–99, 305, 311–12; maternity leave in,
    299, 303, 304; minimum wage laws in, 310;
    protective labor legislation for children in,
    291, 300, 306; protective labor legislation for
    women in, 5, 7, 12, 17, 290–317; ratification
    of Bern conventions by, 51, 313; regulation
    of working hours in, 295, 299, 303; unem-
    ployment in, 305; women as "mothers of the
    nation" in, 291, 294; women's health and
    morality in, 293–94, 308; women's night
    work laws in, 299, 303–4
Greulich, Hermann, 76
Greulich, Margarete, 39, 77
Grimshaw, Patricia, 333
Gripenberg, Alexandra, 48, 50, 240
Gruner, Erich, 67
Guillaume-Schack, Gertrud, 136
Gundelach, Frau (German trade unionist), 137
Gustafsson, Ruth, 265n60

Hagemann, Gro, 19–20
Hainisch, Marianne, 171
Hainisch, Michael, 185n113
Hardie, Keir, 326
Harvard Law Review, 329
health insurance, 3–4, 79, 112, 126

Henry, Alice, 326, 330–31
Herkner, Heinrich, 59n39
Hesselgren, Kerstin, 52
Heyermans, Ida, 203
Hicks, Mrs. Amie, 61n88
Higgins, Henry Bourne, 329, 331
Hirt, Ludwig, 145n16
Hjelt, Vera, 52
Höger, Karl, 162
Holland. *See* Netherlands
Hollanda-Vlaamse Vrouwenbond (Dutch-
    Flemish Women's Association), 58n24
Holst, Henriëtte Roland, 197, 198, 201–2, 204
Houten, Sam van, 191
Howell, George, 106
Huisvrouw, De (The Housewife), 196, 197
Hull-House (Chicago), 326
humanism, 257
Huygens, Cornélie, 197, 204

Ibsen, Henrik, 271
ICW. *See* International Council of Women
    (ICW)
Ihrer, Emma, 136
Illinois, regulation of working hours in, 321, 343
ILO. *See* International Labour Office (ILO);
    International Labour Organisation (ILO)
Indiana, women's night work laws in, 342
individualism, 14
Institute of Social Security, Greek, 315n35
International Association for Protective Labour
    Legislation, 31, 50–51, 239, 245
International Congresses on Protective Labor
    Legislation: description of, 31, 34–36, 38–43,
    50–54, 131; list of, 54–55
International Congress of Women (London,
    1899), 46–49, 56, 141, 239
International Congress of Women (Rome, 1914),
    32, 56
International Congress of Women (Toronto,
    1909), 56
International Congress of Working Women
    (Paris, 1927), 89n75
International Congress of Working Women
    (Washington, D.C., 1919), 26n17
International Congress on Protective Labor
    Legislation (Basel, 1913), 31, 55
International Congress on Protective Labor
    Legislation (Conference Diplomatique pour
    la Protection Ouvrière) (Bern, 1906), 17, 31,
    51, 55, 341–42, 354–55n11

International Congress on Protective Labor Legislation (Congrès International de Législation du Travail) (Brussels, 1897), 31, 54, 62n104

International Congress on Protective Labor Legislation (Congrès International pour la Protection Légale des Travailleurs) (Paris, 1900), 31, 55

International Congress on Protective Labor Legislation (Der Internationalen Arbeiterschutzkonferenz) (Berlin, 1890), 12, 17, 31, 34–36, 51, 54, 76, 111, 133, 214, 238

International Congress on Protective Labor Legislation (First Congress on Workers' Protection; Internationaler Kongress für Arbeiterschutz) (Zurich, 1897), 17, 31, 38–43, 54, 76–77, 88n52, 131

International Correspondence (International Women's Labor Association), 53–54

International Council of Women (ICW), 32, 46, 53, 55, 273, 309

Internationale Frauen-Kongress in Berlin, Der (Berlin, 1904), 49–50, 56, 261n31

Internationale Kongress für Frauenwerke und Frauenbestrebungen (Berlin, 1896), 56

internationalism, of protective labor legislation, 74–75

International Labor Conference (Washington, D.C., 1919), 303

International Labor Conventions (1920), 291

International Labour Office (ILO), 77

International Labour Organisation (ILO): Convention 89 of, 83; founding of, 31, 52; protective labor legislation conventions of, 2, 52, 303; report (1921), 15; and women's night work laws, 52–53

International Open Door Council, 114, 115, 309

International Woman Suffrage Alliance (IWSA), 46, 53, 309

international women's congresses: description of, 32, 44–50; list of, 55–56

International Women's League, 87n30

Iron Ring, Austrian, 155–59

Irwin (Irvin), Marguerite, 37

Italy, women's night work laws in, 2

IWSA. *See* International Woman Suffrage Alliance (IWSA)

Jensen, Jens, 214

Jensen, Johanne, 233n39

Jensen-Sønderup, Jens, 214, 217, 224

John, Angela, 107

Journal des Femmes, 45, 48

Kapital, Das (Marx), 41

Kathedersocialisten, 39

Kautsky, Karl, 57n18, 137, 139, 201

Kautsky, Louise, 36–37, 139, 182n75

Kelley, Florence, 339

Kerdijk, Arnold, 192, 193, 194

Kessler-Harris, Alice, 38, 78, 143, 310, 325

Key, Ellen: defense of special protection for women, 54, 199, 242–44, 245, 252, 257; as a social reformer, 10; and women's equality, 236

Kindig, Louise, 349

Knudsen, Thora, 233n39

Koven, Seth, 142

Krasa, Marie, 185n108

Kristiania (Oslo): First Nordic Meeting on the Woman Question (1902), 232n34, 273; mass meeting of the Labor party (1890), 269

Krog, Gina, 273

Kvinden og Samfundet, 217, 230n11

Labor party, Australian, 319, 330, 331, 333

Labor party, Norwegian, 269, 273, 277

Labor Protection Act of 1912 (Sweden), 261n32

Ladies' Newspaper, The, 295

Law 3524 of 1910 (Greece), 299

Law 4029 of 1912 (Greece), 299

lead exposure, 114, 173

League for Mother Protection, Austrian, 171

League for the Protection of Mothers (Bund für Mutterschutz), German, 142

League for Women's Rights (Syndesmos gia ta dikaiomata tis gynaikas), Greek, 308, 309

League of German Women's Associations (Bund Deutscher Frauenvereine), 140

Lee, Jenny, 325

Leicestershire Stitchers and Seamers Association, 105, 106

Leo XIII (pope), 76

Le Poole, Samuel, 190, 192

Le Rider, Jacques, 15

Leuch, Annie, 80

Lewis, Jane, 47

Lewis, Sara, 332

Liberal party, Danish, 214–15

Liberal party, Greek, 291, 297, 300, 304, 307

Liberal party, Norwegian, 269–70, 271, 275, 276, 277, 278, 281, 283, 284, 286, 287

Liebknecht, Wilhelm, 88n57

Life and Labor, 326

Ligue Belge du Droit des Femmes, 45

Ligue pour le Droit des Femmes (Society for Women's Rights), French, 39

Lindhagen, Carl, 51–52, 254, 266n69

Lindman, Arvid, 254

living wage, concept of, 331, 333

Lochner v. *New York*, 354n3

Locke, Lillian, 331–32

Lohmann, Theodor, 132, 133

London: Congress of the Second Socialist International (1896), 55; International Congress of Women (1899), 46–49, 56, 141, 239

Löwenherz, Johanna, 137

Lytleton, Edith, 111

Macarthur, Mary, 326

MacDonald, Margaret, 326

MacDonald, Ramsay, 326

Machine Act of 1889 (Denmark), 227–28n3

Maier, Gustav, 39

Makropoulou, Anna, 306

Malcolmson, Patricia, 111

Marcus, Moritz, 252, 253, 262n35

Married Women's Property Act of 1870 (Great Britain), 102, 103

Marshall, Alfred, 107

Martin, Maria, 45

Martin, Rudolf, 130–31

Marx, Karl, 41

Maryland, women's night work laws in, 342

masculinity, crisis of, 15

Massachusetts, women's night work laws in, 342, 343

Melbourne Trades Hall Council, 332

Meyer, Johanne, 233n39

Meyerson, Gerda, 235, 261n33

Michel, Sonya, 142

Mill, John Stuart, 175n3, 202

Miners' Federation, British, 107

Mines and Collieries Act of 1842 (Great Britain), 97, 99

Mines and Collieries Act of 1887 (Great Britain), 107

minimum wage legislation, 6; in Australia, 8, 322–27, 329; in Great Britain, 94, 109, 111,

113, 326; in Greece, 310; in the United States, 338

mining industry, regulation of, 6, 77, 97–99, 107, 130, 132, 134, 180n57, 238, 241, 269, 274, 278, 299

Ministry of Industry, Trade and Labor (BIGA), Swiss, 81

Missbrukad kvinnokraft (The Strength of Women Misused) (Key), 242

Mississippi, women's night work in, 343

Modderman, A. E. J., 193

Montefiore, Dora, 50

Morgonbris, 255, 257, 260n14, 262n40

motherhood, maternalist discourse on, 10–14, 19, 23

mothers' pensions, 12–13, 18

Muller v. *Oregon*, 338, 347

Muncy, Robyn, 18

Mundella, A. J., 101, 102

National Anti-Sweating League, British, 113

National Association for Labor Legislation, French, 51

National Association for Women's Suffrage, Swedish, 254, 265n63

National Association of Social Work (Centralförbundet för Socialt Arbete), Swedish, 245–46

National Consumers' League, U.S., 339

National Council of Women, German, 49

National Manufacturers' Association, U.S., 321

National Union of Societies for Equal Citizenship, British, 115

Nebraska, women's night work laws in, 343

Neergaard, Louise, 233n39

Netherlands: industrialization of, 190; labor law of 1889 in, 188, 189–90, 195–97, 204; protective labor legislation for children in, 190–93; protective labor legislation for women in, 7, 12, 188–209; regulation of working hours in, 188, 191, 192–93, 195, 200, 204; social reform in, 191–92, 197; women's morality in, 191; women's night work laws in, 53, 191, 194

new feminism, Dutch, 203

New Hampshire, women's night work laws in, 342

New Jersey, women's night work laws in, 342, 343, 348–49

New Liberal theory, 107, 112

new paternalism, 92

New South Wales Industrial and Arbitration Act of 1901, 326

New York State: restrictions on women's occupations in, 351; women's night work laws in, 14, 342, 346, 347, 349

New Zealand, 318–19

New Zealand Arbitration Court, 325

Nielsen, Andrea. *See* Brochman, Andrea Nielsen

Nielsen, Birgitte Berg, 233n39

Nielsen, Olivia, 233n39

Nielsen, Ragna, 288n17

Nietzsche, Friedrich, 15, 243

Nieuwenhuis, Ferdinand Domela, 195

Ninth International Economic History Congress (Bern, 1986), 20

Nordic Meeting on the Woman Question: First (Kristiania, 1902), 232n34, 273; Second (Copenhagen, 1914), 220, 225

Norske Kvinners Sanitetsforening, 288n8

North Dakota, women's night work laws in, 342, 343

Norway: equal rights legislation in, 278–79, 280–82; failure to ratify Bern conventions, 51, 271, 276; industrialization of, 267, 272; maternity leaves in, 278; national labor insurance in, 270; protective labor legislation for children in, 267, 269, 271; protective labor legislation for women in, 4, 7, 10, 12, 267–89; regulation of working hours in, 8, 17, 269, 270; social democracy in, 15; women's night work laws in, 53, 268–73, 275–76, 285–86, 287

Norwegian Council of Women, 273

Norwegian Feminist Association (Norsk Kvinnesaksforening), 270

O Agonas tis Gynaikas, 317n59

Oastler, Richard, 96

occupational sex segregation, 9, 14, 307, 324–25; opposition to, 45

Ohio, women's night work laws in, 342

old age pensions, 4, 112, 126

Ord, Harrison, 322

Organization for Economic and Cooperative Development (OECD), 318

Organization for Women's Welfare (Gemeinnütziger Frauenverein), Swiss, 79

organized labor. *See* trade unionism

Oslo. *See* Kristiania (Oslo)

Paris: Congrès Féministe International (1896), 43, 44, 55; Congrès Français et International du Droit des Femmes (1889), 44, 55; Congrès Général des Sociétés Féministes (1892), 32, 43, 44, 55; Congrès International de la Condition et des Droits des Femmes (1900), 49, 56; Congrès International des Oeuvres et Institutions Féminines (1889), 55; Congrès International des Oeuvres et Institutions Féminines (1900), 49, 56; Congrès International du Droit des Femmes (1878), 32, 55; Congress for Female Suffrage (1927), 81; Congress of the Second Socialist International (1900), 55; Congress of the Second Socialist International (Congrès International Ouvrier Socialiste, 1889), 33–34, 55, 76, 136; Dixième Congrès International des Femmes—Oeuvres et Institutions Féminine—Droits des Femmes (1913), 32, 53, 56; International Congress of Working Women (1927), 89n75; International Congress on Protective Labor Legislation (Congrès International pour la Protection Légale des Travailleurs, 1900), 31, 55

Parliamentary Inquiry into Factory Work, Dutch (1887), 193–95

Parren, Kallirroi, 295–96

Pateman, Carole, 108

paternalism, 115, 126

Paterson, Emma, 105, 106, 107

patriarchy, 4, 96

Pedersen, Susan, 19

Pennsylvania: regulation of working hours in, 345; women's night work laws in, 342

People v. *Schweinler,* 347–48

Perkins, Frances, 348, 351

Philipsen, Gustav, 214–15

phosphorus, protection from, 51, 186n124, 262–63n42

Piddington, A. B., 327

Plener, Ernst von, 153

Poovey, Mary, 115

Popelin, Dr. Marie, 45

Popp, Adelheid Dworschak, 37, 164, 166, 172, 182n75, 184n105, 185n108

Popular party, Greek, 304

printing industry, 80, 247–48, 274

Proletarische Vrouw, De (Proletarian Woman), 198

Prussia, protective labor legislation for children in, 6

Quack, H. P. G., 202
Quataert, Jean, 139

racialism, 10
Ratan Tata Foundation, London School of Economics, 115
Rathbone, Eleanor, 115, 329
Reeves, W. Pember, 319
Rerum Novarum encyclical, 76
Ritchie v. *The People*, 345
Robbins, Margaret, 326
Roebuck, J., 100–101
Rome, International Congress of Women (1914), 32, 56
Roser, Ignaz, 150, 151, 153
Royal Commission of Labour, British, 63
Royal Commission on Female and Juvenile Labor in Factories and Shops in New South Wales (1911–12), 327–28, 331
Russia, protective labor legislation for women in, 1
Rutgers-Hoitsema, Marie, 50, 53, 201–2, 204, 261n31

Sachs, Hilda Engström, 240–42, 244, 257, 260–61n19
Sadler, Michael, 96
Salomon, Alice, 39, 46–47, 50, 141
Schlesinger, Therese Eckstein, 185n108
Schook-Haver, Theodora, 201
Schopenhauer, Arthur, 15
Schou, Ragna, 220
Schuler, Fridolin, 77
Schwander, Albert, 78–79
Schwerin, Jeanette, 39, 140–41
Scott, Joan W., 83, 228–29n6, 243, 300
Scott, Rose, 330, 332
Second (Socialist) International: description of, 232n30
—Congresses of: description of, 31–32, 33–34, 36–38, 51–52; list of, 55
Second International Socialist Women's Conference (Copenhagen, 1910), 52, 232–33n36
Second Nordic Meeting on the Woman Question (Copenhagen, 1914), 220, 225

Second Women's Congress (Kongress für Fraueninteressen, 1921), 80
September Settlement (1899), 213
sexual division of labor. *See* gendered division of labor
SGB. *See* Swiss Union of Workers (Schweitzerischer Gewerkschaftsbund, SGB)
Sigg, Jean, 39
Simon, Helene, 50
Simon, Jules, 35, 44, 51
Skocpol, Theda, 18
Smith, Adam, 214
Smith, Constance, 113
Sociaal-Democratische Bond (SDB), Dutch, 193, 195, 197, 198–200, 204, 205
Sociaal Weekblad, 196
social contracts, 283
Social Darwinism, 16
Social Democratic Labor party (SDAP), Dutch, 197, 200
social democratic movement, 14, 31, 32, 38, 39–41, 80, 81, 131, 135–40, 160, 161–69, 193, 236–37
Social Democratic party, Austrian, 161–69, 174
Social Democratic party, Danish, 217–19, 220, 222–23
Social Democratic party (SPD), German, 131, 132, 134, 135, 137, 138–39
Social Democratic party, Norwegian, 268, 277–78
Social Democratic party, Swedish, 236–37, 246, 254–55
Social Democratic Women's Association (Social-demokratisk Kvindeforening), Danish, 220, 232–33n36
Social Democratic Women's Conference, Swedish, 246, 248, 252–53
Social-Demokraten (newspaper), 217
Socialist Association of Women, Greek, 308, 309
Socialist Center of Athens, 301
Socialisten, De (Quack), 202
Socialist Federation of the Workers of Thessaloniki, 301
Socialist International of Women, 309
Socialist Labor Party of Greece (SEKE), 303, 307
Socialist Life, 317n59
"Social Question, The," 6, 14, 29, 34, 39, 70, 128, 192, 195, 291
social reform, 10, 14–15, 112; in Australia, 327,

social reform (*continued*)
    330–31; in Austria, 161, 172; in Germany, 126, 127–28, 130, 246; in the Netherlands, 191–92, 197; in Sweden, 245–46, 247; in the United States, 15, 18
Social tidskrift (journal), 245, 260n14
Sombart, Werner, 59n39
South Carolina, women's night work laws in, 342, 343
Spencer, Herbert, 16, 99
Stanton, Elizabeth Cady, 48
State Experiments in Australia and New Zealand (Reeves), 319
Stein, Lorenz von, 156
Steinbach, Helma, 137
Stephens, Rev., 102
Stockholm Women's Club (Stockholms All-männa Kvinnoklubb), 263n45
Strachey, Ray, 323
Strindberg, August, 15
Stritt, Marie, 50
Stumm, Freiherr von, 134
Stuttgart, Congress of the Second Socialist International (1907), 55
Subjection of Women (Mill), 202
suffrage. *See* universal suffrage; women's suffrage movement
Sunday and holiday employment, banning of, 73, 81, 131, 132, 156, 157, 158, 161, 191, 194, 195, 299
Supreme Labor Council, Greek, 298
Sweden: industrialization of, 235, 237; maternity leaves in, 248, 257, 263–64n47; occupational safety in, 237; protective labor legislation for children in, 6, 236, 237, 238, 246; protective labor legislation for women in, 4, 9–10, 12, 17, 235–66; regulation of working hours in, 238, 246, 250, 251; social democracy in, 15, 236–37, 246, 254–55; social reform in, 245–46, 247; women's health and morality in, 236, 241; women's night work laws in, 14, 17, 53, 220, 235–66
Swiss Union for Women's Suffrage (Schwei-zerischer Verband für Frauenstimmrecht), 80
Swiss Union of Workers (Schweizerischer Gewerkschaftsbund, SGB), 80, 83, 89n75
Swiss Welfare Societies, 70
Switzerland: equal pay for equal work in, 82; female education in, 70–71; industrialization

of, 64–65; maternity leave in, 69, 73, 79–80; political structure of, 65–66; protective labor legislation for children in, 6, 66, 68, 69; protective labor legislation for women in, 5, 6, 7, 8, 12, 18, 63–90; regulation of working hours in, 8, 63, 66, 68–69, 70, 73, 78, 81, 158; restrictions on night work in, 63, 66–67, 68, 69, 70–71, 72, 73, 78, 81–82, 83, 158; safety regulations in, 63; unemployment in, 84

Taaffe, Count Eduard, 155, 156, 161
Tailoresses Union, Australian, 332
Ten Hours Movement, British, 95–101, 192
Tennessee, women's night work in, 343
Theimer, Camilla, 171
Theinburg, Gustav Pacher von, 157
Third International, 303
Thyrén, Johan C. W., 266n74
Tönnies, Ferdinand, 59n39
Toronto, International Congress of Women (1909), 56
Trade Code of 1891 (Germany), 131, 133–34, 137, 140
Trades Board Act of 1909 (Great Britain), 18, 111, 114, 327
Trades Boards, British, 5
Trades Union Congress, British, 104, 106

Wawrinsky, Edvard, 263–64n47
Webb, Beatrice: and occupational sex segrega-tion, 109; scrutiny of Australian legislation by, 326; support for minimum wage laws, 19; support for social reform, 112; support for special protection for women, 47–48, 240, 244; and sweated labor, 112, 113–14
Webb, Sidney, 109, 326
Weininger, Otto, 15
Werker, W. H. M., 203
Werker-Beaujon, Corrie, 203
Wiart, Carton de, 39, 40, 88n58
Wichmann, Clara, 203
Wikander, Ulla, 20
Wilhelm II (kaiser), 34–35, 50, 76, 77, 132
Wobbe, Theresa, 142
Women and Economics (Gilman), 201
Women's Bureau of the U.S. Department of Labor, 343, 350, 351
women's citizenship issues, 13, 47–48, 224, 283, 286, 327, 340, 345–46, 352–53
Women's Dressmakers' Union (Damekonfek-

tionssyerskernes Fagforening), Danish, 216

Women's Industrial Council, British, 112, 114, 326–27

Women's Labour League, British, 109

Women's Political Association, Victorian (Australia), 330

Women's Political Educational League, New South Wales (Australia), 330

Women's Progressive Association (Kvindelig Fremskridtsforening), Danish, 215, 216

Women's Protective and Provident League, British, 105–6, 107, 109

women's suffrage movement, 33, 43, 44, 45, 46, 54, 103, 197, 253–55, 274–75, 320, 330–31

Women's Trade Union (Kvinnornas fackförbund), Swedish, 246

Women's Trade Union League (WTUL), British, 109, 112, 326

Women's Trade Union League (WTUL), U.S., 326, 339

Women Tailors' Union (De kvindelige Herresrædderes Fagforening), Danish, 216

Women Workers' Association of England and Ireland, 37

Woorden van vrouwen (Troelstra), 198

Workers' Sickness Insurance Act of 1888 (Austria), 159

Working Center of Athens, 297, 301

Working Center of Piraeus, 298

Working Man's Association (Arbeiterbund), Swiss, 69, 75, 76

Working Women's Associations, Swiss, 71, 73, 80

workmen's compensation, 4

World's Congress of Representative Women (Chicago, 1893), 55

Zetkin, Clara: and social democratic movement, 14, 39, 136; support for protective labor legislation for women, 38, 136–38, 218, 219, 220; and women's equality, 34, 37, 136, 139; and women's right to work, 40–41, 42

Zografou, Evgenia, 294–95

Zurich: Congress of the Second Socialist International (1893), 34, 36–38, 55, 138–39, 164, 182n75, 246; International Congress on Protective Labor Legislation (First Congress on Workers' Protection; Internationaler Kongress für Arbeiterschutz, 1897), 17, 31, 38–43, 54, 76–77, 88n52, 131